The Canadian Criminal Justice System

Second Edition

Thomas Fleming
Wilfrid Laurier University

Subhas Ramcharan
University of Windsor

Ken Dowler
Wilfrid Laurier University

Willem de Lint
University of Windsor

PEARSON
Prentice
Hall

Toronto

To my late brother Scott: wonderful brother, loving father, and acclaimed scientist

—*T.F.*

To Cassia Claire, a beautiful, cherished shining light

—*S.R.*

Library and Archives Canada Cataloguing in Publication
The Canadian criminal justice system / Thomas Fleming... [et al.]. — 2nd ed.

Includes index.
First ed. written by: Subhas Ramcharan, Willem de Lint, Thomas S. Fleming.
ISBN-13: 978-0-13-199246-7
ISBN-10: 0-13-199246-5

1. Criminal justice, Administration of—Canada—Textbooks. I. Fleming,
Thomas, 1951–

HV9960.C2C34 2006   364.971   C2006-905454-1

ISBN-13: 978-0-13-199246-7
ISBN-10: 0-13-199246-5

Editor-in-Chief, Vice-President of Sales: Kelly Shaw
Senior Acquisitions Editor: Ky Pruesse
Executive Marketing Manager: Judith Allen
Developmental Editor: Jon Maxfield
Production Editors: Joe Zingrone, Kevin Leung
Copy Editor: Joe Zingrone
Proofreader: Tara Tovell
Production Coordinator: Janis Raisen
Composition: Laserwords
Art Director: Julia Hall
Cover and Interior Design: Chris Tsintziras
Cover Image: Getty Images/PNC

1 2 3 4 5   12 11 10 09 08

Printed and bound in the United States of America.

Contents

Chapter 4 Law, Social Control, and Theoretical Considerations of Criminality   74

Chapter 5 The Police 98

Chapter 6 The Court System 135

Preface

It has been seven years since the publication of the first edition of *The Canadian Criminal Justice System*. During that period of time, significant changes have taken place in Canada with regard to the law, new developments in criminal justice policy and practice, and the field of criminological research. With the publication of this second edition, we are joined by Professor Ken Dowler of Wilfrid Laurier University, a well-respected expert in theory, crime, and the media.

The second edition contains some completely new chapters written or rewritten for this volume (Chapters 3 and 4). There are a number of new features, including discussion boxes that are intended to provoke in-class and out-of-class discussions on current issues before the courts or of interest to Canadians. This book once again draws together the themes and issues that we feel must be addressed by a book on this area of inquiry. We have endeavoured to make the book highly accessible to students approaching this subject area for the first time using language that is clear, concise, and engaging. It is, of course, up to readers to determine whether we have achieved our goal of a readable, current text that presents a fair and objective analysis of the state of the criminal justice system in Canada.

Students may ask, "Why do we have to study the criminal justice system?" We hope this book provides many answers to that question. The challenges facing police in our society, violence and how to respond to it, how the courts deal with difficult cases, and the spiralling costs of imprisonment are all intriguing issues that students will find are treated in a compelling manner.

We want students to understand how the criminal justice system would respond to them or any other Canadian when a crime is committed, or as you shall discover, not committed. There is a fine balance between individual and civil rights expressed in the Canadian Charter of Rights and Freedoms versus societal needs to control us and establish an orderly society. This is a particularly pertinent issue in the wake of terrorist actions during the past several years, and one that is of great concern to the criminal justice system.

We believe that many distinctive features separate this text from its competitors. The historical and contemporary analysis of the criminal justice system, describing its evolution and future directions, is presented with accessible pedagogy. Key terms, major references, discussion questions, interesting boxed material, and weblinks for further information are provided to assist the student in the learning process. As well, we examine the roles of the police, judiciary, and prisons using analytical tools and examples from contemporary Canadian legal and justice system cases. We have attempted to provide a synthesis of the most important issues that confront our system of criminal justice, and the way in which these issues have an impact on Canadians.

An Instructor's Manual and Transparency Masters are available for downloading from a password-protected section of Pearson Education Canada's online catalogue at vig.pearsoned.ca. Navigate to your book's catalogue page to view the list of supplements. See your local sales representative for details and access.

Acknowledgments

We must acknowledge the critical comments of the reviewers who allowed the authors the opportunity to strengthen the content of the text and improve its readability: David Lynes, St. Francis Xavier University; Gina Antonacci, Humber College; Tess Innocent, Algonquin College; Lynne LeRoy, Durham College; Jim Norgate, Niagara College; John Edward Deukmedjian, University of Windsor; Ken Sauter, Lethbridge Community College; and Walter Greczko, Sheridan College. Finally, the authors collectively would like to acknowledge the contributions of the thousands of students in our courses in criminology who have acted as "guinea pigs" for our ideas, ideals, and critiques, which form the platform for this text on the Canadian criminal justice system.

Thomas Fleming
Subhas Ramcharan
Ken Dowler
Willem de Lint

November 2006

CHAPTER 1

Criminal Justice: An Introduction

Objectives

- To discuss the components of the criminal justice system: the police, the courts, and corrections.

- To outline the processing of criminal cases as they pass through the criminal justice system and the methods used to protect the legal and human rights of those charged.

- To introduce the sociological causes of crime.

- To identify the functions of criminal law and the role of the criminal justice system in administering the law.

- To discuss the internationalization of crime and criminal justice.

What Is Criminal Justice?

The criminal justice system is one of the most fascinating and at times controversial components of the legal institution in Canada. At any given time, vitriolic national debates are being waged over an issue related to the system, be it the police; the judiciary; sentencing; incarceration; parole; or legalizing prostitution, euthanasia, or marijuana. As Schmalleger et al. (2004) note, the concept of justice means different things to different people. Justice can mean "protection from the power of the state for some and vengeance to others, or those who are concerned with individual rights from those who emphasize the need for individual responsibility and social accountability."

Examining the criminal justice system means taking into account public perceptions that crime is on the increase and law and order is breaking down. It also requires that we consider the historical and social underpinnings of the society from which crime and crime-control methods have evolved. Before we get into an analysis of the structural components of the criminal justice system, it is important to understand that the kind of system we have in Canada is a legacy of our political, philosophical, and legal history, developed and moulded over time to reflect our unique social, political, and cultural institutions. How we respond to crime and how we administer the process is clearly going to be markedly different from the methods used in the United States, which has a history, a political system, legal and philosophical values, and social institutions that contrast starkly with Canada's. Of importance, as well, is the impact of racial and cultural diversity on Canada's legal system, criminal justice system, and society in general. Contrary to majority opinion, not all Canadians believe that our justice system treats all racial groups equally. In fact, large segments of Canada's racial minority population were left out of the legal process when laws were being formulated and enacted. Native peoples, for example, are increasingly questioning the process for prosecuting and sentencing offenders, and believe that their socio-cultural value systems define *deviance* differently from mainstream society. As a multicultural society, Canada is being challenged to adapt to, and become more sensitive to, diversity as a first step to understanding crime causation, and to devise methods for effective crime control. We have three major agencies—the police, courts, and corrections—to maintain law and order and protect the public from lawbreakers. These agencies and their network of organizations investigate, detect, prosecute, and punish lawbreakers. This linked body is known as the **criminal justice system** and as Goff (2004) notes, this system allows us to understand the interdependency of the parts of the process and see the many factors that influence decisions in the judicial process. We should note, however, that the idea of a cohesive, integrated judicial system is more a theoretical construct, for often, as Senna and Siegel (1995) note, inter-agency conflict and lack of coordination create breakdowns in the system.

Figure 1.1 illustrates the court procedure in a criminal case, from committing of the crime to arrest, court trial, and corrections outcome. Undoubtedly, no other agency of government provokes so much debate and discussion as the criminal justice system, mainly because it is within this system that the accused is interrogated and charged by the police, tried in the courts, and punished by the state if deemed guilty of an offence.

The Police

The judicial system's initial role begins with the committing of a crime, a report to the police, and a subsequent investigation by the police. It is important to note that the police are the front-line soldiers in the criminal justice system. They not only conduct the criminal investigation, but they also decide whether to proceed with obtaining an arrest warrant from the Crown attorney, the official state prosecutor. Since an **arrest** involves suspension of the individual's rights and freedoms, it is a

COURT PROCEDURE IN CRIMINAL CASES

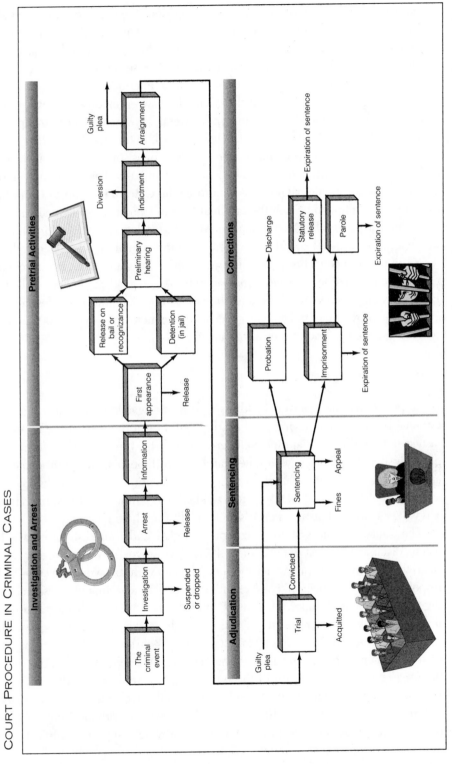

Source: F. Schmalleger, D. MacAlister, & P. F. McKenna. 2004. (2nd Ed.) *Canadian Criminal Justice Today.* Toronto: Pearson Canada.

serious step in the justice process. Furthermore, since the police cannot arrest all offenders who commit criminal or non-criminal deviant acts, the discretionary powers of the police are immense. For this reason, it is important to alter the commonly held perception that some in the police services selectively enforce the law against certain groups of people, for example, racial minorities or the poor.

Schmalleger et al. (2004) note that Canadian law enforcement is extremely complex, with each level of government—federal, provincial, and municipal—creating police agencies to enforce the law. As well, in the last decade there has been a rapid growth of Aboriginal police agencies, quasi-private police agencies, and private security firms that operate on a for-profit basis. The main purpose of all provincial and municipal police is to enforce the **Criminal Code of Canada**, the federal statute comprising the criminal laws of Canada as well as provincial and municipal laws. The Royal Canadian Mounted Police (RCMP or Mounties), the federal police service, enforce all federal statutes in all provinces, including drug and tax offences. They police airports, operate drug and DNA labs, provide national coordination services, and operate the Canadian Police College. Policing is big business in Canada, with over $6 000 000 000 being devoted in 2001 to the provision of policing by government agencies, and over 80 000 police officers being employed in the various agencies.

The Courts

If the police are the front-line soldiers in the war against crime, investigating criminal behaviour and laying charges, the courts form the core of the criminal justice system. For the majority of citizens, the court is the place where they can obtain justice. It is a place where the search for truth begins, pitting the accused and the defence against the state and the prosecution. Undoubtedly, in our adversarial-style criminal justice system the hallmark of the **court system** is that it is where truth and justice, fairness and equality can be obtained.

The Canadian court system is a complex, tangled, and layered structure which will be discussed in great detail later in the text. However, it can be broadly classified into two systems, provincial and federal, each with its own jurisdiction and responsibility. The provincial courts handle the bulk of all criminal cases, including those prosecuted under the Youth Criminal Justice Act. At this level, courts may be organized according to specialties, such as criminal, family, or youth courts. According to Desroches (1995), a provincial court is one of rapid dispatch, with defendants rarely contesting the charges laid. Desroches found in the cases he researched that 90 percent of those charged with robbery pleaded guilty in provincial court. While for most Canadians their only involvement with the court system is at this level, roughly 10 percent of those charged with indictable or serious criminal offences will be prosecuted in the provincial superior courts. These

courts usually sit with or without a jury, but normally have jurors when serious criminal cases are being heard. The provincial appeal courts hear appeals from both the superior and provincial courts, dealing mainly with issues related to procedural errors or sentencing processes. Normally an appeal hearing will involve a panel of judges, who question both the defence and Crown attorneys appearing before them and render their decision after a private discussion among themselves. These decisions can be unanimous or majority, with those dissenting also presenting their rationale for their opinions. While most convictions that are appealed are upheld, appeal courts can and sometimes do accept that a trial judge could have erred in the hearing. When that occurs, the verdict can be overturned or the case sent back for retrial.

The federal court system consists of three levels: a Trial Division, a Court of Appeal, and the Supreme Court of Canada. While the Federal Court Trial Division does not hear criminal cases, it is the tax court of the country, and has jurisdiction on all matters pertaining to federal trade and copyright laws, and judicial review of administrative decisions relating to all Crown corporations and tribunals, including the federal penitentiaries. The Federal Court of Appeal is the appellate division of the federal judicial system and, because of an expanded federal administrative role, has seen its importance increased over the last decade.

The highest court is the Supreme Court of Canada, which hears appeal cases from across Canada on any issue that it deems important. The court consists of a chief justice and eight other judges, selected by the prime minister after consultations with legal representatives and cabinet colleagues (and, lately, Alberta has been pushing the feds for permission to submit their own list of Court nominees). The Court holds great power currently, for in addition to its role as arbiter of the criminal and civil law it is entitled to interpret the **Canadian Charter of Rights and Freedoms** (or **the Charter**), a document that formally outlines the constitutional rights and freedoms of all Canadians. Therefore, the Supreme Court of Canada acts similarly to the United States Supreme Court by not only interpreting the law, but also creating law.

Corrections

Corrections is the name for the system under which convicted offenders are handled. Anyone found guilty of a criminal offence is liable to be sentenced to a term in either a federal or provincial prison. Sentences over two years in length must be served in a federal prison, while those sentenced to less than two years and non-custodial sentences are the provincial government's responsibility. Goff (2004) notes that the federal and provincial incarcerated prison population has been decreasing slightly in Canada—there were roughly 31 000 inmates in 2004, a 2 percent decline from the previous year.

There is considerable debate over the goals of sentencing in Canada. Is the purpose to punish, to rehabilitate, to humiliate, or to seek retribution? Analysis of decisions of judges or guidelines for sentencing provided by the minister of justice suggests that there is considerable latitude for discretionary sentencing by judges in the court system. However, this discretion can often lead to sentencing disparities, as an identical offence can result in many different sentencing options, depending on the province or the values of the judge. The offence of driving while drunk, for example, can see an individual sentenced to a term of imprisonment, a suspended sentence, or community service, and many Canadians are critical of this discrepancy in the sentencing guidelines.

Canada officially espouses the philosophy that its sentencing process is driven by the twin goals of rehabilitation and deterrence. The intent is to deter the offender from repeating the crime, as well as to identify the underlying causes that led to the criminal offence in the first place. Furthermore, in the last decade the courts have been taking into account the impact that a crime has on the victim. Schmalleger et al. (2004) note that, today, victims experience many hardships as they participate in the criminal justice system. They are often uncertain of their role, have little knowledge of the courtroom process, fear retaliation from the defendant, and can find testifying traumatic. Advocates of victims have demanded that the criminal justice system recognize the physical, emotional, and financial consequences of the crime. They believe that the system pays more attention to the perpetrators of crime than to victims. As a result, today, victim impact statements have an important role in the sentencing process, and in some instances victims must be notified when prisoners are being released from prison.

Many criticisms have been levelled at Canada's corrections system. A 75 percent recidivism rate is seen as an example of the failure of the rehabilitation model. The perception that parole boards are too quick to grant freedom to offenders is sometimes reinforced when a parolee commits a high-profile crime, such as sexual assault or murder. In fact, the parole system is highly successful and most parolees do not reoffend while on parole. Critics also believe that prison life has become too soft and cushy, with the authorities condoning a deviant prison subculture. Undoubtedly, the task of the corrections system is a difficult one. It has as its mandate rehabilitating offenders, deterring crime, and punishing lawbreakers—all somewhat contradictory goals. The challenge for corrections and society includes expanding the range of sentencing alternatives, while at the same time continuing the system's traditional mandate of rehabilitation, deterrence, and reducing the prison population.

The Canadian Justice System

The majority of Canadians believe that all the component parts of law and order—the police, courts, and corrections—work together in consensus and for the common goals of upholding the law and keeping order, and, in a civil and integrated way, processing deviants through the various parts of the criminal justice system. For others, the criminal justice system is potholed with conflict and dissension, and is a self-serving body geared to its own self-interest, and not that of society at large. Undoubtedly, the truth lies somewhere in the middle. The criminal justice system, similarly to the society it serves, is an amalgam of institutions, interest groups, and organizations. Often this is an imperfect fit, but in the long run the system must carry out the mandate it has been assigned as efficiently as it can.

The process begins with a police investigation, resulting from either a complaint or a discovery of a crime in progress. After gathering evidence, the police arrest the offender(s), or a justice of the peace issues a summons for the offender to appear in court. An arrest is a serious matter, as it involves potential loss of freedom and brings the criminal sanctions of the state down on the accused. At the stage of questioning and prior to arrest, the individual's protections under the Charter are outlined, including the right to legal counsel and the right not to answer the questions of the police. In the course of the arrest, the accused is fingerprinted, photographed, weighed, measured, booked, and placed in a detention cell. At this stage, the process moves from the police to the courts, with the law stating that within 24 hours of arrest the accused must be brought before a justice of the peace or a magistrate. The purpose is for the court to determine whether the defendant should be allowed bail. Since the Bail Reform Act of 1970, most defendants are released on their own recognizance. However, in the case of more serious criminal charges, the accused will have to post a cash or property bond, and in the rare case that the court believes the defendant may fail to appear for trial, bail is denied. In this situation, the accused is remanded to a detention centre, usually the local city jail, to await a court appearance. Our criminal justice system also allows defendants who are indigent to apply for legal aid and, if granted, a lawyer drawn from a list of available defence attorneys is assigned to the accused.

The formal court process begins with the preliminary hearing, where a judge hears the police evidence, presented by an assistant Crown attorney, and the defence attorney attempts to debunk and deny the validity of this evidence. The judge at this stage seeks to determine only that there are reasonable grounds to believe that the defendant committed the crime. Both the Crown and the defence can call witnesses to prove or dispute the evidence of the other side in our adversarial justice system. Having determined that there is a *bona fide* case against the accused, the judge sends the case to trial. Should the judge believe that insufficient evidence is presented, the case will be dismissed and the defendant freed.

It should be mentioned that the majority of criminal cases never come to trial, and in our criminal courts the majority of those convicted are found guilty of a lesser offence than the one they were originally charged with committing. A study conducted by the Law Reform Commission of Canada (1984) found that 71 percent of defendants pleaded guilty to the original or a lesser charge after the conclusion of the preliminary inquiry. This is because trials are usually long and expensive and both the Crown and the defence work out a plea bargain that is mutually agreeable. In those situations where a trial is the outcome, it can either be before a judge and jury or a judge alone. The process is formal and regulated—rules of evidence, cross-examination by the Crown and defence, and the role of the judge in applying the law are clearly defined. In the case of jury trials, if the jury is unable to obtain a unanimous verdict, a mistrial is declared, and a retrial could be ordered by the Crown attorney. The Crown could decide not to retry the accused, and the accused will then be released.

When the accused is found guilty of a Criminal Code offence, the judge has many sentencing options available. These include probation, community service, fines, imprisonment, or a combination of a fine and imprisonment. A suspended sentence or conditional or absolute discharges are also options available to our judges. Often the sentence is limited to the prior record of convictions of the offender. For serious offences, such as first- or second-degree murder, the sentencing guidelines are specific, with a minimum mandatory sentence required before the possibility of parole. In many instances, the judge will request a pre-sentence report from a probation officer, and will inquire about the offender's socio-economic position, previous criminal record, and family and community status. Recently, victim impact statements have increasingly been allowed in court hearings before sentencing. Because the Criminal Code does not impose strict minimum sentences for most offences, judges have wide discretion in the sentencing process. A major problem with this latitude is that judges in different jurisdictions can impose different sentences for similar offences. Critics of this discretionary sentencing policy believe that specific mandatory maximum and minimum sentences will lead to fairer and more equitable sentencing across Canada.

The final stage in the court process is the right of the accused to appeal the sentence and the conviction imposed by the judge. Provincial courts of appeal handle the majority of these appeals, but in serious cases of a criminal or constitutional

manner, the Supreme Court of Canada could agree to hear the case. However, fewer than 100 cases a year reach the Supreme Court.

Those sentenced to a term in a correctional facility find themselves in either a provincial or a federal institution. The determining factor is length of sentence, with those offenders sentenced to longer than two years ending up in a federal institution. Goff (2004) notes that "offenders can apply for day parole six months before applying for full parole, which can be awarded after they have completed one-third of their sentence or seven years, whichever is the lesser." As well, for those not granted parole the sentencing guidelines allow for mandatory release after two-thirds of a sentence is served. Canada places its prisoners in maximum-, medium-, or minimum-security institutions, depending on the risk and the treatment needs of the offender, and newer prisons are much different from the "fortress, razor wire, and stone wall" structures of the past century. However, in all but minimum-security institutions, rehabilitative programs are almost nonexistent. The challenge for our corrections system is to improve the life chances of the offender, so that on release to day parole, full parole, or to a halfway house, the opportunity to participate in the normative structure of the society will have been enhanced and recidivism reduced.

The goal of the Canadian justice system is not to reduce crime at any cost, but to obtain fair justice for all those accused and to protect the legal and human rights of those charged with criminal offences. This system is known as **due process**. It involves a detailed and careful examination of the facts involved in each case. Under our law, the police are expected to recognize the legal rights of suspects during arrest and questioning. As well, the Crown and the judiciary must recognize and follow the rule of law and constitutional guarantees during the presentation of evidence at the trial. Due process, unlike the alternative **crime control model**, is supposed to ensure that innocent people are not railroaded into guilty verdicts. The crime-control model that is very typical of many US jurisdictions puts the emphasis on the arrest and conviction of offenders, and the enforcement of law and maintenance of order. Our justice system seeks to maintain a balance between the two main schools of thought: those who advocate more crime control methods with less emphasis on due process and others whom the first group might view as having too much leniency toward criminals in enforcing the law while recognizing individual rights.

The bottom line is that the innocent should never be found guilty, and if these injustices ever occur, it must be determined where the system broke down and the problem should be fixed. All parts of the judicial process, from arrest to the courts and finally corrections, have in place limits to the power of criminal justice officials, with the goal of preventing the miscarriage of justice. All offenders are treated as innocent until proven guilty, every effort is made to provide legal representation for the accused, and the police and the prosecution are continually monitored by watchdog agencies. The premise is that the abuse of power by law administration officials is always a possibility—these officials will bend the rules to obtain convictions if given the opportunity. In fact, recent high-profile cases in Canada have shown that innocent people have been convicted of murder and other crimes and that police and court officials have presented evidence that they knew was false. In the past decade, the first-degree convictions of people such as Donald Marshall, Guy Paul Morin, and David Milgaard were all overturned by the Supreme Court of Canada, and after public inquiries further legal measures to control law administration officials were introduced. These high-profile cases of the maladministration of justice show that police and court officials are capable of bending the rules if given the opportunity to obtain convictions. In our due process model of justice, any tampering with criminal procedures, as set by the legal statutes, is a violation of the constitutional and Charter rights of the accused, and can be grounds for acquittal.

The Globalization of Crime and Criminal Justice

The internationalization of crime is a growing concern to law enforcement officials in Canada and elsewhere, and has led to a new field of criminology known as **comparative criminal justice**. Schmalleger et al. (2004) note that by comparing institutions of justice in different countries, procedures and problems can be compared and re-evaluated from a world perspective. Mass communications and travel and technological advances have made it possible not only for organized and international crime to grow, but as well for criminal justice authorities to work together for solutions to common crime problems. International police agencies and the United Nations are increasingly brought together in a new worldwide fight against international crime and terrorism.

A number of international organizations have been formed over the past decades to focus attention on the globalization of crime and international criminal justice issues. The best known of these is the International Criminal Police Association (Interpol) based in France and formed in 1914. Today, over 170 nations belong to this organization, with Canada being one of the founding nations. Interpol's work in Canada is directed by the RCMP, who perform a series of functions including the collection of data and intelligence relating to international law enforcement, and liaising with the central Interpol Secretariat in France. The goal is to coordinate efforts with other countries to track and apprehend criminals operating as part of international cartels and organizations. By working closely with other international crime-prevention agencies, the RCMP has been able to arrest offenders involved in a wide range of offences including terrorism, hostage taking, as well as financial crimes and drug trafficking.

Justice department officials are increasingly being stationed in Canadian foreign embassies both to apprehend criminals fleeing Canadian justice and to obtain information on foreigners planning criminal activities in Canada. While international personal and property crime and drug trafficking have occupied the efforts of Interpol officials in the past, in the last decade the effort for greater police co-operation to fight international terrorism has taken on an increased importance. Both the internationalization of drug trafficking and terrorism are posing major challenges for the world policing agencies. Continued efforts at inter-agency co-operation and the sharing of information, technologies, and expertise are necessary, as the list of crimes of an international nature continues to grow. Recently, money laundering, trafficking in human beings, and child pornography have shown alarming increases, with serious repercussions for criminal justice officials in Canada. It is expected that the United Nations will have a role to play in international criminal justice issues going forward.

Through its Crime Prevention and Criminal Justice Program, the UN gathers information on international crime, and provides a forum for continuous discussions on justice issues throughout the world. Its goals are the prevention of crime in member states; the control of international crime; the consolidation of efforts to combat transnational crime; the creation of more efficient and effective justice administration; and the promotion of high standards of fairness, justice, and professional conduct in member states. The United Nations recognizes that internationally organized criminal groups are one of the major challenges to law and order in its member countries in the twenty-first century. Canada supports the United Nations Crime Prevention Agency because it recognizes that crime is global—criminal activity does not adhere to boundaries, and it cannot live in isolation from what transpires in other parts of the world. We have been influenced by drug trafficking, money laundering, terrorism, alien smuggling, international fraud, and corruption.

Another agency of the United Nations, established in 2002, is the International Criminal Court (ICC). Canada was involved in its creation, and the purpose of this court is to be a permanent criminal court for prosecuting individuals who commit crimes against humanity, including genocide, war crimes, torture, and mass rape. Over 90 countries have ratified its charter, and it has become a global judicial institution with an international jurisdiction. Unfortunately, the United States has not accepted the charter or jurisdiction of the International Criminal Court, leading to strong worldwide condemnation of its actions. Canada, as one of its strongest proponents, has provided prosecutors, judges, and financial support for the ICC's operations.

While the globalization of crime has created shock waves throughout the world community, it has also allowed for enhanced coordination of law enforcement agencies on an international scale. As well, the Canadian criminal justice system can improve by involving itself with its counterparts in other countries. Law-enforcement agencies, the courts, and corrections officials can become more efficient by learning both investigative and crime-prevention techniques from collaborating with other agencies and officials. Improved communications technology, information-sharing methodologies, and new international agreements and partnerships will allow for more success in reducing the globalization of crime.

Conclusion

The tremendous growth in the importance of criminal justice studies in Canada in the past two decades reflects the importance that crime causation, prevention, and administration play in the lives of Canadians. Undoubtedly, the increase in social problems and issues related to drug use and increasing crime rates have boosted interest in the various branches of the criminal justice system. While overall crime rates in Canada have dropped in the last decade, most members of the public still perceive crime and the criminal justice system as important in their lives. Recent Gallup polls (2001) show that over 70 percent of the population believes that the courts are too lenient in punishing offenders, with women and the elderly reporting a higher degree of insecurity in their homes and neighbourhoods. Given these attitudes, it is likely that interest in the administration of justice will continue to be important to the Canadian public. The internationalization of crime and the transfer of crime from other countries to Canada have also taken off in alarming proportions and challenged our criminal justice system. While not an impossibility, creating a justice system that follows due process and protects the legal rights of individuals, while enforcing the criminal laws fairly and efficiently, is a great challenge. In the following chapters, we hope to provide a comprehensive analysis of the operation of the various components of the criminal justice system. As well, we will critically analyze and provide constructive solutions to the dysfunctional parts of that system.

Summary

In this chapter, we have discussed the historical and social underpinnings of the society from which crime and crime-control methods have evolved. Examining the various branches of the criminal justice system—the police, the courts, and corrections—allows us to analyze both the methodology and the practice of criminal justice. While the twin goals of crime control and due process are the linchpins of the system, they often can be in conflict. The crime-control approach emphasizes law enforcement and punishment, while the due process model stresses the rights of individuals to fair treatment before the law, and holds the law-enforcement agencies accountable for upholding justice. Within this mix is thrown the Canadian Charter of Rights and Freedoms, which further enshrines individual rights and limits the prosecutorial power of the criminal justice system. The challenge is to balance the collective needs of the society for effective law enforcement with the need to be fair and equitable and to recognize individual rights.

Key Terms

arrest (p. 2)

Canadian Charter of Rights and
    Freedoms (the Charter) (p. 5)

comparative criminal justice (p. 10)

corrections (p. 6)

court system (p. 4)

crime-control model (p. 10)

Criminal Code of Canada (p. 4)

criminal justice system (p. 2)

due process (p. 9)

Discussion Questions

1. What are the main goals of the Canadian criminal justice system?

2. Discuss the concept of social order in the context of the purpose of criminal law in society.

3. Discuss some of the factors that influence why certain behaviours are defined as criminal and others are not.

4. Outline some changes you would implement in the various parts of the criminal justice system to improve the efficiency of its operations.

5. Does the Charter of Rights and Freedoms affect the promotion of social order and social control in society?

Weblinks

www.criminology.utoronto.ca/library The University of Toronto's Centre of Criminology is an excellent starting point, with a list of links to various online criminal justice resources. The information covers a wide range of subject areas, including public and private policing, violence, deviance and social control, young offenders, criminology, and criminal law.

www.canadalegal.com Duhaime's Canadian Criminal Law Centre site offers plain language articles on criminal justice issues ranging from abortion law to traffic tickets.

www.acjnet.org This site is a gate to Canadian justice and legal information and services. The Access to Justice Network (ACJNet) opens doors to legislation, people and organizations, publications, databases, and discussion forums on justice and legal issues. These resources are organized under subject headings such as: Aboriginal people, crime prevention, plain language, women, and youth.

www.efc.ca/pages/law/cc/cc.html This site provides the text of the entire Criminal Code of Canada.

www.icclr.law.ubc.ca The International Centre for Criminal Law Reform and Criminal Justice Policy is a Vancouver-based, independent, non-profit institute, officially affiliated with the United Nations. The organization is dedicated to national and international efforts to reduce crime and improve justice. Their site contains publications, occasional papers and reports, event and conference listings, an online forum facility, and links to partner institutes around the world.

CHAPTER 2 — Crime Statistics

Objectives

- To provide a statistical analysis of crime in Canadian society, including who commits crime, the prevalence of crime, and the incidence of crime.

- To analyze self-report and victimization data to enhance our understanding of crime, risk factors for crime and victimization, and locations of crime.

- To analyze over- and under-reporting of crime owing to bias in the justice system in the forms of racism, sexism, and classism.

- To provide a comprehensive analysis of crime patterns in Canada by region, type of crime, age, sex, race, social ecology, and demographics.

The Crime Picture

Most Canadians believe that crime is a major social issue. Polls show that Canadians frequently view the "crime problem" as among the top priorities for government intervention. But what is the extent and nature of crime in Canadian society? Who commits crime, what sorts of crimes are most frequently committed, and under what conditions do these crimes occur?

This chapter will provide an overview of the **demographics** (the pattern or distribution in a population) of crime in Canadian society. We will begin by explaining some key terms and concepts that aid in the interpretation of crime rates. Next, we will discuss the sources of knowledge about crime statistics and patterns. Finally, we will discuss some possible reasons for the demographics—reasons that are tied to theories about crime.

A *preconception* is an understanding or a view formed prior to thoroughly reviewing the evidence. Before reading this chapter, you might want to jot down some of your own preconceptions about crime in Canada. Is the crime rate going up or down? Is violent crime on the increase? How does Canada rank compared with other countries in measures of crime?

You might also want to ask yourself what the *sources* are of your preconceptions of the Canadian crime picture. If you are like most people, your sources will be television news and talk shows, major newspaper and magazine stories, and news and information posted on the internet. These are mass media sources because they are a form of communication aimed at very large markets. Unfortunately, the mass media tend to transmit a distorted image of crime. Violent street crimes are widely covered, while non-violent corporate and white-collar crimes are under-reported. Canadian mass media sources also tend to view the crime situation through US lenses, giving the illusion that Canadian society suffers the same degree of social problems that exist south of the border. For example, in a study of local television newscasts, Dowler (2004) finds that there are very few differences in the content and presentation of crime stories between US and Canadian newscasts, although stateside news stories are generally presented in a more sensational way. Furthermore, although the internet contains much accurate and valuable information, it also contains unreliable and inaccurate material.

Your impression of the crime picture might also be informed by your own experiences. Your view of the bigger picture often—and quite naturally—comes from your own experience. Have you been a victim of crime? Was the victimization brutal? Your gut feeling about the extent of crime out there can be shaped and distorted by your individual situation and experience.

Your situation may be unusual in a number of ways that we will discuss, using demographic measures like age, sex, class, ethnicity, and ecology. Even if your situation represents many demographic norms, it still doesn't provide the best place from which to draw inferences on what is happening in the whole of Canadian society. To get a relatively accurate measure of the extent and nature of crime in Canada, we need to look at the number of incidents within *populations*, rather than at the number of incidents an *individual* has experienced. To get a feeling for the difference, speak to some of your classmates and compare notes on your experiences of victimization. The more people you compare notes with, the more you will be able to see how individual experiences are deviations from the average.

You might also compare experiences with criminal acts. Have you ever shoplifted? How often? Ask some of your classmates to describe their criminal history. You may have some apprehension about disclosing your past criminal behaviour, however insignificant it was. Your classmates might also have reservations about sharing their criminal history, however trifling, with you. Nevertheless, these exercises are unsophisticated versions of two of the tools social scientists use to get a picture of crime: victimization and self-report surveys. These, plus official and unofficial statistics, form the basis of a rendering of the crime picture that is *sociologically sound*—or valid and reliable according to social science standards.

Although they may be sociologically sound, we shall also see that each of these techniques is far from perfect. Your own survey of your classmates' criminal histories and experiences of victimization will likely leave you with the suspicion that the true picture has not been fully revealed. Similarly, social scientists using the most advanced methods will also admit that problems persist with the reporting and counting that they use to arrive at their findings. However, it is important to stress that the crime picture drawn in this way is still more reliable and accurate than one drawn from an ad hoc sampling of mass media stories and individual experiences. While the picture of crime in Canadian society presented in this chapter is far from flawless, it is derived from the best methods and tools at our disposal.

The Purpose of Crime Statistics

Why do we record, or try to record, the amount of crime in society? Why is the study of crime often a war of words (and numbers) between those who believe crime is increasing and society is becoming destabilized and those who believe crime is decreasing and society has a handle on its social problems? In part, crime is political, and crime statistics frequently serve political masters. Crime sells votes.

But there are other reasons why crime measurement is important. One reason is that many theories explaining crime depend on some kind of mapping of the frequency and distribution of crime. Without reasonably solid information on the incidence and prevalence of crime, it is difficult to begin the work of explaining crime. Theories of crime causation are important if governments wish to create policies aimed at reducing—or redistributing—criminality in society.

Let us take the example of drunk driving. Before they will see drunk driving as a problem requiring action, governments will want to study the evidence of the prevalence and frequency of this behaviour. The argument that more money, changed laws, or redistributed governmental resources—such as more police officers—are required hinges on some evidence showing that this is a social problem that governmental policy can do something about. To understand the dimensions of the problem, such as increasing frequency, prevalence, and cost, the government needs a picture of the problem based on a collection of records of incidence. If Mothers Against Drunk Driving (MADD) can tell the government that accidents owing to impairment have increased nationally from, say, 5000 in 2005 to 10 000 in 2006, then the federal government may agree that the issue is worthy of further governmental intervention.

So, crime recording provides a picture of a population or of society as a whole from the angle of criminality. How much criminality there is, what kinds of criminality are common, and where the criminality takes place are questions that provide a basis from which policy can attack the social problem of crime. The facts and figures of crime can mobilize political action and social policy.

Methods for Mapping Crime

Terms and Concepts

When you hear criminal justice officials and social scientists speaking about the crime picture, you likely encounter unfamiliar terms and concepts. Before venturing out into the hazardous terrain occupied by numbers and graphs, we will review some of these in order to gain a basic understanding of the terms used in crime statistics.

Prevalence of Crime

The **prevalence of crime** is the number of people participating in crime at a given time. Prevalence is measured by dividing the number of offenders by the size of the population.

If, for instance, there are 50 people in your class and 5 of these students are offenders, then you can determine the prevalence of crime in your class by dividing the population of offenders (5) by the population of your class (50). This gives you a ratio of 1/10.

Incidence of Crime

The **incidence of crime** is the frequency with which offenders commit crime, or the average number of offences per offender. Incidence is measured by dividing the number of offences by the number of offenders.

Let us say that the 5 hypothetical offenders in your class committed the following number of offences: 1 committed 1 offence, 3 committed 2 offences, and 1 committed 17 offences. You would calculate the incidence by adding up the offences and dividing that number (20) by the number of offenders (5). This would leave you with an incidence rate of 4 offences per offender, or 4/1.

Crime Rate

The **crime rate** is the number of offences that occur per population. A population, or a cohort, is simply a group of people with a common demographic. The group can be as large as all of the people in Canada or as small as all of the people in your class. A crime rate is calculated by totalling all the offences occurring in a given population and dividing that number by the population. The population is the *denominator*—the figure underneath the line. The frequency is the *numerator*—the figure above the line. A crime rate uses a given denominator of 100 000. It is usually measured as a frequency of offences per 100 000 people.

Let's take the hypothetical example of your class again. You have 5 offenders who have committed a total of 20 offences in a population of 50 students. You can calculate the crime rate by simply dividing the number of offences by the total population: 20/50 = 2/5. Or, you can calculate it by multiplying prevalence (1/10) by incidence (4/1). This would give you the following: $1/10 \times 4/1 = 4/10$ (or 2/5).

Now, remember that crime statistics are usually presented as a figure per population of 100 000. The easiest way to calculate this statistic is to divide the number of offences by the meaningful population in which those offences occurred to get a percentage and then multiply the percentage (a figure out of 10), by 100 000. In this case, that would give us a rate of 40 000/100 000—presented in short form by just citing the numerator, or 40 000. This is an astronomical rate indeed! Most crime rates are lower than this.

One of the reasons the rate is so high is that we failed to properly account for *time*. In our example, we did not specify a time period in coming up with our rate of 40 000. But a time period is important. When we look at crime, we are always concerned with a rate of crime in a specified period of time. The crime rate is almost always calculated *per year*, but it can also be given per month in month-to-month comparisons.

Let's apply this principle to our hypothetical class. Say those 20 offences were spread out evenly over 15 years. This would give us a rate per year of 1.33; 1.33 divided by the total population of 50 equals a rate of 2066. This figure is more realistic, but it is still higher than what you might reasonably expect to find were you to rely on official statistics.

It is important to remember that a crime rate always refers to the incidence and frequency of offences per a given population. At its most general, the rate consists of *all* offences committed and *all* of the population in a territorial jurisdiction, such as Canada. However, crime rates are also given for specific offences, such as burglary, murder, and auto theft. For example, if there were 70 homicides in the Greater Toronto Area (GTA) in 2006, and the GTA at the time had a population of 2.5 million, we would compute a murder rate of 70/2 500 000 3 100 000 = 2.8 per 100 000.

As an illustration of differences in crime rates for various offences, Table 2.1 compares various offences in Canada for 2004. For example, under homicide, we would calculate the rate by taking the total number of homicides (622) and dividing it by the total Canadian population (31 936 338), and multiplying it by 100 000. It would give us a homicide rate of 1.95, which is rounded up to 2 per 100 000. Similarly, the rate for robbery would be calculated the same way, by taking the total number of robberies (27 477) and dividing it by the Canadian population (31 936 338), and multiplying it by 100 000, which would give us a rate of 86.03, rounded down to 86 per 100 000. Remember, the crime rate for the whole country is calculated using the census population in the denominator. For 2004, according to Statistics Canada, the population was 31 936 338. By 2007, the population is projected to be slightly over 32 500 000.

TABLE 2.1

CRIME RATES FOR SELECTED OFFENCES

	2004		% CHANGE IN RATE	
	NUMBER	RATE[1]	2003 TO 2004	1994 TO 2004
Homicide	622	2	12.3	−5.3
Attempted murder	717	2	0.5	−29.4
Assaults (levels 1, 2, 3)	233 774	732	−2.2	−4.5
Other assaults	12 873	40	1.8	−18.1
Sexual assaults (levels 1, 2, 3)	23 534	74	−0.8	−32.6
Other sexual offences	2 625	8	1.4	−37.6
Abduction	635	2	12.6	−48.9
Robbery	27 477	86	−4.2	−14.0
Violent crime: Total	**302 257**	**946**	**−2.0**	**−9.7**
Break and enter	274 717	860	−4.4	−35.7
Motor vehicle theft	169 544	531	−3.5	−3.5
Theft over $5000	17 294	54	−11.7	−40.8
Theft $5000 and under	680 885	2 131	−3.7	−23.4
Possession of stolen goods	35 400	111	5.8	6.7
Fraud	97 091	304	3.5	−14.6
Property crime: Total	**1 274 931**	**3 991**	**−3.2**	**−24.1**
Mischief	353 661	1 107	−2.0	−19.1
Counterfeiting currency	159 889	500	13.8	333.5
Bail violations	104 334	327	2.3	43.6
Disturbing the peace	117 022	366	12.7	107.4
Offensive weapons	18 002	56	1.2	−13.5

continued

Prostitution	6 493	20	13.1	5.7
Arson	13 148	41	−6.1	−11.7
Other	222 123	695	−4.4	−13.2
Other Criminal Code: Total	**994 672**	**3 114**	**1.8**	**10.4**
Criminal Code: Total:	**2 571 860**	**8 051**	**−1.2**	**−11.8**
Excluding traffic (crime rate)				
Cannabis: Total	**67 832**	**212**	**10.0**	**52.0**
Possession	48 052	150	15.3	53.8
Trafficking	10 470	33	−1.4	16.9
Cultivation	8 328	26	−4.0	120.1
Importation	982	3	45.0	55.8
Cocaine	16 837	53	17.3	23.9
Heroin	792	2	19.5	−55.3
Other drugs	11 674	37	6.9	85.6
Drugs: Total	**97 135**	**304**	**10.9**	**46.6**

[1] Rate is based on criminal incidents per 100 000 population.

Source: Adapted from *The Daily*, Catalogue 11-001, Thursday, July 21, 2005. Available at www.statcan.ca/Daily/English/050721/d050721a.htm.

Problems with Crime Rates

There are problems in calculating crime rates that should induce you to read them with some skepticism. First, what really belongs in the denominator? Some analysts have suggested that to calculate car thefts or property thefts in general, what we really ought to put in the denominator is the property available to be stolen. With car thefts, for example, does it not make sense to consider the number of cars available to steal? Obviously, cities with higher numbers of automobiles would experience higher levels of car thefts. Certainly, we would learn more precisely the extent of auto theft as a problem if we could compare places according to the proportion of cars stolen.

Second, which numbers should be used for the numerator? Above, we used Statistics Canada figures for total Criminal Code offences. StatsCan figures depend on the police becoming aware of an offence and recording it. As we shall shortly see, for the police to record an offence, a number of things need to happen—a citizen has to call the police, and the police have to correctly identify and record the event as an offence.

Third, what is the true relationship between official records and the extent of real crime? We refer to this problem with the term *the dark figure of crime*, which we will discuss next.

CALCULATING CRIME RATE: SPEND-IT-HERE, ONTARIO

Let us take the example of a tourist city, Spend-It-Here, Ontario. Crime reports include all break and enters reported to the police in a given year. Let's say that this figure was recorded as 1500. Therefore, 1500 would go above the line in calculating the crime rate for car theft. If Spend-It-Here has a population of 200 000, that would give us the following:

$$\frac{1500}{200\ 000} = 750$$

The trouble is that Spend-It-Here's population on any given day can also include many non-residents who are not enumerated, which makes the denominator smaller than it should be. If, for instance, there are an extra 15 000 visitors on a Saturday night, and if this is when most car thefts occur, then the denominator of the population of the city ought to be 215 000, giving us a lesser rate of 698.

This is perhaps more extreme in a city like Atlantic City, Las Vegas, or Washington, D.C. In Washington, a great deal of non-residents commute from surrounding states to work every day, making the daily population count much higher than the enumerated residential population. Washington, D.C., has a very high murder rate, but this rate does not include non-residents among the denominator, thus deflating it and inflating the crime rate.

The Dark Figure of Crime

From time to time in your study of criminology you will come across the term **the dark figure of crime**, or simply **the dark figure**. What does this term mean? Simply put, it comprises the amount of actual crime in society, which official crime statistics do not show because not all crimes are reported to, or recorded by, the police. When you hear the radio announcing that the crime rate is up, the report is based on police statistics or on official crime statistics of reported and recorded crime. However, since the first victimization survey in the mid-1960s, criminologists have confirmed what most people in the criminal justice system and in society have long suspected: many people who commit crimes are not caught and brought to justice, and many crimes remain unreported and unrecorded because many victims choose not to pursue the case. The dark figure is this unreported and unrecorded crime; it is a figure that is unknown.

We are beginning to know more about this dark figure, however. We know, for instance, that unreported crimes for some offences are much higher than others. Victimization surveys reveal that the proportion of unreported to reported cases of sexual assault is very high. On the other hand, cases of unreported or unrecorded homicides are very low. The under-reporting of homicide is on the low end of the scale because victims are often missed if they disappear. For these and other reasons, the reporting of homicides is not shadowed by a sizeable dark figure. The exceptions are cases where someone is murdered but the death is officially reported as resulting from natural causes or an accident.

The dark figure is important for a number of reasons. The deterrent effect of punishment holds no sway if the offender is not prosecuted. As well, the picture of crime trends is skewed if "real" criminality is very different from "official" criminality. Insurance programs, compensation programs, and even policy objectives are also best served by the most reliable data about crime.

Before we leave our discussion of the dark figure, one caveat is in order. According to Canadian criminal law, a crime is a violation of the Criminal Code that is attended by the requisite *mens rea* and *actus reus*, as determined by a court of law (we will discuss these elements of criminal offences in Chapter 3). The legal profession would argue that criminologists who claim that there is a dark figure of crime and criminality are using the terms *crime* and *criminality* too liberally, given that only the courts can determine legal criminality, and some of those who make up the dark figure would be found legally not guilty. The problem is exacerbated because "actual" criminality represented in the dark figure depends on information that is most often documented without the benefit of cross-examination. This information may be based on compounded, unchallengeable interpretations of a given event as a legal offence.

Crime Recording

Our understanding of the picture of crime depends on two sources: official statistics and unofficial statistics. As we have learned, **official statistics** detail *recorded* criminal activities. This recording is done by the police, the courts, and provincial and federal corrections agencies. **Unofficial statistics**, on the other hand, are *estimates* of criminal activity based on self-report and victimization surveys.

We have already noted that crime statistics are a necessary starting point for policy and for some theorizing on criminality. However, we will see that official statistics do come with problems, as the numbers that they provide can be skewed by systematic biases and errors. In our discussion of crime reporting, we will begin by addressing the various kinds of official statistics on crime we have in Canada and some specific problems with them. Next, we will look at self-report and victimization reports as a way of augmenting the crime picture with unofficial statistics. Finally, we will look at sources of bias and error in statistics.

Official Statistics

Official statistics begin with individual cases of offences recorded by the police. These cases need to be gathered as a collection of more manageable data. In

Canada, the Uniform Crime Reporting Survey (UCR) allows us to do this. The UCR contains rules, definitions, and categories by which data on incidents are scored according to nationally approved criteria.

The UCR was inaugurated in 1962 as a shared project of Statistics Canada and the Canadian Association of Chiefs of Police. The UCR includes almost all Criminal Code offences, as well as federal and provincial statutes. The Canadian Centre for Justice Statistics (CCJS) assumed responsibility for the program in 1981. The CCJS offers an annual compilation of the UCR.

Before analyzing what these data tell us, we need to consider their limitations. First, not all incidents are reported to the police. Victimization surveys have found that such reporting depends on whether there is a complainant or victim, whether the victim perceives the seriousness of the crime, and whether the victim feels the police can be of help or views the crime as a private matter that can be resolved. Some victims may also fear retaliation, and sexual assault victims are particularly hesitant about having their lives further disrupted by "secondary" victimization through the justice process itself. Some victims also experience a sense of shame, and many do not wish to subject themselves to further violation. The official scrutiny that attends the fact-finding of a criminal event is itself painful, and many victims believe that the criminal justice system will fail to remedy their loss or offer them justice.

Second, often a number of separate offences are committed in an incident, but only the most serious is scored. As Silverman (1980) has argued, the result is that the total crime count is underestimated because those other crimes are lost in the analysis. Another result is the misleading impression that a larger percentage of crimes are serious crimes (Linden, 1996).

Third, the numbers are only as good as their faithfulness to the events they represent. If the police begin to clamp down on prostitution through more "proactive policing," or if they decide to look the other way for possession of small amounts of cannabis even though there are no changes to legislation, then the numbers they feed into the UCR will show increases and decreases that reflect changes in police practices, rather than changes in crime patterns. Also, if the police decide to enforce "zero tolerance" policies with regard to violence in schools or "affirmative arrest" practices in cases of spousal assault—where the police officer is not to use discretion, but is to make an arrest if any sign of physical assault is present on the body of the complainant—then crime rates will rise as a result of these changes in policies.

In addition to the discretion and enforcement practices of the police, there are differences in other subsystems of the criminal justice process that can produce variations in the crime rate. For example, Sprott and Doob (1998) have found huge variations in incarceration rates among provinces, which are partly the result of vast differences in provincial policies and the administration of justice.

Fourth, in addition to changes in crime-control policies, changes in legislation can affect crime rates. If the Criminal Code creates new offence categories or broadens existing ones, crime rates will reflect these legislative changes in the form of increases. Recent changes to drug legislation are a prime example.

Unofficial Statistics

Self-Report Data

In addition to official statistics, criminologists use unofficial statistics to obtain a picture of crime. A **self-report survey**, as the word implies, is one that asks people to report on their own delinquency or criminal past. In our earlier example, your classmates' reports of their past criminal behaviour were rudimentary self-reports. Self-report surveys, then, are merely questionnaires asking for some demographic data in addition to information about the respondents' criminal history.

The first self-report study of crime was conducted by Austin Potterfield in the early 1940s. Of the college students he surveyed, 90 percent admitted to a felony crime. Wallerstien and Wyle (1947) and Nye and Short (1957) did further studies to corroborate Potterfield's initial findings that criminality was widespread across the adolescent population. The dark figure of crime suddenly began to appear, and it loomed large—it seemed that many crimes were neither reported nor recorded.

Self-report studies were important, and not only as a criticism of official data. These studies also held the potential to reveal the work of the criminal justice system. They were key evidence of the claim that there existed law-enforcement biases that gave a skewed or distorted rendering of criminality. Indeed, self-report studies have been important in painting a picture of the relationship between class and crime, as well as in demystifying the assumption that delinquency is an almost exclusively lower-class phenomenon.

In the United States in 1976, a large self-report study, the National Youth Survey, discovered that more than 90 percent of juveniles admitted to at least one act for which they could have served a custody sentence, had they been caught. It also found that the actual rate of delinquency was four to ten times higher than was officially reported in the UCR.

As with official statistics, there are persistent problems with self-report studies. For example, it has been found that lower-class males and black males are more likely to under-report their delinquency (Hindelang, Hirschi, & Weis, 1981). In addition, the method depends on one person's interpretation of events (the perpetrator), which may not accord with how others interpret the events. People can more easily admit to things through confession in a confidential questionnaire, and this sort of confession may exaggerate criminality. There have been strong criticisms of the reliability and validity of self-report surveys because respondents depend on their memory of events, and they may misunderstand questions or simply lie (Huizinga & Elliott, 1986).

Victimization Data

Victimization surveys are another source of unofficial information to augment the crime picture and to cast light into the dark figure. Victimization surveys are questionnaires that ask people to provide information about their experience as the object of criminal activity, rather than as the perpetrator. Respondents are asked to tell if and how often they have been robbed, raped, had things stolen from among their possessions, and so forth. They are asked if they knew the offender; whether they reported the event to the police, and why or why not; and what the circumstances of the crime were. In addition, they are asked detailed questions about their own life circumstances.

Victimization surveys capture many petty infractions and crimes that may occur in the household, such as burglary, domestic assault, and incest, which often are not reported to the police. According to the 1982 Canadian Urban Victimization Survey, personal theft, vandalism, simple assault, and sexual assault were more likely to go unreported than be reported. However, victimization surveys fail to report many frauds, as the victim is often unaware of the crime.

In Canada, there have been several victimization surveys that have taken a national sampling. The first of these, the Canadian Urban Victimization Survey, consisted of a random sample of the population aged 16 and over in seven cities. Over 60 000 telephone interviews were conducted. Residents were asked questions covering a wide range of victimization experiences over the previous year. In 1988 and 1993, the General Social Survey (GSS) was conducted through telephone surveys of a smaller sample of Canadians (10 000). It asked respondents for detailed information on a more limited set of crimes (CCJS, 1994). Finally, a small national sample was taken as part of an international study of crime victimization (van Dijk & Mayhew, 1997; van Dijk, Mayhew, & Kilias, 1991).

In the most recent victimization survey in 2004, it was revealed that a large proportion of Canadians never reported criminal incidents to the police. Only about 34 percent of criminal incidents came to the attention of police (*Juristat*, 2005). Canadians give several reasons for not reporting, which are presented in Figure 2.1.

The relationship between official statistics and victimization rates as reported in victimization surveys is shown in Table 2.2. The table compares the major crime categories in the Uniform Crime Reports index in the United States with responses of victimization from the National Crime Victimization Survey, which began operation in 1972 in the United States. Can you think of why so many motor vehicle thefts are reported?

FIGURE 2.1

MOST COMMON REASONS FOR NOT REPORTING HOUSEHOLD VICTIMIZATION

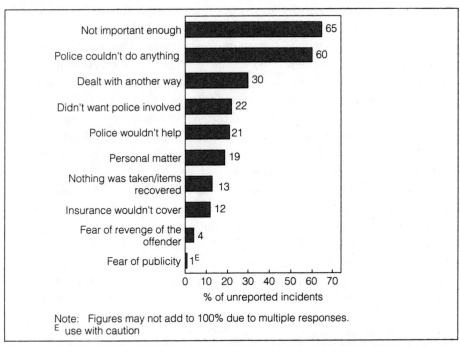

Note: Figures may not add to 100% due to multiple responses.
E use with caution

Source: Adapted from Statistics Canada's *Juristat*, Catalogue 85–002, Criminal Victimization in Canada, 2004, Vol. 25, No. 7, November 2005, page 19. Available at www.statcan.ca/english/freepub/85-002-XIE/0070585-002-XIE.pdf.

TABLE 2.2

COMPARISON OF CRIME REPORTS (2004)

	UNIFORM CRIME REPORTS	NATIONAL CRIMINAL VICTIMIZATION SURVEY
VIOLENT CRIME		
Forcible rapes	94 635	209 880
Robbery	401 326	501 820
PROPERTY CRIME		
Burglary	2 143 456	3 427 690
Larceny	6 947 685	14 211 940
Motor vehicle theft	1 237 114	1 014 770

Sources: UCR fata at http://bjsdata.ojp.usdoj.gov/dataonline/Search/crime/state/Runcrimestateby state.cfm; National crime Victimzation Data from www.ojp.usdoj.gov/bjs/pub/pdf/cvo4.pdf.

Victimization surveys have revealed much about the characteristics of criminal incidents, such as the time, the location, the offender–victim relationship, and the victim's decisions before and after the victimization, such as whether to call the police and the reasons why or why not. Victimization surveys have also helped to change our understanding of crime as a distributed phenomenon, or one that is spread out across time and space in certain predictable ways. By looking at crime from the point of view of the victim, victimization surveys highlight risk factors, focusing attention on the behaviours, locations, relationships, and activities that could increase a person's chances of victimization. In general, much of the dark figure of crime has been revealed through victimization surveys.

There are two noteworthy shortcomings of victimization surveys. One problem is that they depend, for the most part, on the victim's uncorroborated statements. In most cases, these statements are not or cannot be verified. The respondent may be mistaken as to the nature of the event, the time of the event, and the circumstances surrounding the event. People who decide to respond to the survey are likely somewhat keener to talk about their victimization than those who decide not to respond. Some of these methodological problems are addressed and partially resolved in good surveys, but problems remain. A second broad area of concern is how victimization relates to crime. Crime, it must be stressed, is a determination of the court, and many instances of victimization will not constitute legal crimes. The relationship of victimization to crime is not as clear-cut as might be assumed (see Quinney, 1972).

Longitudinal Research

Another noteworthy research technique is known as longitudinal or cohort research. This method involves observing a sample of people or a cohort of people who share a like characteristic over time. The longitudinal method is much like the ongoing British documentary series *28 Up*, *35 Up*, *42 Up*, etc. (as of 2006, the latest instalment of the *Up* series was *49 Up*), which follow a small sample of people by interviewing them every seven years to see how their lives are coming along. Every so often, the sample in a longitudinal survey is investigated on a number of criteria in order to gauge the incidence of crime or victimization.

One of the first of these studies was done by Wolfgang, Figlio, and Sellin in a 1972 study, *Delinquency in a Birth Cohort*. These authors followed 9945 boys in Philadelphia from their birth in 1945 until they were 18 years old. The authors used official police records to identify delinquents and found that over a third of the boys had some police contact. They also found that some of these boys were what they called *chronic offenders* (boys who offended fives times or more up until the age of 18); these boys made up 6.3 percent of the total of the group. When Wolfgang replicated the study in a 1958 birth cohort, he found that the rate of chronic delinquency had increased to 7.5 percent.

The advantage of this kind of study is that it allows researchers to trace patterns in criminal careers or biographies. Such tracing is possible because both official data and some biographical data can be cross-tabulated. The more biographical data used the more that can be discovered above the limited dimensions (such as age and sex) that official statistics make available. In addition, the longitudinal study, if the sample is properly selected, can be a highly reliable indicator of the rates of criminal activity in particular populations.

New Methods

In the United States, the National Incident-Based Reporting System (NIBRS) records crime by detailing the date, time, location, offender characteristics (age, sex, ethnicity, race), victim characteristics (age, sex, ethnicity, circumstances), and offence characteristics. This method is very promising, as it incorporates much of the data that other systems omit, leaving victimization and self-report data to fill in the blanks.

Systemic Biases and Sources of Error

Thus far, we have discussed specific problems in the reporting and recording of crime and the development of crime statistics. There are further structural and systemic causes of error in the development of crime figures. Three sources of error are systemic racism, sexism, and classism. As well, the goals and interests of efficiency in judicial institutions may affect crime statistics.

Racism

Earlier, we mentioned that the police have a great deal of discretion in determining who is selected for criminal prosecution. Such discretion is more pronounced when police are more proactive (in cases where there is no complainant or victim), but it is also relatively greater in minor offences, such as littering, jaywalking, disorderly conduct, and minor traffic violations. The decision of the police and the courts of whether to prosecute may be influenced by professionalism and by weighing the perceived harm to the community or society against the principle of upholding the privacy and liberty of the individual. But it has often been found that professionalism and liberal principles are not the driving forces of prosecutorial decision-making. Instead, as inquiries into the wrongful convictions of David Milgaard and Donald Marshall have found, sometimes even in serious cases the police look for the best available target to clear cases, and they look for them within marginalized groups and minorities—in these cases, Aboriginal Canadians.

Sexism

It has also been contended that sexism may play a role in the over- or under-reporting of crime. In the past, the juvenile justice system was preoccupied with

David Milgaard (right) at a press conference.

status offences, or offences stemming from the moral regulation of girls and young women. Girls were more likely than boys in the early and mid–twentieth century to be apprehended and brought to court for status offences (Chesney-Lind, 1977). More recently, feminists have contended that girls and women are more harshly treated when their behaviour suggests that they are not following traditional roles (Carlen, Christina, Hicks, O'Dwyer, & Tchaikowsky, 1985). A competing view is the *chivalry hypothesis*—the theory that officials in the criminal justice system, from police officers to judges, are more lenient with female criminals, whom they consider "damsels in distress." Today, however, self-report and victimization rates fail to support the chivalry hypothesis. Women appear to be processed by the law in a way that is appropriate to their offending.

Classism

The crime picture is also distorted through classism. Not everyone's interests are equally reflected in decision-making about which kind of conflicts warrant criminalization. Partly, this problem is related to who occupies a position of power in determining right and wrong conduct. People with wealth and status in society can much more easily identify with the interests of others like them. If they occupy the ranks of judges, lawyers, and politicians, then their interests will affect who is processed and how. But they will also influence how social problems are categorized as crime or regulatory offences or as legitimate risks that are not prohibited.

For example, even though many people in high-pollution areas, such as southern Ontario, are put at risk by environmental degradation and the presence of nitrogen oxides, benzene, ground-level ozone, and other pollutants, and many early deaths are attributable to environmental contamination, we still prefer to view repeat health and safety violators as good citizens who should be given a chance to correct their actions. In many jurisdictions, industry and governmental regulators set flexible goals that permit recurrent violations of existing environmental and occupational health and safety codes. Infractions against labour codes are similarly subject to regulatory law, as governments operate to encourage compliance rather than to punish deviation. To get an idea of the differences in the policing of corporate deviance and street crime, try to picture a drug dealer and a police officer sitting down to work out goals or targets for the quantity and quality of infractions (drug deals) that the dealer will be allowed to make. Jeffrey Reiman (2003) argues that there are two sets of laws in our society: one for the rich (the "haves") and one for the poor (the "have-nots").

The discrepancy cannot be justified by citing the greater overall economic importance of corporate polluters and white-collar offenders, because the cost to society of corporate and white-collar crime is estimated to be far greater than the cost of street crime. Rather, the distinction between the two is better understood as a difference of political power. Political power serves the interests of those in society who have a bigger slice of the economic pie. Under this argument, the criminal law is seen as the poor person's law—it is applicable more often and with greater consequences to those in society who have less. This view of the class basis of criminal selection, argued by criminologists such as Richard Quinney, Robert Elias, and Jeffrey Reiman, is important to our picture of the distribution of wrongdoing in society, as it alerts us to the possibility that there is another dark figure of transgressions against society that are not revealed by official crime statistics, self-reports, and victimization surveys (see, for example, Muncie, McLaughlin, & Langen, 1997).

A further problem of classism is that the distribution of resources in society works against the rights of the marginalized. Legal aid programs are intended to right the imbalance for accused people of little means, but for the most part they fail to do so because the quality and availability of legal aid rarely comes close to what is available to those with vast resources for their legal defence. Again, the distribution of wealth in society skews the crime picture to present a much greater distribution of crime in the lower classes.

Institutional Practices in the Police, the Courts, and Corrections Systems

Each subsystem of the criminal justice system—the police, the courts, and corrections—has goals and the means to achieve these goals. These subsystems attempt to maximize their efficiency while operating with some level of accountability and attending to the rule of law. Sometimes, however, the effort to make each of these systems more efficient competes with considerations of due process. Herbert Packer (1964) saw crime control and due process as two competing objectives. But even where law is flexible so that it operates efficiently to control crime, the professionals who work within these subsystems often take shortcuts to achieve their objectives.

Plea bargaining is an example of such a shortcut, because it trades some amount of due process for enhanced efficiency, often rewarding accused persons who agree to such deals with shorter sentences than they would have received had they insisted on a full trial. Plea bargaining is therefore an institutional practice, or a routinized, officially sanctioned procedure used across the whole criminal justice system. Institutional practices like plea bargaining affect the crime picture because they allow for more guilty verdicts than would be possible without them.

Another example relates more to how institutions *think*. Police forces can be understood in terms of their objectives, one of which is to find a suspect who can be processed criminally for a crime. As the Guy Paul Morin inquiry showed, this objective can lead police to seek not so much the person who actually committed the crime, because proving guilt goes beyond the epistemology of police work, but rather a person who can be prosecuted or arrested. Once an arrestable person is found, as discovered in the Morin inquiry, the police may ignore evidence of the suspect's innocence, to the point of failing to disclose such key evidence to prosecutors.

Crime Patterns in Canada

Is Canada a safe country in which to live? Are cities more crime prone than towns? Are women more likely to be victims of crime than men? These are just some of the questions to which a comprehensive **crime map** can provide answers. A crime map is simply a graphical presentation of the official crime statistics published by Statistics Canada. In this section, we will look at how crime is distributed. We will see how it is distributed by region, season, time of day, ecology, age, gender, class, ethnicity, and citizenship. We will also see how the crime rate has changed over time in Canada and how Canada's crime rate compares with those of other nations.

Historical Trends

Probably the most frequently asked question about crime is, "Are crime rates going up?" We look at crime rates as a barometer of social cohesion and quality of life. As Canadians, many of us regard the historically high violent crime rates in the United States as evidence of a lack of social cohesion and of a poorer quality of life than in Canada.

Figure 2.2 shows us what has happened to the crime rates in Canada between 1977 and 2004, the latest year for which figures are available. The crime rate increased consistently between 1977 and 1991. However, since 1994 police have reported that crime has declined for both total Criminal Code offences and property crime. We see an increase in other Criminal Code offences, and violent crime offences have remained relatively stable.

It is impossible to say whether the reduction in crime rates will be long term or whether these recent figures are simply a break before the final assault on the mountain. The main cause of the break may be due to demographics, as there were relatively fewer young people in the population during the years with lower crime rates. As we will see later, young people are more likely to be involved in criminal activity. In fact, the prevalence of offending peaks in the teenage years and then starts to decrease during the third decade of life. In Canada, the number of young people aged 15 to 24 between 1991 and 1996 dropped to 4 million from 4.5 million in the late 1980s.

Comparative Trends

How does Canada's crime picture compare with those of other countries? Is our society more dangerous to live in, or less so? Are we relatively safe from depredation?

Before we look at cross-cultural or comparative data on crime rates, a note of caution should be sounded. We have already pointed out many problems with official reporting methods. When we attempt to compare rates among different countries, these problems become even more pronounced owing to differences in law-enforcement practices, police data-gathering techniques, and definitions of categories. International victimization surveys might provide more reliability in comparing crime rates.

However, there are rather sizable differences in crime rates between countries that are not simply the result of differences in recording and enforcement. For instance, the rates of murder vary significantly, as is shown in Figure 2.3. The highest murder rate in 2003 was recorded in South Africa, at 44 per 100 000. The lowest rate, 0.051 per 100 000, was found in Japan.

We need to remember that crime rates also vary within countries and shift over time. We also must remember that political turmoil, which may be temporary, will have a great impact on crime, although not always on official crime rates, since

FIGURE 2.2

POLICE-REPORTED RATE OF VIOLENT CRIME STABLE WHILE "OTHER CRIMINAL CODE" OFFENCES
ON THE RISE, 1977 TO 2004[1]

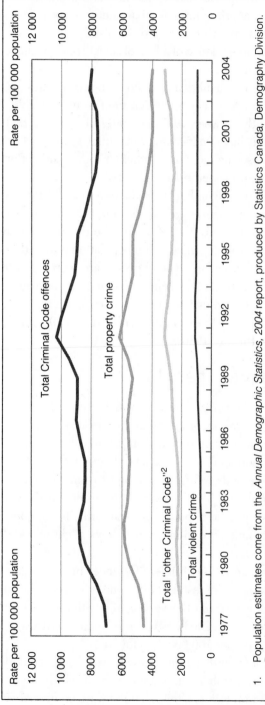

1. Population estimates come from the *Annual Demographic Statistics, 2004* report, produced by Statistics Canada, Demography Division.
   Populations as of July 1st: preliminary postcensal estimates for 2004.

2. "Other Criminal Code" offences include: mischief, counterfeit currency, disturbing the peace, bail violation, offensive weapons, arson,
   obstructing a public or peace officers, indecent acts, prostitution and trespassing at night.

Source: Adapted from Statistics Canada's *Criminal Justice Indicators*, 2005, Catalogue 85-227, December 2005, page 14. Available at
www.statcan.ca/english/freepub/85-227-XIE/0000285-227-XIE.pdf.

FIGURE 2.3

HOMICIDE RATES FOR SELECTED COUNTRIES, 2003

Russia	19.82
United States[1]	5.70
Turkey	5.57
Hungary	2.22
Armenia	2.00
Finland	1.98
Canada[2]	**1.95**
Poland[2]	1.70
France	1.65
England & Wales[3]	1.62
Northern Ireland	1.53
Australia	1.51
Denmark	1.21
Greece	1.12
Spain	1.10
Germany	0.99
Switzerland	0.99
Scotland	0.64
Japan	0.51

1. Federal Bureau of Investigation. (2004). "Crime in the United States – 2003". U.S. Department of Justice. Washington, D.C.
2. Figures reflect 2004 data.
3. Based upon 2003/2004 fiscal year data from Research Development & Statistics (CRCSG) Home Office. "Crime Statistics for England and Wales, 2003–2004". London, England.

Source: Interpol Ottawa.

these depend on the definitions of events by political authorities whose interests may compete with international standards of human rights.

Nevertheless, if we contrast murder rates in Canada, the United States, and England, we are comparing relatively stable democracies, and yet we still see strong differences, with the United States having a rate of 5.70, while Canada has a rate of 1.95 and England comes in at 1.62. Reasons for the differences are many and varied, but some of the most pressing are those related to urbanization, community cohesiveness, economic disparity, and the presence of individualist and libertarian versus socialist or communal social policies and infrastructures (see Hartnagel & Lee, 1990).

For property crimes, the differences between countries are more complicated. These crime rates may also be influenced by the growing internationalization of organized crime affecting major categories such as auto theft.

Homicide in Canada

Figure 2.4 presents homicide rates in Canada from 1961 to 2004. In 2004, the homicide rate jumped dramatically to 622 from 549 in 2003. In 2003, the rate

FIGURE 2.4

HOMICIDE RATE, CANADA, 1961–2004

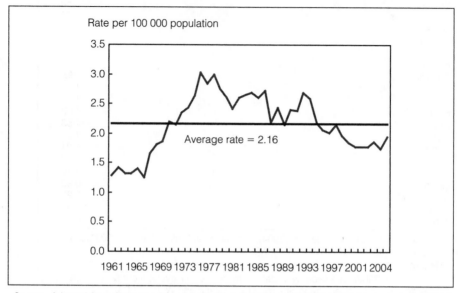

Source: Adapted from Statistics Canada's *Juristat*, Catalogue 85-002, Homicide in Canada, 2004,
Vol. 25, No.6, October 2005, page 3. Available at www.statcan.ca/english/freepub/85-002-XIE/
0060585-002-XIE.pdf.

reached its lowest point in more than 30 years, but increased by almost 12 percent in 2004 to 1.95 victims per 100 000.

In terms of regions, homicide is highest in the Western provinces, with Manitoba experiencing the highest rate at 4.27 per 100 000. The lowest rates were in the Maritimes with PEI (0.00), Newfoundland and Labrador (0.39), and New Brunswick (0.93) leading the way (see Figure 2.5).

Crime by Region

Although murder makes for interesting news and conversation, the reality is that homicide is a very small proportion of all criminal offences. Figures 2.6 and 2.7 on pages 38 and 39 show us property and violent crime rates within the provinces and territories. Among the provinces, property crime rates are highest in British Columbia, while Saskatchewan has the highest violent crime rates.

Crime by Age

A good snapshot of crime in Canada must highlight the effect of age. In Canada in 2003, persons aged 15–24 accounted for 45 percent of property crimes and 32 percent of those accused of violent crime. For homicide, those aged 18–24 had

FIGURE 2.5

HOMICIDE RATES BY PROVINCE

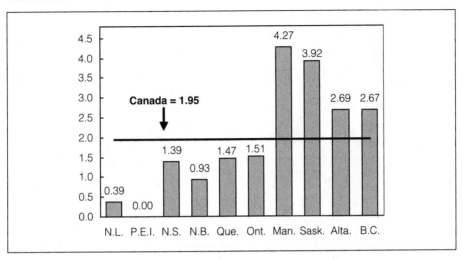

Source: Adapted from Statistics Canada's publication *Juristat*, Catalogue 85-002, Homicide in Canada, 2004, Vol. 25, No. 6, October 2005, page 4. Available at www.statcan.ca/english/ freepub/85-002-XIE/0060585-002-XIE.pdf.

the highest rates, and those rates decline as the ages go up (*Juristat*, 2005). When the distribution of crime is examined according to age, the relationship between crime and age is quite striking.

In Figure 2.8 on page 40, notice how property crime rises rapidly in the teen years but stabilizes throughout the 20s and 30s, with a steady decline as ages increase. The violent crime rate peaks at the age of 16, and than steadily declines through the life course.

As revealed in the graph, violent crimes decline more slowly, and property crimes tend to be more exclusively a young person's phenomenon. The highest incidence for many property crimes occurs between the ages of 15 and 16 and as you can see, both violent and property crime are at their highest percentage at age 15–16.

There are many reasons given to account for the distribution of crime among youths. Adolescent youths are involved in testing the boundaries of the societies in which they live. Family controls are loosened at the same time that there is an increased desire to express individuality and competence in adult roles, whether in socially constructive ways or not. Peer group influences become paramount and often peer group selection demands risk taking and demonstrations of fearlessness. Peer bonds are secured in the solidarity of shared risks.

Again, there are economic, sociobiological, and cultural explanations for the distribution of crime among youths. Young people are acutely sensitized to the

PROPERTY CRIME RATE[1]

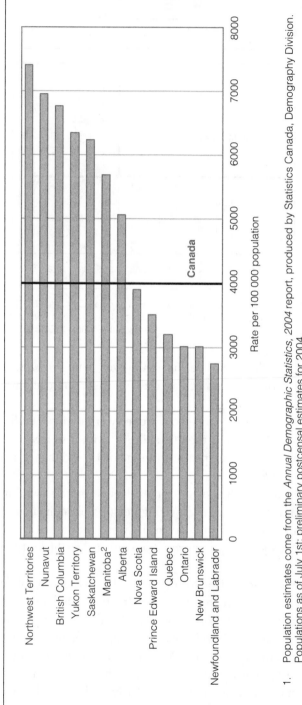

1. Population estimates come from the *Annual Demographic Statistics, 2004* report, produced by Statistics Canada, Demography Division. Populations as of July 1st: preliminary postcensal estimates for 2004.

2. Crime data from April to December 2004 for Winnipeg are estimates (except for homicide and motor vehicle theft) due to the implementation of a new records management system.

Source: Adapted from Statistics Canada's publication *Criminal Justice Indicators*, 2005, Catalogue 85-227, December 2005, page 16. Available at www.statcan.ca/english/freepub/85-227-XIE/0000285-227-XIE.pdf.

VIOLENT CRIME RATE[1]

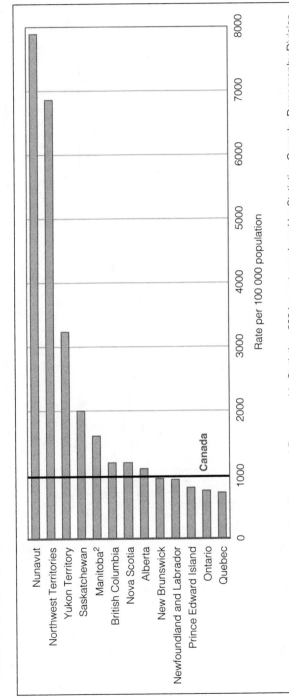

1. Population estimates come from the *Annual Demographic Statistics, 2004* report, produced by Statistics Canada, Demography Division. Populations as of July 1st: preliminary postcensal estimates for 2004.

2. Crime data from April to December 2004 for Winnipeg are estimates (except for homicide and motor vehicle theft) due to the implementation of a new records management system.

Source: Adapted from Statistics Canada's publication *Critical Justice Indicators*, 2005, Catalogue 85-227, December 2005, page 15. Available at www.statcan.ca/english/freepub/85-227-XIE/0000285-227-XIE.pdf.

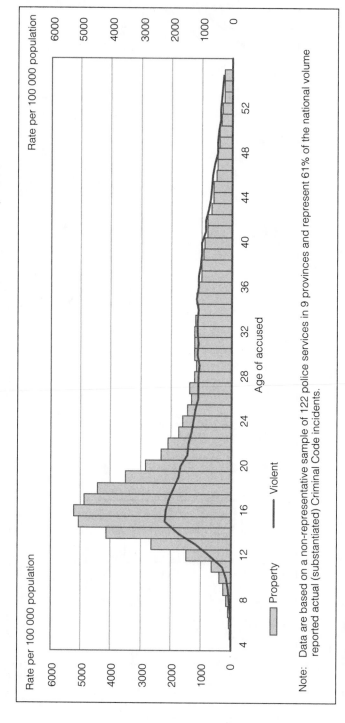

FIGURE 2.8

RATE OF PROPERTY AND VIOLENT CRIME HIGHEST AMONG YOUNG PEOPLE, 2003

Rate per 100 000 population

Rate per 100 000 population

Age of accused

Property — Violent

Note: Data are based on a non-representative sample of 122 police services in 9 provinces and represent 61% of the national volume reported actual (substantiated) Criminal Code incidents.

Source: Adapted from Statistics Canada's publication *Criminal Justice Indicators*, 2005, Catalogue 85-227, December 2005, page 122. Available at www.statcan.ca/english/freepub/85-227-XIE/0000285-227-XIE.pdf.

need to dress fashionably in order to be accepted by their peer groups, but there is a wide variation in their ability to afford the latest fashions. Adolescence is also a time when much energy goes into attracting the attention of peers. The tools to do so may be difficult to attain legitimately. So, biological imperatives and economic necessity come together in criminal activity. The violence, too, is a testing and perhaps a forming of identity, whereby the adolescent becomes aware of the vast social world outside of the family, in which he or she is only one among many. Violence, in this respect, is an attack on this social world in order to assert individualism or empowerment. But as people get older, the vast majority recognize that violence as a means of assertion is counterproductive.

Crime by Sex

Males accounted for almost 81 percent of all Criminal Code violations in 2003. Victimization and self-report surveys also confirm that violent offences are most frequently committed by males. In 2004, the General Social Survey on victimization revealed that 87 percent of violent incidents were committed by males. Research by Hagan (1985) found that males exceeded females in self-reported delinquency in the United States in 1970 by a margin of a little more than two to one.

Looked at historically, the relationship between female and male offending shows a pattern which invites the hypothesis that involvement in the breadwinner role will increase the chances of involvement in criminal offending. For example, between 1912 and 1920 there was a sharp rise in the rate of convictions—from 20 to over 100—of females for indictable offences. The male rate during this period rose gradually from approximately 450 to 500. A similar spike occurred during World War II. The 1970s saw the next upsurge in female criminality. Each of these periods is associated with new role demands or changing roles of women. During wartime, women worked in factories and were more active in the public sphere while many of the men were away at war. During the 1970s, there was a major recession and the women's movement was popularized, leading to a fundamental shift away from the model of the male as the sole family breadwinner. Indeed, Adler (1975) at this time put forth the liberation and opportunity hypothesis that as women began to perform roles previously reserved for men, they would also begin to take on the more aggressive, competitive, and risk-taking characteristics associated with the working world and masculinity. Others, such as Johnson (1986), have argued that women are still committing crimes—credit card fraud and shoplifting—that are associated with their traditional role as consumers and homemakers.

It should be noted that there are other explanations offered for the differences between male and female criminality that are related not to culture and economics, but rather to biology.

Crime by Race

According to Ontario's report on systemic racism in the criminal justice system, *racialization* involves classifying people into racial groups by referring to signs of origin (Gittens et al., 1995). Such signs include skin colour and place of birth. Judgments based on these signs are then made about the character, talents, and belongingness of people in a country. Social constructions of race have been used to rationalize economic exploitation and unequal treatment by social institutions, such as those enforcing criminal justice.

In Canada, Chinese, Japanese, black, and Aboriginal peoples (among others) have been subject to discrimination. During World War II, Canadians of Japanese descent were forced into internment camps, and Aboriginal people laboured under a system of what today would be known as ethnic cleansing, by which their traditions and cultural heritage were subjected to assimilation and genocide by the colonizing Canadians of European descent.

Today, the overrepresentation of Aboriginal and black people in the Canadian justice system continues to be a key dimension of the crime picture. In 2004, Aboriginals represented approximately 3 percent of the Canadian population. However, almost one-fifth of provincial admissions to custody were Aboriginal males and one-third were Aboriginal females. The proportion of federal admissions was 18 percent. For youth, Aboriginals represented 29 percent of those admitted to youth custody (Aboriginal youth comprise only 5 percent of the total population). Especially in Manitoba, Saskatchewan, and Alberta, but also in the other provinces, these groups are charged and imprisoned at much higher rates than are whites. In the Prairie provinces, Aboriginal people account for nearly half of provincial prison admissions, even though they represent less than 15 percent of the population there. For example, in Saskatchewan between 1999 and 2004, approximately 25 000 adults were incarcerated. Of those, 57 percent were Aboriginal.

It should be noted, that with the exception of prison/custodial admissions, official data on the racial composition of victims and perpetrators is unavailable to the Canadian public because police agencies do not maintain records regarding race. The argument is that race statistics may be employed by hate groups to serve their purposes, or that race data will be used to attack public policy toward immigration. Obviously, these concerns are legitimate. There are numerous examples in which a racist agenda is supported through the employment of "official data," without the use of context or appropriate methodology (Russell, 1998). Many Canadian criminologists have debated whether to include race within crime statistics. Gabor (1994) argues that crime statistics based on race should be collected to "shed light" on the crime problem, while Roberts (1994) argues that race should only be gathered on a periodic basis but the dangers outweigh the possible benefits. Although the debate over race and crime statistics is far from over, Dowler (2004) argues that the lack of official statistics on race or ethnicity of suspects/perpetrators might increase the "mysteriousness" of ethnic crime in Canada. Essentially, the public is at the mercy of the media for information. Media reports have increasingly shown a dangerous trend, in which news outlets exaggerate or distort the reality of ethnic crime and continually perpetuate racial stereotypes and myths without appropriate context or information.

In Ontario, the *Report on Systemic Racism in the Criminal Justice System* found that rather than improving in the period covered by their research, the situation in Ontario showed signs of getting even worse. It found a dramatic increase in admissions to prison of black adults between 1986/87 and 1992/93. Black adults were admitted to prison at over five times the rate of white adults, proportionate to the representation in Ontario's population. As well, the admission rate for black women was almost seven times that of white women. The report attributed some of these differences to the greater rate of imprisonment of blacks before trial; by 1992/93, the pretrial admission rate for drug trafficking/importing charges was 27 times higher than the rate for whites. Even for simple possession, the incarceration rate for blacks was 15 times higher than for whites. For the typically more discretionary charge of obstructing justice, the pretrial admission rate for blacks was 13 times higher than for whites. As the commission noted, it was obvious that black people accused were jailed only because they were black, and white people accused were not held before trial because they were white (Gittens et al., 1995).

Some criminologists have argued that criminal justice agents actively discriminate against Aboriginal and black people. This argument has been tested by Hagan (1974). In a study of correctional institutions in Alberta, Hagan found that Aboriginal people were being incarcerated for fine default, and their incarceration for this offence accounted for two-thirds of the sentences for Aboriginal people. These fines originally stemmed for minor offences related to alcohol abuse.

It must be pointed out that some of the disparity between the groups can be accounted for by various quasi-judicial criteria, such as the economic and social standing of the accused. Whether or not accused persons have secure employment and social ties will have an impact on whether they are remanded in custody to await trial, and these factors have spin-off effects throughout the involvement of at-risk people within the justice system.

Apart from quasi-judicial criteria, which have a greater effect on some minorities, there is the actual rate of crime. The higher crime rates among black and Aboriginal Canadians result, at least in part, because these groups commit more crimes than those groups that are under-represented. While some of the discrepancy can be accounted for by selective enforcement, the quasi-judicial criteria, the composition of law-enforcement professions, and other biases in the criminal justice system, the difference cannot be completely accounted for in this way.

The relatively higher economic deprivation of blacks and Aboriginal people does account for some of the wide disparity in incarceration. The social segmentation of some groups inhibits their economic integration (LaPrairie, 1983). LaPrairie views the overrepresentation of Aboriginal people as a result of economic and social disadvantages, including their relative lack of education and employment. The economic argument also can be applied to blacks in Canadian society. In Nova Scotia after World War II, for instance, blacks were subjected to blatant economic, political, and social discrimination to such a degree that their whole community was forced to move from an economically viable area of Halifax. Discrimination has forged an economic legacy of blocked opportunities both in education and employment, which have contributed to overrepresentation in offending, offence categories, and imprisonment.

But it is particularly the relationship between cultural supports and economic opportunity that must be addressed. James (1989) argues that Aboriginal values are placed under stress in a "complex urban society." One key dimension of this stress relates to property values. Aboriginal traditions emphasize the reciprocity of possessions, rather than permanent ownership, and in some such transactions, this translates into theft under the law. When pervading Canadian and Aboriginal values conflict in court, Aboriginal people tend to be the overwhelming losers, thus adding to the escalating spiral of deprivation.

Conclusion

Is the crime rate going up in Canada? Will it continue on the upward slope that we have seen since the mid-twentieth century? Or will it follow the more recent downward trend that we have seen from 1991 to today? It would be fair to predict that we will see another rise in crime rates very soon. One reason for the expected rise is that there will be a change in demographics, so that more youths will be of prime crime age. The greater the proportion of such youths, the greater the likelihood of higher crime rates. Another reason is structural, or related to how society is organized according to the distribution of power. Canadian society is becoming increasingly polarized into haves and have-nots. Economic disparity is identified as a condition in which there tends to be more marginalization and less adherence to norms, both by the rich and by the poor (Braithwaite, 1997; Tittle, 1995). Simply put, when there is an increase in the number of those who have very little and who have a slim chance of improving their lot, there will be more criminalization of such people, both through the enactment of more laws to punish them and through the self-selection of criminal activity by these groups. In Canada, we have already seen cities pass bylaws intended to criminalize homeless persons, creating new categories of offenders. We have also seen policies of zero tolerance enacted in the schools and in the policing of minor offences, which will bring more individuals into the criminal justice system. Finally, our approach to social problems appears to be in a period of malaise—we are politically unwilling or unable to think beyond using the weapons of law enforcement and penalization. Rather, these blunt instruments have become the preferred solution in the absence of the resources of the welfare state.

Summary

In this chapter, we have painted a picture of Canadian crime and the methods we use to create this picture. We began by reviewing official crime statistics in such sources as the Uniform Crime Reporting Survey, and we described the shortcomings of these sources. We then looked at some unofficial sources for uncovering the dark figure of crime, including victimization surveys and self-reports. Finally, we examined recent trends in crime and identified some factors that influence the crime rate, including sex, age, and population demographics.

Key Terms

crime map (p. 32)

crime rate (p. 19)

dark figure of crime (p. 22)

demographics (p. 15)

incidence of crime (p. 18)

official statistics (p. 23)

prevalence of crime (p. 18)

self-report survey (p. 25)

unofficial statistics (p. 23)

victimization survey (p. 26)

Discussion Questions

1. What is one reason that may account for the change in the crime rate in the last decade and a half?

2. Describe two factors that could account for the rise and decline of crime rates.

3. Why are homicide rates seen as fairly good general indicators of overall crime rates?

4. What are some problems with official statistics?

5. What is meant by systemic bias?

Weblinks

www.statcan.ca Statistics Canada's site provides statistics on the topic of justice and crime, categorized by crimes, victims, suspects and criminals, and police and the courts.

www.hc-sc.gc.ca/hppb/familyviolence/bilingual.htm The National Clearinghouse on Family Violence, a Health Canada site, is a resource centre for information about violence within the family. The Clearinghouse provides research findings and information on prevention, protection, and treatment.

www.ncjrs.gov/index.html The US Department of Justice's Bureau of Justice Statistics page is an excellent resource for US statistics on topics such as crime, victims, law enforcement, prosecution, courts, and corrections. There is also a link to the world factbook of criminal justice systems.

www.fbi.gov/ucr/ucrquest.htm This helpful FBI page provides clear and comprehensive answers to the most commonly asked questions regarding the Uniform Crime Reporting Survey (UCR), as well as links to UCR reports and to the FBI home page.

www.ojp.usdoj.gov/bjs/cvict.htm#summary This US Department of Justice website that provides the results of the National Criminal Victimization survey.

www.ojp.usdoj.gov/bjs/welcome.html This is the Bureau of Justice Statistics webpage, and it is an excellent resource for statistics.

www.ncjrs.gov/criminal_justice2000/vol_4/04b.pdf This provides an excellent overview of self-report methodology.

CHAPTER 3 Criminal Law

Objectives

- To outline the use of criminal law to maintain social order and control.

- To offer two main explanations of the purposes of criminal law: the value consensus model and the conflict model.

- To outline the operations of the Criminal Code of Canada and its distinctions among types of criminal offences and defences.

- To discuss the Canadian Charter of Rights and Freedoms.

Defining Criminal Law

The existence of criminal laws is of great importance to keeping order in our society. **Criminal laws** are a collection of rules that have been constructed to address issues of human behaviour. All criminal law is constructed in Canada by Parliament, and applies equally to all citizens wherever they live in our nation. The Criminal Code of Canada also sets forth penalties for transgressions or offences committed by persons. The word *code* is employed since the acts that constitute a **crime** are specifically defined as are the penalties which may be imposed as sanctions for violations of the law. While there are two other forms of law (called *civil law* and *case law*) that govern relations among persons, institutions, and businesses, in this chapter we will focus our attention primarily on the criminal law while providing a brief synopsis of the other forms. We will explore how the criminal law affects the administration of justice and review specific interesting cases that bear upon these issues.

If we adopt the **consensus perspective** of society, which asserts that our ability to maintain law and order is the result of a **social contract** that all of our citizens are a party to, then criminal law may be viewed as an instrument to redress damage to the state as well as individuals. Put simply, acts of crime damage not only the direct victim but also the wider community. Violations of criminal law, for example, can result in the decline of respect for human life, the dissipation of neighbourhoods as safe places to live, or fear for our personal safety as we go about our daily lives. Social order, it may be argued, can only be maintained insofar as the punishment for criminal acts stands as both a **specific deterrent** to the individual and a **general deterrent** to all citizens. In Canada, the prosecution of crimes falls to governments since they are empowered to undertake legal action against offenders. The state, on behalf of our citizens, acts as the injured party. As Ramcharan (2002) has written, the premise is a simple one, "since crime is harmful to society, it is the government's responsibility to seek redress and to obtain justice."

The maintenance of a system of criminal justice that is fair, provides due process and protections for the accused, and applies justice equally to all is the foundation of a civil society. When systems of law or enforcement break down, lawlessness may quickly ensue. The 2005 massive flooding in New Orleans and surrounding areas caused a breakdown in law and order over the period of a few days resulting in murders, armed attacks against the police, and sexual assaults. Thus, it is not sufficient just to have a set of criminal laws—without enforcement, they would be of little use.

Criminal Law: Consensus or Conflict?

Criminologists have made significant attempts over the history of the discipline to develop **macro theories** to explain the operation of society. The consensus perspective arose out of the conservative political thought and criminological writings of the 1950s in the United States. The criminologists of the era reflected the post–World War II view that members of society shared very similar ideas and beliefs producing a consensual social order. In order to produce this uniform type of society there exists a core set of values shared by all individuals.

The consensus perspective is considered to be functionalist in nature. In this view of society, all rules and laws are perceived as operating for the greater good of all, making sure society functions smoothly and efficiently. Since all persons subscribe to the same set of values and share many of the same interests, then society has to ensure that all members who do not act in accordance with these values, by breaking laws, have their behaviour corrected so that it is in keeping with the societal consensus on right and wrong. The consensus perspective became less valuable as a way of understanding society as North Americans entered the turbulent era of the 1960s.

During the 1960s, there were a number of social movements that fought against state policies and for the recognition of human rights and the expression of ideas very different from the mainstream. The "hippie revolution" of the late '60s challenged ideas concerning the organization of society, the value of formal education, the rights of young people, and most important perhaps, the right to freely express oneself. The feminist movement fought for the rights of women. The sexual revolution and the development of birth control pills signalled a challenge to issues of premarital sex and ideas concerning marriage. The era of the 1950s, in contrast, had been highly conservative, a major factor in the development of the consensus view of society as largely homogeneous.

The **conflict perspective** began to emerge during the 1960s as criminological writers began to question the view that there was an overall consensus in society regarding important matters pertaining to the law. Society began to be viewed as consisting of pluralities, that is, groups with different values, ethics, and ideas about how society should operate. While in contemporary Canadian society today we are aware of the diverse nature of our social makeup, it was a new concept three decades ago. Emerging criminological thinkers like Austin Turk (1976) began to view society as composed of a variety of competing interest groups. Groups were vying for power, propelling society toward greater recognition of specific rights and injustices. Groups could be organized vis-à-vis class lines, religious beliefs, ethnicity, sexual orientation, gender, socio-economic status, political interests or anti-social values. Turk argued that groups constantly competed for power—economic clout and the right to make and enforce laws, particularly to promote or repeal laws that would affect the interests of their specific group. Conflict theorists acknowledged, however, that there was a limited consensus on the manner in which disputes were to be resolved in society but their view was not a reflection of widespread common values and interests. Today, critical and radical scholars would not agree with a view of the state as a neutral agent for resolving disputes. Rather, they would view the state and its agents as protecting the interests of certain groups. Osgoode Hall legal scholar Michael Mandel has argued, for example, that judges are merely lawyers for the upper classes (Mandel, 1985)—in essence, Mandel has questioned judges' impartiality in dispute resolution.

Criminal law, for some theorists, represents a powerful weapon in the social control of some segments of society by elites. The "crimes of the powerful" include the use of the criminal law to subjugate groups in society. Reiman (2003) argues that the criminal justice system is predominantly structured to penalize the lower socio-economic classes. Since the majority of those currently in prison in Canada are poorly educated and form part of this group, there is some strength to this contention. Certainly one of the key areas where power is exercised by the rich is in the realm of property laws.

One of the most influential studies of how this occurs was carried out by US criminologist William Chambliss (1975). Examining the notion of vagrancy in eighteenth century England, he discovered that laws were created that gave distinct advantages and protections to businesses and landowners while penalizing poor and homeless persons. Today, we still have a variety of municipal bylaws that penalize begging and sleeping in doorways on public property. Canada's largest city, Toronto, adopted a policy in 2005 that forbids homeless persons from sleeping in public outdoor spaces including the area surrounding Toronto's city hall. Finally, research has shown that corporations have financed lobbying campaigns to ensure that provincial regulations have little impact, particularly in the realm of environmental controls, safety requirements for workers, or business transactions in general. Those who commit property crimes are not in a position to lobby for more lenient treatment under the law. Rather, a great deal of time, money, and effort is invested in ensuring the prosecution of private- and public-property transgressors.

Forms of Law

In Canada, criminal law exists in conjunction with the criminal justice system and is governed by a set of established procedures for dealing with criminal cases. The criminal law is composed of two distinct forms of law that govern the conduct of investigations, the laying of charges, and the behaviour of judges and the courts. **Statutory law** is criminal law that is created through legislation passed by Parliament and in the provinces for regulatory and other matters. Collectively, these laws form the Criminal Code of Canada. **Case law** is created through the decisions of judges and the courts, and forms a guide for future decision-making regarding, for example, which types of evidence are permitted to be introduced into the record and which are not. This type of law is more commonly referred to as the *law of precedents*. Case law exerts a powerful influence in cases brought before the courts in Canada. A decision in a specific case can determine how other cases involving the same charges will be handled by the courts for decades to come.

The Supreme Court of Canada passes decisions which are used as a guideline for the types of arguments both defence and prosecution lawyers will employ in the lower courts (Ramcharan, de Lint, & Fleming, 2001). The judge will consult case precedents when attempting to render a decision. The purpose of precedents is to ensure fair and equal treatment of those accused over time and across all Canadian jurisdictions. Since both sides to a criminal trial are informed in advance by case law of what constitutes acceptable arguments to be advanced to the court, this system ensures that both sides can mount their best possible arguments and submissions. In a sense, case law sets out the rules by which the courts, defence, and prosecution must operate in order for a case to be properly decided.

Civil law is distinct from criminal law since it represents a body of rules that are intended to govern the interactions among persons in society, business, institutions, and various levels of government. When we use the term *civil law*, we are referring to law which is intended to maintain civility in society, that is, a manner of resolving disputes that is formal, ordered, and consistent. Without civil law, it would be difficult, for example, to conduct business—warranties, business claims, and disagreements between contractually bound individuals and businesses would have very little chance of being fairly resolved. This does not mean that civil law invariably produces a fair result for either party. Civil law is meant to regulate, but human beings must make a decision based on the evidence before them. Said evidence is not always complete or adequately presented. When we hear someone utter the words, "I'll sue you!" they are invariably referring to civil law. This law covers matters of contractual disputes; divorce and custody matters relating to children and property; as well as consumer and commercial practices.

When someone pursues a civil matter, he or she is normally seeking some form of compensation usually of a financial nature. As Ramcharan (2002) observes, "violations of civil law are not crimes; instead, they are contract violations." Civil matters require that an individual, body, or corporation bring a lawsuit to the courts; there is no police involvement. Students might be aware of several recent cases in the United States where, while there was not a conviction in a murder case, a civil law case brought against the alleged murderer did succeed. In the cases of both O. J. Simpson and Robert Blake, civil juries made a finding of guilt and assessed millions of dollars in damages. They were able to do so because the standard of proof in civil cases is not beyond a reasonable doubt but instead whether on a balance of probabilities the judge and jury can reach a finding of guilt. The standard of proof in civil cases is thus far lower than in criminal cases.

We have already learned that criminal law is created by Parliament. It is often argued that the law is not responsive to our ever-changing world. That is, it cannot keep up with the rapid changes we experience in our society. Antiquated laws are not eliminated quickly enough or revised to reflect current societal conditions; new laws that allow us to criminalize new forms of behaviour (e.g., technologically based crimes) are not enacted in a timely way. The Law Reform Commission of Canada (LRCC), a creation of the federal Parliament, has been given the task of reviewing our criminal laws on an ongoing basis. The LRCC, while not satisfying the expectations of all Canadians, provides a forum for debate over the form of our criminal law and the sanctions it imposes. In the 2006 federal election, for example, there was a great deal of debate over penalties for crimes involving firearms. Several political leaders called for the establishment of "mandatory minimum" sentences for these types of offences and for repeated violent infractions of the law. While there appears to be public support for these measures, they are unlikely to become law without a great deal of debate over the effect their introduction would have on our police services, our prison system, offenders, and society.

Our Criminal Code is important because it establishes clear offences and penalties for behaviours in Canada. It also ensures that sentences are fair (not excessive or overly punitive) and related to the offence before the court. For the purpose of comparison, readers might contrast the excessive nature of penalties in criminal cases in some states south of our border. It is not uncommon to hear sentences imposed of "400 years" or "six life sentences." We in Canada do not support either the death penalty or sentences of such great lengths. Does this mean we are "soft" on crime, as some critics have alleged? Take a moment to consider this question. Our Criminal Code also ensures that the same transgressions against our law will be charged and punished in a similar manner, ensuring fairness and equal treatment for all Canadians. Finally, criminal law is intended to dissuade vigilante groups from taking the law into their own hands, since we understand that the criminal law will "take its course."

Our Criminal Code also establishes various categories of offences. A crime may be committed by an act. It may also be an omission or failure to act. A crime is categorized by its seriousness and the penalty increases with the seriousness of the offence. **Summary conviction offences** are minor crimes. Crimes included in this category include causing a disturbance or possession of less than 30 grams of marijuana for personal use. In keeping with the less serious nature of summary offences, penalties are less harsh. A first offence will generally result in a fine. Second and later offences may result in probation or a short prison sentence. Given the overcrowding in our prison system, and some attempts to keep people out of it, there has been a sharp rise in judges' use of community service orders for summary offences. Judges have utilized this sentencing option predominantly for young offenders where these sentences are intended to be more productive as learning tools for changing behaviour than fine payments or other options. Through community service, juveniles can see the impact of their crime on victims, learn to empathize with victims, and build community ties that have been shown to be effective in reducing future juvenile criminality. For summary conviction offences, a police officer must witness the offence being committed in order to arrest the suspect or seek an arrest warrant or summons to bring the offender to justice. For indictable offences, in contrast, police need only "reasonable grounds" to believe that the person committed an indictable offence in order to make an arrest.

Indictable offences, as viewers of television's *Law and Order* will know, are more serious offences and carry very harsh punishments. First-degree murder carries an automatic sentence of imprisonment for life. Robbery, drug trafficking, treason, sexual assaults with violence, break and enter of a dwelling house with intent to commit an indictable offence, and arson all are indictable crimes. If a defendant comes before the court with previous convictions and is convicted, a lengthy prison sentence will generally be in order. Punishment can include both incarceration in prison and fines imposed by the court. Since wide latitude is given to judges in sentencing for indictable offences, there has been considerable debate and criticism of the variations in sentences handed down by judges for crimes committed with similar circumstances and defendants' previous involvement with the criminal justice system. Finally, there are hybrid offences, sometimes referred to as *Crown election offences* or *dual offences*. These hybrids may be pursued by the Crown as either summary offences or by an indictment for possession of a narcotic or the proceeds of a drug offence, or laundering the proceeds of a drug offence.

One specific crime contained within the Criminal Code deserves special consideration. **Treason**, as defined under section 46 of the Code, is the offence of engaging in activities, whether employing force, violence, conspiracy, or the communication of military or scientific information intended to overthrow the government of Canada or a province.

Treason also includes the act of obtaining information that is of importance to Canada's defence for the purposes of sharing it with another party or government whose intent is to damage the government or people of Canada. While neither of these offences has been of great concern during times of relative peace, it can be argued that the work of spies in the area of industrial research can have a very significant damaging impact on Canada and its peoples. Recent allegations against Chinese graduate students in various fields of science of spying within Canada for the purpose of stealing new scientific and technological advances comprise an example of possible peacetime treason. You might wish to consider how treason should be evaluated in terms of damage to Canada and what appropriate penalties would be for such crimes. Is the theft of technological or scientific advances merely global competitive business or is it treason?

The Elements of Criminal Offences

The term ***corpus delicti*** means literally "the body of the crime." Under our system of criminal law, it is required that specific facts and features must exist in order for a crime to have been committed. The Crown prosecutor is required to prove the elements of the crime in order to secure a conviction against the accused. In this section of the chapter, we explore the seemingly simple, yet quite complex, elements that are required for a crime to have been committed.

Actus Reus

In order for a crime to be recorded under the law, certain elements must be present. The first of these is termed **actus reus**, which refers literally to the act that has been committed. What constitutes a criminal act can change over time. In an earlier era in Canada, there were no legal prohibitions against the use of LSD or marijuana. These acts now carry criminal penalties. Similarly, until 1983, men could not be charged with the sexual assault of their wives. It is paramount to remember that without an act, no crime can be charged. It is a requirement of Canadian criminal law that the onus be on the prosecution to prove that an individual committed a crime beyond a reasonable doubt. A reasonable doubt is not just any doubt, but one predicated upon evidence before the court demonstrating that an alternate individual may reasonably be judged to have committed the offence or an alternative interpretation of the evidence is possible.

The act and the mental state of the alleged perpetrator are companions in the criminal law. In other words, one must normally have both elements present for a criminal prosecution to succeed. It is a simple concept to understand. Pamela threatens to assault a person. The person calls the police to have her charged. The *actus reus* is the uttering of the threat. The *mens rea* was the intention to commit the act. But what if Pamela were five years old? There would be no intention. Similarly, if Pamela were suffering from advanced Alzheimer's disease there would be no intention. The act also has to be one that is voluntary for the charges to be upheld, since in certain instances, as we shall discover in our discussion of defences, acts are not committed voluntarily. It is also important to understand that an individual cannot be convicted of an offence unless the *actus reus* and the *mens rea* can be demonstrated to coincide.

Actus reus possesses several distinct elements. First, there is the behaviour of the perpetrating individual(s), which must be either a voluntary act or an omission. A voluntary act is one in which the individual freely chooses a particular line of conduct. If one were forced to commit an act under immediate threat of the loss of one's life, this would constitute an involuntary act. The second element is the facts and circumstances surrounding the act. In a sexual assault case, this latter element would be the injuries, both physical and psychological, inflicted upon the victim. The Canadian courts have ruled clearly that psychological harm is to be recognized in assessing whether a crime has been committed and in arriving at appropriate sentencing. The third element of *actus reus* is determining what harm has flowed from the specific act. This final factor must be also be proved. One cannot claim bodily harm if there is no evidence, such as medical reports, pictures, police notes, or witnesses to the injuries. Lying at the heart of all convictions is the need for evidence to prove the case.

Consider the crime of kidnapping. Under section 279(1) of the Criminal Code, "every person commits an offence who kidnaps a person with the intent

(a) to cause the person to be confined or imprisoned against the person's will;

(b) to cause the person to be unlawfully sent or transported out of Canada against the person's will; or

(c) to hold the person for ransom or to service against the person's will.

The above three elements form the *actus reus* of kidnapping. If a person intentionally confines or imprisons a person, the first element is present. Second, it must be proven that the accused actually committed one of the acts of confining, imprisoning, sending, transporting, or attempting to obtain a ransom. The third element is satisfied when it can be proven that the victim was held against his or her will.

It is important for students to comprehend that an act may be proven, even if there is no eyewitness to events, by the use of circumstantial evidence. A person may be charged with murder and convicted of that crime, for example, even if a body has not been found. There are, of course, many reasons why a person might disappear. Someone may tire of a relationship and leave. A person might have received a blow to the head by a falling neon sign and, suffering from amnesia, wandered far from home. A teenager could run away from home to escape abusive parents (Fleming, 1997). The police, however, may rely on circumstantial evidence to ascertain that foul play has occurred. Such evidence played a significant role in the notorious O. J. Simpson trial where no witnesses to the murders existed. However, blood, DNA, and other circumstantial evidence were employed in attempts to convince the jury members that Simpson committed the murders of Nicole Brown and Ronald Goldman.

In a Canadian case, the murder of Elizabeth Bain, the assumption of murder had to be made on the basis of circumstantial evidence. The accused was found guilty of the crime of second-degree murder based upon this evidence and sentenced to imprisonment for life without eligibility of parole for 25 years. In 2000, however, he was freed on bail pending a new trial (see Box 3.1 on the next page). *Different* circumstantial evidence had come to the attention of his lawyers that, in their opinion, appeared to implicate convicted serial killer Paul Bernardo as the murderer of this young woman. While circumstantial evidence may in some cases be very compelling, too great a reliance upon it, as in the Bain case, can lead to a wrongful conviction.

THE MURDER OF ELIZABETH BAIN: A CASE OF CIRCUMSTANTIAL EVIDENCE

On June 19, 1990, university student Elizabeth Bain went missing. Her automobile was found abandoned in Scarborough with blood and brain matter on the seat. It could reasonably be assumed that she had met with foul play, specifically, murder. Two years later, her ex-boyfriend Robert Baltovich, a 24 year old, was convicted of second-degree murder in her death. Baltovich always maintained his innocence throughout the years. The Innocence Project took up his case, and presented an appeal to the courts.

Investigations conducted by private investigators had uncovered many unsettling pieces of information. Bain had been acquainted with Paul Bernardo. She had been seen in the company of a man described by witnesses as resembling Bernardo in the weeks preceding her disappearance. She was murdered in a park where Bernardo was known to have had sexual relations with women. She was killed in the "killing ground," a specific area of the city where Bernardo murdered his victims. Moreover, her car had been spotted at a chicken restaurant that was a favourite of Bernardo's. Her automobile, when found, had the radio tuned to Bernardo's favourite station and a cigarette butt found in the car was his brand.

Robert Baltovich was released on bail in July 2000 (after serving over eight years in prison) pending a new trial.

For further reading on this case, see Derek Finkle, *No Claim to Mercy*, Toronto: Penguin, 2004.

Source: CBC Online, July 15, 2005, and December 2, 2004.

It is not required in all cases that there be consequences which can be traced to a specific act. In the case of perjury, there is no requirement under section 131 of the Criminal Code that there be an effect from the act. The crime is committed as soon as the words have left the mouth of the speaker, and it is not required that they have a specific effect. Similarly, in some cases the prosecutor is not required to prove that a person has engaged in behaviour in order to secure a conviction. This is the case with the offence of possession of instruments for breaking into coin-operated or currency-exchange devices under section 352 of the Criminal Code. Thus, anyone who has such tools in their possession without lawful excuse (e.g., a repair person) in circumstances where it can be inferred they have either used or were going to use them for a criminal purpose, can be convicted of the possession crime, *even though they have not committed an act*. Another example is one well known to most Canadians: driving while impaired by alcohol. All that is required for a conviction is for police to determine that the person in care and control of the vehicle has an alcohol level above legal limits

(80 milligrams of alcohol per 100 millilitres of blood). It also falls to the judge to determine that the individual charged had care and control of the vehicle in question (see Box 3.2 for more discussion about care and control).

A crime may also involve a failure to act. Let's say you assume a legal duty. You are employed by a trekking company to lead teams of tourists into the Rocky Mountains of Alberta. It is winter. You trek 12 kilometres into the wilderness. There is an avalanche that traps two from your party under deep snow. You fear for your own life and leave the group. Several more individuals perish in the snowstorm that follows. Have you committed a crime? Yes! If you voluntarily undertake to assume a duty for an individual(s) you must follow through with that commitment if a failure to do so would be dangerous. As a parent, you are under a legal duty according to section 215 of the Code to provide the "necessaries of life" until your child has reached the age of 16. At this point, parents can literally abandon their children, since they are not committing a legal offence but rather a moral one.

BOX 3.2

YOU BE THE JUDGE: DETERMINING THE ISSUE OF CARE AND CONTROL

In our discussion of driving under the influence of alcohol, we mentioned that the judge must decide based upon the evidence if an individual had "care and control" of the vehicle in question. Let's have you be the judge in several scenarios based on real Canadian cases.

Case 1: Joe is at a party and drinks quite heavily. His friends place him in his car. A police patrol passing by finds him behind the wheel of the car. It is obvious that the car has not been driven in many hours (engines cool down after approximately three hours). He was charged. What issues would you, as the judge have to consider? Think about *voluntariness* (did Joe enter voluntarily?). (Butler, 1939)

Case 2: Patrick, a truck driver, is found behind the wheel of his truck. His blood alcohol is 220/100. The accused's defence is that he was not intending to drive, merely to "sleep off" his drunken state. The keys to the truck were thrown under the passenger's side and he had his feet up on the passenger seat. It was obvious he was going nowhere. Or was he? What factors are relevant to guilt or innocence in this case? (Pilon, 1998)

Case 3: Jerry is drunk and does not want to drive. He goes out to his car with the intention of merely "warming it up" for his friend to drive. Officers find him behind the wheel with the engine running. He is charged with having care and control while impaired by alcohol. Is he guilty or innocent? Why?

Mens Rea

Mens rea is a Latin term that literally means, "guilty mind." *Mens rea* is the mental element of a crime. In other words, one must have the intention of committing a crime to be convicted of a crime. There are several important states of mind that bear on the issue of intent. These are whether the person(s) knowingly, recklessly, fraudulently, or maliciously committed an act. Two types of intention exist: (a) general (or objective) intention, and (b) specific intention. In the law, our concern is the difference between what the accused intended and the intentions of a reasonable person. Crimes that involve this first element require that proof be offered of the intention to actually commit the criminal act. An individual who enters a bank intent on relieving the bank of some of its profits while brandishing a gun runs the risk that someone may be killed. If this should occur, while we may believe that the offender did not want to hurt anyone, only retrieve money, the fact that he or she carried a gun into the bank is evidence of general intent to use the weapon if necessary. Guns are frighteningly effective in bank robberies because of the fact that they can maim or kill many individuals with ease.

A specific intent crime, like theft, requires that the Crown attorney prove there was a special mental element involved (e.g., the taking of an item with the intent to deprive the rightful owner, temporarily or absolutely, of property or their interest in it). In other words, in this form of crime it can be assumed that the perpetrator knew what the direct and immediate consequences of his or her actions would be. Crimes of strict liability do not require the existence of *mens rea* as an element of the offence.

It is also important to remember that *mens rea* and *actus reus* must be seen as occurring together, as linked. Persons are often heard to threaten others' lives in the heat of anger. Has a criminal act been committed if an individual threatens to kill someone on one day but accidentally causes that person's death on another day? The answer is no. The accident that caused the death of the other person was not carried out with intent nor was it the result of reckless behaviour.

There are several other issues that are important for students of criminology to remember about the Canadian legal system. First and foremost, according to the law is the **presumption of innocence**. Everyone in Canada is presumed innocent of crimes that they are charged with until proven guilty. However, we are aware that persons in the general public often assign guilt well before the time of trial, and this form of speculation is often completely incorrect. The second issue is the **right to remain silent**. Anyone who has viewed the television program *The First 48* will be familiar with the admissions that are often given by suspects after intense questioning by detectives when there is not a lawyer present to represent their interests. As soon as a lawyer is requested or arrives, detectives are quick to characterize this action by the suspect as "lawyering up," an acknowledgment that admissions of guilt will not be forthcoming from this individual. Many criminals make the fatal mistake of assuming that being interrogated by detectives without a lawyer present demonstrates their innocence. The number of individuals who have been wrongly convicted of indictable offences should be a sober reminder to anyone suspected of an offence to say nothing until they have obtained legal counsel. Every person charged with a criminal offence in Canada is entitled to due process in determining his or her guilt or innocence. A person's right to a fair trial must be ensured by the justice system. When someone's rights are violated, it may result in an exclusion of evidence or the dropping of charges. Finally, when in court the accused's guilt must be proved beyond a reasonable doubt—not simply any doubt that a juror may have, but rather a reasonable doubt of the person's guilt (for example, one's alibi for the time the offence occurred needs to be corroborated by a reliable witness; otherwise, a reasonable doubt could arise from such a detail). A mistake by a police officer in recording the colour of a suspect's car—dark brown instead of black—for example, does not constitute a reasonable doubt.

Criminal Defences

Once charged with a **criminal offence**, the accused will commonly offer some form of defence to the charges that have been lodged against him or her. There are several specific forms of defence that can be offered by an accused. As a social audience to crime, we often make assumptions about how an innocent person should react to a criminal charge. Some believe that an innocent person would shout his or her innocence to the rooftops. Some of us expect an innocent person to be overwhelmed by the enormity of the injustice being perpetrated against him or her and remain silent. Actually, there are a great many natural reactions to having charges laid against one. *None are consistent with guilt or innocence*, as the general public may believe. It is difficult to appreciate how a person will react until one is actually wrongly charged with an offence. Let us now turn our attention to the possible defences that may be raised by someone accused under Canadian law.

Provocation

One can argue in defence that the victim provoked an attack. This is a common defence in cases of homicide where the accused is seeking either acquittal or conviction on the lesser charge of manslaughter. It's also a common defence raised regarding altercations in a tavern where both participants are likely to have been imbibing alcohol. Common provocations are related to comments on the physical prowess, appearance, origin of birth, race, intelligence level, or sexual prowess (or lack thereof) of the recipient of the remarks. However, you cannot claim that someone provoked you if he or she had a legal right to do so. If, for example, a parking officer is writing you a ticket, you cannot attack him claiming he provoked you because he was performing his legally appointed duty.

The defence of provocation can only reduce the guilt of the accused; it will not completely relieve him or her of criminal responsibility. In cases where provocation has occurred and *can be proven* (normally through impartial witnesses to the event or through the evidence given by the accused), it can have the effect of lessening the sentence to be served when there is a finding of guilt. The defence of provocation may only be raised by an accused in murder cases, so it is a limited defence.

Intoxication

Intoxication is a defence raised in the hope that it will reduce the criminal responsibility of the accused. The issue raised by intoxication revolves around the level of intoxication that the accused induced in him- or herself. Under the Criminal Code, section 33.1, a defence is not available to someone who self-induces intoxication. Section 33.2 is very specific on the issue of criminal fault. It states that, "[when] a person departs markedly from the standard of reasonable care generally recognized in Canadian society and is thereby criminally at fault where the person, while in a state of self-induced intoxication that renders the person unaware of, or incapable of consciously controlling their behaviour, voluntarily or involuntarily interferes to threatens to interfere with the bodily integrity of another person" that person is accountable for his or her actions under the law.

Two 1994 Canadian cases brought the issue of the defence of intoxication to the forefront of the debate on the fallibility of the law and resulted in the writing of section 33 of the Code. In the first case, the husband of the victim had a drinking problem. On the day in question, he consumed a very large quantity of alcohol, approximately three 1-litre bottles of spirits. At the time he was also taking a prescription for Percodan. Upon his return home, he sexually assaulted his wife and was charged by the police. At trial, he was found not guilty since the court was convinced that he could not have formed the necessary *mens rea* for committing the offence since he was under the influence of both alcohol and prescription drugs to such an extent that his reasoning capacities were affected.

The other notable 1994 case, that of *R. v. Daviault*, raised the issue of intoxication. In this tragic case, the victim was a 65-year-old woman who was wheelchair-bound with partial paralysis. The victim was a friend of the accused's wife. The accused, aged 69, was a chronic alcoholic who brought a 1-litre bottle of liquor with him when he came to visit the victim. Before arriving at her home, he had already consumed seven or eight beers in a tavern. The victim drank a partial glass of brandy, then went to sleep. When she awoke in the middle of the night to use the lavatory the accused grabbed her from her wheelchair, threw her on the bed and sexually assaulted her. He left at 4 a.m. During the period from 6 p.m. to 3 a.m., he had consumed the remaining liquor in the brandy bottle. He testified that he could recollect nothing before he awoke nude in the complainant's bed. He denied having sexually assaulted the victim. At trial, a pharmacologist testified that the accused's blood alcohol level would have been between 400 mg and 600 mg per 100 ml of blood after the amount of alcohol that had been consumed. That amount would have surely caused either coma or death in the average person, but the accused had developed a high tolerance to the effects of alcohol. The central point of the pharmacologist's testimony for the purposes of understanding the defence of intoxication was that an individual with such a high amount of alcohol in the bloodstream might suffer an episode of amnesia-automatism or "blackout." This is a state in which the individual is out of touch with reality and the brain is temporarily dissociated from its normal functioning. In this condition, the individual has little or no knowledge of his or her actions and cannot remember them the next day. In such a state, the individual is more likely to act in either a violent or gratuitous manner. The accused was found not guilty since the trial judge found that there was a reasonable doubt concerning the mental state of the accused, specifically whether he could have formed the minimal intent necessary to commit the offence. This raised troubling questions that were addressed by federal Parliament through amendments to the Criminal Code, which assigned criminal fault when persons voluntarily intoxicated themselves.

An earlier British case, reported in Smith and Hogan's (1992) classic law text demonstrated the moral difficulties inherent in the defence of intoxication. A young couple hired a woman to mind their newborn baby so that they might have an evening out. Upon their return, they found the babysitter quietly sleeping in an armchair in front of a roaring fire. They tiptoed past to check on the baby but were shocked to find the baby was not in the crib. They then attempted to rouse the babysitter. This took a great effort, since she was extremely inebriated almost to the point of unconsciousness. The babysitter could give no indication of the whereabouts of the child. She had been enjoying a drink and the fire and had simply fallen asleep. In actual fact, she had consumed an entire large bottle of alcohol. The babysitter protested that she had simply been putting logs on the fire to keep herself warm and someone must have entered the home while she was asleep and kidnapped the child. To the parent's horror, they discovered the baby, wrapped in bundled blankets on the fire. The babysitter had been so intoxicated she had mistaken the baby for a log!

Most observers find it difficult to believe that a person could reach a state of intoxication so great that they would be able to mistake a baby for a log. Yet at the same time we recognize that the leading cause of traffic fatalities in this country is alcohol. Persons are regularly pulled from behind the wheels of automobiles in which they have killed others, incapable of walking or properly speaking and in a semi-comatose state.

The two Canadian cases detailed above caused widespread protest by women's groups concerned with the possibility that rapists would claim a defence of intoxication in order to escape responsibility for their actions.

Mistake

The defence of mistake in Canada is limited strictly to what is termed a **mistake of fact**. What does this imply? There is no defence of ignorance permitted under Canadian law. One cannot state that one had no idea that a particular act was prohibited under the Criminal Code, even if the Code is over 1000 pages in length. In cases of mistaken belief, it has to be demonstrated to the satisfaction of the court that the individual had acted based upon an honest belief. This could be illustrated by a scenario in which an individual is asked to assist in moving the contents of a person's home. Someone might remove items from the home under the supervision of the "owner." Unfortunately, the owner later turns out to be a thief. He insists that the mover was not mistaken about what was transpiring, i.e., the recruited mover knew he was involved in robbing the contents of a home. The mover can provide evidence however that he was acting upon an honest belief substantiated by a telephone conversation inadvertently recorded on his home answering machine and discussions witnessed by impartial observers. Therefore, his defence of honest belief would be substantiated.

One cannot expect full protection of the law when there are multiple layers to a charge. For example, it would not be accepted that someone could argue she believed honestly that the contents of a stolen guitar case were not stolen, or could she? In this category of offence, it has to be established that even though the individual committed an act, she had no reason to believe she was committing a crime. It is incumbent on the defence lawyer to prove that the mistake is an honest one, and that the mistake would have been made by a **reasonable person**. The proof of mistake of fact is borne by the defendant, reflecting perhaps the attempts of accused parties to raise it in cases of sexual assault where they have argued that the victim gave consent.

Ramcharan (2002) has noted that the courts have recognized in recent years that the proliferation of regulatory legislative acts has made it virtually impossible for the average citizen to be aware of the existence of all laws. The Supreme Court has even noted this in a fairly recent decision, pointing to the complexity of laws and overlapping regulations created by federal and provincial governments that have brought society to a point where it is an unreasonable expectation that citizens will have a comprehensive knowledge of the existence of a given law or its application to their actions.

Self-Defence

In certain circumstances, individuals are able to claim the need to act in **self-defence**. Police and prison officers may invoke this defence if charged with an offence. The law permits us to act in self-defence when our lives are threatened. We cannot be held criminally responsible in such circumstances, but it must be remembered that the circumstances surrounding the act of self-defence must be reasonable, that is, one may only use an amount of force that is necessary to repel the attack to avoid injury or death. A homeowner is awakened by the crash of breaking glass in the middle of the night. She gathers her hunting rifle from under the bed, where it is illegally stored in a loaded condition, and makes her way toward the sound. There she sees a figure coming in through the window, who also sees her. Without a verbal warning, she shoots and kills the intruder. Is this a case of self-defence? Since the intruder made no threat or attempt to injure the homeowner, it is not self-defence. The homeowner should have warned the intruder or fired a warning shot. More prudently, the homeowner should have either locked herself in a room and phoned 911 or run from the house. The amount of force used to repel the intruder was not warranted. When the lights were finally turned on, the intruder turned out to be a fifteen-year-old boy with no weapons on his person.

Duress is closely related to self-defence. If you are compelled to commit a crime against your will, you cannot be held criminally responsible. Let us say that a criminal is holding your boyfriend captive and will shoot him unless you rob a bank. This crime is committed under compulsion and you will not be held legally liable. However, you, as the person under duress, must believe that "the threats will be carried out." Further, this defence is not allowed for many serious Criminal Code offences including murder, sexual assault, or kidnapping. Ramcharan (2002) notes that gang members cannot avail themselves of this defence when another gang member is inciting the compulsion. While the defence may be successful where immediate death or grievous bodily harm would result from threats made against the accused, the courts have also found that if there were an opportunity for the accused to leave safely or escape from the situation of duress, then the defence would fail.

As an example, consider a true case: Jill and Jack had a party at their house with three male friends. All of the partygoers were drinking quite heavily. Jill disappeared upstairs with one of the male friends, Sam. After a period of time Jack went looking for her and found her having sexual intercourse with the individual. Jack began to kick and beat the now naked Sam. The two other party guests came upstairs upon hearing the commotion. Jack yelled at them, saying, "Help me beat this bastard or I'll kill you." They complied, citing at court that they were afraid he would carry out his threat. Sam died as a result of being beaten and thrown in the backyard on a very cold winter's day. Did the defence of duress hold up in court? No. The judge stated that the two accomplices in Sam's death could have easily run out of the house to seek help, even if they felt they could not overpower Jack. They were duly convicted of manslaughter.

Necessity implies that you may have to commit a crime in order to achieve a greater good. You are walking down the street on a 100-degree day and see two small children locked in a car with the windows shut tight. The children are pleading to be let out and are entering a semi-unconscious state. You break the window of the automobile to let them out. Your crime involving damage to property will be dismissed by the court, since the damage was necessary to potentially save the lives of the children. While the court has accepted this defence in such minor cases, in more serious cases the defence of necessity has not normally prevailed.

Mental Disorder

The defence of **mental disorder** (formerly referred to as insanity) is perhaps the most misunderstood by the public. It is often argued, for example, that guilty parties feign mental illness in order to escape responsibility for their actions. But faking mental disorder over a lengthy period of time, indeed, even a short one, is a difficult task—particularly the degree of mental disorder required to excuse a criminal action. The defence of mental disorder in Canadian law is derived specifically from the case of Scottish nationalist Daniel McNaughtan who came before the British courts in 1843.

McNaughtan acquired a firearm with the intent to kill the prime minister of England, Sir Robert Peel. This was the same Peel who had lent his first and last names in colloquial form to the title given British police officers, as "peelers" or "bobbies." McNaughtan travelled from his native Scotland to a place near Parliament Hill in London and waited for his quarry. When his target approached, he drew out a revolver and shot twice. A police officer ran to apprehend him from nearby and shouted, "What do you think you've done?" McNaughtan replied, "I've shot the prime minister." From this statement, the police officer deduced that McNaughtan was insane, since he had shot the private secretary of Peel, Henry Drummond, rather than the prime minister.

While McNaughtan appeared mad, he was not. Earlier, Peel had been scheduled to visit Scotland. He did not feel like making the journey, so Peel sent Drummond to sit in the coach and pretend to be him. Since this was before the days of cameras, the Scottish citizens had no idea that the person in the coach was not Peel. McNaughtan had actually seen Drummond pass him in the streets of his hometown. But why did he wish to assassinate Peel? McNaughtan was a Scottish nationalist who hated the British government. They had imposed increasingly harsh taxes on the Scottish people, including recent taxes on both the purchase of wool and the sale of finished products, a mainstay of the cottage industries that supplied many with their survival. Times under British rule had been extremely difficult for the Scots, by nature a fierce warrior race who had often sparred with the British.

McNaughtan was tried as a madman who in an insane fit had tried to kill the prime minister but was so deluded as to not know whom he was killing. This was a political trial with the plain intent of ensuring that McNaughtan not be given the chance to use the court to protest the miserable treatment being given the Scots people by the British. If he had been allowed to do this, or if McNaughtan was hanged for his crime, it might have roused the Scots to commence a new war against British rule.

McNaughtan was sentenced to Broadmoor Hospital for the criminally insane following his conviction. He was not insane, as guards often noted on the logs kept for each patient. He eventually died of diabetes mellitus at the age of 63. Following McNaughtan's conviction and given the fact that he was not hanged, Queen Victoria ordered a panel of judges to consider new laws regarding the defence of insanity. This was prompted by her disgust at McNaughtan's sentence, since Drummond had been a friend of the Queen. The jurists devised the **McNaughtan rules** which became the standard by which insanity is judged in our laws. The McNaughtan rules state that in order for a person to be found not guilty by reason of insanity, they must not "know the nature and quality of the act they have committed" (Fleming, 1993).

Very few people argue for a defence of mental disorder in Canada; roughly 3 percent of cases involve a consideration of this problem. The mental disorder defence is a legal test, not a psychiatric determination of the accused's state of mind *at the time of the crime*. Both prosecution and defence in such cases seek expert witnesses who will support their point of view on the mental state of the accused when they committed the crime(s) in question. This reflects the adversarial nature of the criminal justice system in which we operate. Those students who have had an opportunity to read about or observe the O. J. Simpson trial, for example, will be cognizant that each of the sides involved often refers to their own efforts as a "search for the truth" while denigrating the efforts of the opposing side as mere showmanship. In actuality, both sides are committed to do all they can, short of breaking the law, to ensure that they win.

When a person enters a mental disorder plea, there is often considerable disagreement amongst psychiatrists about his or her state of mind. The most important consideration is not whether the person suffers from a mental condition at the time of examination, but whether this mental condition existed at the time he or she committed the crime and whether it was sufficient to release the accused from responsibility. Those accused may be in some instances so mentally ill that they are unable to instruct their counsel on how to conduct their defence. These individuals would be adjudged **unfit to stand trial** under Canadian law and referred for psychiatric treatment. This should have been the determination of the judge in a recent US case involving the shooting and murder of many passengers on a commuter train. Their assailant went through a variety of lawyers who were assigned to assist him, firing all of them. He eventually undertook his own defence. While in court, his mannerisms and phrases often aped those of high-profile trial lawyers. It was obvious that this individual was mentally disturbed. He maintained, while questioning witnesses whom he had shot at close quarters, that his victims were mistaken, and, indeed, that he had never had a gun in his possession on the day in question. He was eventually convicted and sentenced to life imprisonment. His conviction was appealed by well-known criminal attorney William Kunstler, who would cite these behaviours as the grounds for a reversal of conviction. While there is no doubt that the assailant did fire the shots in question, there is great doubt as to his state of mind at the time of the offence, given his behaviour post-arrest and at trial. This highlights the substantial differences between psychiatric versus legal definitions of mental illness. While the MacNaughtan rules may act as a guide to the legal determination of mental illness, there is often significant debate among psychiatrists as to the mental state of an accused—debate that may determine whether he or she appears for the defence or the prosecution. It is common for two or more medical experts to disagree as to 1) whether a mental illness exists in an accused, and 2) the nature of the illness(es).

Serial murderers have often claimed to be criminally insane, but very few have been successful in this argument. While their acts are certainly bizarre, unforgivable, and unforgettable, there is little evidence to indicate that they are unable to distinguish between right and wrong. It is more consistent to think of them as individuals who understand that something is wrong but choose to do it anyway, for a variety of questionable reasons (Fleming, 1998).

Automatism

Arguably the most fascinating of all defences is that of automatism. Simply stated, persons who commit crimes when they are acting as an automaton are not guilty of an offence punishable by law. The most famous case in Canadian legal history involving this defence is that of Ken Parks, as chronicled by June Callwood in her book *The Sleepwalker* (1990). Ken Parks had led a quite unremarkable life up until the night of May 23, 1987. Ken and his wife lived in a small commuter city just east of Toronto called Pickering.

On the night in question, Ken Parks was watching television around midnight and dropping off to sleep on the couch. Parks was a large man over six feet five inches (196 centimetres) tall and twenty-three years of age. Ken and Karen's marriage was not going well at that time. Parks had been fired from his job for embezzling funds to support a gambling habit that he had developed. He had forged phoney purchase orders and taken the $32 000 in payments to pay for his losses. Like all embezzlers, he rationalized that it was only a temporary loan and he would one day pay them back. Unfortunately for Parks, he was caught before he could win back his losses. He was jailed overnight, after which he stole all of his wife's savings and took money from loan sharks reasoning he could win back the money he had embezzled and get his job back. He lost this money too.

Parks had not been sleeping well during this entire period. In the two nights before May 23, he had enjoyed no sleep at all. The last thing that he could remember was nodding off during *Saturday Night Live*. After that, he woke up from a horrifying dream. Parks could see the face of his mother-in-law pleading for help and heard distant screams. He called for his wife's brother and sister; they seemed to need help but he could not find them. Something was wrong, he thought. He must look for help. Next he heard a telephone and then ran to the underground parking garage. In his hand was a knife. He threw it on the floor of his car and drove to a police station. Was he still dreaming? When he entered the Scarborough police station in the middle of the night, Parks's hands were covered in blood and he was bleeding profusely from wounds to them. He walked to the desk officer and put his elbows up on the night desk. He said that he had just killed two people. Ken Parks was soon under arrest for the murder of his mother-in-law and a serious assault on his father-in-law. It had not been a dream. But what, if anything, was Ken Parks guilty of?

Parks had fallen asleep on the couch in his townhouse living room that night. Then he had gotten into his automobile and driven along highway 401, taking the cut-off for his in-laws' house. Parks had his wife's keys so that he could park and enter the house from the basement garage. After entering, he had proceeded to the master bedroom where his father-in-law had awoken to find a man sitting on his chest and beating his head bloody to unconsciousness. Then Ken proceeded to stab his mother-in-law to death. The two children in the house had awoken to hear the attack punctuated by the assailant's grunting noises. They crawled out through a bedroom window across the roof to escape.

Ken Parks was found not guilty of the murder of his mother-in-law. He had murdered her while in a dissociative state similar to sleepwalking. Parks's father had also suffered from this same defect of the mind. The father was known to get up in the middle of the night and prepare an entire meal in his sleep. However, were the father to be awoken from the sleepwalking state, he could become violent. Parks suffered from a form of non-insane automatism, which could be medically treated so that violent behaviour would not recur. The events leading up to the night in question were characteristic of factors associated with an upcoming autonomic episode; severe stress in the life of the individual, sleeplessness, marital turmoil, loss of employment, and shame were all present in Parks's life. Let us consider another recent related case: the acquittal of Jan Luedecke (see Box 3.3).

Consent

The final defence available to accused persons under Canadian law is that of consent. Consent is an issue that is predominantly associated with sexual assault cases. The issue is whether the complainant consented willingly to the behaviour in question. This is a difficult issue, on one hand because there are typically only two witnesses to such an event. However, juries are generally predisposed to believe that a complainant is in the position to indicate whether he or she gave consent to the act or not.

BOX 3.3

A CASE OF SEXSOMNIA

While the case of Ken Parks is the best-known example of automatism as a successful defence to a criminal charge, a recent case illustrates its use in a different type of assault.

In what has been described by the courts as a "rare case," Jan Luedecke was acquitted of sexual assault "after a judge ruled that he was asleep during the attack—a disorder known as "sexsomnia." Justice Russell Otter deemed his conduct to be "not voluntary."

The victim, a middle-aged woman who had only just made Luedecke's acquaintance the night of the attack, was apparently woken from her sleeping state on the couch to discover the accused having sex with her. Luedecke's maintained that he was sleeping on the same couch and "woke up when he was thrown on the floor."

The expert witness in the case testified that the accused had sexsomnia, "which is sexual behaviour during sleep." The condition is known to be aggravated by the use of "alcohol, and sleep deprivation and is genetic in origin." The court was told that the defendant had on four other occasions had "sleep sex" with his various female girlfriends.

1. Do you think that the accused should have been acquitted?
2. Is it likely that other defendants will attempt this defence?
3. Do you think an appeal of the verdict by the victim will be successful? Why?

Source: "It's ruled sleep sex," by Natalie Pona, *Toronto Sun*, November 30, 2005.

Persons cannot give voluntary consent to an act if they are

1. unconscious; or
2. under the influence of alcohol to such an extent that it impairs their cognitive abilities.

They also cannot give voluntary consent if there is a gun being held to their head. Further, if an individual refuses sexual intimacy by saying "no," this has to be taken as a refusal of consent. This is a difficult question for juries to decide, particularly if the credibility of the victim is in question. Canadian criminologist Ron Hinch found that police in a study he conducted in Nova Scotia routinely listed as "unfounded" those sexual assault cases in which the victim was a prostitute; had a history of mental illness, drug abuse, or alcoholism; or had a criminal record related to sexual offences. Police were assuming a great deal of discretionary power in screening out victims whom they felt would not provide credible testimony at court.

The Canadian Charter of Rights and Freedoms

The Canadian Charter of Rights and Freedoms, entrenched in the Constitution Act of 1982, was one of the most significant additions to the Canadian legal system. The role of the judiciary has become one of interpreting whether federal or provincial legislation contravenes the core values of the Charter and the nation. One of the major requirements of the Charter is to allow the judiciary the right to define as unconstitutional legislation that contravenes the protected rights of citizens. However, it is not an easy task to define many of these protected rights in ways that allow for consensus in an increasingly heterogeneous society. Whereas prior to the proclamation of the Charter, Canada was governed by the doctrine of parliamentary supremacy, the Charter is today the overarching document, with the courts entitled to test all laws against the values it enshrines. Since 1982, when the Act incorporating the Charter was signed, the Supreme Court of Canada has found that many pieces of legislation and some sections of the Criminal Code contravene the Charter rights of individuals or groups and thus has invalidated these particular legislative acts.

The Charter guarantees the rights and freedoms of Canadians, subject to certain limitations. As shown in Box 3.4, the Charter is composed of several sections guaranteeing fundamental freedoms, legal rights, equality rights, enforcement rights, voting rights, mobility rights, language rights, and Aboriginal rights (see http://laws.justice.gc.ca/en/charter/index.html for the complete Charter). It also provides opportunities for those whose rights are infringed upon to obtain remedies and redress from the courts.

BOX 3.4

KEY SECTIONS OF THE CHARTER OF RIGHTS AND FREEDOMS

The Charter of Rights and Freedoms: Legal Rights and the Canadian Criminal Justice System

Legal Rights

7. Everyone has the right to life, liberty and security of the person and the right not to be deprived thereof except in accordance with the principles of fundamental justice.

8. Everyone has the right to be secure against unreasonable search and seizure.

9. Everyone has the right not to be arbitrarily detained or imprisoned.

10. Everyone has the right on arrest or detention

    (a) to be informed promptly of the reasons thereof;

    (b) to retain and instruct counsel without delay and to be informed of that right; and

    (c) to have the validity of the detention determined by way of habeas corpus and to be released if the detention is not lawful.

11. Any person charged with an offence has the right

    (a) to be informed without unreasonable delay of the specific offence;

    (b) to be tried within a reasonable time;

    (c) not to be compelled to be a witness in proceedings against that person in respect of the offence;

    (d) to be presumed innocent until proven guilty according to law in a fair and public hearing by an independent and impartial tribunal;

    (e) not to be denied reasonable bail without just cause;

    (f) except in the case of an offence under military law tried before a military tribunal, to the benefit of trial by jury where the maximum punishment for the offence is imprisonment for five years or a more severe punishment;

    (g) not to be found guilty on account of any act or omission unless, at the time of the act or omission, it is constituted an offence under Canadian or international law or was criminal according to the general principles of law recognized by the community of nations;

    (h) if finally acquitted of the offence, not to be tried for it again and, if finally found guilty and punished for the offence, not to be tried or punished for it again; and

    (i) if found guilty of the offence and if the punishment for the offence has been varied between the time of the commission and the time of sentencing, to the benefit of the lesser punishment.

12. Everyone has the right not to be subjected to any cruel and unusual treatment or punishment.

13. A witness who testifies in any proceedings has the right not to have any incriminating evidence so given used to incriminate that witness in any other proceedings, except in a prosecution for perjury or for the giving of contradictory evidence.

14. A party or witness in any proceedings who does not understand or speak the language in which the proceedings are conducted or who is deaf has the right to the assistance of an interpreter.

Equality Rights

15. (1) Every individual is equal before and under the law and has the right to the equal protection and equal benefit of the law without discrimination and, in particular, without discrimination based on race, national or ethnic origin, colour, religion, sex, age or mental or physical disability.

    (2) Subsection (1) does not preclude any law, program or activity that has as its object the amelioration of conditions of disadvantaged individuals or groups including those that are disadvantaged because of race, national or ethnic origin, colour, religion, sex, age or mental or physical disability.

Enforcement

24. (1) Anyone whose rights or freedoms, as guaranteed by this Charter, have been infringed or denied may apply to a court of competent jurisdiction to obtain such remedy as the court considers appropriate and just in the circumstances.

(2) Where, in proceedings under subsection (1), a court concludes that evidence was obtained in a manner that infringed or denied any rights or freedoms guaranteed by this Charter, the evidence shall be excluded if it is established that, having regard to all the circumstances, the admission of it in the proceedings would bring the administration of justice into disrepute.

Source: http://laws.justice.gc.ca/en/charter/index.html.

Conclusion

In this chapter, we have analyzed the goals and purposes of Canadian criminal law in the context of the criminal justice system. It is within the justice system that the law is administered and enforced. While law serves many purposes, one of its main roles is to reflect the values of society, and just as Canadian society continually evolves and changes, so must the criminal law. What is defined as a violation of the law and harmful to the social order must always reflect the experiences and opinions of society. Similarly, criminal law must distinguish between serious indictable offences and summary conviction offences. The presumption of innocence on the part of the defendant is the linchpin of our criminal justice system, and the guilt of the defendant must be established in a court of law, such that it is proved beyond any reasonable doubt that a crime was committed. Canada's legal system allows for a series of defences. The purpose of the defence is to show that the defendant should not be held accountable for his or her actions, even though he or she may have violated the Criminal Code. New and innovative defences are continually being tested in our courts, but mental disorder and self-defence remain the two most important defences. Finally, we have addressed one of the most important additions to our legal system, the Canadian Charter of Rights and Freedoms, which was incorporated into the Constitution in 1982. That this document has had a profound influence on our society and in our courts is without dispute. Although it is not without its critics, the Charter is the document that guarantees our legal rights and that places in the hands of the courts the role of final arbiter of our values, as well as our belief in what constitutes a just and fair society.

Summary

The basic premise of Canadian criminal law is that social order and social control are challenged by the commitment of criminal acts, and that these acts injure not just individuals but society itself. For the purposes of criminal law, criminologists see two opposing perspectives: the consensus perspective sees society as characterized by a core set of values held by all citizens. When these values are deviated from, society seeks ways to punish offenders through the Criminal Code. The conflict perspective, on the other hand, sees society as composed of various interest groups, with the criminal laws mainly protecting the power and property of those who are rich and influential and who enact the laws.

Guilt for any criminal law infraction must be proved by the prosecution in a court of law, and the accused is presumed innocent until proven guilty. There are many defences that an accused can claim to rationalize her or his behaviour, including the defence of mental disorder. One of the most significant additions to our legal system is the Canadian Charter of Rights and Freedoms, which outlines the protected rights of citizens, including the legal rights of accused persons when they become part of the criminal justice system. As well, the Charter defines the rights of the accused to legal counsel and guarantees a fair trial, release on bail, and protection from harsh or unjustified punishment. While law serves many purposes, one of its main roles is to reflect the values of our society, and from this perspective what is a violation of the criminal law must always reflect the experiences and changes in society.

Key Terms

actus reus (p. 54)

case law (p. 50)

civil law (p. 51)

conflict perspective (p. 49)

consensus perspective (p. 48)

corpus delicti (p. 53)

crime (p. 47)

criminal offence (p. 59)

criminal laws (p. 47)

duress (p. 63)

general deterrent (p. 48)

indictable offence (p. 52)

intoxication (p. 60)

macro theories (p. 48)

McNaughtan rules (p. 65)

mens rea (p. 58)

mental disorder (defence) (p. 64)

mistake of fact (p. 62)

necessity (p. 64)

presumption of innocence (p. 58)

reasonable person (p. 62)

right to remain silent (p. 58)

self-defence (p. 63)

social contract (p. 48)

specific deterrent (p. 48)

statutory law (p. 50)

summary conviction offence (p. 52)

treason (p. 53)

unfit to stand trial (p. 65)

Discussion Questions

1. Discuss the goals and purposes of criminal law.

2. Discuss the differences between the defences of necessity and duress.

3. Discuss the defence of mental disorder and its relevance to criminal law.

4. The emphasis in the criminal law is on property offences. Discuss reasons for the lesser emphasis on white-collar and environmental crime in Canada.

5. Discuss the importance of Charter provisions in protecting the legal rights of the accused.

Weblinks

www.canadalegal.com/gosite.asp?s=4286 This site is run by Professor David Paciocco, an expert on the law of evidence. He explains in detail the role of defence counsel. He begins by asking, "How can you defend those criminals?" and goes on to explain how.

home.istar.ca/~ccja/angl/index.shtml The Canadian Criminal Justice Association (CCJA) is dedicated to the improvement of criminal justice in Canada. The website offers the CCJA's Justice Report, position papers on special issues such as crime prevention and young offenders, excerpts from the *Canadian Journal of Criminology*, and links to other sites of interest.

http://laws.justice.gc.ca/en/charter/index.html The website of the Canadian Charter of Rights and Freedoms, with the full text made more accessible through links to specific areas.

www.extension.ualberta.ca/legalfaqs The Legal Studies Program at the University of Alberta offers a Canadian legal FAQs site, with questions and answers provided by topic and by provincial or federal jurisdiction.

www.lexum.umontreal.ca/index.epl?lang=en The Faculty of Law at the University of Montreal has a searchable online collection of case law, including Supreme Court of Canada decisions on the Canadian Charter of Rights and Freedoms.

CHAPTER 4

Law, Social Control, and Theoretical Considerations of Criminality

Objectives

- To outline the methods by which the criminal justice system uses criminal law to control society and affirm the dominant social values.

- To discuss the influence of the criminal law on social control and social change.

- To discuss theories explaining why people commit crime or deviance.

- To outline classical, positivistic, and sociological perspectives on crime.

- To discuss the impact of economic and corporate interest groups.

Law and Society

What is the role of the law in society? How does the judicial system decide what is "wrong," and whose interests does criminal law serve? When we examine the criminal justice system, we may conclude that Canada has made a deliberate policy decision to use the criminal law as an instrument to control Canadians' moral conduct and to affirm certain dominant moral values. However, many critics believe that using the law to promote morality is not only problematic and possibly futile, but also has major repercussions on our understanding of crime in Canada and our attempts to solve it. Hills (1971) believes that the consequences to societies that use the law to symbolize morality include overburdening law-enforcement and judicial administration. As well, when minor "morality crimes" are brought before the courts, the effectiveness of the justice system to deal with more serious crimes is compromised. Furthermore, by branding certain behaviours as criminal, the criminal justice system may actually encourage the growth of organized crime.

According to Larsen and Burtch (1999), criminal law is the best example of an influential group's attempts to control the behaviour of Canadians. The law acts as an instrument of coercion by imposing **criminal sanctions**, or penalties to enforce obedience to the law, on behaviour that is considered threatening to the dominant group's values. However, while agreeing that certain types of behaviour, such as murder, robbery, and assault, are a threat to society, these authors believe that using the criminal law to control morality is unacceptable. They argue that the state may inadvertently be contributing to problems of crime control by attempting to control moral behaviour in **victimless crimes**—crimes that are considered to have no victims because the participants are willing, such as drug use, prostitution, and pornography. By prohibiting the goods and services that the public demands, the criminal law may serve to inflate the price of the illegal product and encourage organized criminals to provide the demanded services. These prohibitions serve the role of creating monopolistic, strongly organized crime syndicates, whose huge profits allow them to expand and diversify. Of more serious concern is the fact that when the demand for the product is created by a physical addiction, such as drug addiction, high prices lead to the vicious cycle of secondary crime. Offenders commit crimes so that they can procure the money to purchase the illicit products.

Hills (1971) also believes that criminal sanctions against such victimless behaviours as gambling, sexual deviation, obscenity, drugs, or prostitution are almost unenforceable. Legislating private moral behaviour where the social danger is absent or difficult to assess can mean diverting the scarce resources of the justice system from those deviant behaviours that generate national consensus. In the absence of victims willing to testify in court against such crimes, the police often rely on informers and contacts with the underworld. Recent judicial decisions have shown that Charter infringements on the legal rights of defendants, involving illegal search and seizure, false arrests, harassment, entrapment, and other illegal police practices, have been inordinately high in public morality crimes. Increasingly, critics have suggested that using the criminal law to prosecute victimless crimes provides the breeding ground for bribery and police corruption. Furthermore, because of the sporadic nature of law enforcement and the absence of any clearly definable social danger, these laws are violated with impunity, encouraging disrespect for the legal process and cynicism toward the criminal justice system.

When victimless crimes are prosecuted, judges often have to impose severe and mandatory sentences on offenders. The Supreme Court of Canada deemed as "cruel and unusual punishment" the sentence of seven years for marijuana possession. It is important for the Canadian judicial system to review the impact of the criminalization process for the wide variety of moral crimes. Would it not be more in keeping with the goal of moral and societal responsibility if the law were to concentrate on prosecuting possession and trafficking of hard drugs such as heroin and cocaine? Similarly, in terms of societal harm, would it not be more responsible to focus on prosecuting purveyors of child pornography and child prostitution?

It is clear that criminalizing morality diverts scarce law enforcement resources from the more serious crime problems, on which there is societal consensus. Crimes of violence, property crime, and white-collar crime pose a greater threat to the values of society. Relying on the law to deal with the public drunk, the prostitute, or the user of soft drugs such as marijuana is too often a repetitive process of arrest, short-term incarceration, and rearrest. The only outcome is a continuous overburdening of the branches of the justice system—the police, the courts, and the prisons. The final proof of the futility of the process is that in the history of prosecution for these offences in Canadian courts, very few of the major traffickers in gambling and drugs, and few, if any, of the producers of child pornography, are ever arrested and successfully prosecuted. Canada must seriously ponder the effects of overcriminalization and an overreliance on the criminal law to legislate morality. By arresting and convicting large numbers of people for such crimes as soft drug use, prostitution, gambling, or public drunkenness, the police and the criminal justice system are playing to the court of public opinion and to those who believe that such laws protect the moral standards of the community.

Criminal Law as a Mechanism of Social Control

Informal and Formal Social Control

Rush (1994) notes that **social control** is the way in which societies encourage conformity. As a result of social control mechanisms, the majority of society's members accept the normative controls of the state; they know that supporting the legal norms will be rewarded and that non-conformist behaviour will result in sanctions, including fines and imprisonment. Social control operates on both informal and formal levels. **Informal social controls** are the unwritten codes of behaviour that the majority of small groups follow in everyday social interaction. While there is no formal sanction for failing to follow informal codes of behaviour, conformity is maintained through social pressure from other group members. **Formal social controls** are those that are legislated and form the written body of our civil and criminal legal codes. Statutory law, for example, dictates interpersonal behaviour through our highway traffic laws or behaviour related to business practices. When these formal social controls are violated, the negative sanctions can be severe.

Grana and Ollenburger (1999) note that the internalization of formal and informal social controls is an ongoing part of the socialization process. Through this process we learn who we are, how we should relate to society, and what our relationships are with others. Built into the socialization process are the control mechanisms that dictate how we learn skills and knowledge, how we can realize our aspirations, and how we can recognize our limitations. We also learn who in society occupies the positions of influence and power. Through socialization, the individual learns to accept, distrust, or reject authority and to admire, fear, or hate others in the society. For all of us, sanctions—whether they are positive or negative—are affected by our gender, ethnicity, and social status.

Criminal Law and Social Change

It is clearly documented that the criminal law has been used to promote social control and to transform society. The colonization of Canada by the English and French in the seventeenth century is a classic example of the use of law to define the legal role and status of Aboriginal peoples. Through coercion, threats, and criminal sanctions, the colonizers forced Aboriginal people off their land and onto reserves. With the passing of legislation titled the Indian Act, Aboriginal people became wards of the state and totally dependent on the federal government for the necessities of life. Caputo, Kennedy, Reasons, and Brannigan (1989) argue that colonizers used the law to deculturate and destroy the social and economic organization of Aboriginal people in Canada. Today, Aboriginal people have been left with an incarceration rate that is 10 times higher than for any other racial or ethnic group in Canada. This use of the criminal law to create subordinate and dominant groups is an example of the negative effects that the law has on a changing society.

In some cases, laws can create positive changes in society. For example, Grana and Ollenburger (1999) note that changing patterns of domestic relationships cause changes in divorce law, which also have an effect on society's view of marriage. Since its advent in 1982, the Canadian Charter of Rights and Freedoms has had a dramatic effect on criminal law and on the concept of justice in society. The fact that the courts could actually create laws, rather than simply enforce them, is creating a new function of the law as an instrument of social change. Vago (2000) notes both the positive and negative effects of using the law for this purpose. Because both criminal and civil law have the power to impose negative sanctions, they can encourage society to overcome its resistance to change. For example, if the law supports equal employment opportunities for designated groups, then employers, although they may be reluctant, will have to accept these legally sanctioned societal changes to avoid the negative sanctions imposed for non-compliance. This is a clear example of the coercive effect of the law. Because many people see the law as representing authority and believe that it is their obligation to obey it, they see the need for compliance. As well, because the law represents social order for the majority of Canadians, they accept its role in the socialization process and prefer consensus on issues rather than conflict. Legally dictated societal change, therefore, is accepted. However, when laws are created that further social ends, but that go against the social, economic, or moral principles of powerful interest groups, then conflict rather than consensus could be the outcome. For example, gun-control laws in both Canada and the United States have met with immense opposition because these laws conflict with the views of many powerful interest groups. In this case, the effectiveness of the law as an agent of social change has been diminished. As Vago notes, the views of the powerful can negate the views of the oppressed or the majority.

Society also enacts public policy through the criminal law. In the past 25 years, major changes to public policy, including the legalization of abortion, the decriminalization of homosexuality, the abolition of capital punishment, and the enactment of gun-control legislation, have been administered through the criminal law and the criminal justice system. The state is always attempting to control behaviour, and using the law is the most effective method of ensuring compliance. Criminal law can be a major means of societal change. Acceptance of laws will be positive if laws are presented as rational and fair to all groups. Similarly, when enforcement is immediate, the criminal justice system is committed to public policy, and the punishments are clearly defined, then compliance will outweigh resistance.

What Causes Crime?

Why do people disobey the norms of society? Why do some people continually break the law? Why do some individuals steal, rape, kill, and maim? For more than two centuries, criminologists have been pondering these questions. Some criminologists argue that criminals are rational actors who choose their actions. Simply, criminals have free will and engage in criminal behaviour accordingly. Conversely, other criminologists suggest that transgressors of the law are influenced by their social, economic, and cultural environments. Essentially, larger social forces are *criminogenic*, or crime causing. For this reason, many sociologists and criminologists look to the operation of the market or the state, or at relative economic deprivation, as the reason for criminality. Nevertheless, the majority of criminologists argue that there are many causes of crime and that the explanation of crime is multi-faceted. In the next section, the major theoretical perspectives on criminality will be briefly discussed.

Theoretical Considerations of Criminality

Exploring the causes of crime is of great importance to criminologists. Generally speaking, there are four major branches of criminological theory: *classical, biological positivism, sociological,* and *conflict/critical theories.* There is considerable debate about the merit of each approach and various theories are tested by researchers to determine their relevance in explaining crime. It is beyond the scope of our text to provide a comprehensive analysis of criminological theories. However, we will briefly summarize the major theories.

Demonic or Religious Explanations of Criminality

Before we can discuss the major theoretical perspectives, it is important to provide a historical background on how crime has been viewed. In past centuries, the cause of crime was seen as the result of evil or supernatural forces. Deviant members of the community were supposedly possessed by evil forces and the solution was to wipe out the evil from the individual. During the fifteenth-century Spanish Inquisition, the Catholic Church obtained confessions through brutal tortures, both before and during public executions. In the late seventeenth century in places such as Salem, Massachusetts, famous witch trials were conducted. Guilt was determined by many novel devices in a trial by ordeal, which was designed to reveal a sign of God's will. Brutal execution practices included burying alive, burning at the stake, quartering, beheading, stoning, and breaking on the wheel. Death was the major method of punishment. Non-lethal forms were also unsavoury, including branding, pillorying, and whipping.

The brutality and the perceived unfairness of the punishment became revolting to an increasing segment of the population. Seventeenth- and eighteenth-century Enlightenment thinkers captured much of this sentiment, leading to a rethinking of sin as crime and of atonement as punishment. As a result, the classical approach was formed as a way to reform the barbaric and unfair punishments that were standard in the dark ages. Classical theory offered a *naturalistic* rather than a supernatural explanation for criminal behaviour. Both Enlightenment and classical thinkers would argue that crime was not a possession of the person by evil, external forces. Rather, crime was a product of the rational individual's free will.

Classical, Neoclassical, and Choice Theories

The Classical school of thought began in the late 1700s and early 1800s and had its roots in the Enlightenment. Simply put, the school held that men and women were rational beings; that crime was the result of the exercise of free will; and that punishment would be effective in reducing the incidence of crime since it negated the pleasure to be derived from crime commission.

The Enlightenment and the Birth of the Classical School

The Enlightenment was a reform movement that spread throughout Europe by philosophers who rejected the belief that Church doctrine was a sufficient and rational account of how people existed in relation to institutions, society, and other people. In his 1748 treatise, *l'Esprit des Lois* ("the spirit of the laws"), Baron de Montesquieu repudiated torture and espoused a rational basis for the administration of criminal law. In 1762, Jean-Jacques Rousseau wrote the *Social Contract*, in which he argued that people could be made bad not by God, necessarily, but rather by social institutions; therefore, he believed a concerted effort should be made to reform these institutions.

The classical school applied the philosophy of this large body of work to the area of criminal law and punishment. Two main proponents of **classical criminology** were Cesare Beccaria of Italy and Jeremy Bentham of England. Both believed that the criminal law should mainly operate to deter crime, and that this function could best be achieved through principles of rationality, transparency, proportionality, and humaneness (see Box 4.1).

BOX 4.1

MAJOR PRINCIPLES WITHIN THE CLASSICAL SCHOOL

Rationality	People have free will to commit crime and make rational decisions to engage in criminal behaviour. As a result, deterrence is an important factor in policy-making because potential offenders would think rationally about the rewards and punishments of a given offence.
Transparency	Laws need to be known prior to the commission of a crime. Potential lawbreakers must be aware of the law and the punishments must be clear and just.
Proportionality	The punishment must be commensurate with the criminal act and the harm caused. The focus is to eliminate arbitrary and unjust punishment.
Humaneness	The punishment must be just and fair and not tied to the power of those in positions of authority. Humaneness is strongly tied to the concept of proportionality and reflects the level of social harm that the crime inflicts.

Bentham is important mainly for his *happiness principle*, which brought the notion of hedonism into the business of governance. Recognizing the pursuit of happiness as a legitimate part of humanity, Bentham sought to work *with* the idea of happiness rather than against it. He came up with his famous dictum: the greatest happiness for the greatest number. Because crime reduced the sum total of happiness, it needed to be deterred. It could be deterred, in turn, through a *pleasure/pain calculus*, in which the individual seeks to maximize his or her own happiness and to minimize pain. Bentham called the weighing of pleasure and pain the **hedonistic calculus**; the pain from crime always had to be greater than the pleasure derived from it.

Cesare Beccaria is most famous for his small volume, *On Crimes and Punishments*, first published anonymously in 1764. Like other texts challenging doctrine or policy, it was denounced by the Catholic Church. Following Enlightenment thinkers and Social Contract thinkers, such as John Locke and Thomas Hobbes, Beccaria argued that punishment was a necessary instrument of deterrence, or crime prevention. He said that it was "always better to prevent crimes than to punish them" (1764/1963). He insisted, however, that only laws, and not magistrates, ought to be able to decree punishments for crimes. Only the legislator represents the will of the people, so it is the rightful maker of laws. So vigorous was his opposition to the arbitrary power of magistrates that he also argued against the right of judges to interpret law. Beccaria believed, furthermore, that legal punishment ought to be reserved for acts that were harmful to society; in this way, he hoped to restrict the scope of punishment to secular considerations (see Box 4.2).

BOX 4.2

THE PRINCIPLE TENETS OF CLASSICAL THEORY

1. The Social Contract, where an individual is bound to society only by his or her own consent. Therefore, society is responsible for him or her.
2. Free will, where individuals are free to make their own choices to act.
3. People seek pleasure and avoid pain.
4. Punishment should be used as a deterrent to criminal behaviour.
5. Punishment should be based upon the seriousness of the crime.
6. Punishments for identical crimes should be identical.

Modern Classical/Choice Theory

The focus of the classical school was on the operation of the criminal law, rather than on the causes or conditions of crime. It was unnecessary to think much about criminals per se, because they were, like other members of society, simply rational thinkers who could be deterred from crime through good policy. Even today, this concept of rational choice holds immense popularity among contemporary criminologists. In a backlash against liberal criminal justice policies of the 1960s, classical theory enjoyed renewed interest in the 1970s. Many criminal justice practitioners, theorists, and researchers argued that a lot of people choose crime of their own free will. Today, classical theory continues to exert much influence in contemporary penology in arguments favouring incapacitation and "just desserts." It has also resurfaced in a number of criminology theories, including deterrence theory, rational choice theory, and routine activities theory.

Deterrence Theory

Deterrence theory holds that people can be discouraged from committing crime by punishment and preventive measures. *General deterrence* refers to the use of punishment to inhibit crime rates or the behaviour of specific populations, rather than specific people. Essentially, general deterrence theory predicts an inverse relationship between crime rates and the certainty, celerity (swiftness), and severity of punishment. *Specific deterrence*, on the other hand, entails discouraging the activity of a particular individual through such steps as incarceration, electronic monitoring, or shaming. The specific deterrence effects of incarceration or other penal sanctions are measured through *recidivism rates*, or the chances of a person's returning to criminal activity upon release.

Rational Choice Theory

Modern-day proponents of **rational choice theory** argue that some offenders, at least, are rational decision-makers who seek to benefit from criminal behaviour. In the view of Cornish and Clarke (1987), offenders make decisions and choices in committing crime. Generally speaking, everyone is a rational calculator and exercises free will, but some are limited in their ability to calculate. Cornish and Clarke further argue that we need to be crime-specific. According to the authors, rational choice theory has more promise by emphasizing the particular crime rather than the general disposition to offend. In other words, the decision to commit an offence would depend considerably on the type of crime.

Proponents of a rational choice model theorize that decisions to offend are based on the offender's evaluation of a situation. In fact, there are two steps to decision-making in offending: the involvement decision (deciding to become involved or to stop participating in a form of offending) and event decisions (the tactics of carrying out an offence). Thus, rational choice theorists seek to evaluate the offender's decision-making. They do this by seeing offences as having properties—including skill levels, payoffs, and costs—that structure an offender's choices.

Routine Activities Theory

Routine activities theory is a brand of rational choice theory which suggests that lifestyles contribute significantly to both the volume and type of crime found in any society. Routine activities theory has been described as a victimization theory because it places emphasis on the role of the victim within the criminal act. The theory assumes that crime is opportunistic—by nature, people will, in the absence of deterrence, exploit illegal chances that come their way. Routine activities theory involves the convergence of three distinct variables: suitable targets, capable guardians, and motivated offenders.

By *suitable targets*, Felson and Cohen (1979) are referring to the importance to criminal opportunity of perceptions of target vulnerability. In explaining the increase of crime contiguous with the post–World War II increase of wealth, Felson and Cohen noted that there was a dramatic expansion in the production and proliferation of portable durable goods, like televisions, stereos, computers, and even large items such as automobiles. These goods were suitable as targets because they had value in the black market. All of a sudden, there was much wealth in the form of these goods, which could be targeted by those motivated enough to do the taking.

By *capable guardians*, Felson and Cohen are referring to the absence or presence of protection for targets. Something that is well guarded against theft or damage is less likely to be targeted. Another sort of capable guardian is the police. It is logical to assume that if the police are present or available then the likelihood of a crime occurring would be minimal.

By *motivated offender*, the authors are referring to the absence or presence of people who are sufficiently motivated to commit a criminal act. A number of motivators exist. In structural terms, motivation is more likely to be prevalent in societies that value wealth. When legitimate opportunities to gain wealth are scarce, people are also more likely to be motivated to commit criminal acts to satisfy this goal.

The combination of a motivated offender and a suitable target with a lack of capable guardianship thus produces a situation in which crime is more likely to occur. If you leave your bicycle unlocked outside a hostel, it is quite likely to be stolen. If you leave it unlocked at a family gathering on your brother's farm, it is more likely to be left alone, particularly if your family gets along.

Biological Positivism

With the emergence of scientific methodology and the positivist school in the nineteenth century, thinking about crime and punishment turned toward examining the criminal and correction. *Positivism* was primarily a reaction to the Enlightenment. Whereas Enlightenment thinkers stressed the negative influence of traditional institutions—such as the Church and the class system, which granted only some people rights—the founders of positivism tried to reconcile reason and experience with traditional institutions like the Church. This philosophy endorsed positive change to the social system. It was committed to reconciling social traditions with emerging knowledge based on scientific evidence and methodology, and it recognized that individuals are determined more than they are freely choosing. However, it also required that existing institutions adapt to scientific discoveries about the nature of humanity and society and acknowledge the leading role of scientific knowledge in societal evolution. The nature of human existence did not have to be taken as a given, but rather could be perfected through social engineering. In the main, **positivist criminology** took a narrow view of positivism, focusing on its methodology and its approach that the human condition is determined but changeable.

If people prone to committing crimes were not possessed by evil and were not simply rational actors who needed to be deterred, then what were they? The answer would spring from the method. Positivist scientific method involved deductive reasoning through systematic observation, accumulated evidence, and objective facts. When the "evildoer" became the "criminal" in popular understanding, early Italian school criminal anthropologists like Cesare Lombroso, Enrico Ferri, and Raffaele Garofalo could set about discovering any unique traits to account for the deviation of this "class" of persons from the population as a whole. They did so, typically, by separating a sample of convicts from a control sample of soldiers or others representing the general population. They then set about distinguishing the two populations through systematic observation and scientific measurement. Thus, Lombroso "discovered" that criminals have more physical abnormalities than the general population; using Darwinian theory, he argued that these traits were "atavisms," or throwbacks to previous evolutionary stages of human development. Lombroso's later work and the work of the other Italian school positivists also explored the environment as a conditioner of criminal behaviour.

In the early twentieth century, positivist criminologists studied various causes of criminality, including "feeble-mindedness" and genetic or hereditary traits; body types or somatotypes (Sheldon, 1949); psychological influences; and sociological influences (after Quetelet's work in 1831 on social statistics). For instance, following Alfred Binet's invention of the intelligence quotient (IQ), many attempts were made to link criminality to inferior intelligence. With intelligence testing, governments could categorize people into distinct population groupings. A royal commission on the feeble-minded was appointed in Ontario in 1920 to examine the possibility of categorizing and institutionalizing these people. This work became problematic when better methodology found, for instance, that soldiers were at least as likely to be feeble-minded as prisoners. *Eugenics*—social engineering through the controlled breeding for inherited qualities—thrived up until the 1920s in scientific circles and was enforced as late as the 1970s by Alberta's provincial government.

While work dedicated to uncovering traits that separated criminal and non-criminal populations waned during the mid-twentieth century in favour of truly sociological approaches (which we will take up in the next section), the belief in the malleability of the criminal continued to inform penological studies. Correctional literature developed a treatment philosophy that thrived in policy documents until the 1970s. Albeit controversial, in recent years, a more conservative attitude toward crime and punishment has rejuvenated trait theory and the implication of biological factors in criminal behaviour. Pierre van den Bergie (1974), Edmund O. Wilson (1975), and James Q. Wilson and Richard Herrnstein (1985), among others, revived the assumption that biology is related to behaviour. This approach includes biochemical theories related to hormones and diet, neuropsychological theories related to brain chemistry and structure, theories related to genetics, psychological trait theories, and sociobiological theories, which see crime as an offshoot of behaviour that maximizes the chances of an individual's genetic reproduction within environmental constraints. These theories are too complex and numerous to be reviewed here.

Sociological Theories of Crime

Throughout history, the individual was seen either as being born to commit crime or as making rational decisions to commit acts of deviance or criminality. Social relationships and factors were not considered. But we live in a society full of complex relationships with other people and institutions. Those interactions shape us. They give or deny opportunity, reward or punish behaviour, and help to set our expectations of ourselves and of society. In the last three sections, we divide the sociological theories into social structure and social process theories.

Social Structure Theories

In order to understand crime, we cannot ignore features of social organization or structure. *Social structure theories* seek explanations within the characteristics of society itself. In this respect, social structure theory is macrotheoretical, because it focuses on crime rates, rather than on criminal behaviour (Williams & McShane, 1999). Essentially, social factors and conditions influence individuals' attitudes and behaviours. In terms of criminality, advocates of the structural approach argue that economic, educational, religious, and political systems would have great influence over crime rates within society. Within the social structural theories, there are a number of important theories—social disorganization theory, strain theory, and cultural deviance theory—that we will briefly review.

Social Disorganization Theory

Building on the previous work of their University of Chicago colleague Robert Park, Clifford Shaw and Henry McKay (1942) hypothesized a relationship between **social disorganization** and the movement of populations through Chicago. Shaw and McKay used various census data to confirm that there is an internal migration in the city from the transitional zone outward, and that crime rates also decline the farther into the suburbs a person moves. They believed that highly transient communities were more crime prone because they were socially disorganized. A highly transient community can be found where members of the community move in and out, which makes the area highly unstable. Simply put, the residents who live in such areas are more interested in "upgrading" by moving into a suburban community, which leaves the poorer residents to toil in the area. In contemporary terms, these areas would include low-cost housing projects or areas with low levels of home ownership rates. Because a highly transient community is one in which people take up what they hope is temporary residence, the area lacks sufficient interest from residents in durable, formal, and informal social controls. People do not develop a stake in the community. As a result, these transitional areas are more likely to be socially disorganized. Not all the blame should be placed on the residents—these areas also lack essential services, such as social programs, education, health, and housing. In essence, the sources of control, such as family, school, business community, and social services are weak and disorganized.

Anomie, Strain, and Opportunity

In his book *Suicide: A Study of Sociology*, Emile Durkheim (1897/1951) found that suicides were more numerous during periods of economic and political instability and crisis. He argued that a condition of social disorganization characterized by economic and political instability is one in which the norms of society are also no longer effective in regulating behaviour. This is a condition of normlessness, or *anomie*, to which suicide is a response. In addition to suicide, the absence of sufficient regulation in society also unleashes the passions and aspirations of individuals in other acts, some of which will be criminal.

Taking Durkheim's idea of anomie, Robert K. Merton later modified it and developed **strain theory**, which argued that societies stimulate aspirations as socially approved goals, but that the legitimate means to achieve these goals are unequally distributed (1938). Merton suggests that the accumulation of money, as well as the status that results from material wealth, is the universal goal of US citizens. There are also socially structured means for achieving this goal, such as schooling. However, the availability of education (the means) is unevenly distributed in society—especially within the United States, where school funding is tied to the tax base of the community, and in which poorer communities are unable to provide capital for school resources. Simply stated, the theory argues that crime is the result of frustration and anger experienced by individuals who are unable to attain financial success through legitimate means. Essentially, both criminals and non-criminals desire similar goals; however, the means to attain those goals may vary.

Merton saw a number of possible outcomes in the relationship between culturally defined goals (accumulation of money) and socially approved means (legitimate or legal ways to acquire money). Merton labelled these outcomes the *modes of adaptation* (see Figure 4.1).

FIGURE 4.1

TYPOLOGY OF INDIVIDUAL MODES OF ADAPTATION

Modes of Adaptation	Cultural Goals	Institutionalized Means
Conformity	+	+
Innovation	+	–
Ritualism	–	+
Retreatism	–	–
Rebellion	+/–	+/–

Source: R. Merton. 1957. *Social Theory and Social Structure*. Glencoe, IL: Free Press.

According to Merton, the individual who wants to achieve the cultural goal via institutionalized or legitimate means is a *conformist*. For instance, rather than steal or deal drugs to gain extra income to pay off debt or buy a house, an individual may take on an extra job, work overtime, or go back to school to gain more resources for the cultural goal of financial success or security. The individual who aspires to the goal but has insufficient means must adapt through an *innovation* of means, which may be an innovation involving criminality. For instance, rather than working a legitimate job, an individual who is an innovator may engage in illegal activities such as drug dealing, theft, or prostitution to acquire wealth or income. Other modes of adaptation are *ritualism*, in which the individual has no great aspiration for the cultural goal and so is content to follow institutionalized means—in other words, the individual goes through the motions. A *retreatist* is someone who neither aspires to cultural goals nor follows its prescribed means; a drug addict/alcoholic is an example. Finally, a *rebel* seeks to substitute society's cultural goals with different ones, possibly through political revolution.

More Recent Developments in Strain Theory

Steven Messner and Richard Rosenfeld (1994) have added to a growing list of theorists in the strain tradition by arguing that the "American Dream" of material success attained through individual competition is a double-edged sword. Individual success often comes at a cost, and that cost is in other societal tasks that are not primarily economic in nature. Education, for example, once ideally an end in itself, is increasingly supported only where it can be shown to add economic value to individual and social life. Messner and Rosenfeld argue that the American Dream itself exerts pressure toward crime because it invites an "anomic cultural environment" where people adopt an "anything goes" attitude in the pursuit of personal goals.

This theory is much like *relative deprivation theory* (Blau & Blau, 1982), which views much of violence and crime as the result of frustrations experienced by people who are relatively poor and who live near others who are economically advantaged. Elliott Currie (1998) also argues that market societies are particularly prone to violent crime because they chip away at informal support networks, withdraw public provisions, and force most people to make a hard choice between low-wage labour and unemployment. Much of this argument restates Willem Bonger's work, first published in 1916, in which he argued that the drive to economic success in capitalist societies pushes rich and poor alike into criminality.

Cultural Deviance Theories

Cultural deviance theories begin with the premise that we live in a complex society in which there is disagreement about conduct norms, particularly among different levels of the class structure and across ethnic groups. Thorsten Sellin (1958) argued that members within a subculture have to adapt to the conduct norms of these groups, which may put their conduct in conflict with the conduct norms (and legal norms) of the dominant culture. Such conflict occurs, for example, with the Rastafarian culture, as smoking marijuana is part of Rastafarian spiritual practice, but possession is illegal in Canada.

Various cultural conflict and cultural deviance theorists (see, for example, Miller, 1958; Wolfgang & Ferracuti, 1967) looked at differences in values and norms between the dominant culture and subcultural pockets of inner-city populations. They argued that these subcultures could be distinguished in their focus on machismo, honour, excitement, fate, autonomy, and street smartness and toughness. These values place their members in conflict with the dominant culture, because membership in the subculture sometimes require actions, such as defence of honour, that will be defined as illegal. Two prominent cultural deviance theories include Albert Cohen's delinquent boys and Richard Cloward and Lloyd Ohlin's differential opportunity.

Delinquent Boys

Albert Cohen (1955) argues that at least some of the crime attributed to people from lower-class backgrounds is committed by **delinquent boys** who act to show their rejection of middle-class values, which they cannot hope to measure up to. Some of them react through negativistic and non-utilitarian criminal activity in order to reclaim their status. Cohen argues that a "middle-class measuring rod" consists of a number of values, including ambition, individual responsibility, cultivation of skills, respect for property, and deferred gratification. These values, Cohen argues, are more formidable challenges to people whose backgrounds have deprived them of various forms of capital (social, economic, or moral).

Differential Opportunity

Missing from Merton's strain theory, in the opinion of Cloward and Ohlin (1960), was reference to the fact that illegitimate means are not equally available to everyone. These authors argue that while people may be strained in their ability to meet goals with the means at their disposal, people do not necessarily have access to the means of crime—thus the term, **differential opportunity**. They suggest that just as legitimate opportunity structures exist, there are also illegitimate opportunity structures, which not everyone has access to. Perhaps there have been times when many of us would have joined a criminal gang, had it been available and accepting of us, but thankfully for law-abiding citizens such access is not routinely available for most adolescents.

Social Process Theories

While social structure theories were more likely to focus on social conditions or structural components that have an impact on criminality, social process theories are more socio-psychological in nature. In brief, social process theories see learning and interaction as important parts of influencing criminality. Simply put, social process theories examine the means by which criminal behaviours are developed. Social process theories include social learning theories, social control theories, and labelling theories.

Social Learning Theories

Social learning theories maintain that socialization plays an important role in the development of criminal behaviour. Proponents of social learning theory suggest that youthful offenders are taught to believe that criminal or deviant behaviour is acceptable and possibly legitimate behaviour.

Differential Association

One of the first major events in the sociological understanding of crime was Edwin Sutherland's pronouncement in 1934 that criminality is normal, learned behaviour. In his theory of **differential association**, Sutherland argued that criminal behaviour is learned in interaction "with other persons in a process of communication" (1966). It is learned within intimate personal groups, and the learning includes techniques for committing crimes and the motives, attitudes, and rationalizations that the groups use to favourably define the behaviour, even though it may violate the law. Simply put, the more time a person spends in the company of those who violate the law, the more a person learns of the techniques of crime and the more a person learns to see the activity in a favourable light.

Differential Reinforcement

Adapting the views of B. F Skinner and operant conditioning, Burgess and Akers (1966) contend that the learning of criminal behaviour is heavily influenced by the rewards or punishments meted out by family and/or friends. Potential offenders decide to commit an offence by weighing the potential rewards or risks. Like differential association, **differential reinforcement** purports that criminal behaviour is learned within close, intimate personal groups; however, Burgess and Akers further argue that the mass media can also influence the learning of behaviour.

Neutralization or Drift Theory

Neutralization or **drift theory** was proposed by David Matza and Gresham Sykes. According to neutralization theory, in order to commit delinquent acts, youth learn ways to neutralize conventional values or attitudes. They will drift back and forth from conventional and criminal behaviour. The offender will learn how to rationalize his or her actions before the behaviour. Simply stated, in order for an individual to commit a crime, he or she must mentally justify the actions. Otherwise, the person will not be able to override dominant social values which teach that criminal or delinquent behaviour is wrong. Matza and Sykes (1961) developed five ways that criminals rationalize or neutralize their actions, which include:

1. Denial of Responsibility—the offender would justify the criminal act by claiming it was beyond his or her control or it was not his or her fault.
2. Denial of Injury—the offender would justify the criminal act by claiming that it did not really hurt anyone.
3. Denial of Victim—the offender would justify the criminal act by claiming that the victim deserved what he or she received. The victim was asking for it.
4. Condemnation of Condemners—the Coffender would justify the criminal act by claiming that the focus should not be on the act but on those who have condemned the act (essentially shifting blame to others).

5. Appeal to Higher Loyalties—the offender would justify the criminal act by claiming that the loyalty to the group (peer, family, or otherwise) supersedes legal codes and/or other norms/values.

Social Control Theories

Social learning theories advance the notion that potential offenders learn the attitudes, techniques, and rationalizations for committing crimes. Essentially, they argue that human beings are born good but learn to be bad. On the other hand, **social control theories** assume that humans are born bad but learn to be good. Advocates of the control perspective would argue that crime is an innate or natural behaviour and that social control mechanisms, both informal and formal, operate to prevent potential criminals from acting out. Albert Reiss (1951) contended that a failure of personal controls leads to criminality. However, Reiss failed to consider the impact of family, environment, and community controls. Building on Reiss's ideas of lack of personal control, Walter Reckless and Travis Hirschi developed **containment theory** and **social bond theory** respectively.

Containment Theory

Walter Reckless (1967) claimed that each person has inner and outer controls that pull or push potential offenders toward delinquency. For Reckless, containment was the ability to resist criminal inducements. One of the major strengths of this theory is that it provides a psychological as well as a sociological component to criminal behaviour. According to Reckless, positive self-esteem insulated individuals from criminal behaviour. He further argued that there were three crime-producing forces, which included internal pushes, external pressures, and external pulls. Internal pushes include personal factors such as restlessness, discontent, hostility, rebellion, mental conflict, anxieties, and the need for immediate gratification. External pressures include adverse living conditions, relative deprivation, poverty, unemployment, limited opportunities, and general inequalities—simply put, outside factors that may influence criminal behaviour. External pulls include deviant companions, criminal subcultures, and media influences.

Social Bond Theory

Travis Hirschi (1969) claimed that a person's bond to society prevents him or her from engaging in criminal behaviour. Essentially, the weakening of ties that bind people to society produces criminality. Individuals with a greater bond to society have a greater "stake in conformity" and are less inclined to commit criminal acts. For Hirschi, there were four elements of the social bond to conventional society— they include *attachment, commitment, involvement,* and *belief. Attachment,* which Hirschi suggested is the strongest bond, refers to how connected individuals are to family, friends, or community. A strong attachment to these three things would restrain criminal behaviour. *Commitment* is the amount of time and energy that is spent in conventional activity; essentially, young persons with lofty goals or aspirations will be less inclined to engage in delinquency. For example, a young person who makes a strong commitment to become a police officer will not likely jeopardize her or his career by engaging in crime. *Involvement* is a situationwhere a person is too busy in conventional activities such as work or school to commit criminal acts. Essentially, he or she has little time for criminal activity. For instance, a high school dropout would have more time to hang out on the streets and become involved in delinquent behaviours, while a student who keeps a part-time job at the local mall and is involved in extracurricular activities such as sports will be too busy to engage in delinquent acts. Many youth advocates argue that getting teenagers involved in sports and other extracurricular activities will provide kids with the opportunity to engage in positive behaviour and stay off the streets. *Belief* is a set of moral convictions such as honesty, morality, fairness, and responsibility. Teenagers who are socialized with strong morals are less likely to become involved in criminal behaviour. For example, studies consistently show that individuals with strong religious beliefs are less likely to be involved in delinquent or criminal behaviour.

Social Reaction and Labelling Theories

Much thinking about crime causation focuses on the biology, nature, and social environment of the individual—whether the individual chooses to commit criminal acts or whether these acts are externally determined. **Social reaction theories** follow social learning inasmuch as they agree that criminal behaviour is learned. But they also place more emphasis on the interaction between social control agents, such as the courts, the police, and schools, and the individual. They remind us that what Sutherland calls definitions favourable to the commission of crime are followed by societal reaction to the criminal act. These reactions then help to shape the individual's identity. According to **labelling theories**, when a judge tells a youth, "You are first and foremost a thief," this formal, powerful reaction "labels" the youth, and the youth is more likely to act according to this label.

Howard Becker went even further than this, however. He broke from the consensus view of criminality by saying that "deviant behaviour is behaviour that people so label" (1963). He argued that rather than focusing on how the individual is deviant, we need to recognize that there is no deviance until social groups create deviance by making rules "whose infraction constitutes deviance." Becker argued that much more attention needs to be given to the *social reactors* rather than to the individual designated by agents of social control as the criminal.

Labelling theorists like Lemert (1967) argued that in no small part the social reaction to the first act of deviance (*primary deviance*) imposes social penalties that cause further deviance, in a spiral that will eventually lead the individual to behave in accord with the view of the social reactors that he or she is indeed, first and foremost, a deviant. This labelling effect, in which the individual accepts the social view of himself or herself and acts accordingly, Lemert referred to as *secondary deviance*.

Labelling theory has influenced social policy. In the 1960s and 1970s, policies were launched to minimize the labelling of youths, including programs that sought to correct youths within the community. *Diversion* is a program that came straight out of labelling theory. This program allows youths to avoid the stigma of delinquency by giving those convicted of minor criminal offences the chance to be placed in informal programs at arm's length from the correctional system.

Conflict Theories

While consensus theories are concerned with explaining the causes of deviation from social norms, **conflict criminology** is concerned with explaining how social control agents and agencies behave. The conflict perspective holds that there is an ongoing contest for power in society, and that the criminal law and the various agencies of law enforcement act, either directly or indirectly, in the interests of the powerful.

The central task of criminology from a conflict perspective is not to explain what causes criminal behaviour, but rather to explain the process by which certain behaviours and individuals are formally designated as criminal. For many consensus theorists, the social reaction to crime consists simply of actions that crime control authorities take to represent society's interests in being protected from crime. Conflict theorists argue that this social reaction is really an opportunity to consolidate power around specific interests and values that the powerful in society wish to uphold. While most conflict theorists would accept that there is widespread interest in peaceful coexistence, they believe that this interest ought to be distinguished from a consensus about the specific values and interests that an act is alleged to have threatened. Conflict theorists argue that the norms, values, and principles that the law seeks to defend are politicized to serve the

ends of the powerful. In this way, conflict theorists see the law as serving political interests in resource distribution by those who have more power in the shaping of public issues. They see the work of law-making and of norm clarification zealously championed by powerful interests who are attempting to maintain and justify their special claims. An example of this is the role of economic or corporate interest groups within the criminal justice system.

Economic and Corporate Interest Groups

Despite the media publicity surrounding the Enron, WorldCom, Conrad Black, and Martha Stewart cases, there has been a clearly biased interpretation of the criminal law in the non-prosecution of **corporate crime**—crime committed by businesses. Larsen and Burtch (1999) outline the ability of powerful economic and **corporate interest groups** to exploit human and natural resources, pollute the environment, form illegal monopolies, fix prices of goods and services, and manipulate the stock market, and yet to have all of these activities classified as legal behaviour. These authors believe that although corporate criminality is widespread in Canada, seldom are any of the activities clearly defined as Criminal Code violations, and thus they are not prosecuted. Furthermore, if prosecution occurs it is usually through quasi-judicial tribunals, and fines are the major form of deterrence. Since these fines are paid out of corporate profits, the punishment fails to deter the deviant behaviour.

That corporate crime affects large numbers of Canadians is undeniable. Yet that those inappropriate behaviours are rarely defined and regulated by criminal law is also undeniable. Corporate interest groups often control and manipulate the law-making process and influence the legislators. The norm has been for special regulatory agencies, rather than the punitive criminal law, to handle morally reprehensible behaviour by the business class. Furthermore, although some of these behaviours may be classified under the criminal law, they are poorly enforced, reflecting the symbolic nature of legislation and enforcement. Larsen and Burtch believe that because of the immense influence of corporate interest groups on lawmakers, these interest groups are often involved in the process of defining inappropriate corporate behaviour.

Given the influence of corporate interest groups on lawmaking, it is not surprising that street and property crime dominate Canada's Criminal Code. Corporate special interest groups protect their position of influence and power by attributing criminality to the powerless in society and using the criminal justice system as an instrument of coercion and force. It is clear that the individuals and groups who are most likely to be affected by law enforcement are those whose behaviours the dominant interest groups perceive as threatening. The danger in our society occurs when the values and norms of particular interest groups become incorporated into criminal law and the justice system. In our heterogeneous society, those who do not subscribe to these values and norms run the risk of being discriminated against by the legal system that was supposed to protect their rights.

If, in fact, the probability of being labelled deviant and subject to the criminal law depends on a person's social and economic position, then Canada's criminal law and justice system needs to be revised. When special interest groups use the legal system to maintain inordinate power and influence, the result is not only dysfunctional, but also conflictual. Unfortunately, in the court of public opinion, corporate crime ranks low on the scale of criminal behaviour. The public has accepted the belief that street crime is the form of crime that is most harmful and threatening to society and local communities. Therefore, street crime continues to attract the greatest public condemnation and most of the resources of the police and the courts. The public has bought into the idea that corporations are the purveyors of prosperity who keep the economy running and the Canadian people prosperous and economically satisfied. While many interest groups have successfully manipulated the law-enforcement process, none has been as influential as the corporate interest group. Inevitably, the outcome of this influence is the compromising of the Canadian criminal justice system.

Conclusion

Law, social control, and crime causation are major areas of study for many criminologists. Law is the major method of control in our society, and it uses punishment to regulate behaviour. Vago (2000) notes that Canada's highly structured and formalized criminal justice system uses elaborate techniques and methods to limit and control deviant behaviour. The Criminal Code, which contains all of Canada's criminal laws, incorporates the punishments for law violators, who are punished according to society's perception of the severity of the deviance. However, the use of the criminal justice system to control victimless crimes has generated considerable debate. Many critics believe that attempting to control crimes such as drug addiction, gambling, or prostitution through the legal system is not only expensive, but is also an ineffective method of controlling this type of behaviour. Criminologists are interested in understanding the role of law in regulating social control and the debates that emerge out of this regulation. Criminologists are also interested in explaining the nature of crime and the reasons why it exists. Without a doubt, the causes of crime are multi-faceted and no single theory can explain criminality. The causes of crime can be rooted in the social structure of society or within the personality characteristics of offenders. Today, many theories are brought together by integrated theories of crime causation, which help explain more of the differences between those who commit crime and those who do not.

Summary

This chapter has analyzed the role of law as a mechanism of social control. Individuals are socialized to behave in normative and societally accepted ways, and those who deviate from societal norms are subject to sanctions. These methods of social control can be either formal or informal. Canada relies on the criminal law as a method of controlling the moral conduct of Canadians and of affirming society's dominant moral values. The law acts as an instrument of coercion, but critics are increasingly questioning whether the criminal process should be used to control moral behaviour in "victimless" crime. Instead, they suggest that the police and the law should concentrate on the more serious crime problems on which there is societal consensus, such as robbery, sexual assault, murder, and fraud and embezzlement.

This chapter has also presented a brief overview of the history of crime theorizing. In general, theoretical perspectives shift between theories which argue that the criminal actor is a rational calculator, and theories which argue that the criminal is determined by social, biological, or environmental forces. In searching for causes of crime, we have seen that theorists have not only probed within the human body for evidence of abnormalities, but have also turned to contexts, including social disorganization and strain, and to the operation of the criminal justice system itself, which is embodied in the spirit of conflict theory.

Key Terms

classical criminology (p. 80)

conflict criminology (p. 93)

containment theory (p. 91)

corporate crime (p. 94)

corporate interest groups (p. 94)

criminal sanctions (p. 75)

cultural deviance theories (p. 88)

delinquent boys (p. 88)

deterrence theory (p. 82)

differential association (p. 90)

differential opportunity (p. 89)

differential reinforcement (p. 90)

formal social control (p. 76)

hedonistic calculus (p. 81)

informal social control (p. 76)

labelling theories (p. 92)

neutralization (or drift theory) (p. 90)

positivist criminology (p. 84)

rational choice theory (p. 82)

routine activities theory (p. 83)

social bond theory (p. 91)

social control (p. 76)

social control theories (p. 91)

social disorganization theory (p. 86)

social learning theories (p. 89)

social reaction theories (p. 92)

strain theory (p. 86)

victimless crimes (p. 75)

Discussion Questions

1. Discuss the ways in which the criminal law acts as an instrument of coercion and social control.
2. Discuss how criminalizing morality influences the criminal justice system.
3. What role does conflict criminology play in contemporary criminal justice?
4. What criminological theory best explains criminal behaviour or actions? Why?
5. In your opinion, are crimes such as drug use, prostitution, and child pornography victimless? Why or why not?

Weblinks

www.crimetheory.com This site provides an interactive and informative overview of major criminological perspectives and theories.

www.criminology.fsu.edu/crimtheory Maintained by Cecil Greek, this website provides overviews of the major theoretical perspectives in criminology.

www.ccja-acjp.ca/en/aborit.html Put forward by the Canadian Criminal Justice Association (CCJA), this bulletin is on Aboriginal peoples and the criminal justice system, and deals with the historic, demographic, social, political, and economic factors affecting Aboriginal peoples in Canada's justice system.

www.law.cornell.edu/wex/index.php/white-collar_crime Developed by the Cornell Law School, this is an excellent overview of white-collar or corporate crime in the United States.

www.edwardhumes.com/books/mean/index.shtml This site provides an excellent overview of unethical behaviour within the criminal justice system.

www.methodist.edu/criminaljustice/criminologylinks.htm This site provides an exhaustive and informative list of resources for criminology theory.

CHAPTER 5

The Police

Objectives

- To describe the branches of law enforcement in Canada and their roles within the criminal justice system.

- To discuss the role of the police in crime prevention, law enforcement, public order maintenance, victim assistance, and emergency services.

- To portray both sides of the public debate over the issues of the powers, discretion, autonomy, and accountability of the police.

- To highlight the important initiative of community policing and the restructuring necessary to make this policy effective.

Historical Development

Citizens in many other countries, where the police do not serve to muster nationalistic pride, are often perplexed at how Canada came to use a police figure as a national icon. To understand how the RCMP (or the Mounties) has come to have this symbolic value, we need to examine the history of Canadian policing.

In the eighteenth and early nineteenth centuries in Canada, policing was provided by four kinds of arrangements. First, there were regulations (called, interestingly, *police regulations*), which required householders to prevent disorder and crime. For example, they required that householders make available ladders and buckets in case of fire and keep basement entries to their houses locked to prevent unwanted entry. Second, in towns there was often a nightly watch, which was staffed by able-bodied males as a duty of residency. Those on nightly watch would do set rounds, looking for suspicious activity or people and for signs of fire, and they would arrest and bring to a constable or a justice of the peace any person found breaching the peace or breaking the law. Third, there were amateur constables, appointed annually from the town or county rolls, who made arrests or carried out warrants on a fee-for-service basis (for example, getting a set amount for bringing a felon to jail). Fourth, in cases of public disorder or riot, there was a volunteer militia, which consisted of able-bodied men in the community who could be called on to suppress the affray.

Reformers of the day criticized these arrangements. They argued that the volunteer militia was a blunt and rusty instrument because of its sporadic use and lack of training. The watch was often subjected to ridicule for attracting fools and hoodlums, since the "better class" of men often deputized substitutes instead of doing their turn. The amateur constabulary suffered under a similar reputation in some parts of the country, as it was difficult to control and the men were viewed as either too inactive or too eager in collecting fees. Whether these charges were founded or not, in the 50-year period leading up to Confederation, a series of reforms took place at municipal, provincial, and federal levels, displacing the informal, voluntary, and part-time policing arrangements with full-time, publicly paid, uniformed police.

Federal Policing

In the latter half of the nineteenth century, large tracts of land west of the Great Lakes were claimed by Britain but inhabited by Aboriginal peoples and eyed by expansionist Americans. Rupert's Land, an area of land extending south and west from Hudson Bay, was purchased from the Hudson's Bay Company by the federal government in 1870. The government felt an agency was needed to act as a liaison between settlers and Aboriginal people in order to prevent the sort of violent expropriation of Indian territory that was common in America, especially following the Riel Rebellion in 1869–70, when Louis Riel led the Red River Métis in protest against the takeover of their land by the government. The Dominion Police Force was created in 1858 by the federal government under the Act Respecting Police of Canada, but this force was limited to protecting federal buildings and to enforcing federal statutes, such as treason and sedition, and later to enforcing laws prohibiting counterfeiting. While it had jurisdiction for the whole of the country, in practice the police force served only central and eastern Canada. Consequently, in 1873 an act of Parliament (the Act Respecting the Administration of Justice and the Establishment of a Police Force in the Northwest Territories) established the **North West Mounted Police (NWMP)**. This force was modelled after the Royal Irish Constabulary and was mobilized with the tacit responsibility of easing adversities of settlers in the West, appeasing Aboriginal resistance, and deterring US colonization of British land.

Members of the NWMP faced great hardships both in trekking out to the area that later became Alberta and Saskatchewan (known as "The Great March") and in maintaining their spirits in the harsh, virtually unpopulated northwest. A great number of the initial authorized 300 members deserted or were disciplined for drunkenness or insubordination. Nevertheless, the force gradually began to attract adventuresome young men of a high calibre who sought challenge in the harsh conditions and in their mission to "maintain the right." Soon, stories of great feats of heroism began to circulate and to define popular conceptions of the Mounties, who went to great lengths to "always get their man." The Mountie who travelled hundreds of miles criss-crossing the Yukon in search of the "Mad Trapper" is one such legend. In 1905, by royal decree, the NWMP became the Royal North West Mounted Police (RNWMP) and began taking up provincial duties under contract to provinces. In 1920, the Dominion Police were merged with the RNWMP to become the **Royal Canadian Mounted Police (RCMP)**.

In the early years, it was unclear whether a federal police force was needed. The British North America (BNA) Act of 1867 provided under section 91 that law enactment be a federal responsibility and law enforcement a provincial responsibility. Although there was little or no parliamentary debate when the Act constituting the federal force was passed, many doubted the lasting need for such a force, given this distribution of authority and the temporary practical requirements for the colonization of the northwest. In addition, provincial governments were up and running in the Western provinces and (some argued) were capable of providing their own police services. Atlantic MPs, in particular, argued that there was no use for a federal force. The dual role of the federal force as police officers and magistrates in remote regions where magistrates were still not available was also criticized. Finally, some considered the Mounties' conduct in labour disputes at the Canadian Pacific Railway and during the Winnipeg General Strike as inept. Between the late 1800s and the early 1920s, consequently, numerous attempts to have the force disbanded took place.

However, these storms were weathered with renewed support from federal governments in view, particularly, of worries about labour unrest and the popular belief in a budding communist threat. In addition, Saskatchewan and Alberta had already established a precedent in the jurisdictional issue by contracting with the federal government for police services, beginning in 1905. Such contracting was extended to municipalities, beginning with Flin Flon, Manitoba, in 1935. Opposition to RCMP expansion dwindled, and the force continued to expand in strength from its initial 300 in 1873, to 750 at the turn of the century, and to 1600 in 1920, when instead of being dismantled, it absorbed the Dominion Police. During the Depression, the size of the RCMP also grew by taking over policing duties from hard-pressed provincial forces. Since the 1950s, all the provinces except Ontario and Quebec (in addition to the Yukon and the Northwest Territories, Nunavut, and some 198 municipalities) have had contracts with the RCMP to provide regular policing services.

Through the post-war years up until the 1980s, the federal force maintained its responsibility to counteract political insurgency—a role required by its 1920 absorption of the Dominion Police. Indeed, RCMP officers have infiltrated many political organizations regularly since World War I. However, this dual function of investigating political organizations and enforcing the Criminal Code became a source of widespread concern in the aftermath of the October Crisis of 1970, when Prime Minister Pierre Trudeau controversially invoked the War Measures Act. After investigating RCMP wiretapping and counter-insurgency activity, the 1977 Keable Inquiry recommended that a separate agency undertake the role of intelligence gathering for national security. This is now the mandate of the Canadian Security Intelligence Service (CSIS), which was created in 1984.

Today, the RCMP includes some 16 000 women and men (excluding civilians and public servants). The RCMP's federal responsibilities are authorized under the Royal Canadian Mounted Police Act of 1959, according to which it is responsible for federal statutes, including excise and customs, narcotics control, the Indian Act, and federal properties. But RCMP officers also have the powers of peace officers. Members of the RCMP are required to enforce Canadian laws, prevent crime, and maintain peace and order. Finally, the RCMP also serves other police agencies in providing investigative and informational services, such as the Canadian Police Information Centre (CPIC), established in 1972, which is a database available to police officials that stores criminal-related information entered by the country's police agencies.

Provincial Policing

According to section 91 of the BNA Act, upon entry into Confederation the provinces were to enact legislation to assume responsibility for the administration of justice and the enforcement of laws. In 1858, the colony of British Columbia was the first to create such a territorial force, although Quebec is credited with establishing the first *provincial* force, the **Sûreté du Québec (SQ)**, in 1870. Newfoundland established the Royal Newfoundland Constabulary in 1872. Ontario also made an abortive attempt to establish a force at the end of the nineteenth century, with the first provincial officer being hired in 1874 and legislation allowing the ad hoc appointment of provincial constables passed in 1877. It finally drafted a viable act for a fully provincial force in 1909, when it passed legislation establishing the **Ontario Provincial Police (OPP)**. Like the RCMP and other territorial and provincial forces, the OPP and its predecessor, the Niagara River Police, helped to secure the frontier, especially where precious metal deposits or the whisky trade made the frontier attractive to those seeking quick profits and relaxed social controls. Provincial forces established in Alberta, Manitoba, and Saskatchewan were short-lived. Saskatchewan and Alberta had

their own provincial police forces by 1917, but the Saskatchewan Provincial Police was disbanded in 1928 in favour of a contract with the RCMP. Alberta's provincial policing was taken over by the RCMP in 1920. Today, only Quebec's and Ontario's provincial forces survive. (The Newfoundland Constabulary no longer acts as a provincial service, but it is responsible for providing services to three areas of Newfoundland and Labrador: St. John's, Mount Pearl, and the surrounding communities which comprise North East Avalon, Corner Brook, and Labrador West.)

The OPP enforces the Criminal Code in areas that do not have municipal or federal jurisdiction. Since 1945, it has provided policing by contract to municipalities that do not wish to institute their own forces. In Quebec, the SQ has jurisdiction over the whole province and may intervene in municipalities at the behest of the provincial government. In Ontario, the OPP may be called in when local police boards request additional policing or when the **Ontario Civilian Commission on Police Services (OCCPS)**, the provincial body that oversees the police forces, finds that a municipality is failing to meet the standard of service. Provincial police also oversee the delivery of policing to First Nations communities and are responsible for the policing of provincial property, such as the Ontario legislature and the National Assembly in Quebec City. As well, the OPP regulates private security in Ontario. In cases of labour demonstrations or political protests, the OPP may be called in to maintain order. Provincial police also offer specialized services, such as marine, investigative, and tactical support services, to municipalities that are unable to provide them.

Regional and Municipal Policing in Ontario

The first municipal police force in Canada was established in Toronto in 1935. Soon afterward, London, Montreal, and Quebec City established municipal forces. Table 5.1 provides an overview of police agencies in Ontario.

The responsibilities of municipal police forces in Ontario are set out in the Police Services Act, which was amended in January 1998. Every municipality is required to provide adequate and effective police services in accordance with its needs (section 4.1). Section 4.2 of the Act states that these services must include, at a minimum, crime prevention, law enforcement, assistance to victims of crime, public order maintenance, and emergency response. In addition, under section 4.3, the municipality must provide adequate infrastructure and administration to maintain these services, including vehicles, equipment, supplies, buildings, and communication services.

Also, as per the Ontario Police Services Act, each municipality that maintains a police force is required to have a police services board. This board consists of a majority of municipal appointees depending on population size:

- less than 25 000: 2 municipal, 1 provincial
- regional and more than 25 000: 3 municipal, 2 provincial
- more than 300 000: 4 municipal, 3 provincial

It is worth noting that the provincial–municipal split favours municipal control and not provincial control as it did in the past. These police boards are overseen by the OCCPS, which ensures that all boards comply with standards and also conducts investigations and inquiries when there are substantiated complaints about the delivery of service. They may also make recommendations, or they may suspend the chief or the whole board, disband the police force, and require the OPP to take over policing if they find that the police service is unable to meet standards.

Throughout the 1960s and 1970s, the police were amalgamated in regional services, stimulated in part by requirements to provide specialized services,

TABLE 5.1

POLICE RESOURCES IN ONTARIO, 2004

	Population	Population density	Police officer Male	Police officer Female	Police officer Total	Other personnel	Population per police officer	Police officer per 100 000 population
		persons/km²						
Population (100 000+)								
Barrie	124 641	1619	141	25	166	67	751	133
Chatham-Kent	109 708	26	143	15	158	73	694	144
Durham Regional Police	563 220	223	609	135	744	250	757	132
Guelph	115 071	1328	138	24	162	62	710	141
Greater Sudbury Police	160 839	48	190	44	234	116	687	145
Halton Regional Police	427 219	442	399	108	507	187	843	119
Hamilton Regional Police	519 734	465	605	129	734	262	708	141
Kingston	121 474	130	140	30	170	49	715	140
London	356 436	845	425	76	501	200	711	141
Niagara Regional Police	431 265	231	577	72	649	343	665	150
Ottawa Police Service	829 578	299	860	216	1076	501	771	130
Peel Regional Police	1 108 112	1997	1359	247	1606	669	690	145
Thunder Bay	117 941	174	179	33	212	94	556	180
Toronto	2 603 182	4133	4514	777	5291	2293	492	203
Waterloo Regional Police	475 739	348	510	120	630	215	755	132
Windsor	221 463	1836	369	65	434	139	510	196
York Regional Police	889 002	509	863	162	1025	397	867	115
Population (50 000 to 99 999)								
Brantford	91 584	1280	121	18	139	83	659	152
North Bay	57 493	138	72	14	86	50	669	150
Oxford Community	61 561	56	64	15	79	28	779	128
Peterborough Lakefield	78 560	716	98	17	115	49	683	146
Sarnia	74 543	421	98	11	109	48	684	146
Sault Ste. Marie	76 791	250	112	18	130	53	591	169
South Simcoe Police	56 133	116	61	8	69	21	814	123
Ontario Povincial Police (OPP)								
Caledon	63 260	92	35	20	55	5	1150	87
Lambton Group	52 801	20	52	10	62	6	852	117
Nottawasaga	57 203	62	38	13	51	4	1122	89
Norfolk	63 439	22	75	12	87	10	729	137
Stormont/Dundas/Glengarry	67 810	21	66	14	80	9	848	118
Wellington County	86 502	34	73	18	91	11	951	105
Population (15 000 to 49 999)								
Amherstburg	21 649	76	26	4	30	3	722	139
Belleville	48 273	109	68	13	81	32	596	168
Brockville	22 366	1079	37	5	42	23	533	188
Cobourg	30 517	110	31	4	35	25	872	115
Cornwall Community Police	47 333	765	68	11	79	43	599	167
Essex	21 114	56	24	4	28	3	754	133
Kawartha Lakes Police	23 778	94	27	8	35	21	679	147
Lasalle	29 489	452	27	4	31	16	951	105
Leamington	29 103	68	36	3	39	18	746	134
Midland	16 523	568	21	4	25	8	661	151
Nishnawbe-Aski	18 380	8	103	14	117	31	157	637
Orangeville	28 226	1813	31	3	34	21	830	120

Note: **Use caution in comparing forces:** The number of officers may not reflect the number available for general community policing because some officers in certain communities are restricted to specific locations (e.g., ports, airports).

Source: Adapted from Statistics Canada's publication *Police Resources in Canada*, 2005, Catalogue 85-225, December 2005, page 48. Available at www.statcan.ca/english/freepub/85-225-XIE/0000585-225-XIE.pdf.

which are more expensive for smaller municipalities to deliver. Now, for instance, in the Greater Toronto Area, York Regional, Durham Regional, and Halton Regional police forces provide regional service delivery. While having some advantages, regionalization is also criticized for sacrificing local responsibility for more homogenized and standardized police delivery.

Police Roles and Functions

Legislation compels jurisdictions in Ontario to narrow the terms according to which police services may be provided. According to section 42(1) of the Ontario Police Services Act, police constables have duties that include the following:

- preserve the peace
- prevent crimes and other offences and encourage crime prevention
- assist victims of crime
- apprehend criminals
- lay charges and participate in prosecution
- execute warrants
- perform lawful duties assigned by the chief of police
- enforce municipal bylaws (where applicable)
- complete prescribed training

As we've already noted, the Ontario Police Services Act also requires that municipalities provide crime prevention measures, law enforcement, public order maintenance, emergency response, and, most recently, assistance to victims of crime.

Crime Prevention

When Robert Peel drafted legislation in 1829 to institute a uniformed, full-time, publicly paid police force in Metropolitan London, he stressed a preventative role for his "bobbies" or "peelers," as they came to be known. Peel argued that his police should be judged by the absence of crime. Since then, the traditional role of the police has been crime prevention. But it has more recently been asked whether it is realistic to entrust this role to the police. After all, the causes of crime are multiple and varied, and neither the police nor any other single agency has the resources or the authority to sufficiently intervene into the lives of people to achieve this goal.

Are the police successful at crime prevention, and should we expect that they be? There is powerful debate about the impact that police have on crime rates. Early studies reveal that the presence of more police is associated with more, not less, crime and is in fact not a deterrent (see Kelling, Pate, Dieckman, &

Brown, 1974). However, Marvell and Moody (1996) collected data from 56 US cities, over 20 years and found that an increase in police decreased the crime rate. They concluded that for every police officer hired, there are 24 fewer crimes. A recent study of Montreal by Lemieux (2003) finds that an increase in police presence significantly decreased both property and violent crimes. Despite these assertions, there is still considerable debate over the role that police play in reducing the crime rate. Many critics argue that politicians and police interest groups overstate the role that the police have in preventing crime for political and budgetary reasons. Many criticisms of the ability of the police to deter crime focus on the relationship between police presence and crime absence. This relationship is often difficult to expose because the police themselves "make crime" in the sense that they are the ones who certify that an act is criminal. Some critics argue that increasing police or toughening laws will increase crime rates by penetrating into the dark figure of crime.

A counter-argument has often been that the absence of police patrol during police strikes, such as in Montreal in 1969, New York in 1971, and Stockholm in 1970, is associated with an escalation of certain types of opportunistic crime. An important study by Sherman and Weisburd (1995) finds that police presence in the form of increased patrols of "hot spots" does reduce reported crime. More recent research confirms that active or aggressive policing of hot spots decreases crime (Weisburd, 2005). Many Canadian police forces engage in "crime mapping" to determine hot spots and actively deliver more resources to areas that are deemed crime prone.

A classic example of crime prevention is found in the much-touted "broken windows" thesis of J. Q. Wilson and G. Kelling (1982), which is credited with a substantial decrease in crime in New York and other US cities. Also known as "quality of life policing" or "zero tolerance policing," this strategy seeks to reduce major crimes by displaying zero tolerance for minor acts of disorder, which are seen as creating a crime-permissive environment. Recent research supports the broken windows policing model, Worrall (2006) finds a connection between arrests for minor offences and reduction in serious crime, while Golub, Johnson, Taylor, and Eterno (2003) find that quality of life policing is effective in reducing the crime rates.

Despite the success of broken windows policing in cities such as New York and Boston, there are negative repercussions. Although crime declined dramatically in New York, citizen complaints toward the police increased. Many opponents of zero tolerance policing argue that aggressive policing will only generate negative feelings toward the authorities and violate the civil rights of citizens (Davis, Mateu-Gelabart, & Miller, 2005). Despite the negative consequences of the broken windows approach, the rash of gun homicides in Toronto propelled many to argue that a more aggressive approach, like zero tolerance policing is needed on the streets of Toronto (see Box 5.1).

THE TRAGIC DEATH OF JANE CREBA AND THE CALL FOR TOUGHER POLICING

On December 26, 2005, 15-year-old Jane Creba was caught in the crossfire of the Boxing Day shootings in downtown Toronto and was mortally wounded. Creba, an intelligent, athletic, and attractive teenager came to symbolize the so-called "year of the gun," in which Toronto gun murders doubled from 27 to 52. Although gun homicides in Toronto pale in comparison to US cities of similar size, the Boxing Day murder epitomized the fear that Toronto, too, was becoming increasingly violent like other stateside urban centres. As a consequence, the media, politicians, and citizens clamoured for tougher laws and increased police action. Chief of Police William Blair vowed to get tough on criminals and Mayor David Miller pledged to reduce gun-related crime. In the midst of an election, political parties weighed in and Conservative leader Stephen Harper promised tougher laws, more police, and increased penalties, which, after his election as PM on January 23, 2006, he enacted. Similarly, many pundits citing US examples argued that "broken windows" or "zero tolerance" policing was the only way to reduce the increasing gun violence. Absent from this call for get-tough policing were the negatives associated with tougher policing, such as increased citizen complaints, police harassment of minorities, civil rights violations, and lower overall satisfaction with police services.

Most critics would acknowledge that much of the maintenance of order and peacekeeping work that police do reduces some crime. Many police reformers who are seeking a more communicative, low-key police presence argue that crime can be reduced when police are more integrated into the communities they patrol. When police are problem-solving or troubleshooting—for example, when they negotiate with leaders of a demonstration before the event rather than react to them after the demonstration has begun—they are doing crime prevention according to the broad view of their mandate. In this way, they prevent crime not by clearing criminals out of an area, but by pre-empting the conditions that precipitate the criminal act.

Crime prevention is not merely a police goal—it is required of police. In the case of Jane Doe in Toronto, the Toronto Police were sued by a woman who, while in her apartment, was sexually assaulted by a serial rapist who had been targeting her neighbourhood. In this case, the police were accused of not doing their duty to prevent law violation because they failed to inform those who were possible targets in the area.

Emergency Service Provision

The police are, along with firefighters and paramedics/ambulance services, one of the few public agencies available around the clock for emergency services. Many police activities are marshalled under the rubric of emergency services, from answering suicide and animal rescue calls to providing disaster relief, quelling riots, and responding to common criminal incidents. In much emergency work, the police are caught in a dilemma: if they restrict the scope of their availability to calls involving the need for law enforcement expertise, they can preserve and better define their professionalism in the most glorious of their functions. However, if they do narrow their services in this way, they also make themselves too inaccessible and push other service providers into their monopoly, which is law enforcement where legitimate force may be needed.

Periodically, governments have toyed with offloading some of the emergency response activities of public police to other service providers, especially where privatization and the rationalization of public services have been well developed. After all, do you need someone with police training and powers to rescue a cat from a tree or to direct traffic at an intersection because a traffic light is malfunctioning?

Thus far, the police have jealously guarded within the organization their response capabilities and have augmented them with civilians. Perhaps they look at it this way: sure, we do a lot of grunge work that sullies us, but all that grunge work insulates us too, and at the core of the craft of what we do is law enforcement.

Law Enforcement

Perhaps the role that the police themselves most identify with is **law enforcement**. Police officers often refer to themselves and are referred to by others, especially in the United States, as *law enforcement officers*. Of course, there are many kinds of laws and many kinds of officials with the duty of enforcing them. Officers of the Security and Exchange Commission enforce laws concerning the transaction of shares on the stock exchange. Officials at the Ministry of the Environment enforce, or oversee the enforcement of, regulatory standards and laws pertaining to levels of pollutant emissions from industrial plants. Most people, however, think of uniformed public police officers first when they think of law enforcement officers.

Police officers enforce the Criminal Code of Canada, provincial statutes, and municipal bylaws (RCMP officers also enforce some other federal legislation). Law enforcement is both reactive and proactive. Police officers may anticipate the violation of the law in certain circumstances, and so they will proactively intervene. In fact, many law violations have such built-in presuppositions, including possessing tools for the purposes of breaking and entering and communicating for the purpose of prostitution. Much proactive enforcement of laws against drug trafficking is also anticipatory of future crime, which drug enforcement officers may facilitate while skirting carefully around legal prohibitions against entrapment.

Police officers enforce the law by identifying violators and bringing them before the appropriate judicial authorities for further disposition. In doing so, the police use their formidable powers to take personal freedoms away when they believe there are sufficient grounds to do so. If the violation is serious, the police may remand the offender in custody until a justice of the peace can hear the case. Police officers may also enforce the law by distributing information about law violations, issuing summons for court appearances, and offering warnings, by way of deterrent, when violations are minor.

Public Order Maintenance

Enforcement of the law is complicated by the other roles of the police. If it were a matter of enforcing the law, and doing this alone, the police role would be more manageable, if still often controversial. However, the police also have the roles of **peacekeeping** and **order maintenance**. Police acting as peacekeepers take an active role in settling disputes and keeping them from getting out of hand. Order maintenance requires police to take a more passive role—their presence acts as a sufficient general deterrent.

Police spend a lot of time cooling tempers between spouses in domestic disputes, landlords and tenants, motorists, neighbours, and other potential adversaries. Many police researchers have noted that police use their discretion *not to arrest* where making an arrest is an option that can be legally justified. The Criminal Code indicates that a police officer *may arrest* an individual found committing an offence. However, much of the time, arresting one or more persons is not the best way to handle a dispute in either the short or the long run. Major riots in both the United States and England have been caused by arrests that onlookers perceived as being unwarranted (for example, in Detroit in 1967 and Brixton in 1981). Police officers themselves have been attacked by wives whose husbands they arrested for assault. Order maintenance often means the restraint of law enforcement.

Police achieve their peacekeeping mandate in a number of ways. First, they are visible. Although in some cases, such as at tense public demonstrations, too much police visibility can exacerbate the situation, in most cases in consensus societies, the presence of police brings a kind of official or state order. Second,

although they may not be visibly present everywhere, their availability is known. The threat or promise of police attendance offers a form of peacekeeping at a distance. Third, the police offer a form of state-funded dispute resolution. They provide 24-hour arbitration—a service that often prevents escalation in the dispute and thus avoids conflict resolution through the use of force.

Victim Assistance

As many police officers will tell you, much of modern policing is driven by complaints. Studies on police discretion have shown that the wishes of a complainant are important to the decision of whether to arrest. Reactive 911 policing depends on complainants' calls for service. Historically, the police and state prosecutors were mobilized to augment, and then to displace, with state interests, the role of the victim in the justice process for alleged wrongs suffered. The idea that the police and prosecutors stand in for the victim and through their intervention make the formal role of the victim redundant is one that is currently being reconsidered. As we shall see further in Chapter 10, victims, once marginalized in the formal process, are again assuming a role of importance.

Much of the current focus on the victim is a product of formal institutional neglect or indifference. But it is also the consequence of what may be a "recivilianization" or even a "reprivatization" of the criminal process. When the police begin to view their role as serving the victim rather than community or public interests, the historical rift between private and public prosecution may be closed. However, at present most police agencies have restricted themselves to informing complainants or victims of the progress of prosecutions against the accused.

Conflict in the Roles of Police

Because police have such varied duties, role dilemmas inevitably occur. Should the police be more proactive in preventing crime? If so, how should they be proactive? Should they be more proactive in stopping criminals, or should they attempt to eliminate criminogenic conditions—the circumstances that offer opportunities of crime to motivated offenders? If they are to be more proactive in stopping criminals, then they are quite right to devote resources to organizing sting operations and to the infiltration and surveillance of criminal networks. If their proactivity is to be addressed toward eliminating the conditions or circumstances that attract criminal activity, then they may be better off devoting their energies to early interventions, such as diversionary or victim–offender reconciliation programs, and to problem-solving community policing interventions. Historically, there has been a shift toward more proactive policing on both fronts. But this is not to say that reactive policing is not alive and well. You have only to pick up the phone and dial 911 to confirm that it is.

As well, the police are a 24-hour service. But how much should they develop the role of meeting customer satisfaction, or of serving clients and markets? Would this orientation, set out in some policy documents, undermine their mandate to serve citizens under the rule of law?

But the most pressing and persistent role dilemma remains the one between maintaining order and enforcing the law. Much of the controversy surrounding police arises out of questionable decision-making and mobilization. To stress again a central feature of the problem, the economic incentives to the individual officer derive mostly from arrests and the resulting overtime and court time that accrue. Peacekeeping and order maintenance, like much non-specialist work, is seen for the most part as belonging to the larger question of the good arrest decision, rather than as an end in itself. What is needed, as Robert Peel recommended in establishing the first London police force, is the rewarding of police for the peace they bring, rather than for the crime they solve or the people they arrest. Such a strategy for evaluation will by necessity make policing much more integrated with other mechanisms of local governance. To take a favourite example, police ridership on public transportation would be a crime prevention measure, because police presence reduces fear of crime.

Police Powers

All police officers have the traditional power of the common-law constable, which entails their right to seek an arrest and initiate a prosecution without a warrant. However, it should be noted that the capacity of the individual police officer to fulfill this common-law right is constrained by law, by the power and authority of other players in the criminal justice process, and also, more problematically, by political interference.

What are **police powers** in Canada? The police enforce warrants of the court, but they may also pursue warrantless arrests, under section 495(1)(c) of the Criminal Code. They have the power to preserve the peace and to arrest people when they have a good faith belief that a crime has been or will be committed, and they may enforce statutes and bylaws. Police may also search premises when they are in hot pursuit of a suspect, or when they have a search warrant under section 487 of the Criminal Code. They may install wiretaps or intercept communications under section 184, and they may obtain DNA samples under section 487.05.

Finally, police may use force under section 25. They are limited in their use of deadly force in situations where police officers perceive themselves or other citizens to be under immediate threat of serious bodily injury or death. Although section 25 does not restrict the officer from using deadly force in preventing the escape of a person when no other means exist to prevent that escape, section 37 limits the use of force according to an equivalency of "excessiveness"—the degree of force should not exceed the severity of the assault that it is intended to prevent. Also, police standards require that an investigation take place when an officer has discharged a weapon, and when an officer has killed or injured another person. In Ontario, the Special Investigations Unit (SIU) investigates such occurrences.

Discretion

Just how much power do the police have? While we may talk of legal parameters on the use of force, real power is measured by the lack of constraints or by the autonomy to choose a course of action. **Police discretion** is the freedom of police officers to choose between two available courses of action. It has long been contended that the police enjoy what is called *low-visibility discretion*. This means that others, such as other officials, cannot readily review police officers' choice of action. The police make their decisions usually without the presence of respectable third parties, and they have the tacit sanction of superior officers. Police often use this power and the wide scope of the law in deciding not to arrest when an arrest is legally permissible. The fact that they have, in many instances, a full cartridge of statutory capacity at the ready gives the police the leverage to resolve matters without having to resort to enforcing statute, and to have these resolutions agreed to (see Box 5.2 on the next page).

Let's take a simple example. Officer Joe comes upon you and a friend while you are firing beer bottle caps into a ravine from a park bench late one night, both of you with an open beer in your 18-year-old fists. Officer Joe is likely to approach you (depending on his professionalism) with an attitude of neutrality and firmness. You notice that he gives you and your friend a great deal of slack— Officer Joe might even be very friendly. But Officer Joe knows that there are at least three charges he can levy against you and your friend, including drinking under age, possessing an open container of alcohol in public, and littering. What he most likely wants to know is whether your attitude suggests that these transgressions are isolated and largely out of character, or whether you and your friend are serious deviants on your way to lengthy criminal careers. What Officer Joe will do is give you and your friend an "attitude test" to determine to which side of this equation each of you belongs. If you pass, Officer Joe can give you a warning and provide a form of informal social control in the garb of officialdom. By doing so, he will hope to bring you back into the fold of law-abiding and respectable citizens. The result is that order has been maintained, and it may also be said that he has enforced the law, but he has acted as a charismatic authority enforcing justice without the encumbrances of judge, jury, and legal process. The low visibility of the encounter is ensured because either you will fail the test and he will formally begin prosecution or you will pass and be happy not to challenge his decision not to charge you.

It has often been noted that the distribution of decision-making power (or discretion) within police organizations is an inversion of that found in most other organizations. In most organizations, the decision to deploy the special capacities of the organization is reserved for the top echelons. But the nature of the special capacities of police work (such as legal powers and the right to use force) has kept much decision-making with the front ranks. There is some suggestion, however, that new communications technologies may be changing this situation.

In the example above, what if Officer Joe were wired to a sophisticated miniature video and audio system that enabled sergeants in a monitoring and control station to observe the unfolding events and to call up data on you and your friend, leading them to suggest or insist on courses of action? It has at times been an administrative dream to know and see all from a distance, but even if such devices could routinely be used, the split-second nature of real-time interaction would still require that police work remain very much a matter of front-line officer discretion. To use a sporting analogy, many football quarterbacks now have radio transmitters in their helmets so that coaches can instruct them on the play, and many on-air television announcers are wired to take instructions from producers or directors behind the cameras. Even in these fields, we can see the limits of the human ability to balance the initiation of action and the taking of instructions. Often, we see television announcers and football quarterbacks caught in a stasis of indecision as they try to field two sources of input simultaneously. The terrible consequences of too much off-site discretion in policing have been seen in Ontario, where in 1988 an OPP Tactical Rescue Unit shot and killed an innocent, suicidal young man when the off-site commander issued an instruction to "take out" the suspect (Forcese, 1999).

Some researchers still conclude that there are clear-cut reasons for police decisions. In a recent Canadian study, Carrington and Schulenberg (2003) found that environmental, organizational, and situational factors play a role in police discretion with young offenders. Environmental factors are outside forces that the police have very little ability to change. These could include the availability of youth diversion programs or community resources. Availability of programs is

BOX 5.2

POLICE DISCRETION WITH YOUNG OFFENDERS: CONSEQUENCES OR SANCTIONS COMMONLY USED BY POLICE

1. Take no further action
2. Give an informal warning
3. Involve parents
4a. Give a formal warning; and/or
4b. Arrest, take to police station, and release without charge
5a. Arrest, take to police station, and refer to a pre-charge alternative measures; or
5b. Lay a charge without by way of an appearance notice or summons, then recommend for post-charge alternatives measures
6. Arrest, charge, and release on appearance notice, a summons, or (more commonly) a promise to appear (PTA) without conditions
7. Arrest, charge, and release on PTA with conditions or an officer in charge (OIC) undertaking
8. Arrest, charge, and detain for a judicial interim release (JIR) hearing
(The severity of options 6, 7, and 8 could be mitigated by recommending post-charge alternative measures.)

Source: Carrington and Schulenberg (2003).

a crucial determinant in deciding whether a charge should be laid. Such availability varies widely across Canada and these programs are more likely to exist in larger metropolitan areas. Nevertheless, many police officers report that the programs are inadequate for youth with serious problems such as drug or alcohol abuse, mental health issues, or anger management problems. As a result, Carrington and Schulenberg report that the lack of suitable diversion programs is tied to the upswing in the laying of charges and the increased use of detention. Environmental factors can also include considerations such as community size—rural police agencies are more likely to use informal sanctions out of necessity.

Organizational factors involve the make-up or structure of the police agency or service and/or police strategies. Carrington and Schulenberg report that police agencies with youth squads or dedicated youth officers make more use of parental involvement, referrals to external agencies, pre-charge diversion, and less use of formal charges. They also report that agencies employing school liaison officers with enforcement duties are more likely to make use of informal actions. Community policing may influence the discretion of police officers. Police services that allocate significant resources to community policing are more likely to use informal action, make more referrals to external agencies, and use more pre-charge alternative measures to avoid sending youth to detention facilities. In addition, agencies with more crime prevention programs have lower rates of charging young offenders.

Situational factors involve the circumstances of the crime, offender, offence and victim. Carrington and Schulenberg report that legal factors, such as seriousness of the offence, presence and type of weapon, harm done to a person or victim's property, and the youth's criminal history are the most important determinants of whether police officers decide to lay a charge. The strongest single factor for an officer in deciding to make an arrest is the number of prior apprehensions. In addition to legal history, youth demeanour, parental involvement, and race are factors that have an impact on police discretion. In their study, Carrington and Schulenberg report that three-quarters of police officers interviewed claim that the demeanour of the accused is an important factor in their decision-making. A youth who accepts responsibility for his or her crime, shows remorse, and respects the law is less likely to be charged. The extent and nature of parental involvement is also an important indicator—youths from unstable homes are more likely to be formally charged. Similarly, youths who are affiliated with gangs are also more likely to be formally processed. With similar conditions or circumstances, Aboriginal youths are more likely to be charged than their white counterparts. Carrington and Schulenberg report that the views of police officers about discretion are consistent across the country and that there is little variation among police services.

Accountability

Because the police enjoy awesome powers to take away rights and freedoms with low visibility, few discussions of the police will fail to mention **police accountability**. What are the mechanisms in place to ensure that police themselves follow the letter or the spirit of the law?

Accountability refers to the requirement among public servants to provide an account for actions taken or not taken. Police notepads, for example, belong not to the officer but to the department and are often entered as evidence. Police are accountable for what they write in these books.

Because there are several levels of policing in Canada, there are also different and sometimes overlapping mechanisms to ensure accountability. Unfortunately, it has been nearly impossible politically to make these mechanisms fully independent. Civilian review of police conduct has been successfully resisted. In Ontario, the closest approximation to a civilian review agency was the short-lived Public Complaints Commission, staffed in large part by lawyers and ex–police officers. It disbanded in 1995. That being said, a police officer is liable for violating the policy and procedures of his or her department and can also be tried civilly or criminally.

Mechanisms to deal with police misconduct exist in all Canadian jurisdictions; however, given the layers of administration, procedures may vary somewhat across Canada. Currently, in Ontario there are three avenues for the redress of wrongdoing by a police officer. First, there is the internal investigation of complaints. Mid- to large-sized police agencies have their own internal affairs division, which investigates complaints about officer conduct. These investigations may be aided by external investigators who are called in from outside agencies, particularly when a complaint alleges an organization-wide problem. Sometimes this practice is more commonplace, as in Montreal, where the police force regularly calls upon the Sûreté du Québec to look into matters of officer conduct. In Ontario, members of the public who are dissatisfied with the outcome of their complaint may appeal to the OCCPS.

Internal review processes have been criticized on a number of grounds. First, critics claim that the processes fail to promote structural changes because they take a case-by-case approach. Second, critics contend that internal reviews focus on protecting the organization from bad publicity rather than on protecting the public from bad cops. Third, critics claim that the practice of conducting background investigations of complainants deters potential and actual complainants from pursuing the process. Fourth, many consider the penalty structure of the internal process too lenient, as police officers are mostly given small financial penalties for actions that many members of the public would condemn as illegal and irreconcilable with the status of a police officer.

Another review mechanism is external review by outside monitoring agencies. All provinces except Newfoundland and Labrador have local or municipal boards or commissions that are authorized to oversee the delivery of municipal police services. Saskatchewan, New Brunswick, and Alberta also have police commissions that oversee provincial police forces. In Ontario, the Ontario Civilian Commission on Police Services and the Special Investigations Unit are empowered to review police conduct. Indeed, the SIU does not require the initiation of a complaint, but instead investigates every case involving serious injury, sexual assault, or death that may have been caused by the actions of a municipal, provincial, or regional police officer. The agency operates directly under the attorney general and has the authority to decide whether charges are warranted.

Yet another avenue available is civil procedure. Individuals can launch lawsuits against public police organizations for negligence in the provision of security. In 1998, Jane Doe won a 12-year-long case against the Toronto Police Service and was awarded $220 000 by a court in Toronto after the judge agreed that police tried to use her as "bait" to capture the balcony rapist.

An unofficial but powerful mechanism of accountability is the local and mass media. Likely a few times a year, your daily newspaper runs a story about police wrongdoing in mid- or large-sized metropolises. These stories are provided not only to titillate, but also as part of the professional mandate of the media to act as a fourth estate in governance. While this function of the media as a watchdog on the police is far from neutral, as the media outlets select and present stories in formats and according to viewpoints that cater to powerful interest groups, it is another vehicle by which police may be held to account (see Ericson, Baranek, & Chan, 1987, 1989).

Autonomy

The common-law office of the constable dates back to medieval England, where it was established in 1285 in the Statute of Winchester, and was brought to Canada in the Parish and Town Constable's Act of 1793. Just how much autonomy today's police officers take from the historical autonomy of the constabulary office is much debated (see Stenning, 1983). It is also questionable just how much the decision-making authority of the office of constable is superseded by the authority of the chief of police.

There are both institutional and organizational factors that guarantee autonomy for the police constable and the police function. Institutionally, we in Canada distinguish ourselves from totalitarian regimes in that the executive function of government is institutionally separated from the judicial and legislative branch. There is a further separation between the police function and political authority.

BOX 5.3

THE TRAGIC DEATH OF NEIL STONECHILD AND THE ACCOUNTABILITY OF THE POLICE

On October 24, 2004, one of Canada's most tragic cases of police misconduct concluded with the final report into the death of Neil Stonechild. Initially ruled a self-inflicted accident, Neil Stonechild, a 17-year-old Aboriginal from Saskatoon, Saskatchewan, was found frozen to death in the outskirts of Saskatoon on November 29, 1990. With temperatures dropping as low as −28 Celsius, Stonechild was found with one shoe, a blackened sock on one foot and in an attempt to keep warm his hands were curled up in a sports jacket. The case was largely forgotten until two Aboriginal men, Rodney Naistus and Lawrence Wegner, were found frozen to death within one week in 2000 and Darrell Night came forward to say that he too had been left on the outskirts of Saskatoon in sub-zero temperatures. After a decade of cover-ups, racism, and a botched investigation, the Stonechild case was finally revisited with a public inquiry that began on September 8, 2003, and concluded on May 19, 2004.

Despite police denials, Justice David Wright ruled that there was enough evidence to suggest that Stonechild was in police custody the night that he died. The strongest evidence came from Stonechild's friend Jason Roy who testified that he saw a terrified Stonechild in the back of a police cruiser the night he died. Roy, then 16, claimed that Stonechild screamed, "Help, these guys are going to kill me." The controversy over police involvement in the death caused a firestorm of outrage within the Aboriginal community, where it was common knowledge that police regularly took troublemakers out of the city to make them walk home. These dumpings were called "starlight tours." In March 2004, Dan Wiks, the former Saskatoon police chief, admitted that the investigation into Stonechild's death was "shoddy" and that the police had misled the public about the case. Saskatoon police admitted that they ignored tips, lost evidence, and lied to the Stonechild family. Despite the poor police investigation and subsequent cover-up, there was not enough evidence to bring criminal charges against the officers involved. However, the inquiry report made eight recommendations which included the following:

- undertake a thorough review of the Coroner's Act
- attract more Aboriginal candidates to municipal police services
- make it easier to complain about behaviour by police
- improve in-depth training on race relations for police officers
- have the larger municipal police services designate an Aboriginal person to act as a liaison and an informal ombud to deal with complaints and concerns from Aboriginals and persons from minority communities
- review the anger management and dispute resolution course policies
  For more information on the case and the inquiry, you can check
  www.stonechildinquiry.ca.

Institutional independence is also guaranteed in the convention that although political authorities, such as municipalities or provincial governments, may give direction on matters of policy, police forces retain decision-making authority over operations or how specific cases or even kinds of cases are handled. Such operational independence is bolstered by the fact that police-monitoring entities are often staffed by political representatives who, owing to their relative ignorance of policing, the political constituency of their representation, or their short duration as commissioners, are prone to deferring to police expertise (see Stenning, 1983).

Organizationally, constabulary autonomy is simply an expression of effective police work. The effectiveness of police as peacekeepers and law enforcers has long depended on optimizing each police officer's strengths within the police agency and jurisdiction. Subsequently, the agency reflects the peacekeeping and law enforcement capacity that each police agent can bring to bear, determining the basis of the term *police strength*. (However, under community policing initiatives, there has been much reinvigoration of unofficial agents in police provision.)

In addition, autonomy is supported because it is inconvenient for the entire police organization to be seen as directly responsible for the actions of its individual members. A police officer is personally and criminally accountable for his or her actions. The fact that the individual officer is mainly responsible for police wrongdoing can keep the organization as a whole relatively unencumbered when official actions draw criticism or legal action.

Police Work

So you want to be a police officer? Get in line. There are hundreds of applicants for each job in policing. This is not meant to depress or deter you, but it should alert you to the necessity of planning ahead. The role of policing goes some way to predicting the criteria for officer selection, but there are distinctive elements of the process of candidate selection and evaluation that reflect how role requirements may be ranked.

While this chapter on policing has spent relatively little time addressing considerations of law application and the use of force, these are the two areas stressed most strongly in formal police training. In police selection and training, both subjective and objective evaluation criteria are applied and successful socialization to the job—as in many other professions where teamwork is essential—also depends on the recruit's ability to socialize within the police environment.

Selection

The selection of police officers is at heart a complex undertaking because it involves a number of interests and dilemmas. There is a public interest in ensuring that public policing is representative of the community. There is a professional and occupational interest in ensuring that police officers have sufficient proficiency in those competencies that are crucial to their work. There is a further professional and occupational interest in demonstrating that the police tradition has always reflected the highest ideals and noblest intentions. However, in the transition to more representative policing over the past three decades, the greatest obstacles to progress have been the narrow interpretation of the core competencies of police work and the relative rigidity of those gatekeepers invested with decision-making power over entry and promotion. Police practitioners have overemphasized physical attributes, and those authorized to determine the candidacy and progress of police officers have too often been drawn from the ranks of the police.

The basic qualifications for employment as a public officer usually include the following:

- Canadian citizenship
- minimum age (18 or 19)
- physical and mental fitness
- good moral character and habits
- four years of secondary school

Normally, police agencies also require the candidate to meet a certain standard of visual acuity and to possess a valid driver's licence. In addition, Ontario, following the work of the Ministry of the Solicitor General's Strategic Planning Committee on Police Training and Education (Ontario, 1992) and its Police Constable Selection Project, has identified eight areas of core competency required of candidates for police constable:

- analytical thinking skills
- self-confidence
- communication skills
- ability to be flexible in dealing with diversity
- self-control
- facility for relationship building
- achievement orientation
- physical skills and abilities

It is worth noting that a criminal conviction does not by itself disqualify the applicant. Those with a criminal conviction on record may still be hired if they have received a pardon or if they have received a discharge and their record has been sealed by the RCMP.

Controversy remains regarding how tests that distinguish between men can also be used to distinguish between women, particularly women of Asian descent who are often of a slighter build. Even downgrading the physical requirements for women fails to address the more fundamental issue of how competencies are prioritized. On the one hand, it is stated that standardized tests are the only fair device of selection, but on the other hand that the profession demands the widest spectrum of representation in order to match police service membership to communities. Tests still privilege physical characteristics—including physical strength—under the premise that certain abilities are a requirement for officer and community safety, but it is obvious that there can be no physical equivalency between the average Asian-Canadian woman and European- or African-Canadian man. The acceptance of women into policing is not yet complete when women are still being evaluated according to antiquated, male standards that focus on physical strength. Multiculturalism is also an incomplete policy if distinctions between the innate proficiencies of various ethnic groups are not considered in police candidacy criteria. The focus by the police on physical attributes stems in part from the nature of the job, in which a diverse range of physical and mental competencies comes into play. However, police services as a whole are not served when focusing on physical competence if the selection process filters out candidates who may expand on the typical officer profiles. In any event, police services may yet require more of officers who seek postings to work that require a greater array of competencies than measures of physical strength. We must consider whether all the energy put into selection is a consequence of the fact that although the service still has a great capacity to insist on standards of entry, the power of police associations has undermined the service's ability to maintain standards of performance once the officer has reached first-class status. It should be noted that studies evaluating the effectiveness of women in policing have found them to be just as capable as men.

The selection process usually also includes interviews (screening and board interviews) and is completed after a successful background check (which establishes such things as credit history) and interviews with people who may have knowledge of the applicant's character, judgment, and values.

Training

There are three forms of police training: recruit, in-service, and field training. *Recruit training* is the initial block of intensive exposure to law, policy, procedures, and skills development, which is now universally delivered at a specialized training facility like the RCMP's Training Depot or the Ontario Police College (OPC).

Most time spent in the basic training program is devoted to traffic law and accident investigation, criminal offences and provincial statutes, laws of arrest and evidence, and communications. The second largest block is devoted to firearms training, police vehicle operation, and defensive manoeuvres and skills development in executing arrests and in the use of force. There is also some instruction on race relations, police ethics, and general handling of stress, victims, and relations with the public.

During *in-service training*, individual services provide instruction in their forms, policies, and procedures. This training can take anywhere from a few hours in smaller forces to up to eight weeks in the larger forces. Further in-service training is ongoing, such as in firearms recertification.

A key element of police training is *field training*, in which the trainee is assigned to a coach officer for instruction in the finer points of police duty, including how to work the on-board, computer-aided dispatch system and the protocols for handling the everyday workload.

Police Officer Numbers and Workload

In 2005, there were 61 000 police officers in Canada, an increase of more than 1000 officers from the previous year. Table 5.2 shows the trends in police personnel and expenditures since 1962.

It is important to keep in mind that raw numbers by themselves do not tell us what we need to know about the relative strength of police officer numbers. To gauge their strength, we need to know how many police officers there are per population. In 2005, there were 189.2 officers per 100 000 population, which reveals a slight increase from 2004 (see Figure 5.1 on page 124).

In the meantime, some have argued that the workload of police officers is an important measure of police work. Workload is typically measured in Criminal Code incidents per officer. Figure 5.2 on page 125 reveals that in 2004, incidents per officer was 43. Incidents per officer have increased dramatically since the 1960s and 1970s, but have remained relatively constant through the 1980s and 1990s, with highs in 1991 and 1992.

Table 5.3 on page 126 shows that workload varies by more than a 2 to 1 ratio between major jurisdictions across the country, with Toronto having the relatively low number of 27 incidents per officer and Vancouver the very high 80 incidents per officer. Needless to say, an officer assigned to the downtown core of Vancouver has a higher workload than one assigned to Montreal's downtown core. This higher workload also means that those officers are less likely to be engaged in activities more indirectly related to the administration of Criminal Code incidents, such as community policing.

TABLE 5.2

TRENDS IN POLICE PERSONNEL AND EXPENDITURES, CANADA, 1962–2005[1]

	Population[2]	Police officers	Civilian personnel	Total personnel	Police: civilian ratio	Population per police officer	Police per 100 000 population	Actual[3] Criminal Code incidents	Incidents per officer	Total expenditures
	000s									$000s
1962	18 583	26 129	5699	31 828	4.58	711.2	140.6	514 986	19.7	..
1963	18 931	27 333	5935	33 268	4.61	692.6	144.4	572 105	20.9	..
1964	19 291	28 823	6655	35 478	4.33	669.3	149.4	626 038	21.7	..
1965	19 644	30 146	7133	37 279	4.23	651.6	153.5	628 418	20.8	..
1966	20 015	32 086	7583	39 669	4.23	623.8	160.3	702 809	21.9	..
1967	20 378	33 792	8018	41 810	4.21	603.0	165.8	784 568	23.2	..
1968	20 701	34 887	8351	43 238	4.18	593.4	168.5	897 530	25.7	..
1969	21 001	36 342	8963	45 305	4.05	577.9	173.0	994 790	27.4	..
1970	21 297	37 949	9936	47 885	3.82	561.2	178.2	1 110 066	29.3	..
1971	21 962	40 148	10 597	50 745	3.79	547.0	182.8	1 166 458	29.1	..
1972	22 218	41 214	11 762	52 976	3.50	539.1	185.5	1 189 805	28.9	..
1973	22 492	43 142	12 297	55 439	3.51	521.3	191.8	1 298 551	30.1	..
1974	22 808	45 276	12 085	57 361	3.75	503.8	198.5	1 456 885	32.2	..
1975	23 143	47 713	13 794	61 507	3.46	485.1	206.2	1 585 805	33.2	..
1976	23 450	48 213	14 377	62 590	3.35	486.4	205.6	1 637 704	34.0	..
1977	23 726	48 764	15 231	63 995	3.20	486.5	205.5	1 654 024	33.9	..
1978	23 963	48 705	15 749	64 454	3.09	492.0	203.2	1 714 300	35.2	..
1979	24 202	48 990	15 001	63 991	3.27	494.0	202.4	1 855 271	37.9	..
1980	24 516	49 841	16 410	66 251	3.04	491.9	203.3	2 045 398	41.0	..
1981	24 820	50 563	16 999	67 562	2.97	490.9	203.7	2 168 202	42.9	..
1982	25 117	50 539	17 738	68 277	2.85	497.0	201.2	2 203 665	43.6	..
1983	25 367	50 081	17 342	67 423	2.89	506.5	197.4	2 148 633	42.9	..
1984	25 608	50 010	17 503	67 513	2.86	512.1	195.3	2 147 656	42.9	..
1985	25 843	50 351	17 702	68 053	2.84	513.3	194.8	2 174 175	43.2	3 542 240
1986	26 101	51 425	18 273	69 698	2.81	507.6	197.0	2 277 749	44.3	3 771 205
1987	26 449	52 510	19 558	72 068	2.68	503.7	198.5	2 368 958	45.1	4 027 809
1988	26 795	53 312	19 407	72 719	2.75	502.6	199.0	2 390 008	44.8	4 389 414
1989	27 282	54 211	19 526	73 737	2.78	503.3	198.7	2 425 936	44.7	4 684 760
1990	27 698	56 034	19 259	75 293	2.91	494.3	202.3	2 627 197	46.9	5 247 646
1991	28 031	56 768	19 440	76 208	2.92	493.8	202.5	2 898 989	51.1	5 426 887
1992	28 367	56 992	20 059	77 051	2.84	497.7	200.9	2 847 981	50.0	5 716 833
1993	28 682	56 901	19 956	76 857	2.85	504.1	198.4	2 735 623	48.1	5 790 165
1994	28 999	55 859	19 492	75 351	2.87	519.1	192.6	2 646 209	47.4	5 783 656
1995	29 302	55 008	19 259	74 267	2.86	532.7	187.7	2 639 654	48.0	5 808 607
1996	29 611	54 323	19 603	73 926	2.77	545.1	183.5	2 644 893	48.7	5 856 055
1997	29 907	54 719	19 679	74 398	2.78	546.6	183.0	2 534 766	46.3	5 989 022
1998	30 157	54 763	19 383	74 146	2.83	550.7	181.6	2 461 156	44.9	6 209 756
1999	30 404	55 321	20 168	75 489	2.74	549.6	182.0	2 356 831	42.6	6 396 534
2000	30 689	55 954	19 907	75 861	2.81	548.5	182.3	2 352 768	42.0	6 798 531
2001	31 021	57 076	19 982	77 058	2.86	543.5	184.0	2 374 811	41.6	7 269 977
2002	31 373	58 422	20 732	79 154	2.82	537.0	186.2	2 417 444	41.4	7 827 195
2003	31 669	59 412	21 476	80 888	2.77	533.0	187.6	2 579 172	43.4	8 324 176
2004	31 974	59 800	22 212	82 012	2.69	534.7	187.0	2 571 860	43.0	8 823 028
2005	32 271	61 050	23 391	84 441	2.61	528.6	189.2	..	..	

1. A new survey was implemented in 1986. To maintain historical continuity, figures prior to 1986 have been adjusted.
2. 1962–1970 final intercensal estimates at June 1st, without adjustment for net census undercounts; from 1971 onward estimates are adjusted to July 1st and include adjustments for net census undercoverage, non-permanent residents and returning Canadians; 1971–1995 revised intercensal estimates; 1996–2000 final intercensal estimates; 2001–2002 final postcensal estimates; 2003–2004 updated postcensal estimates; 2005 preliminary postcensal estimates. Population estimates provided by the Demography Division of Statistics Canada.
3. Data provided from the Uniform Crime Reporting Survey, Canadian Centre for Justice Statistics. Excludes Criminal Code traffic incidents.

Source: Adapted from Statistics Canada's publication *Police Resources in Canada, 2005*, Catalogue 85-225, December 2005, page 25. Available at www.statcan.ca/english/freepub/85-225-XIE/0000585-225-XIE.pdf.

FIGURE 5.1

POLICE OFFICERS PER 100 000 POPULATION, CANADA, 1962–2005

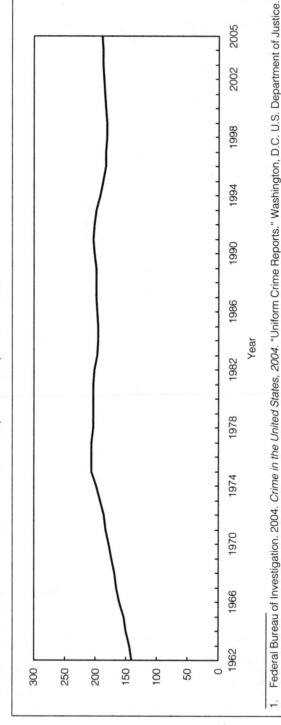

1. Federal Bureau of Investigation. 2004. *Crime in the United States, 2004.* "Uniform Crime Reports." Washington, D.C. U.S. Department of Justice.
2. Australian Institute of Criminology. 2004. *Australian Crime: Facts and Figures 2003.* Canberra, Australia.
3. Nasreen Bibi, Michelle Glegg and Rachel Pinto, 25 July 2005, "Police Service Strength—England and Wales, 31 March, 2005." *Home Office Statistical Bulletin.* 12/05.
4. Police per capita figures for England and Wales were calculated using the Home Office police officer figures and Office for National Statistics population data.

Source: Adapted from Statistics Canada's publication *Police Resources in Canada, 2005,* Catalogue 85-225, December 2005, page 11. Available at www.statcan.ca/english/freepub/85-225-XIE/0000585-225-XIE.pdf.

CRIMINAL CODE INCIDENTS PER OFFICER, CANADA, 1962–2004

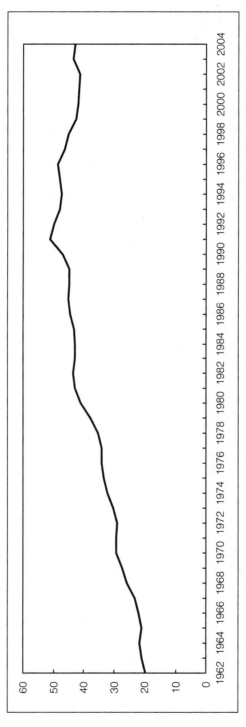

Source: Adapted from Statistics Canada's publication *Police Resources in Canada, 2005*, Catalogue 85-225, December 2005, page 12. Available at www.statcan.ca/english/freepub/85-225-XIE/0000585-225-XIE.pdf.

TABLE 5.3

POLICE OFFICER WORKLOAD, BASED ON CRIMINAL CODE INCIDENTS, 2005

	POPULATION (2004)	OFFICERS PER 100 000	CRIME RATE PER 100 000	INCIDENT PER OFFICER
Winnipeg	695 187	178	12 167	68.35
Regina	200 977	180	15 430	85.72
Toronto	5 211 843	172	4669	27.15
Halifax	379 770	152	9924	65.29
Edmonton	1 003 399	162	11 332	69.95
Vancouver	2 173 679	146	11 814	80.92
Calgary	1 049 006	152	7101	46.72
Hamilton	691 088	145	5764	39.72
Ottawa-Hull	873 397	137	5663	41.34
Montreal	3 633 264	179	8173	45.66

Source: Adapted from Statistics Canada's publication *The Daily*, Catalogue 11-001, Thursday, December 15, 2005. Available at www.statcan.ca/Daily/english/051215/d051215d.htm. Also adapted from Thursday July 21, 2005 at www.statcan.ca/Daily/english/050721/d050721a.htm.

These numbers notwithstanding, police numbers (or strength) are often bolstered not according to a need represented by a rise in crime statistics, but rather according to the prevailing political viewpoint on the importance of law and order in government policy. Prime Minister Stephen Harper has courted public opinion using the US-style "tough-on-crime" approach. Despite a steady decline in the violent crime rate, many politicians have learned that a law-and-order platform still wins votes, and such policy often includes the promise of more police hiring, even if, as we have seen thus far, much of that new hiring is in fact swallowed up in force replenishment.

Composition of Police

Especially during the late 1980s and early 1990s, public police services were active in attempting to make the composition of police forces representative of the communities served. However, much work is still to be done to make policing more inclusive to minorities. Visible minorities constitute 10 percent of the employed labour force, but they represent only 3 percent of police officers (CCJS, 1999b). According to Stenning (2003), visible minorities account for 4 percent of officers in Montreal, 10 percent in Toronto, and 7 percent in Vancouver, despite the fact that visible minorities account for approximately 37 percent of the populations in Toronto and Vancouver. Greater representation of Aboriginal people in policing has been achieved, at 3 percent of all police officers, nearly double their 1.7 percent representation in the total employed labour force (CCJS, 1999b). However, critics argue that more Aboriginal representation is required, especially in larger urban centres and cities in which Aboriginal tensions with the police are rampant.

While there were no female full-duty public police officers prior to 1973, there has been a gradual increase in female participation in policing (see Figure 5.3 on the next page).

Table 5.4 shows that in 2005 women represented only 17.3 percent of non-civilian police. However, there has been a gradual increase in the proportion of female officers, almost doubling from 1995.

In a comparison of provinces, British Columbia reports the highest proportion of female officers (21 percent), followed by Quebec (19 percent). The lowest proportions are in the Maritimes, which include PEI (12.7 percent), Nova Scotia (13.4 percent), and New Brunswick (13.6 percent) (see Table 5.5 on page 129).

Internationally, Canada ranks seventh in terms of female representation. Almost doubling the United States; however, both Norway and Australia have twice as many female officers as Canada (see Table 5.6 on page 129).

The Cost of Policing

An evaluation of policing costs should take into consideration the wider impact of decisions about resource distribution. Critical criminologists insist that the costs of policing need to include the repercussion of more arrests on costs further down the justice system, as more court resources and more correctional resources are used. Conservative criminologists would argue that the benefits of prosecuting crime outweigh the costs to the system; in other words, human resources and technology costs of policing should be measured against property losses, higher insurance rates, and the pain and suffering of victims. Evaluations of the impact of social policy decisions are still in their infancy. In the meantime, most discussions about the costs of policing will be about the costs of police services, rather than about the relative costs of competing policy decisions regarding crime prevention.

TABLE 5.4

POLICE OFFICERS BY SEX, CANADA, SELECTED YEARS

	Male		Female		Total
	number	%	number	%	
1965	29 956	99.4	190	0.6	30 146
1970	37 763	99.5	186	0.5	37 949
1975	47 151	98.8	562	1.2	47 713
1980	48 749	97.8	1092	2.2	49 841
1985	48 518	96.4	1833	3.6	50 351
1990	52 461	93.6	3573	6.4	56 034
1995	49 630	90.2	5378	9.8	55 008
2000	48 304	86.3	7650	13.7	55 954
2004	49 941	83.5	9859	16.5	59 800
2005	50 471	82.7	10 579	17.3	61 050

Source: Adapted from Statistics Canada's publication *Police Resources in Canada, 2005*, Catalogue 85-225, December 2005, page 16. Available at www.statcan.ca/english/freepub/85-225-XIE/0000585-225-XIE.pdf.

FIGURE 5.3

PROPORTION OF FEMALE POLICE OFFICERS, CANADA, 1965–2005

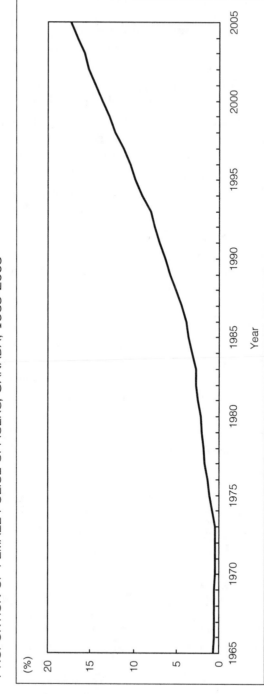

Source: Adapted from Statistics Canada's publication *Police Resources in Canada, 2005*, Catalogue 85-225, December 2005, page 16. Available at www.statcan.ca/english/freepub/85-225-XIE/0000585-225-XIE.pdf.

POLICE OFFICERS BY SEX, PROVINCES/TERRITORIES, 2005

	Male		Female		Total
	number	%	number	%	
British Columbia	5898	79.0	1571	21.0	7469
Quebec	11 960	81.1	2793	18.9	14 753
Nunavut	100	82.6	21	17.4	121
Saskatchewan	1664	82.7	347	17.3	2011
Ontario	19 531	83.4	3889	16.6	23 420
Alberta	4491	84.2	844	15.8	5335
Newfoundland and Labrador	665	85.7	111	14.3	776
Yukon	103	85.8	17	14.2	120
Manitoba	1939	85.9	317	14.1	2256
Northwest Territories	149	86.1	24	13.9	173
New Brunswick	1121	86.4	176	13.6	1297
Nova Scotia	1406	86.6	218	13.4	1624
Prince Edward Island	186	87.3	27	12.7	213
RCMP* Headquarters and Training Academy	1258	84.9	224	15.1	1 482
Canada	**50 471**	**82.7**	**10 579**	**17.3**	**61 050**

* Royal Canadian Mounted Police

Source: Adapted from Statistics Canada's publication *Police Resources in Canada, 2005*, Catalogue 85-225, December 2005, page 17. Available at www.statcan.ca/english/freepub/85-225-XIE/0000585-225-XIE.pdf.

PERCENTAGE OF FEMALE POLICE OFFICERS, INTERNATIONAL RANKING, 2002

Ranking	Country	Female	Ranking	Country	Female
		%			%
1	Norway	30.7[1]	15	Finland	9.8
2	Australia	29.9	16	Iceland	9.1
3	Netherlands	19.2	17	Denmark	8.5
4	Sweden	18.7	18	U.S.A.	7.2[3]
5	United Kingdom	17.8	19	Japan	7.1
6	Hungary	15.3[2]	20	Greece	7.0[4]
7	**Canada**	**15.3**	21	Luxembourg	6.8
8	New Zealand	14.8	22	Austria	6.3
9	France	13.3[2]	23	Italy	5.1
10	Ireland	12.1[2]	24	Turkey	4.5[2]
11	Czech Republic	12.0	25	Germany	3.9
12	Belgium	10.7	26	Portugal	3.8
13	Slovakia	10.1	26	Spain	3.6[2]
14	Poland	9.9	27	Mexico	2.1

1. Data from 1994.
2. Data from 2000.
3. Data from 1999.
4. Data from 1997.

Source: Social data ranking of developed countries, the Organisation of Economic Co-operation and Development (OECD) and the United Nations Surveys of Crime Trends and Operations of Criminal Justice Systems, Eighth Wave, the United Nations Office on Drugs and Crime (UNODC). Population source: World Bank.

Still, we should always be asking ourselves if we are getting the most out of our public policy. The United States is often perplexing to European visitors because, while it practises the most zealous accounting for the expenditure of public monies, it also seems to have infinite resources for building prisons and hiring police officers. Indeed, in California more money is now spent on putting people in jail than on educating people.

Juristat reports that policing accounts for roughly 61 percent of the total money spent on criminal justice. In 2004, police expenditures totalled $8.8 billion, which translates into a cost of $276 per Canadian (see Table 5.2 on page 123). Of this amount, 80 percent goes to salaries, wages, and benefits. Ontario and Quebec both pay more per capita than the national average, while the Maritime provinces pay the least (CCJS, 2005).

Community Policing

From the first fleet of automobile patrol cars in the early 1910s to the proliferation of fleets of patrol cars equipped with two-way radios from the 1930s to 1950s, police organization was driven toward a model of reactive, call-for-service patrol. This model meant that in the first half of the twentieth century, police organizations were changing their mandate from peacekeeping to law enforcement. Although the typical police officer in the 1950s was not unavailable to keep the peace, in the larger urban centres the patrol officer was more likely to be seen only when someone placed a service call to the station or when the officer noticed something happening while en route between such calls.

But in the organization of reactive patrol, police had forgotten much of the legacy of Robert Peel's principles, in which crime prevention, rather than clearance of Criminal Code violations, was to be the best goal and measure of policing. In fashioning themselves more as impartial servants of the law, they had also distanced themselves from local problems that required peacekeeping and order maintenance expertise. In short, while police organizations between the 1920s and 1960s modernized themselves with sophisticated communications, command and control, and intelligence-gathering systems, many had also lost touch with the communities they policed.

This distance became obvious in the many urban riots in the United States in the mid-to-late 1960s, in which police practices were cited by the Kerner Commission as a major precipitator of the riots (Peak, 1997). Many of the police incidents were deemed discriminatory or racist, but this finding only confirmed that the police had become out of touch with the interests and concerns of the large constituencies they were accountable to. They came in, made arrests, and left, leaving a wake of dissatisfaction. Added to these findings was a famous study by George Kelling and colleagues (1974), which found in a controlled experiment of random patrols in Kansas City that increasing the number of patrol cars in a test area failed to decrease crime there. This finding suggested that police patrol had little effect on crime.

By the early 1970s, many police organizations had responded with isolated programs. These programs included training in race relations; unit beat policing, whereby police officers are assigned regularly to the same beat; and public relations liaisons with schools. In the late 1970s and early 1980s, however, a distinct and positive philosophy of community policing began to emerge. Its advocates touted it as a reinvention of the way police would deliver services. Among those credited with bringing a philosophy of community policing to life are Robert Trojanowitz, Herman Goldstein, George Kelling, and James Q. Wilson.

What Is Community Policing?

Community policing entails returning to the principle of policing being carried out by the community as a whole rather than by one specific agency of government. When you think of policing, you probably visualize the police, including the uniform, weapons, technology, and various cultural idiosyncrasies associated with the police personality. Policing, however, is more than the modern organization that most of us have come to depend on for problems related to personal security.

Because professional police organizations have become so central to our understanding and expectations of policing delivery, community policing is mostly understood as a partnership between the local professional police organization and various other agencies, be they voluntary, private, or public.

Community policing also involves change to public police organizations. Recent changes to the OPP, for example, have altered its organizational structure to enhance the appearance, at least, of an organization dedicating resources to front-line delivery. Thus, reorganization according to community policing often includes the following changes:

- decentralizing decision-making (becoming less paramilitaristic)
- reducing bureaucracy
- rewarding non-conventional initiatives in crime prevention

BOX 5.4

TRADITIONAL VERSUS COMMUNITY POLICING

TRADITIONAL POLICE PRACTICE: THE THREE R'S	PRINCIPLES OF COMMUNITY POLICING: THE THREE P'S
Random patrol	Prevention
Rapid response	Problem solving
Reactive investigation	Partnership with the community

- reducing specialization or creating a generalist orientation (e.g., focusing on problem-solving)
- instituting practices of the "learning organization"

For the most part, it has been a tall order for Canadian police organizations to follow through on the restructuring that community policing calls for. Two of the biggest forces, the RCMP and the OPP, have done much restructuring but are still labouring under the vestiges of central command, large bureaucracies, traditional rewards (for law enforcement), and specialization. Reforms face resistance from the line officers, and community policing also competes for resources with traditional, reactive law enforcement. At budget time across the country, the police often remind the public that the community policing programs it wants can come only through greater financial investment.

Conclusion

How policing will look as we move ahead in this new millennium is impossible to predict. However, certain patterns and key developments may be worth noting and watching:

One trend, of course, is the continual development of technology. The capacity of technology to reduce the human labour required to perform specific tasks is too often overestimated. In police work, new technologies have often been credited with awesome improvements to service delivery. Telegraphy, fingerprinting, radio-cars, the Canadian Police Information Centre (CPIC), and DNA profiling have each offered great innovations in the way the police perform. Closed-circuit television and video surveillance allow forms of virtual patrol.

Another trend is the growth in private security. In your daily life, you are more likely to come across a private security officer than a public police officer. Private security outnumbers public police in Canada by a ratio of 2 to 1. The public police are said to be able to perform a smaller relative share of the policing role; the RCMP, for example, have been reducing their capacity to cover economic crime and are increasingly ceding this responsibility of law enforcement to private security and intelligence services.

Further, there is a trend in which, despite long-standing efforts at prevention, police organizations are developing a number of tiers. No longer is it possible to see public police officers as the generalists that early versions of community policing supported. Rather, we see in other nations, such as the Netherlands, new subconstable ranks and private and volunteer patrols, in which the most visible policing is no longer the full-duty constable, but rather a hybrid of public and private or lay and professional service providers. The responsibility of public police in the area of patrol may be one of community safety coordination or "beat management," rather than direct enforcement (see the Salinas, California, Police

Department website at www.salinaspd.com). Here, the police are seen as accreditors and coordinators of patrol, rather than as those who provide that patrol themselves. This kind of "governing at a distance" may happen to other areas of traditional delivery, as well. More and more in advanced democracies, specialists are required for effectiveness, from crime scene investigations to strategies of crime prevention, yet local authorities can no longer afford front-line patrol by full-duty police officers, and volunteer and private delivery is filling the gap.

This brings to bear a third dynamic, which is the relative power of local versus extra-local and national versus transnational police authorities. As the information age causes increased globalization, more crime and criminal depravations occur via the information and exchange channels we use. Patrolling and securing these new channels of communications require strategies oriented to a different version of jurisdiction than has typically been the case. Policing the global marketplace requires "global cops" (or police with excellent connections) and agreements with other forces in faraway places.

What all this means is that policing is changing dramatically and rapidly. What we have been accustomed to expect for many decades may no longer be serviceable by the role and resources of the public police as we know them today.

Summary

In this chapter, we have highlighted several important features of Canadian police organization, history, and administration. First, we showed that Canadian police history is unique in that it developed with aspects of both British colonial and US municipal policing. Canada's federal police, the RCMP, were important emissaries of the advantages of British rule and have maintained much legitimacy, despite periodic doubts as to the need for a federal force. We then reviewed police powers and responsibilities, and noted the influence of community policing. Finally, we reviewed some of the selection and training methods and practices and offered some brief remarks on possible future issues facing police work.

Key Terms

law enforcement (p. 108)

North West Mounted Police
(NWMP) (p. 99)

Ontario Civilian Commission on Police
Services (OCCPS) (p. 103)

Ontario Provincial Police
(OPP) (p. 101)

order maintenance (p. 109)

peacekeeping (p. 109)

police accountability (p. 116)

police discretion (p. 112)

police powers (p. 112)

Royal Canadian Mounted Police
(RCMP) (p. 100)

Sûreté du Québec (SQ) (p. 101)

Discussion Questions

1. What are the three levels of public police jurisdiction in Canada?
2. What is meant by *community policing*?
3. Why was the North West Mounted Police (NWMP) established as a federal police force?
4. List some of the functions or services provided by the public police. Which do you believe take precedence? At times of budget cutting, what areas do you think are most likely to feel the sting of the cuts first?
5. What might be expected of the future of public policing? Do you believe that the public police are endangered by increasing privatization?
6. List and describe the factors that have an impact on police discretion.

Weblinks

www.torontopolice.on.ca This link provides information about the Toronto Police Service.

www.opp.ca This link provides information about the Ontario Provincial Police.

www.walnet.org/jane_doe This site provides an overview of the Jane Doe case, which was discussed in the chapter.

www.rcmp-grc.gc.ca The RCMP has a thorough and informative site with links to information on their forensic services, the national DNA databank, peacekeeping, and recruiting info, as well as the latest news releases.

ww2.psepc-sppcc.gc.ca/abor_policing/index_e.asp The Aboriginal Policing Directorate is responsible for administering the First Nations' policing policy and providing national leadership regarding the delivery of policing services for Aboriginal people off reserve.

www.interpol.com The website of Interpol, the international police force, provides fascinating information on international crime issues such as trafficking in human beings, terrorism, drug trafficking, and internationally wanted criminals.

www.theiacp.org/pubinfo The International Association of Chiefs of Police site offers links to police training information, legislation and policy, research initiatives, and publications.

www.applicanttesting.com In Ontario, police candidates secure qualifications through Applicant Testing Services (ATS), a private agency contracted by the Police Learning System to provide constable-selection services. This website provides an overview of the qualifications and testing procedures that candidates must take.

CHAPTER 6

The Court System

Objectives

- To illustrate how the court system establishes guilt or innocence, imposes sentences, and maintains social order and control.

- To examine the roles and functions of the provincial courts, the federal courts, and the Supreme Court of Canada.

- To analyze the processing of a criminal trial through the court system and the roles of judges and juries.

- To examine the Youth Criminal Justice Act and outline its positive and negative features.

The Criminal Court Structure

That the courts play a critical role in the criminal justice system is without question. Regardless of their complex and labyrinth-like nature, the courts collectively remain the arbiter of justice and the search for truth. The criminal trial, which pits the resources of the defendant against those of the state, is seen by the public as the final process whereby guilt or innocence is determined, and where the judge imposes a sentence. It is through our justice system that social control and order is maintained. Because the court system is established to protect the rights of those charged with a criminal offence, it monitors other branches of the justice system, specifically the police and the prosecution. It is that dual role of protecting the accused from abuse while controlling and punishing the guilty that makes the court the hallmark of our democracy. Since the introduction of the Canadian Charter of Rights and Freedoms in 1982, even greater responsibility has been placed on our courts to protect the rights of individuals from the power of the government and bureaucracy. Furthermore, the concept of judicial independence is embodied in the principles of fundamental justice, and Canadians expect their cases in the courts to be heard before a judiciary that is fair, impartial, and not subject to political pressure from any branch of the government.

The Canadian judiciary can be divided into three sections: the provincial courts, the federal courts, and the Supreme Court of Canada. The provincial and federal courts both have trial and appellate wings; topping the hierarchy is the Supreme Court of Canada, which serves as the appeal court of last resort for both systems. Canada has a national legal structure in the sense that the Supreme Court is accepted as the final arbiter of disputes from across the land by the federal and all provincial governments.

The Provincial Court System

Most criminal trials are heard in the **provincial courts**. The British North America (BNA) Act of 1867 allowed for each province to establish a system of courts responsible for both civil and criminal cases, ensuring that the provinces would retain authority to set up a general system of courts. The Act allowed the provinces to establish lower-level and appellate courts, but it gave the federal government the power to appoint and pay judges for higher levels of courts. Only in lowly magistrate courts could the provinces appoint the judges. Furthermore, responsibility for creating criminal law and statutes was delegated to the federal government under the BNA Act, while the provinces were mandated to enforce the law and to conduct criminal prosecutions in court. Schmalleger et al. (2004) note that in the last two decades the court system has been greatly simplified—every province has a provincial court as the central criminal trial court and also a superior court.

The workhorse of the court system is the provincial court. All criminal and civil cases enter a provincial court, and the vast majority of less serious cases are tried there. Within the provincial court system are separate divisions, including small claims, family, youth, traffic, and criminal courts. The criminal division deals with all offenders charged who are over 18 years of age; the **youth court** handles offences committed by those under age 18. The provincial governments appoint provincial court judges and pay their salaries.

The most serious criminal offences, such as first-degree murder cases, are tried in provincial **superior courts**. As stated earlier, under the Canadian Constitution, the federal government appoints and remunerates judges of the courts of appeal and the superior courts.

The role of the provincial court is to arraign the accused; set bail; ensure that the Crown makes proper disclosure of evidence; determine the amount of bail; decide on the method of trial; and, 90 percent of the time, conduct the criminal trial. If the defendant pleads guilty or is found guilty after a hearing, the judge in provincial court also imposes the appropriate sentence. Schmalleger et al.

note that provincial courts do not hold jury trials; instead, the presiding judge is empowered to interpret both fact and law. In most instances, the goal is swift and decisive justice, with informal and uncomplicated jurisprudence the expected outcome. Because of the great number of cases and the need for swift justice, only the provincial superior courts use the complete extent of the justice system— juries, prosecutors, defence lawyers, witnesses, and expert witnesses, such as the ones we have all been exposed to in courtroom dramas and movies. This formal procedure can be long, expensive, and difficult, involving many "legal eagles" and expert witnesses, as illustrated by the Paul Bernardo murder case. While there is a place for both the formal procedural model and the more informal hearings in the courts of the nation, the overload of the court system is creating pressure for cases to be quickly resolved and for decisions to be based on uncomplicated issues of law and fact.

All provinces have **courts of appeal** as part of the superior court system. The appeals court usually consists of a panel of judges. At this level, there are no juries present; instead, three to five judges examine evidence and revisit the findings of the original judge, and they extensively question the defence and prosecution lawyers, who appear before them. The court of appeal usually renders a decision after long and extensive debate and discussion in private. This decision, often made in writing, can be a split decision with minority dissent, or it can be unanimous. The role of the appeal court is to review the transcript of the lower court to ensure that the hearing was fair and in accordance with statutory and case law. Brockman and Rose (1996) note that most convictions are reaffirmed on appeal. However, sometimes the appeals court will find that the trial judge erred in his or her decisions in terms of allowing or not allowing certain evidence to be heard. As well, the judges may determine that the statute relating to the case was improperly interpreted. Should the appellate court find these aberrations in law or fact, many options are possible, all within the premise that the original verdict will be set aside. Some of the options include sending the case for retrial or overturning the conviction and acquitting the defendant. Depending on the nature of the offence and the statute in dispute, decisions of provincial appellate courts can be further appealed in the court of last resort, the Supreme Court of Canada. The Supreme Court will usually review the cases that are appealed to them and decide on which cases they will hear and which decisions of the appeals courts they will rule as final. However, in split decisions of the appeals court or on questions of law, a Supreme Court appeal is almost always granted.

The Federal Court System

Side by side with the provincial court system is the **Federal Court of Canada**, divided into a trial and an appellate division. This court is not involved in criminal cases, but instead deals exclusively with legal actions brought against the federal government and federal agencies. Appeals from the decisions of the trial division can be made to the Federal Court of Appeal and finally to the Supreme Court of Canada.

The Supreme Court of Canada

The **Supreme Court of Canada** is an immensely powerful institution. Because of its ability to review all decisions of the provincial and federal courts, it has the power to define which lower-court decisions reflect best the laws and the Constitution of Canada. Schmalleger et al. (2004) believe that the evolution of the Supreme Court is a classic example of institutional development in Canadian history. In its earliest years, it was not influential in developing legal doctrine, but today it is a system that wields great legal power in most aspects of Canadian life. Its influence has grown owing to its willingness to confront social change and the resulting legal ramifications. As well, it acts as an alternative to the arbitrary decisions of the lower courts, and it counters manipulation of the justice system by provincial and federal governments. The Canadian Charter of Rights and Freedoms, created in 1982 as part of our constitution, delegated the Supreme Court as the repository of judicial review of government actions and laws. The Court has willingly accepted its role as the arbiter of Charter-protected rights, and consequently its workload and importance have increased. When the Court agrees to hear a case, it reviews the records and invites written and oral presentations

from all parties involved in the case. While the Court gets hundreds of requests petitioning for appellate review, only about 100 cases are selected to be heard annually. These cases usually involve some aspect of case or statute law, or an issue of national importance. As is the case with other appellate courts, a majority decision is sufficient to prevail as a verdict in the Supreme Court, and in most instances transcripts of both majority and dissenting opinions are provided. The federal cabinet may also request a ruling from the Supreme Court on a matter of constitutional importance. This special role tends to further the power and influence of the Court with respect to law and the political structure of Canada.

Trial and Case Resolution

While the rules of procedure and evidence governing criminal prosecution in the court system are complex, one of the most important and fundamental principles is the **presumption of innocence**. In our judicial system, the defendant is considered innocent until either convicted or acquitted. The role of the Crown is to prove guilt; the onus is not on the accused to prove his or her innocence of the charge. Two further tenets of our justice system are that a person cannot be held criminally responsible for an act committed owing to a mental disorder, and planning or attempting to commit a crime is a criminal offence punishable by law. Crimes are also divided into two categories. **Summary conviction offences** are less serious types of crimes, and **indictable offences** include more serious crimes, such as murder, robbery, sexual assault, kidnapping, or fraud.

The Decision to Go to Trial

In most provinces the police lay the criminal charge, and under the discretionary clause, the recommendation is to proceed only if there is a reasonable prospect of conviction and if pursuing the charge is in the public interest. Although the police usually lay the charge, that decision will normally be either ratified or rejected by the **Crown attorney**, the prosecutor who acts on behalf of the government in prosecuting an indictable charge. Crown prosecutors represent the attorneys general of the provinces, or in the case of federal prosecutions, the minister of Justice. Their responsibilities include presenting to the court all of the evidence gathered by the investigative police officers, disclosing all facts to the defence, and maintaining an impartial role as officers of the court. The police officer lays out the information pertaining to the charge before a justice of the peace, outlining the alleged infractions of the Criminal Code that the accused has committed. Should the justice of the peace accept the bona fides of the charge (that the charge is made in good faith), then several options are in place to ensure that the accused will appear in court for the trial. In the case of less serious offences, the justice of the peace issues the accused a notice to appear in court and defend the charge. In more serious cases, the police will issue an arrest warrant. After arrest, the decision must be made whether to release the defendant on bail or detain him or her in police custody. The Charter of Rights and Freedoms protects Canadians from arbitrary detention and presumes that release from police custody after arrest will be the norm. Only if the police have reasonable grounds to believe that the accused will fail to appear in court or that it is in the public interest to detain the accused, will detention withstand a Charter appeal on the grounds of arbitrary detention.

The Bail Reform Act of 1976 established a legal framework to provide for the release of the accused from custody. Bail is considered to be an urgent necessity for the accused, as otherwise they could lose their jobs, leading to the financial ruin of themselves and their families. Furthermore, when submitted to lengthy pretrial incarceration, defendants will have more difficulty retaining legal services or assisting in preparing their defence. The literature is replete with evidence that pretrial incarceration creates a presumption of guilt and a self-fulfilling prophecy, with conviction and a prison term the inevitable outcome. As a result of these reforms and Charter protections, the majority of those arrested for Criminal Code violations today are granted some form of bail. However, if the suspect fails to attend the trial, the security will be forfeited, and a warrant will be issued for the suspect's arrest. While continued detention without bail is no longer the norm in the court system, the Supreme Court has upheld the right of the Crown to object to bail when the suspect has been charged with an indictable offence after having been previously released on bail for a separate indictable offence. Furthermore, the Court has ruled that the onus is on the accused to establish that they should be granted bail when they have been charged with trafficking in or importing narcotics.

For summary conviction offences, the Criminal Code sets out clear rules for trial and conviction. Accused persons should appear in person before a judge, but they may have a legal representative appear and plead on their behalf. The vast majority of these offences are heard in provincial court. More than 75 percent of all cases examined in the Toronto provincial courts were dispatched with three or fewer court appearances, with sometimes no more than five minutes for each court appearance.

The Criminal Code states that unless specifically expressed by law, those accused of indictable offences should be tried before a judge and jury. However, exceptions provided in the law have become so common that it is today rare for an accused to be tried by a judge and jury. In the main, indictable offences fall into three categories. In the first category are the most serious offences, including murder. The Criminal Code allows for persons charged with these offences to be tried by a superior court judge without a jury, provided the judge and the provincial attorney general both agree on this approach. The least serious of the indictable offences in the Criminal Code, which include theft, fraud, and embezzlement, are heard by the judge alone. A catch-all category of offences also exists—these include armed robbery, sexual assault, attempted murder, and dangerous driving. This last type of situation allows the accused to choose trial either by judge and jury or by judge alone.

All those accused of an indictable offence first appear in provincial court. If the offence falls into a category to be tried in provincial court, it continues there to its conclusion. Others will be moved to the superior court, depending on the severity of the offence. However, it is important to note that before these cases are forwarded to the superior court for trial, a provincial court judge must conduct a **preliminary inquiry** to determine whether there is sufficient evidence to warrant a committal of the accused for trial. The preliminary inquiry is an important phase in our criminal court process. The purpose is not to establish the guilt or innocence of the accused, but rather to find out whether the Crown has sufficient admissible evidence to result in a guilty conviction when presented in a trial. Both the Crown and the accused have the right to call and cross-examine witnesses. However, while the Criminal Code provides for an elaborate mechanism under which a preliminary inquiry can be conducted, the actual preliminary inquiry is usually a perfunctory examination of the case. Furthermore, in more than three-quarters of cases, inquiries last for less than a day. The judge conducting the preliminary inquiry has two options at the conclusion of the hearing. Based on the evidence presented, the judge can order the accused to stand trial for the offence charged or substitute another charge. As well, the accused can be discharged if the judge believes that on the basis of the evidence, the Crown has presented an insufficient case. The goal of the Crown is to make a prima facie case (one with enough evidence to make a judgment), not to prove the guilt of the accused in the preliminary trial. As a result of evidence provided at the inquiry, the Crown can change the nature or severity of the charge, illustrating the power of the Crown in our justice system.

The Criminal Trial

The actual criminal trial before a judge and jury is a well-choreographed affair. Both the Crown counsel as prosecutor and the **defence counsel** make opening statements to the judge and jury, in which they outline their respective positions and evidence. While no evidence is presented at this stage, the goals of the defence are to poke holes in the Crown's case and to present support for the defendant's alibi or character. The presentation of evidence is the centrepiece of the trial, and the Crown counsel marshals the prosecution's case. The Crown counsel's purpose is to prove the guilt of the defendant, and the evidence can be of two types—direct and circumstantial. **Direct evidence** is factual documentation, such as wiretaps, videos, photographs, or testimonials by eyewitnesses. **Circumstantial evidence** is not as clear-cut, and the judge and jury will have to evaluate its veracity. Unlike direct evidence, such as physical material, weapons, fingerprints, or recorded confessions, circumstantial evidence includes such things as a witness who saw the accused running from the scene of the crime or who heard the accused threatening the victim on a previous occasion. In today's modern criminal trial (especially in Canada), DNA evidence is becoming a major tool of forensic detection in connecting the accused to the victim, even though eyewitnesses may be lacking.

Judges have the important role of deciding which evidence a jury will hear. In making this decision, the judge also needs to ensure that a jury will not be biased as a result of the content or presentation of evidence. An error in allowing or disallowing the use of evidence can be grounds for an appeal of the jury's verdict, particularly by the defence in the wake of guilty verdicts. Schmalleger et al. (2004) note that witness testimony is the major tool by which evidence is introduced in court trials. Witnesses can include victims, investigative officers, the defendant, and, in today's courts, experts from specified fields. Whether to call the accused as a witness is a major issue for defence lawyers to broach. The defendant's right to remain silent and refuse to testify is protected under both common law and the Charter of Rights and Freedoms. Furthermore, the Supreme Court of Canada has ruled that if a defendant refuses to testify, prosecutors and judges should refrain from commenting on this fact, other than to instruct a jury that silence does not equal guilt. It is the duty of the Crown to prove its case, with or without testimony from the accused. All witnesses can be cross-examined by the other side, and the purpose of the cross-examination is to verify the witness's credibility and memory of the events. The hope of the lawyer conducting the cross-examination is to find discrepancies in the testimony of the witness and discredit the evidence that is being presented. In some instances, witnesses perjure themselves or knowingly make untrue statements in the courts, leaving themselves open to criminal prosecution. Furthermore, if perjury is proven in a court trial, the witness can damage the case in the eyes of the jury and affect the trial's outcome.

Plea Bargaining

Plea bargaining is a process whereby the defendant, prosecutor, and defence counsel negotiate a plea of guilty. While it can occur prior to the trial, it also can occur during the course of the trial when the defendant and defence counsel believe that a more lenient sentence could be brought about more expediently by negotiation than by allowing the trial to continue. In most instances, a plea bargain involves a reduction in the severity of the charge and the sentence. As well, in the case of multiple charges some of the charges could be stayed or withdrawn and only the main charge prosecuted. In the process of plea bargaining, the prosecution and defence often make a joint submission to the judge on an appropriate sentence, and while judges do not have to accept the recommendation, in most instances they do. Plea bargaining obviates the need for a lengthy trial to resolve a criminal case, and is based on the premise that such an outcome is in the best interests of all parties. Schmalleger et al. believe that prosecutors benefit by a quick conviction without the necessity of committing large amounts of time and financial resources to the case. The defendant and his or her counsel benefit by having multiple charges withdrawn, thus reducing defence costs, and a lesser sentence is obtained.

While the parties to the court process see plea bargaining as an essential and effective mechanism (and one that prevents the breakdown of the criminal justice system), public opinion of the practice is usually negative. As Schmalleger et al. note, the classic example of a plea bargain—the receipt of a 12-year prison sentence for a guilty plea to manslaughter by Karla Homolka in exchange for her testimony against her husband in his first-degree murder trial—was viewed by the public as a grave injustice. To the public, this husband and wife pair were sadistic killers who should have both been convicted of first-degree murder, and it was a travesty that she plea bargained her way to a manslaughter conviction. In a 1996 public opinion survey, the Law Reform Commission found that over 79 percent of respondents strongly disapproved of plea bargaining. They felt that both society and the victim are not served when the offender is able to plead to a lesser charge. It has been suggested that judges should become involved more openly in the process—then the public would be more convinced in the legitimacy of plea bargaining. As it stands, most people believe that the prosecution and defence get together in informal deal-making and decide on a plea and sentence. The reality of the coercive power of the state in fact makes the plea bargain often more favourable to the prosecution than the defence, and most defence lawyers believe that their clients plead guilty to the lesser charge because they are convinced that the state would obtain a guilty verdict even though the evidence might not support the charge. From this perspective, the public's perception of a defendant getting away with a lighter sentence may not reflect reality. How the courts function is critical to the efficient operation of the criminal justice system. The reality of our courts' operations means that it's impossible to achieve full trials of all cases—the resolution of criminal cases through negotiation is a fact of life in the court system. Maintaining a balance between the speedy resolution of cases and obtaining justice for defendants and victims is the challenge that the courts face in the plea bargain process.

The Jury Process

At the conclusion of the criminal trial, both sides make their closing arguments. This is a process of summation, review, and analysis of the evidence. For the prosecutor, the purpose is to hammer home the evidence presented and prove the guilt of the accused. For the defence counsel, the purpose is to discredit the prosecution's evidence and case and cast doubt in the minds of the jury members. If the accused has not taken the stand, the defence also must convince the jury that this should not be perceived as a reason for a guilty verdict. In cases of circumstantial evidence, the defence will want to show the lack of direct proof of the accused's guilt. Finally, before the case goes to the jury for deliberation, the judge's role is to outline the main evidence as presented and to remind the jurors of their duty to be objective and impartial in reviewing the evidence. In his or her charge to the jury, the judge will also outline the various verdicts that the jury can return, the burden of proof that the Crown must show, and of the need to return a unanimous verdict. The jury, after receiving its instructions from the judge, often retires to the jury room and begins deliberating. Jurors can from time to time request additional transcripts of the evidence or further clarification of the rules of evidence or legal issues from the judge. While in most instances juries return their verdicts within hours or days, in more complex cases this process can last weeks. If a jury, after a long period of deliberation, informs the judge that it is unable to reach a unanimous verdict, the judge can discharge the jury and order a new trial. Judges have also been empowered to attempt to break deadlocks by using every persuasive technique to clarify the evidence for jury members who cannot accept the reasoning of their colleagues. However, the Supreme Court of Canada has stated that while judges can attempt to prevent hung juries, a juror should not be coerced to change his or her mind simply to conform to the majority opinion.

Critics of the legal system point to the jury system as one of its main weaknesses. They believe that the ability of the jury to sort through the evidence and accurately determine a defendant's guilt or innocence is questionable. These critics assert that when faced with increasingly complex legal issues, many jurors not only do not understand trial court language and practice, but also may not even understand the instructions or charge from the judge. Furthermore, in highly publicized cases, it is difficult to separate emotions from fact. With today's increasing use of technical evidence and expert witnesses, it is not surprising that jurors could be lost as to the importance of legal technicalities or could fail to comprehend the expertise of expert witnesses. The calling into question of jury members' impartiality was brought home to the public by the obstruction of justice trial of Gillian Guess, in which it was found that while part of the jury for a murder trial, she was having a sexual affair with one of the accused. Moreover, fellow jurors told the court that Gillian Guess bullied and badgered her colleagues into bringing in a not guilty verdict.

Alternatives to the current system could be to hold the trial before a panel of judges or to use professional jurors, who would be trained in the necessary skills, such as due process, objectivity, and observation. However, the concept of a "trial by judge and a jury of one's peers," which comes from centuries of British jurisprudence, is difficult to eradicate. As well, this right is enshrined in section 11(f) of the Charter. While there is room for improvement in the selection, training, and maintaining of the quality of jurors, our view is that the system does protect society from arbitrary justice and bias.

Appeal

At the conclusion of the trial and the finding of guilt or innocence, either the prosecution or the defence can appeal the court's decision. Appeals can involve questions of law or fact, and there are different appeal procedures for summary conviction and indictable offences. An appeals court has various options when a case is presented before it. If it believes that there is no merit to the appeal, it may decide not to hear it. Alternatively, it can hear the appeal, discuss it, and direct that the offender be acquitted or order a new trial. In most appeals, it is not the conviction that is appealed, but the sentence. In this case, the appeals court could uphold the sentence, reduce the sentence, and in rare occurrences increase the sentence. In some instances, it could substitute a lesser conviction and commensurate sentence. In many cases, the appellant will apply for bail while the appeal is heard. Because in the bail hearing the appeals court examines the sentence and evidence, frivolous appeals for bail solely to avoid incarceration are uncommon in the Canadian court system.

The final arbiter of the appellate system is the Supreme Court of Canada. The Criminal Code provides for appeals to the Supreme Court of the decisions of the lower courts of appeal. The right of appeal must relate to a question of law, and it is automatic if a judge of the court of appeal has dissented in the judgment. As well, the accused can obtain the permission of the Supreme Court to appear to argue a question of law. The Crown can also use these same grounds to appeal a decision of the appeals court.

Youth Criminal Justice

One of the startling facts about modern Canadian society is the high rate of crime perpetrated by our youth. While young people between 12 and 18 years of age account for 10 percent of the population, they commit 20 percent of violent crime, and the number of youths charged with homicide increased by 10 percent from 1995 to 1998. While violent crime committed by female youths is considerably less common than for males, the rate for female property crime increased faster during this period than for their male counterparts. Statistics also show that guns were involved in a higher percentage of violent crimes among youths than adults. We should note, however, that the majority of criminal activity by youths involves property crime—the highest occurrences being theft, break and enter, and motor vehicle theft.

By the beginning of the twentieth century, the criminal justice system understood that a more effective and humane way of dealing with delinquent youths was to separate their handling in the justice system from that of adults. Schmalleger et al. (2004) note that the transition to youth courts was not immediate. It was not until the passage of the Juvenile Delinquent Act of 1908, and amid widespread disagreement as to how juveniles should be treated, that juvenile courts were established nationally. The philosophical principles of those early juvenile courts included the belief that children were worth saving, and that non-punitive treatment was beneficial. Judges were granted wide discretion in handling cases, and children in youth court were to be protected from the stigmatizing effect of formal judicial hearings. Court hearings were to be private and the names of youths and their identities were to be protected. For justice to be effective, rulings had to be individualized and non-criminal outcomes were best instituted if primary considerations were to be the needs of the child. In addition, the Juvenile Delinquent Act specified that delinquents were to be kept in custodial facilities separate from adults. While the intent of this legislation was to remove youths from the criminalization process, by the 1950s child advocates believed that the system was not working. The total power given to the courts had not shown a decrease in acts of delinquency, and the rehabilitation process had not delivered. Critics also believed that the power to allocate indeterminate sentences often made for harsher rulings for youth than for adults convicted of the same offence. By the 1980s, a widespread debate on the future of youth justice raged in Canada. With an increase in youth crime, high youth unemployment, and a cry in the streets for law and order, the government enacted the Young Offenders Act (YOA) in 1984. This legislation was a compromise between the benevolent welfare model and the "get tough" law and order model favoured by the police and some justice officials. The YOA standardized the age of young offenders at 12 to 17 years, defined criteria and procedures for a diversion from court, mandated the use of legal counsel, and permitted youth courts to issue only determinate sentences. The goal of the YOA was to ensure that in court the youth would be allowed full equality before the law, including legal counsel. Going forward, trials would be held before a judge without a jury, and if the offence were serious and indictable, and the offender 14 years of age or older, the case could be transferred to adult court. Because of public protests as a fallout from the widespread perception of lenient sentences in youth court, amendments to the YOA allowed for tougher sentences, greater enforcement of the laws, and a shift toward the crime control model of youth justice. The shift in judicial decisions from a rehabilitative to a punitive model has been seen by the increase in long-term sentences, with the rate of custody in Ontario the highest in the nation. However, probation designed to provide supervision of youth offenders in the community is the most frequently used type of punishment. For critics, this community-based type of program is ineffective. They cite high recidivism rates as examples of the ineffective role of probation officers in providing supervision and counselling for troubled youths. These law and order advocates believe that institutionally based programs can be more effective than community-oriented ones.

One of the important questions that society seeks answers to is why violent behaviour among our youth has increased in the past decade. The availability of weapons (including guns), the rapid growth in our urban centres of youth gangs, and an increase of hate crime initiated by youth gangs, are all part of youth criminal activities today. Gang-related youth violence is a phenomenon of our times. Modern youth gangs are often involved in illegal drugs, extortion, and robberies. Also, guns are the weapons of choice, and drive-by shootings are increasing in our urban centres. In addition to Aboriginal gangs, our large cities increasingly have youth gangs who come from all social classes, cultures, races, and ethnic backgrounds. Schmalleger et al. note that efforts to control youth gangs have included youth service programs, improved community policing, and drop-in centres for troubled teenagers. The pressure to belong can often overtake rational behaviour in many of our young people.

One of the saddest aspects of modern society and the family as an institution is the large number of teenage runaways and homeless youths in our midst. Of these, almost 66 percent leave home because of physical and/or sexual abuse, and 33 percent because of emotional abuse. Studies show that the majority of these youths who remain on the streets for longer than two weeks will resort to theft or prostitution as a means of support, and 20 percent will come into contact with police and social services agencies. Mental health issues, drug use and abuse, and increased teenage suicide are common in this group of street kids. The tragedy is not only that thousands of our children are living on the streets and turning to criminal behaviour, but also that the conditions of oppression, normlessness (anomie), and sexual and physical abuse in the home are the driving factors behind teenage runaways.

While youth crime is a complex phenomenon, there are some common characteristics that can be documented. Broken homes, poor role models, inadequate parental supervision, poor interpersonal relationships, inferior education, and poverty are all strong indicators that problem families and delinquency and youth crimes are related. Change must involve all components of the community, including schools, families, neighbourhood groups, law enforcement, courts, and employment agencies. Families are the backbone of children's early socialization, and the values instilled can be instrumental in later life. Finally, the impact of the peer group cannot be underestimated. Young persons' friends have a large role in shaping behaviours—parental monitoring of their children and friends' behaviour is crucial to the supervision role.

Youth Criminal Justice Act (YCJA)

In February 2002, the federal Parliament passed the **Youth Criminal Justice Act (YCJA)**, which replaced the Young Offenders Act. The new YCJA builds on the strengths of the YOA and introduces major reforms that were highlighted by critics of the YOA. The hope of the YCJA is that a fairer and more effective youth justice system is now in place that meets the needs of the youth population as well as the wider public. Over the past 20 years, many problems and issues relating to the youth justice system have been documented. The major criticisms include the fact that, contrary to public perception, incarceration of our youth is endemic. Canada has the highest youth incarceration rate in the Western world, including the United States. Because the system does not make a clear distinction between serious/violent and less serious offences, the courts have allowed disparities and unfairness in youth sentencing to perpetuate. In many situations, the effective reintegration of young persons after release from custody has been an abysmal failure. Because of a failure to adjust to the community norms and values, recidivism becomes the norm. The Youth Criminal Justice Act attempts to address these and other shortfalls of the youth criminal justice system. It should be noted though that government legislation, while important for setting the stage for effective change, is just one of many variables that are necessary for successful reform. For example, community crime prevention efforts, including community policing, public education partnerships with schools, child welfare, and mental health agencies, are all essential ingredients that must come together in local communities. One of the important goals of the Youth Criminal Justice Act is to ensure that the society recognizes its responsibility to address the developmental challenges and needs of young persons. Only if communities and families work in partnership to address the underlying causes of youth crime, and provide guidance and support aimed at reintegration into the community, will success at amelioration occur. While acknowledging the hurt and concerns of victims, and their right to be part of the rehabilitation process, the youth justice system must change its modus operandi—only the most serious deviant behaviour should be its concern, and the overreliance on incarceration must be curtailed. Another critical goal is to ensure that the YCJA and youth system reflect the fact that young persons lack the maturity of adults. For example, procedural protections should be increased, and rehabilitation, reintegration, and timely intervention emphasized. In terms of interventions, the goal should be reinforcing respect for societal values, encouraging reparations, and respect for gender, cultural, or ethnic differences. Victims' rights are to be respected and, similar to the situation with parents' rights, they have the option to participate in court hearings.

In keeping with the research findings suggesting that causation of youth crime is multi-variant, it is central to the 2002 YCJA that all those involved in youth behaviour modification be party to group-conferencing on a given case. The goal is for expertise to be disseminated to all parts of the justice system, be it to police officers, judges, prosecutors, or youth workers, to help with decisions on appropriate measures for a case. This expertise can include appropriate extra-judicial measures, conditions for release from pretrial detention, appropriate sentences, or plans and methods for integrating the young offender back into the community after detention. Ideally, the conference will involve some form of restorative justice for the victim, as well as the coordination of methods for assisting the troubled youth.

In addition, if under the charge laid a custody sentence is unlikely, then the judge is required to release the young offender to a relevant protection authority until the case is heard. The presumption is that the young person is not a danger to the public. As a final alternative, even if the charge is sufficiently serious that a custody sentence may be the outcome upon the finding of guilt, the onus is on the judge to undertake a search for a responsible adult to take care of the young person until the trial date. These measures are strong incentives for the justice system to minimize pretrial detention of youths and reflect the provisions of the Criminal Code that pretrial detention be minimized. Past youth justice acts have been criticized for not clearly delineating the purposes or principles of sentencing, and for the fact that principles were generally inconsistent and not prioritized. Because judges were not given clear legislative direction in sentencing, actual sentences could differ markedly in severity for the same offence. In particular, research has shown that Canada has one of the highest rates of incarceration in the Western world, and that custody sentences can range from a low of 5 per 1000 youths in Quebec, to 25 per 1000 youths in Saskatchewan. As well, the youth incarceration rate was not only higher than the adult rate, but for eight of the most common offences in youth court, young offenders received longer periods of custody than adults would for the same offence. The vast majority of custodial sentences for youths have been for non-violent offences, such as shoplifting, minor theft, breach of probation, or possession of stolen property. The most calamitous fallout from the old YOA was the large number of first offenders guilty of minor theft who were sentenced to custody terms.

Under the Youth Criminal Justice Act, all of these criticisms have been addressed. The YCJA provides specific sentencing guidelines, and emphasizes that the purpose of youth sentences is to hold young persons accountable through appropriate sanctions. These should ensure meaningful consequences and promote youths' rehabilitation and reintegration into society. Also, youth sentences will not be more severe than for adults, and the goal must be the reintegration of a young person into mainstream society. The young person should acknowledge his or her responsibility for the crime and the harm perpetrated. Under the sentencing guidelines of the new YCJA, a custodial sentence can be awarded only for violent offences, serious indictable offences, or for the failure to comply with non-custodial sentences. Where the judge believes that it would be impossible to avoid imposing a custodial sentence, reasons must be provided for this exceptional action. As in cases before regular adult courts, the special circumstances of Aboriginal youth are stressed in the YCJA, with the directive that all other avenues should be exhausted before custodial options are considered. This proviso has been instituted because of the extraordinarily large numbers of Aboriginal youth in custody. Youth court judges have also been given more options for sentencing. These would include a reprimand for minor offences or attendance orders, and commanding a youth to attend rehabilitative or educational sessions. The YCJA calls for a more intense support and supervisory system, with a smaller caseload for probation officers and more support to encourage behavioural change. Should there be the need for intensive rehabilitative custody based on repeat serious and violent offences, or mental psychological or emotional problems, the YCJA ensures that an appropriate program be found. The goal is to provide an individualized treatment plan that would facilitate rehabilitation. The practice of sending a 16- or 17-year-old charged with a serious criminal offence (such as murder or attempted murder) to adult court and sentencing the young person as an adult has been changed in the YCJA. Now, the youth court determines the guilt or innocence of the youth, and under specific circumstances the court can request an adult sentence. The YCJA sets as the standard for pronouncing an adult sentence that the ruling would be a sentence sufficient to hold the young person accountable. If the youth sentence is of sufficient length to provide accountability, then the court must impose a youth sentence.

Finally, one can note that a marked strength of the new YCJA is its many provisions to assist in the youth's reintegration into the community. The focus of a custodial sentence must be on providing a release and sustainable program that encourages the youth not to reoffend. For serious offences, part of the sentence must be custodial and the rest community service. While the risk to reoffend is always possible, supporting and addressing the youth's needs and setting out a reintegrative plan with effective programs is essential if successful re-entry is to occur. Under the YCJA, the criteria of placement must always be the least restrictive level of custody and a separation of youths under age 18 from adults in custodial facilities. It has always been the practice that the identity of young offenders should be protected, since publishing the name could impede rehabilitation efforts. Only if a youth court has imposed an adult sentence can identifying information be published. As an analysis of the new YCJA has shown, its provisions seek to achieve a fairer and more effective youth justice system. Outlining measures to ensure that less serious cases are handled outside the court process, it also provides for a fairer sentencing process, a reduction in the high rate of youth incarceration, and a more effective reintegration of young offenders back into society.

Sentencing and Alternatives

On conviction under the Youth Criminal Justice Act, the youth court judge will order a predisposition report, which is mandatory before a custodial sentence can be imposed. The judge then has a range of options for the disposition or sentencing. For most youths, a non-custodial sentence is the norm. Schmalleger et al. (2004) note that the most common disposition is probation, with 50 percent of offences handled in this way. This often means that the youth is released into the custody of a parent or guardian and will be compelled to undertake education or skill-upgrading courses or counselling, with the normal probation period being 12 months. Fines and community service comprise roughly 10 percent of the sentences. While the idea of restitution to the victim fits in well with the new emphasis on victims' rights, the reality is that few youthful offenders can pay a fine, so community service is the next best thing. When taking into account that some probation sentences also include community service, this is becoming increasingly important as a sentencing option. These will include service to parks and recreation departments, food banks, or charitable and volunteer organizations. Lately, youth court judges have been advising victims that they can pursue parents of guilty youths in small claims court to recover damages. On the one hand, the goal is to instill a sense of parental responsibility and authority, but, on the other hand, this could elicit unfair punishment of parents. Because many of these parents are poor and/or single, this measure could exacerbate family problems and also defeat the purpose of having youths held responsible for their own actions. There is considerable criticism of probation and community-based programs by those who advocate stricter justice for youths. However, the concept of rehabilitation that drives the YCJA must ensure that a sufficient number of probation officers is provided to ensure supervision and counselling to troubled youths. While the media highlight high recidivism rates, the success stories of youth who go on to reintegrate into society receive little fanfare.

Thirty-five percent of youth court dispositions are to open or secure custodial centres, such as a youth centre or training school. Open custody could include group homes or community residential centres. Secure custody facilities such as youth detention centres are operated by provincial governments.

Youths confined to secure custody normally receive a maximum sentence of two years, but in first- or second-degree murder convictions the sentences can be as long as six years. The youth court judge is often walking a tightrope between the common public perception of too lenient sentencing and a Youth Criminal Justice Act that has as it goal rehabilitation and reintegration into the community. For first-time offenders, probation and community service remains the norm. However, for repeat offenders, who account for more than 45 percent of youth court cases, custodial sentences have increasingly been called for.

The purpose of alternative measures and diversion programs is to facilitate the reconciliation of victim and offender, to compensate the victim and most importantly to avoid a formal hearing in youth court. The goal is to allow the young offender to be rehabilitated in the community and to avoid the stigma of being labelled a criminal. All alternative measures programs across Canada are designed to allow young people to take responsibility for their criminal behaviour, to meet with their victims, and to work out mutually satisfactory methods of restitution.

The major objectives of these programs are to reduce the number of cases that come before youth courts, to bring about a positive change in the attitudes of young offenders, and to lower the rate of youth crime and recidivism. Young offenders in Ontario who have been exposed to alternative measures programs show marked improvement in attitudes toward victims and in recidivism rates. Further diversion programs are usually less expensive than the courts, and since this a fairly new alternative to youth court, it is imperative that sufficient time is given for evaluation. It is clear that reverting to a more punitive deterrent model for youths will in the long run have a negative impact on rehabilitation, and slow the re-entry of young offenders into mainstream society.

Jones and Krisberg (1994) comment on the complexity of problems facing our youth today. Broken homes, poor parental supervision, poverty, low self-esteem, poor interpersonal relationships, and peer group pressure can all be contributors to delinquency and, later on, adult criminality. The development of programs that involve all parts of the community, including schools, social service agencies, neighbourhood groups, and law enforcement officials, are of critical importance. The phenomenon of rising numbers of street kids shows a strong correlation between physical and sexual abuse at home and runaway kids who soon fall into a pattern of drug abuse and violence. The societal goal should be the creation of a home environment where parents and children share emotional involvement and common values, with a subsequent positive socialization. In this complex modern society, youth problems will be ever-present, and society must utilize all available tools to alleviate these problems.

Diversion and Alternative Measures Programs

The purpose of alternative measures and **diversion programs** is to facilitate the reconciliation of victim and offender, to compensate the victim, and, most important, to avoid a formal hearing in youth court. The goal is to allow the young offender to be rehabilitated in the community and to avoid the stigma of a criminal label. All alternative measures programs across Canada are designed to allow young people to take responsibility for their criminal behaviour, to meet with their victims, and to work out mutually satisfactory methods for restitution. This process also allows young offenders to perform community service and to attend counselling and treatment programs. As well, early intervention programs have as their goal the prevention of criminal behaviour in youths who may be at risk but who have not committed a serious criminal offence.

The major objectives of these programs are to reduce the number of cases that come before youth courts, to bring about a positive change in the attitudes of young offenders, and to lower the rate of youth crime and recidivism. As well, these programs cost less than the court process. Because these programs have been operating for a little over decade, it is imperative that society allow sufficient time for evaluating their operations. Reverting to a more punitive and deterrent-laden model for youths will have in the long run a negative impact on rehabilitation, and it will hinder the re-entry of youthful offenders into society.

Conclusion

The issues discussed in this chapter occupy a central role in an analysis of the Canadian criminal justice system. The criminal court and trial are the basis of our democratic principles of fairness and justice. The adversarial process that pits the Crown against the defence, with a judge and or jury being the final arbiter of justice, is based on centuries of jurisprudence. While there are weaknesses in the court structure and process, nothing that has been advocated can improve on the peer-based fact-finding process of our judicial system.

That our youth have special status and courts to adjudicate their deviant conduct is as it should be. In our changing society, with increasing challenges to established institutions and norms, it is not surprising that deviant and criminal behaviour among youth has been increasing. The easy availability of drugs; the decline of the family as the major socializing agent in society; and the increase in family violence, abuse, and breakdown have all contributed to societal deviance. Faced with increasing youth crime rates and more serious violations by youth of the Criminal Code, the justice system has been forced to reconsider its goals and purposes in terms of youthful offenders. Diversions and other alternatives to custody measures are being criticized as failing to reduce recidivism rates among delinquents. While recognizing that the challenge to find answers to increasing rates of violent behaviour among youth is daunting, we believe that the only long-term method for success must remain rehabilitation. Closed custodial incarceration only exacerbates the institutionalization process, creating a social system based on violence, exploitation, and a subculture of learned deviant behaviour. A punitive approach may appease public opinion, but it fails to address the underlying causes of non-normative behaviour in our young people.

Summary

The Canadian court system is a complex network of provincial and federal trial and appellate courts, and at the apex is the Supreme Court of Canada. Provincial courts are located in most Canadian cities—they have the power to hear all criminal cases, as well as small claims and business and family disputes. The superior provincial courts hear more serious criminal cases. Federal courts hear cases falling under the Federal Court Act and usually involve tax, immigration, and administrative tribunal matters. Each of these courts allows motions to the appeal division, and the Supreme Court of Canada can decide to hear cases from any of these jurisdictions if they pertain to a constitutional or legal interpretation issue.

Whereas the police lay charges, it is the role of the Crown attorney to review the evidence and decide if it justifies prosecution. The Charter of Rights and Freedoms protects all citizens from arbitrary detention and provides for the right to bail and a fair trial. Because of the crowded court docket, plea bargaining is becoming increasingly common. In this process, the Crown and the defence together decide on a common plea and sentence, which they present to the judge. However, in the case of serious criminal offences, a judge and jury trial is still the norm. In this situation, it is the duty of the Crown to prove the defendant guilty, and it is the role of the defence counsel to poke holes in the prosecution's case. Regardless of the verdict, the decision can be appealed to the higher court, either on grounds of law or fact.

Juveniles have always been treated differently in the courts of Canada, and today the Youth Criminal Justice Act is the guiding principle for the administration of juvenile justice. The goal is the rehabilitation of the offender and diversion from the formal court system. For more serious offences, the youth is allowed full equality before the law, including legal counsel. As in most situations involving criminal justice, there is continuing debate as to whether youthful offenders should be punished more severely, such as by long periods in detention centres. The public pressure is for increased enforcement and retributive justice. However, because of the complexity of the causes of youth deviance, any policy that hinders the re-entry of offenders into the wider society will be counterproductive.

Key Terms

circumstantial evidence (p. 142)

courts of appeal (p. 137)

Crown attorney (p. 139)

defence counsel (p. 141)

direct evidence (p. 142)

diversion programs (p. 153)

Federal Court of Canada (p. 137)

indictable offence (p. 139)

plea bargaining (p. 142)

preliminary inquiry (p. 141)

presumption of innocence (p. 139)

provincial courts (p. 136)

summary conviction offence (p. 139)

superior courts (p. 136)

Supreme Court of Canada (p. 138)

Youth Criminal Justice Act
   (YCJA) (p. 148)

youth court (p. 136)

Discussion Questions

1. Plea bargaining is an increasingly important part of the court system. Discuss the pros and cons of this practice.

2. Discuss the success of alternative measures programs for young offenders.

3. What are some of the factors that have led to calls for a review of the current jury system?

4. Discuss the various stages in a criminal jury trial.

Weblinks

www.lexum.umontreal.ca/index.epl?lang=en This site, hosted by the Law Library of Canada and Quebec, provides links to Canadian judicial websites, including the Supreme Court, the Federal Court, and provincial courts.

www.rand.org/pubs/monograph_reports/MR699-1 RAND, a public policy research institute, has posted the complete text of their report, *Diverting Children from a Life of Crime: Measuring Costs and Benefits*. The report is conveniently posted as separate chapters, and with figures and tables also provided as a separate file.

canada.justice.gc.ca/en/ps/yj/index.html The Department of Justice hosts a youth justice website, with links to relevant legislation and articles on the topic.

www.brooksandmarshall.com/lobby.html The First Line Criminal Law Information, a web resource provided by a Canadian private firm, offers articles on such topics as being arrested and charged under the Criminal Code and dealing with police searches and seizures.

CHAPTER 7

Corrections

Objectives

- To acquaint readers with the criminal justice process in Canada from charge to trial to sentence.
- To outline the principles that underlie sentencing decisions in Canada.
- To describe the plea-bargaining process and its objectives.
- To explore the trial process, including the role of the prosecution and defence attorneys.

From Charge to Trial

Once a crime has been committed and a suspect apprehended, the police lay charges. In Canada, charges are laid by the police, as opposed to the US system where the office of the district attorney charges suspects. The police conduct an investigation of the crime and then propose to charge the suspect with one or more offences. They may also find that there is insufficient evidence to pursue a successful prosecution. Finally, they may find that evidence exonerates a suspect(s) (e.g., "ironclad" alibis or other forms of irrefutable evidence that indicate innocence). It is quite common for police to "upcharge" or to "overcharge" suspects. Upcharging means charging a suspect with a more serious crime. In cases of homicide, for example, the police may upcharge in order to strengthen the position of the Crown prosecutor when plea bargaining. If, for example, the evidence does not support a charge of premeditated murder, police can switch to the lesser charge of manslaughter. It is much more difficult to charge a person with a more serious form of a crime once an initial charge has been laid, and this practice would be unfavourably viewed by judges. Overcharging can also involve adding a series of charges to the offence(s) with which the accused is being charged in order to ensure that a conviction will be possible on at least some of the charges. It is also advantageous to the Crown in plea negotiation to have numerous charges with which to construct a deal, as the Crown may decide to drop some charges in order to focus on others.

Television viewers are familiar with the guarantee of rights, referred to as the *Miranda warning*, which is issued to suspects upon arrest in the United States. Police officers are compelled at the point of arrest to warn suspects that they have certain rights, including the right to remain silent, to contact an attorney, and to have an attorney appointed if the suspect cannot afford one. The rights of Canadians who are charged by police are contained in the Charter. Fundamental among these rights is the right to life, liberty, and security of the person. All Canadians have the right to know the reasons for their arrest or detention. They also have the right to counsel. Police must inform suspects of the specific charges being made against them. Further rights guaranteed by the Charter include

- the right to have a trial conducted in reasonable time;
- the right to avoid self-incrimination;
- the right to be considered innocent;
- the right to obtain a jury trial;
- the right not to be denied bail without just cause;
- the right to avoid double jeopardy (being tried twice for the same offence);
- the right not to be submitted to cruel and unusual punishment; and
- the right to have an interpreter during the trial.

BOX 7.1

WHAT IS A "REASONABLE" AMOUNT OF TIME TO WAIT FOR A TRIAL?

The lapse of time between charge and trial may be several years in the case of a serious offence. Cecilia Zhang, a young Toronto girl, was kidnapped from her home and murdered in late 2003 by a 21-year-old visa student, Min Chen. He wanted to remain in Canada, and sought to extort $25 000 from her parents in order to enter an arranged marriage to keep himself here. According to his allocution, he inadvertently suffocated Cecilia in a panic when she cried out for assistance. Chen's trial, held in May 2006, did not take place for more than two years after the initial offence. In your opinion, is a lapse of several years a "reasonable" amount of time before the commencement of a trial for a serious crime? You may want to consider the amount of scientific analysis and legal preparation that is required by both the Crown prosecutor and the defence to present their cases. Do you think there should be specific guidelines that govern the amount of time allowed before a case comes to trial? In Canada, cases must not be unreasonably delayed. A major delay occurred in the case of *R. v. Askov*, which caused an uproar. Following the Askov situation, a great number of cases were dismissed because of unreasonable delays.

In Britain, recent legal amendments have removed the right of the accused to remain silent. The courts in Britain now interpret silence to mean that the individual is revealing guilty knowledge of the crime committed. The right to silence is important because those accused often give incriminating information to the police in the hope that the charges will be dropped if they just "explain" everything and then can go home. Readers familiar with the television program *The First 48* have been privy to detectives' interrogation of homicide suspects. In this fascinating glimpse into the world of interrogation, it is readily apparent that most suspects will, without a lawyer being present, answer police questions in order to demonstrate their innocence in a criminal matter. This is a foolhardy approach in a system which is adversarial in nature, and in which detectives are well trained in obtaining incriminating evidence, particularly when lawyers are not present. For some accused, this offering of information reflects their nervousness at the time of being charged and the human desire to communicate, even when it is not in their interest. Peter Demeter, a Mississauga contractor who murdered his wife, hired a leading criminal attorney to handle his case. The lawyer requested a $10 000 retainer and then indicated that he would give Demeter $10 000 worth of advice. That advice was simply to say nothing to the police. However, Demeter thought himself cleverer than the police and invited detectives into his home for drinks, all the while talking about his relationship with his wife and his theories about the crime and how it might have been committed. Eventually, he managed to talk himself into a life sentence in prison for her murder (Jonas & Amiel, 1978).

Following arrest, most people are released until the date of their first appearance before the court; thus, the individual is generally free to remain in the community for several months. For the small number of offenders who are charged with extremely violent crimes, or who present a substantial risk of fleeing from the jurisdiction, or are repeat offenders, the court will require remand to a jail or detention centre. Accused offenders are given a notice to appear, which states the time, date, and place of the trial. As well, those accused must present themselves at a police station to be fingerprinted before their court appearance. If the police decide not to arrest the person at this time, they may still do so at a later date by asking a judge to issue an arrest warrant or a summons to ensure that the individual will be in court on the appropriate date. If the individual fails to appear for the court date, an arrest warrant is issued, which allows the police to pick the person up and bring him or her to a jail pending a hearing.

Some offenders are brought before a justice for what is termed an *initial hearing*. This is an opportunity for the charges that are being laid to be read to the accused. The initial hearing is a short process and is adjourned until the accused can obtain legal counsel to assist him or her in the case before the court. When counsel is present at the initial hearing, a number of courses are open to the prosecution:

- In cases of a summary or a minor indictable offence, a plea from the accused may be taken.
- A trial date can be set when a plea of not guilty is registered.
- A preliminary hearing may be set for more serious charges.
- The accused is required to select the manner of trial, either before a judge sitting alone or before a judge and jury. If the accused elects for a trial before a provincial court judge, he or she can make a plea at this time. If the accused chooses a trial before a superior court judge, sitting either alone or with a jury, a preliminary hearing date must be set.

Preliminary Inquiry

Under Canadian law, in cases of serious offences a preliminary inquiry must be held before proceeding to a full court trial. The preliminary inquiry serves to determine whether the prosecution can produce sufficient evidence to warrant proceeding to a full trial. This process has two functions: it eliminates the need for costly trials when there is flimsy evidence against the accused, and it protects the right of the individual not to be subjected to a full criminal trial with all its stresses when a strong case cannot be made. The process is surprisingly similar to a full trial. The prosecution presents evidence to demonstrate to the judge that there are sufficient grounds for a full trial. As in a full court trial, the prosecution will also call all relevant witnesses.

The role of the defence attorney is also the same in a preliminary inquiry. This procedure allows the defence to cross-examine the witnesses, understand the strengths and weaknesses of the prosecution's case, and evaluate the quality of the witnesses and evidence that will be brought to bear against the client in the event a full trial is warranted. This evaluation of the evidence is important if it is obvious that a trial is warranted, since it allows the defence to formulate a trial strategy. The accused's attorney also presents witnesses and evidence. While those accused have the right to take the stand in their own defence at this hearing, they rarely do so. Unless the accused can provide an ironclad alibi—for example, "I was in England at the time; here is my plane ticket, hotel bill and other receipts, and pictures of me in front of Buckingham Palace with the Queen on the 24th"—it is usually wise to observe silence until the trial. Hearing the evidence against them and the witnesses for the prosecution may assist the accused's lawyer in presenting evidence at the full trial, where it will have the greatest impact and may come as a surprise to the prosecution. At the conclusion of the presentation of the evidence, the judge must determine whether there are sufficient grounds to commit the case to a full trial or whether the defendant should be discharged. Any case can be committed to a full trial without going through a preliminary inquiry at the discretion of the prosecutor.

The Criminal Trial

Jury trials are rare in Canada. A jury trial is a costly process, particularly when the case is before the courts for an extended period of time. While the O. J. Simpson case was instructive in some aspects of the criminal trial process in the United States, it would be atypical in Canada. Plea bargaining is the most common way of resolving charges in the criminal justice system (see the section on plea bargaining later in this chapter). Cases that proceed to trial typically involve contentious issues of evidence, a higher level of complexity, a truly innocent accused, or the prospect of lengthy jail time when there is no plea bargain available or offered.

Juries are selected randomly from the tax assessment or voter registration lists of communities within the court's jurisdiction. Once chosen, jury members are sent a notice by the sheriff's office to register for jury duty or to provide sufficient reasons for why they cannot serve. Certain professionals are excluded from jury duty, including police officers, criminology professors, and members of the clergy, reflecting the fact that they may exert undue influence upon other jury members' decisions.

A jury in Canada consists of 12 people. Those selected for jury duty are examined to determine their suitability. The prosecution, the defence, and the judge question prospective jurors to ascertain their willingness and ability to sit fairly in judgment. A person who admits to being prejudiced against the accused, to having already formed an opinion for any reason, or to being unable to judge the case on the evidence put before them in the court is dismissed. When a case is highly controversial and has received a great deal of pretrial publicity, the defence and prosecution may issue a considerable number of challenges before they select a jury. Many lawyers now employ specialists who advise them of jurors whom they believe would be more sympathetic to their clients or might find in their favour. Lawyers may base their challenges on the information these experts pass on to them. This portion of the criminal trial is known as *voir dire*.

An artist's sketch of a jury. Most Canadian courts do not allow photographs to be taken during the proceedings.

The Courtroom Proceedings

Once a trial commences, it takes the form of a complicated human drama governed by strict rules of procedure. Over the years, television dramas like *Perry Mason* and *Law and Order* have given Canadians a perspective on criminal trials that is not based in reality. Trials are rarely sensational, as courtroom observers will attest. Although the evidence given may be shocking, such as in a murder trial, the daily grind of a trial is typically formal and dry. The prosecution is required to present a full case against the accused and to prove guilt beyond a reasonable doubt.

The trial is an adversarial process, rather than a truth-seeking forum, despite the famous protestations of Johnny Cochrane and Marcia Clark during the mid-1990s trial of O. J. Simpson for the murder of his former wife Nicole Brown. The prosecution brings witnesses to the stand and presents evidence and any other materials that may be legally placed before the court to secure conviction. The defence attorney is required to provide the best possible case, short of breaking the law, in protecting his or her client according to Edward Greenspan (Greenspan & Jonas, 1987), one of Canada's most high-profile defence lawyers. The defence attorneys will cross-examine witnesses, challenge testimony or witnesses where appropriate, and do essentially all that is within their legal powers to secure their client's release by creating a reasonable doubt. "Beyond a reasonable doubt" implies not that all doubts of innocence are erased, but rather that the evidence before the court is sufficient to find the accused guilty.

There are few surprises in the conduct of a criminal trial. There are no last-minute confessions from the stand, there should be no manipulation or mis-direction of the process by judges, no speeches by the defence or prosecution when cross-examining witnesses. The judge ensures that due process and fair play are observed by both sides. In some instances, failure to follow simple rules of procedure will result in the judge ordering that evidence be struck from the court record and the jury ignore the evidence presented, or it may result in a mistrial. A mistrial occurs when procedures are severely flawed, the evidence is insufficient to warrant a defence being made, or evidence has been misleading, making it impossible to reach a fair verdict. After the judge declares a mistrial, a new court date may be set by the prosecution if sufficient grounds for proceeding still exist.

Opening Statements

Both the prosecution and the defence present opening statements to the judge and jury, if present in the trial. In their opening statements, both sides hope to present an overview of their cases and alternative theories of what actually occurred. The opening statement is key because if it is not followed through in the trial, serious consequences may ensue in the form of an unexpected verdict. The O. J. Simpson trial is a model of how *not* to present either a defence or a prosecution case. Vincent Bugliosi, a prominent criminal trial attorney who prosecuted the Manson family (and hundreds of murder cases in Los Angeles), demonstrates in his book on the case, *Outrage: The Five Reasons Why O. J. Simpson Got Away with Murder* (1996), that in his opening statement defence attorney Johnny Cochrane promised to present a number of witnesses and pieces of evidence that were never delivered. The prosecution neglected to point this omission out in its summation. This was a significant error that Bugliosi contends contributed strongly to the acquittal of Simpson. In most trials, this failure of the defence to follow through on the opening statement could easily have resulted in doubt about the defence's credibility being placed in the jury's mind. A key witness who was promised is never called. Does this mean that the witness did not want to testify? Was Mr. Cochrane not being truthful? Does this mean that he is not truthful about other matters? Did this witness have evidence that would have shown the accused's guilt? Questions such as these reveal how central a good opening statement is to a successful case. Judges and juries want to be shown a road map and to be led down it. Only poor preparation makes the opening statement unreliable.

The opening statement is an opportunity for the attorneys to red-flag certain evidence or testimony as crucial. If an attorney states, "Watch for Mr. X—his testimony provides a solid alibi for my client," you can bet that the jury will perk up when Mr. X is called to the stand. If, on the other hand, he never takes the stand, doubts will be raised. The opening statement also provides the defence with an opportunity to remind the jury that the burden of proving guilt is on the prosecution and to instruct jurors on how they can acquit the defendant. The prosecution is likely to emphasize the serious nature of the offence and the responsibility of the judge and jury to see that justice is done.

The Calling of Witnesses

The prosecution's case includes the calling of witnesses, usually police officers; experts; and witnesses who can provide information on various aspects of the offence that is under consideration by the court. The prosecutor questions the witnesses on what they have seen or heard directly. Information about someone that a person hears from another party is considered hearsay and is not permitted to be entered into evidence (see Box 7.2). As well, the opinions of most witnesses have no place in a criminal trial. However, experts with proven credentials in areas of specialization, including psychiatry and forensics, may present expert opinions to the court, as long as the opinions are based on direct scientific inquiry, an interview with the accused, or physical evidence that has been examined. Examples of expert opinions include blood-splatter analysis, crime scene analysis, and firearms testing.

BOX 7.2

ADMISSIBLE AND INADMISSIBLE HEARSAY EVIDENCE

Not all hearsay is inadmissible in a court of law. In his important book on the subject, *Canadian Evidence Law in Nutshell*, noted legal scholar Ronald Delisle addresses both sides of the hearsay issue. There are several dangers to hearsay evidence that underscore why it is only allowed in very specific situations. First, if a witness were giving evidence he or she heard from a third party, it could not be tested by lawyers on either side if the person of origin for the information were not in court. Second, how would one determine if the author of the evidence was being truthful? Third, what are the powers of perception of the original person who viewed the actions or heard the words now before the court? Finally, did the witness now in court understand the meaning of the words as the originator of the statements intended them? In most cases, these questions cannot be answered and therefore the evidence must be excluded.

In some cases, hearsay evidence may be admitted. Here are some of the exceptions to the general rule that hearsay evidence cannot be introduced into a trial:

- If there is an admission—in other words, a statement made by a party when tendered by the opposing party.

- When an accused does not reject an accusation as false, their failure to deny it, when a reasonable person would have done so, will be admitted as evidence of an implied admission.

- The acts or statements of co-conspirators may be admitted since they have been involved in a "common purpose" under the law.

- If a person makes a declaration against his or her interest, this may be admitted.

- A dying declaration may be admitted if it is given when it is clear in the mind of a testifying individual that death is close at hand.

Source: Adapted from *Canadian Evidence Law in Nutshell*, Ronald J. Delisle. 2002: 83–98.

After the prosecution has directly examined each witness, the defence attorney engages in cross-examination. For people who have never appeared at trial, this is a most stressful and anxiety-provoking experience. The defence has the task of trying to clarify or "shake" the witness's testimony through a series of carefully considered questions. Following the preliminary hearing, the defence should be aware of the witnesses they will confront and of the points that the witnesses were unclear or seemingly unsure about. Skilful cross-examination can tie a witness in knots and thus cast doubt upon his or her testimony. Witnesses who are considered unreliable, including criminals, drug addicts, alcoholics, paid police informers, and people who have been granted special consideration for their testimony, will receive rough treatment, at least verbally, from a skilled attorney.

Once the prosecution has presented its case in full, it "rests" its case, and it is now the turn of the defence. The defence calls witnesses to build its case in a parallel manner to the prosecution. Following the presentation of the defence's case, the prosecution may present rebuttal witnesses. These witnesses are intended to refute the testimony or evidence presented by witnesses for the defence. For example, if a witness claims to have been with the defendant at the time of the crime, the prosecution can present a rebuttal witness who knows that the witness is lying. The defence may, of course, also examine these witnesses.

Closing Arguments

Following witness testimony, the prosecution and the defence present closing arguments. Both sides restate their cases, either for innocence or for guilt, presenting the evidence in a way that is most favourable to their arguments. The defence presents its arguments first, followed by the prosecution. During these statements, the attorneys are prohibited from commenting on any evidence that was not presented at court. It is at this point that they can make a powerful statement to the jury if there is a chain of evidence to support their contentions. Juries respond well to cases that are presented in an orderly and logical manner, in which the opening remarks, evidence, and closing arguments are cohesive. This presentation requires a great deal of thought and planning on the part of the attorneys. A measure of the research required to present a compelling defence is Edward Greenspan's assertion that when asking a question of a witness, one should always know the answer in advance (Greenspan & Jonas, 1987).

At the conclusion of the case presentation, the judge will give instructions to the jury. These instructions may relate to the type of charges that the jury is to consider—complex legal issues that the jury needs to understand or the type of evidence and standard of proof that are required as proof of offences. The judge's charge to the jury must not prejudice its decision, however, since that would leave the verdict open to appeal. The judge will normally discuss the *burden of proof* that the state's case must meet and the meaning of *reasonable doubt*.

The jury then retires to deliberate on the case. This process may take a few hours or days. The judge will normally call the jury back to the courtroom to inquire about its progress if there is a substantial delay. Members of the jury may ask to view evidence in order assist their decision-making. In a long trial, the jury may be sequestered. When sequestered, jury members are usually lodged in a hotel either for the entirety of the trial or for the period of deliberations. If they are allowed to return home in the evening, they are cautioned not to discuss the case with anyone.

If it cannot reach a decision, the jury is considered to be "hung." At this point, jury members are discharged from their duties, and the onus is on the prosecution either to bring or drop further legal action against the defendant.

In June 2000, convicted people began to be sampled for their DNA in the courts' holding facilities. Before sentence is passed, normally a period of time transpires during which presentence reports are constructed to assist the judge in finding an appropriate sentence. This stage normally takes place within a few weeks of the conclusion of the trial. Convicted people have the right to appeal the decision of the court. Usually, the appeal process is lengthy and may involve the appeals court or, if a significant legal issue is being decided, the Supreme Court.

In the next section we will explore the process of sentencing and its underlying principles in the Canadian criminal justice system.

Sentencing Options

Incapacitation

One approach to sentencing in Canada, **incapacitation**, involves imprisonment of offenders. Through separating offenders from society, protection is provided to law-abiding citizens. In some parts of the world, incapacitation may mean execution, the amputation of a hand to prevent pickpocketing, or similar punishments to prevent the repetition of a crime. A new form of incapacitation is electronic tethering or monitoring of offenders, who are confined to their homes. The philosophy guiding incapacitation is that confined prisoners will be unable to commit further crimes because they are isolated from society.

Historically, the British government took the issue of incapacitation one step further by removing criminals not only from civil society but also from the country itself. Under the transportation policy, convicted criminals were shipped to Australia, Africa, and the American colonies either to serve a term of imprisonment or to toil as indentured servants for five to seven years. By removing the criminal element from society, it was also felt that they would not reproduce more criminals. This approach punished prisoners by taking them from their families and loved ones and moving them into environments that the British

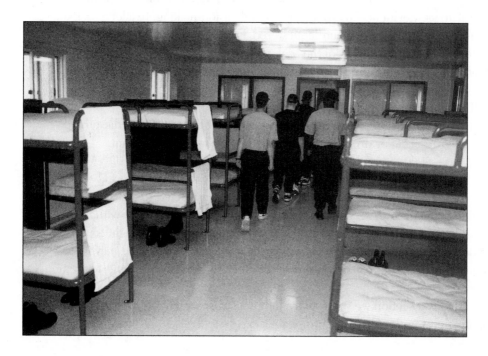

considered uncivilized and primitive. Transportation of offenders to America ended with the US Revolution and the severing of ties with England, particularly in matters related to the dumping of "undesirables" into the new republic.

Deterrence

Deterrence is the attempt to prevent crime by imposing penalties that are constructed to convince potential offenders that they will lose, rather than benefit, from committing criminal acts. There are two forms of deterrence: general and specific. General deterrence involves discouraging criminal acts through penalties, which induce in people the fear of punishment. Specific deterrence refers to inflicting punishments on specific individuals to deter them from future criminality.

Under this approach, it is assumed that people will be deterred after they rationally consider the potential punishment that awaits them. However, given the influence of drugs and alcohol and the frequent spontaneity of the decision to commit crime, it is unlikely that most criminals weigh the consequences of their actions. Furthermore, given the variability in sentencing decisions in Canada, it is also unclear how the criminal justice system could determine, in advance, the penalty to be imposed. The creation of mandatory minimum sentences, as suggested by Stephen Harper's federal government, could be argued by some analysts to provide offenders with a clear knowledge of the exact penalty for certain crimes since extra-legal factors (character, criminal record, or lack thereof, etc.) are not relevant. As well, although repeat offenders may be familiar with criminal law and the sentences typically handed down for specific crimes, deterrence appears to have little effect on first-time offenders.

With serious crimes, there is little doubt that individuals recognize that a severe penalty will follow apprehension. But does this knowledge affect their decision to commit crimes? Canadian homicide statistics, for example, clearly demonstrate that the death penalty or the lack of it is not a deterrent to potential murderers (Fleming, 2000). As a deterrent, the death penalty has two disadvantages: first, it has no effect on the rate of homicide, and second, it is irreversible. However, despite the knowledge gained from criminological analysis, a majority of Canadians, and certainly most policing agencies, support the reintroduction of the death penalty. Given the evidence, the death penalty can serve only as a retributive measure. It appears that the ideas of Jeremy Bentham were correct—that is, there must be a certainty that punishment will be imposed in order for it to be effective. Yet, because sentencing is variable and extra-legal factors may affect judges' decisions in imposing sentences, this end cannot be reached under current Canadian law. We must also understand that the majority of defendants, who are drawn disproportionately from the lower socio-economic classes, will have few resources to obtain the best quality of legal representation available to corporations or wealthy accused persons.

Rehabilitation

Rehabilitation is intended to provide opportunities for offenders to change themselves and thus avoid future involvement in crime. This approach involves training, education, and treatment programs that encourage offenders to develop a socially acceptable, productive, and law-abiding lifestyle.

The rehabilitative movement arose in concert with the increasing medicalization of deviance and crime after 1900. There can be little doubt that for some offenders rehabilitative programs are effective. However, it has been argued that high recidivism rates indicate the failure of this approach. In Canada, over two-thirds of offenders are estimated to reoffend following incarceration. Some critics have argued that no matter how high the quality of such programs, the community is structured in such a way as to promote failure for many ex-inmates. A more radical hypothesis would suggest that society views certain individuals and social groups, particularly those drawn from the lower socio-economic strata of society, as "social junk" to be constantly recycled for criminalization and imprisonment (Reiman, 2004).

Just Desserts/Retribution

Another goal of sentencing is to punish offenders for their crimes. The previously discussed sentencing approaches focus primarily on what the offender might do in the future or on the effect that various forms of sentences could have on them. The **just desserts** approach, however, focuses on the act or events that led the individual to be convicted. The underlying philosophy is that the criminal has benefited from the crime and now must pay society back for his or her misdeeds, presumably to make things "even." Under this principle, large financial penalties would be imposed for the crime of engaging in fraudulent business practices. In this way, the financial gains that offenders made from their illegal acts would be far outweighed by the fines imposed by the courts. However, while this measure appears on the surface to be reasonable, there are sentencing discrepancies that undermine its effectiveness. If our focus shifts to the area of environmental crime, the problem with this sentencing approach becomes apparent. Brady (1990), in examining the sentencing of individuals versus corporations for such environmental offences as dumping toxic chemicals into waterways and improperly disposing of toxic waste, found that individuals paid penalties roughly equivalent to those of corporations charged with similar offences. For corporations, therefore, the fines are merely a token amount. In cases such as these, the principle of just desserts may be better applied to individual criminal offenders than to corporations.

Restorative Justice

Restorative justice places the victim more centrally in the criminal justice system by focusing on the harm that the offender inflicts not only on the community but also on the victim. Victims have traditionally expressed dissatisfaction with the police and with the handling of their cases in court. For victims, crime is deeply felt and emotionally charged, and they often view their treatment by the criminal justice system as a second form of victimization. Victims report frustration at the failure of police to inform them of the status of their cases. They also often find it difficult to address the complex emotional and psychological issues that arise from their victimization. Since they have generally been unable to confront the perpetrators outside of the courtroom, they often report a sense of being denied justice.

The process of healing and closure for victims was finally addressed in recent Criminal Code of Canada amendments that permit victim impact statements (VISs) to be used in court (see Chapter 10, "Victims of Crime"). The VIS allows a victim the chance to confront an offender directly with the suffering his or her crime has produced and to influence sentencing options. Victims' rights have become an important element in Canada's justice system through a variety of programs, including the following:

1. *Victim–witness assistance programs.* These programs assist victims and witnesses in their journey through the criminal justice process.
2. *Victim funds.* These programs require offenders to pay into funds that compensate victims for medical expenses, physical or psychological damage, and wages lost as a result of victimization.
3. *Restorative programs.* These programs allow offenders to meet with victims. Restorative programs are useful in helping victims to deal with psychological trauma and in assisting criminals to understand the extent of the suffering they have inflicted directly on victims.

The judge and/or jury may consider all of the approaches listed above when imposing sentences. Historically, each approach has enjoyed a brief period of ascendancy. In the 1960s and 1970s, rehabilitation was a primary goal of sentencing. Rising crime rates in the 1980s and the perceived dissatisfaction with the rehabilitative movement led away from rehabilitation toward a more repressive model of punishment. Today, with the focus on the baby boom cohort, concerns over crime and fears of crime (whether grounded in reality or not) may come to dominate sentencing goals. In an era of conservative approaches to law and order, strict adherence to principles of punishment and responsibility will continue to be championed.

Sentencing Dispositions

In Canadian courts, there are generally five types of sentences or dispositions that the judges may impose upon conviction of offenders:

1. fines
2. suspended sentences
3. probation
4. incarceration
5. capital punishment

Fines are typically awarded in criminal cases involving minor crimes. Fines are also frequently combined with another sentencing alternative, such as probation. A **suspended sentence** may be imposed in cases where the court perceives that the offender needs treatment, rather than confinement. Under this form of sentencing, a sentence is handed down, but it is unenforced provided the offender commits no further crimes. Not only is it more effective and positive for some offenders to remain in the community, but also costs to the justice system can be reduced. Offenders who run afoul of the law because of persistent intoxication in public places are often granted this form of sentence, since jails are considered inappropriate for people who are considered to suffer from a recognized medical illness (Fleming, 1974). Supervision is rarely imposed upon the person; instead, failure to obtain proper treatment or rehabilitative intervention can result in the offender's committing a new offence, which will bring him or her back before the courts. At this point, the judge may order the offender to serve the original custodial sentence that had been suspended. Similarly, the judge may impose **probation**, commonly referred to as community supervision (discussed in full in Chapter 9, "Alternatives to the Prison System"). Under probation orders, the individual is required to report regularly to a probation officer for supervision and to abide by certain conditions in order to avoid returning to court. Incarceration removes the offenders committed of serious crimes from the community in order to ensure its protection. Capital punishment is no longer an option in Canada, having been abolished in 1976.

The Imposition of the Sentence

Imposing sentences is one of the key duties of judges. Juries do not have sentencing authority, but administrative tribunals may impose sentences in noncriminal cases.

In felony cases, sentencing is related to a wide variety of information that is available to the judge. As mentioned above in the "Restorative Justice" section, one of the most important sources of information is the victim impact statement, which emerged in the 1990s as a response to victims' rights advocacy. However, there is little evidence to support the idea that victim impact statements have a demonstrated effect on increasing sentences, owing to the strictures of law and the limited number of possible sentences that are open to judges. Instead, the process provides the victim with a form of active intervention and the offender with an opportunity to learn.

In considering the type of sentence that should be imposed, judges will often review a presentence report. These documents include the social, criminal, and personal history of the offender. Presentence reports also attempt to evaluate the individual's suitability for various treatment programs.

The imposition of sentence often involves conviction on more than one charge. The convicted person is sentenced on all charges. When the sentences are concurrent, they commence on the same day and end following the serving of the longest term imposed. For example, if an offender receives 3 years for carrying a concealed weapon and 10 years for armed robbery, after serving the 10-year sentence (less parole eligibility), he or she would be freed from confinement.

Another form, the **consecutive sentence**, is typically much more ominous than the **concurrent sentence**. In this case, the offender referred to in the above scenario would serve the 3-year sentence first, followed immediately by the 10-year sentence. The full length of the term if served would be 13 years. However, consecutive sentences are rare—they are usually reserved for offenders with a long record of serious crimes against people or for those who have committed several heinous crimes at one time. Given recent medical advances that have extended people's lives, some judges sentence particularly dangerous felons so that they will be held until the end of their natural (or extended) lives.

Factors Considered in Sentencing

Sentencing does not simply involve applying a fixed penalty to the offender. All Criminal Code offences carry maximum sentences. Misdemeanour offences carry a maximum sentence of two years less a day in confinement, served in a provincial institution, and/or a fine of up to $1000. Felonies typically invoke longer sentences of from 2 to 25 years, depending on the crime committed. However, it is rare for an offender to receive the maximum on being convicted for a first offence. A mandatory minimum sentence is imposed for several crimes: for example, first-degree murder and drug trafficking. In some US states, mandatory minimums are imposed for possession of even a very small quantity of drugs. Michigan, for instance, imposes a mandatory life sentence on people found in possession of little over an ounce of cocaine. While it could be argued that mandatory minimums have a powerful deterrent effect, it could equally be argued that they fail to take into account mitigating circumstances in sentencing. So, if a first-time cocaine user happens to buy slightly more than an ounce for personal use, believing it to be only an ounce, the judge would be forced to impose a life sentence with no possibility of parole. Many countries have strict prohibitions against possession of illegal drugs, and life terms and the death penalty are common sentences.

At the time of sentencing, the judge is called upon to consider a number of extra-legal factors. These factors may be grouped into two broad categories: mitigating factors and aggravating factors. *Mitigating circumstances* may be defined as factors that when considered individually or together justify a more lenient sentence. These factors diminish an offender's responsibility for a crime. For example, first-time offenders deserve consideration, given their lack of a criminal record. An offender who has performed community service, been responsible, and acted selflessly may be granted a lesser sentence. Old age or a pre-existing medical condition that requires monitoring also may influence a judge's sentencing. For example, the late Harold Ballard, a well-known entrepreneur and former owner of the Toronto Maple Leafs hockey team, received in the 1970s what many consider a lenient sentence for fraudulent business practices because he was ill at the time of sentencing. More frequently, the submission of a guilty plea results in sentence reduction, since a costly trial is avoided (Beddoes, 1989).

Aggravating factors are those that can increase a sentence. Obviously, a previous criminal record can have a negative impact on the sentence if the current offences are consistent with those committed in the past. For some offences, the judge seriously considers evidence of the offender's deliberation and planning, since these qualities reveal that the crime was not an impulsive action. Judges also may view particularly violent or prevalent crimes in their communities as warranting lengthier sentences. A Toronto case from a few years ago involved the carjacking of a prominent attorney and his wife. The assailants severely beat both victims. The judge handed down lengthy prison sentences of 16 and 18 years to the two perpetrators in order to deter others from committing similar crimes. Since carjackings are rare in Canada but common in many US states, the judge determined that an effective way to dissuade others from engaging in this behaviour was to be extremely harsh in sentencing. However, the question remains, How effectively is the sentencing publicized to would-be criminals?

Plea Bargaining

Plea bargains have been compared to game shows: they invite the offender to "make a deal." But are plea bargains a good deal for everyone? Do they circumvent the judicial process in allowing the Crown attorney to determine sentences instead of requiring a formal hearing? These are important questions, since society depends on the judicial process to provide due process to every person charged with a crime. Plea bargains have been known to account for as much as 90 percent of the criminal cases that come to the courts (Klein, 1976). It is a sad reality that most people charged with offences are, in fact, guilty. On the advice of defence counsel, they may opt to plead guilty in return for a reduced sentence.

The plea-bargaining process involves consultation between the defence attorney for the accused and the Crown attorney representing the state. The defence, typically meeting in the Crown's office, will suggest an appropriate sentence in private consultations. Again, *Law and Order* fans will be familiar with the plea process. Almost every episode of the television drama contains one or more scenes in which a defence attorney proposes a plea bargain to the prosecutor. In the real world, a period of negotiation follows until a sentence agreeable to both parties is decided on. In Canada, the accused enters a plea of guilty at court, after which the Crown offers a sentencing recommendation. The judge normally accepts the Crown's recommendation but is not strictly required to do so. Since judges, Crown attorneys, and defence attorneys work together in court on a daily basis, tacit co-operation is required to ensure the smooth flow of cases through the justice system. Accused people also benefit from providing evidence or testimony that results in another crime being solved and another person subsequently being convicted. While the criminal underworld considers turning a fellow criminal in a serious offence, the practice is quite common among career criminals. CrimeStoppers and TIPS programs, which allow individuals to benefit financially from anonymously turning in offenders, also have been highly successful.

The most famous plea bargain in Canadian criminal history was granted to Karla Homolka, the former wife of multiple murderer Paul Bernardo. Homolka benefited from her willingness to provide information as the only living witness to the torture and murders that she and Bernardo committed together. Rather than receiving a life sentence, which would have confined her to a prison cell for a minimum of 25 years for her part in three homicides, she was convicted of the lesser charge of manslaughter and received a 12-year sentence (which is reduced by parole eligibility). In 2005, Homolka was released from prison after serving her full sentence. While there were attempts to impose restrictions on her life after prison, including denying contact with victims' families, her legal team successfully argued against the legality of further restrictions. Homolka, having learned the French language while incarcerated, settled in Quebec.

Most experts and the public view sentencing as being differentially administered across Canada. Similar offences committed by relatively comparable offenders can produce widely varying sentences. Some criminologists believe that a movement toward structured sentencing would create both uniformity and fairness. Under this model, judges would have no discretion in the sentencing process. Crimes would have set penalties. Extra-legal factors would have no relevance in the process. This form of sentencing appears appropriate for very serious crimes. There are, however, serious drawbacks to its use. First, it does not allow for rehabilitative progress to result in an early earned release. Without incentives such as early release programs, it may prove difficult or impossible to motivate prisoners to engage in treatment or educational programs. Second, this form of sentencing denies consideration of the person's contributions to the community and lack of previous criminal behaviour. Third, given the size of the prison population in Canada, authorities would quickly be overwhelmed with prisoners whose release date could not be shortened for any reason.

Capital Punishment

Death is the most serious sentence that can be imposed on an offender. Capital punishment is no longer a sentencing option in Canada. The last executions in Canada took place at Toronto's Don Jail in 1962. Hanging was often employed in cases of capital murder between Confederation in 1867 and the repeal of hanging in 1976.

The repeal of the death sentence in Canada can be traced to several cases of wrongful execution in England and Canada. In Canada, both the Coffin and Truscott cases were central to this debate (see Chapter 9). One book in particular, *A Calendar of Murder: Criminal Homicide in England since 1957* (Morris & Blom-Cooper, 1963), was instrumental in demonstrating the often slim circumstantial evidence that could result in a death penalty. These two eminent researchers underscored the true nature of most homicides as tragedies of human weakness and frailty, rather than coldly calculated acts. The authors produced a short vignette on the details of each murder committed in England during 1960. Rather than displaying the ingenuity, callousness, and cunning of the homicidal foes of Sherlock Holmes, the average murderer acted spontaneously out of a fairly limited range of motives. These motives, including jealousy, anger, revenge, hatred, sexual infidelity, and greed, have also been documented by Canadian criminologist Neil Boyd (1989). Boyd argues that Canadians are most likely to be murdered in an argument or quarrel, reflecting the actions of desperate people in difficult circumstances. Offenders and victims in homicides are frequently under the influence of illegal drugs, alcohol, or a mixture of several chemicals. Since most murders are committed in the heat of passion, spontaneously and without deliberation, it rapidly became apparent to researchers, juries, officers of the court, and parliamentarians that death was an inappropriate sentence.

Conclusion

The principles of sentencing have remained relatively stable through countless centuries of the administration of justice. However, the principle of retribution, which once figured prominently in the sentencing process, has gradually given way to more informed and humane principles that more broadly serve societal interests—specifically, deterrence and rehabilitation. This move away from retribution is symbolized by the abolition of capital punishment in Canada.

The trial process in Canada includes both informal and formal interactions between the defence and the prosecution, with a view to resolving issues of guilt and innocence and determining sentencing. Plea bargains are common in the court process in Canada and represent a trend toward minimizing the use of formal trial procedures in determining sentences.

Summary

In this chapter, we have explored the correctional system, focusing on the issues behind sentencing and sentencing determinations. We have analyzed, in terms of their goals and effectiveness, the principles underlying sentencing in the Canadian justice system and their role in sentencing decisions. As well, we have discussed the goals of sentencing, including deterrence and rehabilitation, and have examined plea bargaining as a central component of the administration of justice in Canada.

Key Terms

concurrent sentence (p. 171)

consecutive sentence (p. 171)

deterrence (p. 167)

incapacitation (p. 166)

just desserts (p. 168)

probation (p. 170)

rehabilitation (p. 168)

restorative justice (p. 169)

suspended sentence (p. 170)

Discussion Questions

1. What is the purpose of the criminal trial?

2. How should sentencing goals be weighted in determining an appropriate sentence?

3. Which of the goals of sentencing is most important to society? Why?

4. What societal factors might be associated with the decline of the rehabilitative movement in sentencing?

5. What are the purposes of plea bargaining?

6. Should plea bargains be permitted in Canadian courts?

7. List three forms of hearsay that are admissible in a court. List three dangers associated with hearsay evidence that normally prohibit its use in a trial.

Weblinks

www.canadalegal.com/gosite.asp?s=1457 Written in plain language and with all legal terms explained, this article, by a Nova Scotia law firm, provides information on how an adult gets sentenced for a crime.

www.acjnet.org/splash/default.aspx The Canadian Association of Provincial Court Judges provides a link to articles on sentencing issues, with topics such as sentencing reform and dangerous offenders.

www.legalinfo.org The Legal Information Society of Nova Scotia (LISNS), committed to "helping Nova Scotians understand the law," provides a clear, easy-to-understand overview of what is involved in sentencing.

CHAPTER 8

The Prison System

Objectives

- To outline the historical development of prisons in Canada.

- To compare Canada's rate of imprisonment with that of other countries.

- To examine federal corrections in Canada.

- To distinguish between various security classifications in Canadian prisons.

- To describe life inside prisons and the inmate subculture.

- To explore significant issues concerning Canadian prisons today and in the future.

- To understand women's experience of prison.

The problem of how society will deal with those convicted of criminal offences in Canada is one that confronts judges daily. One of the most frequent sentences for offenders is imprisonment in a provincial or federal prison facility. Increasingly during the past 200 years, the justice system has embraced prisons as receptacles for unwanted Canadian men, women, and children. Criminologists have questioned the continued and increasing use of prison as the first choice among sentencing options (Morris, 1997). The "punishment industry," by which we mean the entire range of activities within corrections, is well funded by governments and seems to have an almost infinite capacity for expansion, in the view of some writers (Culhane, 1985, 1987). It may surprise you to know that by 2000, Canada had built over 60 federal prisons and over 100 provincial facilities—in fact, there are more prisons than colleges and universities in this country. Despite the number of these facilities, there are very few sources of information that allow Canadians to learn about life "inside." Only a handful of documentaries have been produced showing prison life, and very little media attention has been paid to the plight of prisoners and prison conditions. While Canadians will be familiar with calls to make prison tougher, increase sentences for violent crimes, or stories in the media arguing that prisons have a country club atmosphere, the average Canadian has almost no real knowledge of prisons. In one sense, as a society we don't want information on prisons, since we want them to house criminals away from us. For many, prisoners "deserve what they get" and prison conditions are of little concern to them. For some, prison sentences should be substantially increased for all offences since criminals are "getting off easy."

The reality of prisons and prison life in Canada is a much more complex series of issues than most Canadians realize. The above "get tough" sentiments have to be tempered by another area of widespread ignorance for most Canadians: the astronomical costs of keeping people confined. In this chapter, we want to present an overview of the prison system, its costs and benefits, and its role in the criminal justice system.

For many Canadians, prisons remain an enigma. Some view prison as a place purely reserved for punishment, while others stress its rehabilitative potential. It is a widely held belief that prisons are similar to social clubs where prisoners live a life better than many average citizens. The ability of convicted murderer Karla Homolka to pursue a university degree in prison is one issue that angers many Canadians who feel that prisons may reward criminal behaviour. Pictures of Homolka and other prisoners in the newspaper enjoying a social evening while inside prison angered many readers. Frustated by what they perceive as a system that appears to reward illegal behaviour, citizens cite their own inability to afford a university education in condemning educational and training opportunities offered to prisoners.

Few Canadians want to become educated about prisons; the prevailing view is that inmates should be apart from the rest of society. The majority of prisons are located in isolated rural areas far from major cities. Prisons, therefore, not only remove prisoners from society but also take them far from their communities, creating what might be thought of as double isolation for prisoners. Since our prison population is drawn in large measure from the poorest in society, the location of prisons in hard-to-reach locations means that many prisoners' families have difficulty visiting them.

What little Canadians know about prison life has generally emerged from television programs or movies that focus largely on prison life in the United States. The popular A&E documentary series *American Justice*, for example, has provided viewers with a view of US prisons and interviews with men and women, from minor offenders to those awaiting execution on death row. One dramatic view of prison life in Canada was provided in the training video shot by correctional services personnel when quelling a disturbance at the Kingston Prison for Women in 1995. This disturbing video featured naked women being beaten by male guards and left wet and virtually naked on cold prison floors. It was a vision that shocked Canadian sensibilities regarding the nature of imprisonment in their country.

In this chapter, we will examine the components of the correctional system in Canada. We will begin by focusing on the history of the prison system and its underlying philosophies of correction and control. Next, we will analyze the current population of the prison system and explore the key issues that face prisoners, including the prison subculture, violence, and suicide. Although men overwhelmingly form the largest portion of the prison population, we will also discuss women in Canadian prisons. We will then consider current and emerging crises in the prison system, including the housing of prisoners with HIV and AIDS and the difficulties that the growing geriatric prison population presents. We will discuss next the challenges of prison privatization and its relation to prison conditions. Finally, we will suggest alternatives to prison that have emerged in recent discussions among prison reformers, inmates, and criminologists.

The Evolution of Prisons in Canada

The first large houses of confinement in Canada were designed on the model of British institutions. Prisons were meant not only to physically confine those who required punishment and removal from society but also to symbolically represent the severity of punishment through the austerity and the sheer enormity of their scale. Few visitors or innocent passersby could fail to be forewarned of the severity of punishment upon viewing the first federal prison, opened in Kingston, Ontario, in 1832. Designed to accommodate long periods of confinement as the preferred method of punishment, it stood as a silent but ominous monument to the consequences of crime. Punishment had by this time largely moved from the public square into the privacy of the institution, and prisons provided an ideal location for attempting to transform those who failed to abide by the law. An ominous grey building constructed with grey limestone common to eastern Ontario, and reminiscent of cemetery mortuaries, it represented a form of living death for inmates, who lost their civil status and rights upon entry, effectively placed in a kind of purgatory far from civilization and its rules. Its aim was to produce fear in incoming prisoners, an important first step in the correctional philosophy of the era, ensuring an orderly institution, and to produce what Foucault (1977) referred to as "docile bodies," persons who did not think to challenge the existing order or the laws of society. Docility was produced with the denial of a person's freedom, arbitrary prison rules, harsh punishment, brutality from guards, and substandard living conditions.

The Kingston Penitentiary.

According to Curtis and Blanchfield's (1985) illustrated history of Kingston Penitentiary, in May 1849, George Brown, editor of the *Toronto Globe* (later *The Globe and Mail*) undertook an investigation of the conditions in the penitentiary. What he discovered was an institution where violence and human degradation were everyday events. Brown's investigators severely criticized the practice of corporal punishment, or whipping, which was inflicted on children who were incarcerated at the prison. But their concern was not echoed in either public or parliamentary intervention in the lives of these tortured youngsters. Curtis and Blanchfield report the cases of two children that are illustrative of the approach of the prison to discipline:

> Convict Peter Charbonneau [was] a ten-year-old serving seven years. The punishment book noted that Charbonneau's prison offences were of a trifling nature, like staring, winking and laughing—behaviour one would expect of a young boy. But for this he was stripped of his shirt and publicly lashed fifty-seven times in eight and a half months.
>
> There was also the case of Antoine Beauche, sentenced to three years in November 1845. The report notes that this eight-year-old received the lash within a week of his arrival and was given no fewer than forty-seven lashings in nine months.

Women convicts were not spared . . . One fourteen-year-old, Sarah O'Connor, was flogged on five occasions during a three-month period. Another, Elizabeth Breen, aged twelve, was flogged five times in four months. (pp. 42–43)

The food in this early prison was kept intentionally routine and dull. The food purchased at the local market was typically unfit for human consumption. Most meals were soggy and flavourless, as they were cooked in steam boilers. Bread was the staple of all diets but was reported to often be mouldy. Brown also reported on the numbing routine prisoners were subjected to:

Silently and obediently, day after day, week after week, year after year, the inmates at Kingston were supposed to shuffle along the corridors to their work every morning, their heads inclined at an angle that would prevent them from looking at the man ahead, work all day at a bench without making the slightest gesture to anyone around them, shuffle to the mess hall and eat meals that were calculated to keep them alive without appealing to 'luxurious' tastes and not communicating with anyone. (pp. 42–43)

The long-term impact of the so-called "silent system" was to break prisoners when they recognized that the numbing routine of the prison was unchanging, and that rebelling against it would be like throwing oneself head first into a stone wall.

Early prisons were home to all kinds of criminals and "misfits," mixing men, women, children, the mentally ill, and syphilitics together with dire results. Societal members viewed prisons in much the same way as they had previously viewed leper houses—as a holding place for all those who were "bad" and "evil." It was a place to isolate "social ills" from respectable society. One of the widely held ideas of the era was the belief that criminals were "born." The work of the early Italian criminologist Cesare Lombroso lent an air of "scientific" strength to this belief as he wrote and lectured throughout Europe on this idea. Upper and middle class persons were reassured that they were indeed "different" from the criminal classes, and that this difference occurred at birth. Given this idea, there was no use in attempting to rehabilitate "born" criminals; rather they must be properly isolated from society in prisons, transported out of the country, or killed. The first French prisons, had been located in former leper colonies. It is little wonder that prisoners became the new "untouchables" in our society. Prisons were places invested with mystery and terror, designed to instill fear and also to ward off public interest and criticism.

Over the first 100 years of its existence, the federal prison system in Canada expanded with the construction of 8 more institutions. Between 1950 and 1990,

16 more were built, double the number built in the first 100 years. Readers might want to consider whether this meant that there were more criminals in society, or more acts that became criminalized under the law. Perhaps it reflected an increasing focus on the use of prisons to deal with social problems in an increasingly violent society. There have been many points of view on the need for expansion of prisons at such a fast pace, and much debate about the reasons for this approach.

North American prisons, in general, were based on two significant approaches to punishment and correction in the nineteenth century. The first approach is referred to as the **Pennsylvania system**. Prisoners were relegated to small cells where they were to read the Bible (a somewhat difficult task for the many illiterates who occupied cells). They were allowed to exercise in a small yard for less than one hour per day. Heavily influenced by the Quakers, this approach to imprisonment kept inmates on their own, in a form of solitary confinement. While more benevolent than modern forms of complete segregation, this approach was also strongly connected to religious and moral ideals: inmates were supposed to contemplate their acts and repent.

The second major approach to imprisonment in the nineteenth century was referred to as the **Auburn system**. The architects of this system believed that hard labour was the path to reform of the convict. Prisoners were put to work performing jobs necessary to the functioning of the prison. They also worked in animal husbandry and agriculture to produce food for the inmate population. The Auburn system has also been referred to as the *silent system*, since prisoners were forbidden to speak to one another at any time. *Birdman of Alcatraz*, a film depiction of the life of Robert Stroud, contains scenes that show the "no talking" rules. Similarly, in the classic 1949 film *White Heat*, actor James Cagney's character breaks the silent system by screaming and smashing things in the lunchroom (and the heads of several guards) when other inmates whisper to him the news of his mother's death.

What also distinguishes this second system is that unlike earlier prisons and jails, the institution was built with *tiers* or *blocks*: multiple floors containing individual cells stacked one on top of another. This design was adapted from the original concept of British seventeenth-century philosopher and writer Jeremy Bentham. He proposed the construction of the **panopticon**, a circular, multi-tiered institution that would require few guards to maintain control. Tiers permitted guards to "lock down" segments of the prison, whole tiers, or individual cells. The tiers also allowed more prisoners to be housed in one building, as they were stacked rather than spread out. The Auburn-style prison was the model eventually adopted for the first Canadian federal prison in Kingston.

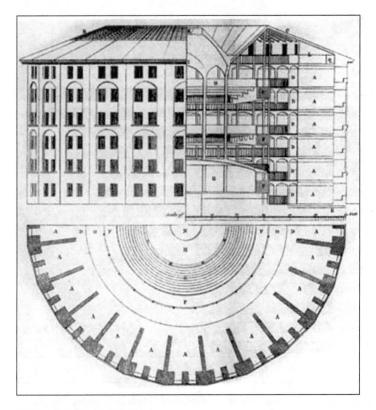

Jeremy Bentham's panopticon.

Prisons in Contemporary Canada
Rates of Imprisonment

Canada has a high rate of imprisonment among Western nations (see Figure 8.1 on the next page). The **incarceration rate**, which is the number of people jailed per 100 000 population, was 129 in 1997; 123 by 2001; and 116 by 2002 (CSC, 2005). The incarceration rate has been rising rather consistently since the opening of the first prison in Canada. However there are fluctuations that occur. Falling rates of imprisonment in Canada may seem to make sense. It could be argued that governments are becoming sensitive to the costs associated with imprisonment. We are likely seeing the impact of alternatives to prison and other forms of diversion from secure forms of custody. But comparisons with other countries indicate that Canada's rate of imprisonment has little to do with crime rates; rather, they reflect a country's policies toward dealing with crime.

FIGURE 8-1

NUMBER OF INMATES PER 100 000 GENERAL POPULATION

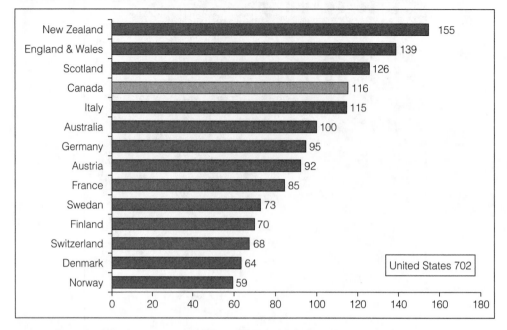

Note: The incarceration rate is a measure of the number of people (i.e., adults and youth) in custody per 100 000 people in the general population. Different practice and variations in measurement in different countries limit the comparability of these figures.

Source: US Department of Justice; Canadian Centre for Justice Statistics, Statistics Canada; Council of Europe; and the Ministry of Justice, New Zealand.

Switzerland (68) and Denmark (64) have rates that are almost half those of Canada. Does this mean that residents of these countries are less criminal than Canadians? Research would suggest that there is little difference in the respective levels of criminality in both countries; instead, the differences may be attributed to very different approaches to punishment. Countries with high incarceration rates have chosen through legislation and penal policy to use prisons as the major form of social control. The United States, for example, imprisons 702 adults per 100 000 population.

It would appear that there is an almost limitless capacity for societies to create and fill prison spaces. Empty prisons are not seen in Canada. However, the questions of what kind of society a high rate of imprisonment produces, and what kind of society produces high rates of imprisonment are troubling. If there are few alternatives to prison, rates can be expected to climb accordingly. Similarly, some criminologists would argue that the ever-expanding number of prisons has produced a **prison industry**. This industry is a huge employer of thousands of prison employees and tens of thousands employed in support industries. By 2005, the staff of CSC totalled more than 15 900 workers directly employed in the prison system. The total expenditures of CSC in 2003/04 was a staggering 1.5 billion dollars. Of this amount, fully $976 million was spent on salaries and benefits of employees, $100 million on capital expenditures and $435 million on operating costs (CSC, 2005). The many industries and services that support prisons' functioning would arguably add tens of thousands more employees. This figure would not include the thousands of persons involved in the criminal justice system whose work actually results in the imprisonment of Canadians. Criminals are the raw product required to keep the industry working and growing, if we accept this line of thinking. Consistently high incarceration rates in Canada over the past century also reflect the view of many small communities that prisons are a permanent source of jobs, prosperity, and community stability when few other economic opportunities exist.

A high rate of imprisonment leads to a considerable number of Canadians having criminal records. In 1998, Canada had an adult population of 23 086 400 (adults are persons over 18 years of age). By 1998, 2 617 380 Canadians possessed a criminal record. This is approximately 10 percent of the adult population, or 1 in 10 people. According to the CSC, the number of persons incarcerated in federal facilities as of April 11, 2004, was 12 034 men (2193 of these were Aboriginal) and 379 women (of which 108 were Aboriginal). This figure does not include children or provincial inmates. According to the CCJS, there were over 37 000 inmates registered in Canada's 151 provincial/territorial institutions and 48 federal facilities on October 5, 1996. Those who were between 20 and 39 years of age were overrepresented in this one-day snapshot of corrections. Interestingly, inmates were more likely to be unmarried, to have fewer years of education, and to be unemployed than the general population of Canada at the time of their admission. Most inmates had a previous record of conviction, with 83 percent of the individuals in provincial/territorial facilities falling into this category and 72 percent having served a previous term of incarceration in a provincial/territorial prison. In terms of offences, 73 percent of federal inmates were serving time for an offence against the person, in particular homicide/attempted murder and robbery. In provincial/territorial prisons, 33 percent of offenders were in prison for crimes against the person, particularly sexual assault and robbery. Table 8.1 on the next page profiles the total inmate population in 2004.

TABLE 8.1

PROFILE OF THE FEDERALLY INCARCERATED INMATE POPULATION,
APRIL 11, 2004

	MEN	WOMEN
Age Groups	**(12 034)**	**(379)**
Less than 18	5	—
18–19	125	6
20–29	3354	125
30–39	3889	138
40–49	2950	73
50+	1711	37
Serving a first federal sentence	7796	316
Length of Sentence		
Under three years	2746	140
Three to under six years	3422	117
Six to under ten years	1679	39
Ten years or more	1477	15
Life or indeterminate	2710	68
Offence		
Murder—first degree	693	16
Murder—second degree	1648	50
Schedule 1* (excluding sexual offences)	5837	214
Schedule 1 (sexual offences)	1814	9
Schedule II* *	1466	74
Non-scheduled	1828	44

Note: individuals may appear in more than one category
*Schedule 1 refers to sexual offences, and other violent crimes excluding first and second degree murder.
**Schedule II consists of serious drug offences and conspiracy to commit serious drug offences.

Source: CSC Canada, 2005.

Security Classifications

Prisons in Canada exist primarily to confine lawbreakers. Therefore, it is crucial, from a management perspective, that the risks associated with each prisoner be assessed at the time of their entry into prison through **security classifications**. The initial classification will likely be at a higher security level, and later, as a prisoner approaches release, a lower level of classification may be appropriate. Incoming prisoners are assessed for classification according to the risk they pose for escaping, for being a danger to other inmates or correctional officers, and for breaking the rules of the prison. Another factor might be the assessment of the harm offenders could pose to the community if they were to escape. A serial killer might show little interest in escape, for example, but if he or she were to escape, the danger to the community would be great.

Classification occurs after the parole officer assigned to the case reviews the details of the crime. The parole officer also reviews the offender's past record of offences and institutional behaviours (for repeat offenders). Upon the offender's entry into the institution, a placement officer conducts an interview with the new prisoner to assess the appropriateness of the institutional classification to the prisoners' needs. The placement officer reviews the inmate's previous record of behaviour (where it exists) and decides on specific programs, if any are available at the institution, of benefit to the inmate. People who require treatment for sexual offending can be directed to a prison that might not match their security classification but that would provide necessary treatment.

According to Ekstedt and Griffiths (1988), the CSC has developed specific definitions for three security classifications and a fourth, "mixed" category:

1. *Maximum security.* The prisoner is likely to attempt or complete an escape and poses the threat of committing serious harm in the community.

2. *Medium security.* The prisoner is likely to attempt escape but does not pose a risk of behaviour that would cause serious harm to the outside world.

3. *Minimum security.* The prisoner poses little risk for escape. If the prisoner were to escape, he or she would not cause harm.

4. *Multilevel.* The prisoners are from two or more categories and are mixed, owing to space constraints and to a need to encourage positive role modelling.

Table 8.2 breaks down the security classification of male and female inmates as of April 11, 2004.

TABLE 8.2

SECURITY CLASSIFICATION OF INMATES, 2004

SECURITY LEVEL	MEN	WOMEN
Maximum	1737 (14%), of which	36 (9%), of which
	367 (17%) are Aboriginal	13 (12%) are Aboriginal
Medium	7359 (61%), of which	170 (45%), of which
	1397 (64%) are Aboriginal	58 (54%) are Aboriginal
Minimum	2226 (18%), of which	140 (37%), of which
	318 (15%) are Aboriginal	27 (25%) are Aboriginal
Not yet classified	712 (6%), of which	33 (9%), of which
	111 (5%) are Aboriginal	10 (9%) are Aboriginal
Total	**12 034 (100%), of which**	**379 (100%), of which**
	2193 (18%) are Aboriginal	**108 (28%) are Aboriginal**

Source: CSC, 2005.

TABLE 8.3

REGIONAL DISTRIBUTION OF PRISONS IN CANADA, 2004

SECURITY LEVEL	ATLANTIC	QUEBEC	ONTARIO	PRAIRIE PROVINCES	PACIFIC
Maximum	1	3	2	1	1
Medium	2	5	5	1	3
Minimum	1	3	4	6	4
Multilevel	2	2	1	4	2

Source: CSC, 2005.

By 2004, the CSC, which is responsible for the operations of federal prisons, had 54 institutions in its system (two more than when the first edition of this book was written). These include treatment centres and annexes with various prisons. They also manage 17 community correctional centres and 71 parole offices across the nation. Additionally, they also manage five regional headquarters and staff colleges, what is termed *a correctional management learning centre*, an addictions research facility, and a national headquarters. The CSC also partners in 200 community-based non-governmental residential facilities across the country. Reflecting the concentration of Canadians in large urban centres, prisons are generally more numerous in provinces with larger populations (see Table 8.3). Currently, 5 prisons are open in the Atlantic region, 12 in Quebec, 14 in Ontario, 13 in the Prairie provinces, and 8 in BC. It is interesting to note that the three Prairie provinces share roughly the same number of prisons as Ontario despite their smaller total population. Several criminologists have pointed out that Aboriginal Canadians make up a disproportionate number of inmates in the Prairie system (Hylton, 1983). According to the CSC, Aboriginals made up 16 percent of the federal offender population in 2004 but only 3 percent of the Canadian population.

The number of inmates that each prison can hold varies from a low of 78 to a high of 501. The average capacity of institutions is 259 people. Minimum-security facilities are smaller, since there is an emphasis on preparing the prisoner for imminent re-entry into the community. There is a greater need at this juncture to monitor the inmate's behaviour. Minimum-security institutions house 121 people on average, while medium- and maximum-security facilities house 379 and 235 respectively. The majority of institutions are between 10 and 50 years old. Only 6 prisons that are over 50 years old are still in operation.

Prison Architecture

The four levels of prisons have very different physical structures. The architecture of each structure reflects the level of security required to ensure confinement of prisoners and their progress toward freedom in the community.

Minimum-security prisons have, at least outwardly, the appearance of college campuses. It is rare that any form of fence or wall surrounds them. Security levels are very low because inmates are near the point of return to the community. They have a lot to lose by attempting escape at a time so near to release. Few offenders are tempted to escape. The promise of light at the end of the carceral tunnel becomes, itself, a form of self-imposed wall. Prisoners do not even wear special clothing. Visitors would find that prisoners and staff are dressed similarly. While formal cells are not evident, prisoners are allocated private or semi-private rooms.

The emphasis at minimum-security facilities is on preparation for return to the community. Prisoners are encouraged to engage in life skills courses, which are designed to assist them in reintegrating into the community. Life skills classes focus on seeking employment and accommodation following release and on fundamentals for living on the outside. Given the subculture of prison life, with its own specific rules and argot, this is a time to relearn how to live in the outside community and to "shake off" the "joint." In other words, prisoners require time to adopt the language and interpersonal skills that will lead to success in the community.

Mixed institutions combine both minimum- and medium-security inmates. The mixed institution is an interesting and potentially positive development in correctional approaches. The advantage of a mixed institution is that it allows medium security prisoners to observe what awaits them as they move to minimum-security status. Given the influence of prison subcultures, there is the potential to create more positive outcomes for prisoners. The more positive aspects of the minimum-security designation can be seen as an inducement, perhaps, for inmates to focus on developing acceptable behaviours and on working toward their own release, as they can view release becoming a reality for other prisoners. This sense of the possibility of release prevents inmates from being further entrenched in the inmate subculture, which has little relationship to success upon release.

Mixed- and medium-security institutions are enclosed by chain link fences topped by barbed wire and razored wire. Prisoners have greater freedom in these facilities than in maximum-security facilities and may have access to educational programs, as well as treatment courses.

Maximum-security prisons are built with a focus on preventing escape. To deter escape, these prisons have high brick or wire fences and are equipped with electronic surveillance systems designed to prevent escape from the inside and rescue attempts from the outside. Prisoners' movements are highly supervised and monitored. Cell counts are conducted at various points throughout the day to ensure that all prisoners are on site and accounted for.

Protective custody units are also a part of maximum-security prisons. Often prisoners have to be protected from other prisoners because of the crimes that they have committed. Serial killers, including Clifford Olson and Paul Bernardo, are held in special sections of the building. Members of the general population of inmates are not allowed into these special units, which require more correctional officers per inmate in order to guard the prisoners. Inmates who require protective custody include those who have been or would be the targets of sexual or other physical assaults, or even murder attempts if they were to remain in the general population. Sex offenders are universally reviled in prison society because inmates have families outside of prison who are vulnerable to sex offenders. Rapists and pedophiles are at the greatest risk in prison.

Inmates who are "rats"—that is, who co-operate or give evidence against other inmates to the authorities—also require protective custody. In protective custody, they are safe from other prisoners but must spend 23 hours a day locked in their cells.

Solitary confinement is used in maximum-security prisons in order to punish prisoners who fail to obey institutional rules or who commit violence against others. There are strict rules concerning the use of solitary confinement as a form of punishment. However, Canada has had a poor record of abuse with this form of prisoner control. Several cases brought to the courts by prisoners have demonstrated correctional officials' willingness to place prisoners in "the hole" for periods of hundreds of days (Jackson, 1983). Segregation still remains a concern in 2006 according to the 2004/05 report of the correctional investigator.

Maximum-security prisons are holding places for people serving life and other long-term sentences for serious offences against persons and/or property. Treatment programs aimed at personal control, such as substance abuse and anger management programs, are often mandatory for prisoners in both maximum- and medium-security facilities. While there are a variety of programs available for inmates, including university degree programs, there is a distinct shortage of programs for prisoners who are serving long-term sentences (Fleming, 1995). Canadian prisons are not unique, however, in their inability to respond to the needs of "lifers" and other long-term prisoners.

Inside the Prison

Prisons emerged as a place of punishment. They are constructed both in terms of their architecture and the culture that develops inside to punish the inmates. From the time of John Howard's famous journeys to observe prison conditions in eighteenth-century Europe, there has been little to recommend prisons other than as places to be avoided. Prison means the loss of one's freedom, employment, family, and friends. It imposes a stigma on the individual upon returning

BOX 8.1

ISSUES IN THE COST OF PRISON

Consider the amount that is spent on each prisoner in Canada (see Table 8.4). Remember that in 2001 the Canadian Centre for Justice Statistics reported that there were 58 000 inmates in federal and provincial institutions, of which 25 000 were young offenders aged 12–17. Compare it to the cost of a typical undergraduate education. The four-year cost of an undergraduate degree for tuition, books, a computer and transportation is approximately $39 000 (excluding accommodation, food and ancillary expenses). It might be argued we would be better off financially and in terms of law and order if we simply sent inmates to university at approximately one-third to one-half the cost of imprisoning them. Also, remember that the additional annual cost of supervising a person on parole is $19 755 per year (CSC, 2005). Is prison "a luxury we can no longer afford?" If we found more cost-effective alternatives for a large majority of prisoners who are non-violent, the savings would be enormous. As a taxpayer, do you think this is a good use of your taxes, and would you like to spend tax money to help build more prisons and put more offenders inside their walls?

to society that makes reintegration into the community difficult. Some prison critics have referred to prisons as garbage pails for society (Fitzgerald, 1986).

Prison was seen to have a rehabilitative function, at least in the stated philosophy of prison officials during the last 150 years. Recently, however, penal administrators have begun to admit that there is no reality behind the rhetoric. The prison system, for historians like Michel Foucault, is merely a mechanism of circular elimination. By removing unlawful individuals from our society, prisons also effectively removed their plight from public view and attention. While the costs of imprisoning people are very high and continue to rise, we accept the costs as the price to be paid for not having to deal with the problem of crime in our communities. Again, the prison remains a place of punishment and control into which the public rarely has the chance, or the desire, to gaze.

TABLE 8.4

THE COSTS OF IMPRISONMENT IN CANADA

Women	$150 867 (multilevel security)
Men	$110 223 (maximum security)
	$71 640 (medium security)
	$74 431 (minimum security)

Source: CSC, 2005.

Some inmates have recounted their prison experiences once outside the prison walls. Roger Caron's book *Go-Boy!* (1978) provides a rare and illuminating insider's account of prison life in Canada during the 1950s, 1960s, and 1970s. Caron was fortunate to recover the manuscript of his book following the 1971 Kingston riot. It is a valuable document, since almost all the information we have about prisoners is strictly controlled by the CSC. Prison mail is routinely censored, and, since most prisoners have little education, few inmates have written books about their experiences on the inside.

Aside from Caron's books, two other accounts have been written by former or current inmates since the inception of the prison system in Canada. Bonnie Walford, a woman serving a sentence for murder, wrote about her own experience and that of other women in her book *Lifers* (1987). Julius Melnitzer, a former lawyer, recorded his experiences as a prisoner in *Maximum, Minimum, Medium* (1995). In the United States, books by prisoners are also rare, but some insightful works have been written by Caryl Chessman (1954), Eldridge Cleaver (1967), and Jack Abbot (1981). Our knowledge of life inside prisons has been greatly enhanced by these personal accounts, by criminological studies (Cayley, 1998; Gosselin, 1977), by journalistic accounts (Marron, 1996), and by a book written by a former prison psychiatrist (Scott, 1982). As well, *The Journal of Prisoners on Prisons* has for many years provided an important forum for both prisoners and academics to write about life inside.

Daily Life in Prison

The strongest characteristic of daily prison life is its highly scheduled, inflexible routine. This routine varies across the four forms of prison in Canada, but the account of Kurt, a life prisoner, is typical:

> "I work in textiles, making clothing to supply other jails across Canada—underwear and shirts—and I enjoy it. Go back, have lunch, come back and work. Three afternoons a week I attend school—SFU [since cancelled]. I look forward to getting back to three o'clock lockup.
>
> We eat around three-thirty. . . . Then I look forward to gym.
>
> Then we . . . pretty well sit around from six till lockup. I would say like, organized things."
>
> John, another lifer, summarizes life inside as repetitive and boring: "It's just over and over and over the same thing. I hate every second I have to be here. You know when you lose your freedom, you've lost everything." (Murphy &; Johnson, 1997, pp. 25–26)

The Inmate Subculture

Upon entry to prison, inmates enter a unique world of norms and rules, termed the **inmate subculture**. Prisoners have even developed their own jargon, called **prison argot**. Some examples of commonly used words that have developed in Canadian prisons to substitute for common words in English are *diddler*, *fish*, and *shank* meaning "child molester," "newcomer," and "homemade knife" respectively. As in wider society, prison subcultures develop their own rules of permissible conduct and penalties. However, inmate codes of conduct are not written down; instead, new inmates learn the codes of conduct by talking to other inmates and by observing interactions among prisoners and between correctional officers and prisoners.

Inmates vary in the degree to which they internalize these rules and norms. Some who feel at ease or empowered in prison subcultures become highly institutionalized. They find it difficult to "shake off" the "joint" mentality—that is, to return to civilian modes of thinking and acting. Despite life skills training, these prisoners find it difficult to succeed in the community.

Most of the rules reinforce the interests of the inmate group against the guards and prison administration. John Irwin (1970), a former prisoner turned criminologist, found that the rules helped to bind inmates together as a group. The rules include not being a "rat" (giving information to the authorities), displaying toughness, and refraining from arguing with other prisoners.

In Canada, research by Marron (1996) has addressed the issue of whether the inmate code exists in Canadian prisons. Given Caron's (1985) account, one would have thought that such an exercise was unnecessary. Marron found that interview subjects consistently identified a set of informal rules of conduct. These rules included doing your own time, staying out of the illegal prison economy, not trusting anyone, and showing respect for other inmates. Inmates are advised by other inmates to avoid purchasing products in the illegal prison economy (such as drugs, moonshine, cigarettes, and pornography), since, if they fail to repay debts, they risk being seriously assaulted or having to remunerate through sexual acts. Prisoners must also acknowledge the place of other prisoners in the institutional hierarchy. Inmates serving life sentences, so-called "lifers", are accorded the highest status in the inmate subculture, as are prisoners who commit serious violent offences. Not only are they serving long sentences, but they are also considered dangerous because of their acts on the outside. New prisoners occupy the lowest rung of the hierarchy.

Violence in Prisons

There is little doubt that prisons are violent places. Violence can take many forms. Inmates may threaten or assault others to gain property. Staff may assault inmates to display their power. In some instances, inmates assault staff. The CSC reported 142 major assaults of this type in the first nine months of 1991–1992, the last time data was provided on this matter. Stabbing constituted roughly 40 percent of assaults in prison. As a result, cells are regularly searched, or "turned over" by staff, to find illegal weapons and other forms of contraband. Other reported assaults include punching or kicking (33 percent), clubbing (19 percent), sexual assaults (4.7 percent), and burning (2.4 percent). However, given the inmate subculture and the threat of reprisal, there is likely a large dark figure to crimes committed in prison—that is, crimes that are committed but never reported. The majority of assaults occurred in maximum-security prisons (over 50 percent). Drugs accounted for 29 percent of disputes, retaliation for 19 percent, attacks on informants for 10 percent, and sexual motivations for 7 percent.

Staff are rarely the targets of serious physical attacks, in keeping with the assertions of both researchers and inmates that the inmates, rather than correctional officials, control prison society. Only two to four serious assaults of staff occur each year. Given the low staff-to-inmate ratio, it is surprising that more attacks do not occur. The checks and balances of the inmate code, although of little relevance to life outside the institution, make it possible for staff to run the prison. However, at certain times, inmates may rebel against prison conditions and cause a riot.

Prison Riots

Prison riots are a rare event in Canadian institutions as they are in prisons around the world. The largest riot in Canadian prison history occurred at Kingston in 1971 (see Box 8.2 on the next page). It has been the subject of both criminological analysis and an insider account (Caron, 1978). Riots appear to arise naturally from prison conditions, but this does not mean that they are predictable. Generally, they arise from inmates' concerns about mistreatment or intolerable conditions that prison officials have ignored. Tensions appear to reach a crescendo, and prisoners feel that only direct action will result in change. Taking over the prison provides a forum for them to express demands formally and to receive wider public attention concerning their plight. A minor altercation between staff and prisoner may ignite a wider revolt among prisoners. Most prison riots require planning by the prisoners and thus are not truly spontaneous.

Prisons are what sociologist Erving Goffman (1961) termed *total institutions*, with strict rules of conduct. They are often overcrowded, outdated facilities, with little in the way of rehabilitative programming for long-term prisoners. Double bunking (the practice of assigning two inmates in a cell), which has been declared legal by the Canadian courts, creates significant intrusions on personal privacy. There is little opportunity for either privacy or personal expression. We know that humans when placed in overcrowded accommodations of any kind are more prone to violent outbursts and ill health. Experts also view prison riots as a method for inmate societies to rid themselves of informers and also to permit new individuals and groups to attain power. Changes in prison administration or the transfer of inmates who are powerful in the subculture can create a gap in the power structure of the prison, making it vulnerable to riots. Finally, as an institution that houses violent people in a violent subculture, prisons might be expected to have riots.

Prison riots, as opposed to strikes, are not generally organized, but they do require some planning among a select group of inmates. The plans remain clandestine but are circulated as a rumour to other inmates. There are several phases that characterize prison riots: explosion, organization, confrontation, termination, reaction, and explanation. As Caron (1978) describes it, the explosion is a period in which inmates engage in a frenzy of drinking, drug use, violence, and sex after overwhelming staff and taking hostages. Pent-up frustrations and a lack of freedom lead to an explosive release. Inmates then organize into smaller groups led by other inmates. Typically, various forms of confrontation with the authorities follow, including threats and small skirmishes. Termination occurs either through a negotiated end to the riot or through the physical retaking of both the buildings and the prisoners. The army may assist correctional authorities in retaking control. Claire Culhane (1985) and others have documented the ramifications of riots for prisoners during the reaction phase. These consequences may include lengthy periods of solitary confinement or lockdowns, denial of privileges, and physical and psychological attacks by correctional personnel. The final phase is one of "damage control," when correctional authorities issue explanations to inmates and the public to divert public attention from inmate complaints and prison conditions.

BOX 8.2

THE KINGSTON PENITENTIARY RIOT, 1971

Riots can provide an opportunity for inmates to act violently against other inmates, particularly sex offenders and informers, who are normally segregated in protective custody. Here is Roger Caron's eyewitness account of the riots at Kingston Penitentiary in 1971:

> On the extermination list was a tall, stooped offender dubbed "The Camel"... In his late twenties, the Camel was serving a life sentence for raping two very young girls. When the bingo broke out he had somehow been living quietly in the prison population . . . he had survived several beatings and a stabbing, but had stubbornly refused to be locked away for his own protection. That stubbornness was coming back to haunt him now that there were so many convicts prowling the tiers thirsting for victims . . . the two dragged the rapist struggling and screaming from his cell. With great effort the three cons tried mightily to throw him over the railing to his death far below. The Camel had developed great strength in his hands, which he now used to grip the railing, stubbornly refusing to let go even when one of the men bit and kicked at his fingers. Finally in exhaustion the three cons gave up and settled for punching and kicking him until he curled up in a ball. Later one of the inmates was asked why they changed their minds, and they replied: "Because he was screaming too much." (Caron, 1985, pp. 126–127).

Curtis and Blanchfield (1985) reported that "virtually every moveable item was destroyed" in the rampage. As their anger mounted, the inmates broke into RANGE 1D, which housed the "undesirables"—sex offenders and rats. The rioters pried open the cell doors and dragged the occupants into the Main Dome of the prison in a circle around the bell, hated by inmates, that rang out to mark all events in the prison day. The inmates beat and brutalized the fourteen undesirables during the night, two of whom died as a result of the attacks. Most of the inmates surrendered voluntarily the next day and released their guard prisoners unharmed before being temporarily transferred to Millhaven Penitentiary. Like most riots, the events had provided a way for inmates to vent their pent-up rage and violence but did little to change the conditions under which inmates were living and continued to live once the prison was repaired and reopened.

The Correctional Investigator

The **correctional investigator (CI)** is a position that is mandated by law. This person acts as an ombud on behalf of federal offenders. The role of the CI is to "investigate and resolve individual offender complaints" (Annual Report, 2004/05). In reviewing the annual report the total number of complaints received is quite illuminating.

In women's facilities a total of 435 contacts were initiated with inmates. The CI conducted 105 interviews over 28 days spent in 9 institutions that spawned complaints. In the Atlantic region, 604 complaints were received, 176 interviews conducted and 31 days spent in the 5 prisons where complaints emerged. In Ontario, 1783 complaints were received, 528 interviews conducted and 98 days spent in the 11 institutions where complaints originated. In the Pacific region, 1162 complaints were investigated in 433 interviews and 69 days were spent in the 8 institutions. In the Prairies, 1716 complaints were investigated in 558 interviews and 97 days were spent in 11 institutions. Finally, in Quebec 1920 complaints were received, 686 interviews conducted and 103 days spent in institutions investigating. In total there were 7617 complaints, 2486 interviews, and 427 days spent in institutional investigation. Review the total number of inmates incarcerated during this period (previously discussed) and the high volume of complaints becomes apparent. But what did prisoners complain about?

The complaints fall into a number of unique categories, which provide a general idea of what concerns merited complaints to the CI. Complaints concerned the following issues with the number of complaints in brackets: administrative segregation (468); case preparation for release (348); issues regarding cells or cell placement (660); claims against the Crown (71); community programs, conditions of confinement, death or serious injury (469); diet (66); discipline issues (73); discrimination (16); employment (104); file information (access, disclosure, and correction issues) (351); financial matters (261); grievance or food services 458); health care access and decisions (891); program access and quality (220); and mental health (44). Additionally, there were 429 complaints directly against staff, 215 regarding the safety or security of the offender, 183 on security classification, 211 regarding telephone access, and 121 on temporary access decisions. While these do not represent all categories of complaints, they reflect a system in which a great number of complaints are generated on a regular basis. In total, there were 7648 complaints that emerged from 13 248 inmates.

To give readers some context in which to understand these figures, let us first consider some statistics on prison conditions as reported by the CSC in 2004/05 and, second, some of the concerns and recommendations of the CI for 2004/05. There were 52 major violent incidents that occurred in this time frame—a decrease from 70 the previous year. According to the CSC, major disturbances saw a dramatic decrease of 87 percent, but this is simply a reduction from 8 incidents to 1. Nine inmates committed suicide—a drop from the 5-year average of 11.4. One major assault occurred on a staff; none occurred the previous year. The average number of major incidents per 1000 inmates decreased from 4.8 to 3.0.

The CI expressed a number of more general concerns that arose after his interviews with prisoners and his staffs' visits to correctional institutions. First, he found that women were over-classified, that is classified as requiring a higher level of security than their record or crimes would dictate. Why this occurred appears to be related to a lack of spaces at various levels, and in some instances this resulted in the unacceptable practice of housing women in men's facilities. He also found that the CSC was lacking the funds to support an adequate mental health service for prisoners, and that front-line staff were inadequately trained to intervene in mental health crisis situations. Aboriginal offenders' needs were also not being adequately met, and the CI recommended the immediate hiring of a deputy commissioner for Aboriginal offenders. In the area of inmates' grievances, harassment, and allegations of staff misconduct, the CI urged immediate action and the implementation of proper evidentiary procedures to ensure what he termed, "fair and expeditious" resolution of inmates' grievances and complaints. Of particular concern were the last two problem areas listed above. There were serious inadequacies noted in the preparation of cases for parole consideration and access to programs that would improve an inmate's chances of success at parole. This complaint seems to provide another explanation of why many inmates either do not apply or are not successful at parole. Finally, for the fourth year in a row, the CI urged that the CSC cease its illegal practice of classifying all persons charged with first- or second-degree murder as maximum security for the first two years of their sentence when they are serving a minimum sentence. The fact that the CSC has ignored the CI's request to cease a long-standing illegal practice is not a positive reflection on its ability to respond to fair criticism. (Annual Report of The Correctional Investigator, 2004/05).

Correctional Officers

Research has identified three types of correctional officers, or guards. First, there are officers who are friendly to inmates. They treat inmates as human beings and talk with them about the community, news, family, prisoner issues, and life. A second group adheres strictly to the rules and generally does not engage inmates in casual conversation. The third group is composed of violent bullies who manipulate prison rules to vent their own anger toward inmates.

In understanding the adaptive styles of correctional officers, it is important that we consider that they are, in fact, committed to the prison environment. With regular and overtime shifts, they will spend more waking time in their lives with prisoners than with significant others in the community. This large amount of time spent within an environment that carries a significant daily potential for conflict and periodic episodes of violence contributes greatly to the degree of stress officers experience in their work (Correctional Officers of Canada, 2004).

Women in Prison

The Dark Past of P4W

The Kingston Penitentiary for Women (P4W) was built as a small prison for females. It opened its doors in 1934 at the height of the Great Depression. Arriving inmates were placed on the "range"—the older portion of the prison, which contained two tiers of barred cells. According to Bonny Walford, a prisoner serving a life sentence, the range held approximately 70 inmates. It was hardly a place for the contemplation envisaged by early prison philosophers:

> The range is incredibly noisy; each inmate has her radio, stereo or television on loud enough to drown out everyone else's. It is absolute madness . . . this is where most of the fights, trouble, and brew-making go on. There are double the number of guards. (Walford, 1987, p. 2)

P4W was surrounded by 4.5-metre-high walls. A tennis court, gym, bingo room, and baseball diamond were provided, as well as jogging and cycling paths (Walford, 1987). A well-known feature of the prison was the two-bedroom family visiting unit (FVU). An inmate who had maintained good behaviour could apply for three-day family or conjugal visits every six weeks. These visits allowed brief respite from prison life and a chance to visit with family, partners, and children.

As in the men's prison, cells were small and contained only a bed, dresser, toilet, and sink. There were also two wings where "peace and quiet" was the rule. There were no cells in these wings, but rather a series of 25 rooms, each with a bed, desk, dresser, chair, and wardrobe. The dimensions of the rooms were 2 by 3.5 metres, and each had a screened and barred window with an exterior curtain. Toilet and bathing facilities and a washer and dryer were located at the end of the hall. Inmates' visiting between rooms ended at 11 p.m., after which time they were allowed to watch television with headphones. Walford states, "The wing is a very cosy and peaceful home to the residents. Pettiness and fights are not tolerated in the wing" (1987).

Despite having some comfortable features, P4W was an institution with a violent culture perpetuated by corrections officers. On February 21, 1995, television viewers across Canada watched a video of women prisoners being strip-searched, stripped naked, and left shackled to the walls and pushed with batons. Correctional officers equipped with riot gear pulled the women from their cells. As Marron relates, the video "conjured up images of political atrocities, pornography and extreme sexual abuse" (1996).

THE P4W VIDEO AND VIOLENCE AGAINST PRISONERS

A Native woman who had been stripped while she was apparently half-asleep looked disoriented and totally humiliated, as she was forced to back up against a wall with a transparent plastic riot shield pressed against the front of her naked body. Another naked woman kneeled with hands behind the back of her head, motionless as if in a yoga position, asking in vain for a gown, while a chain was fastened around her waist and two guards stood in front of her with their batons raised like erect penises. But perhaps the most disturbing images were of a woman protesting and struggling as two men pinned her, face-down on the floor, and helped a female guard rip her clothes and tear them from her body.

Source: Marron, 1996, p. 124.

The Honourable Louise Arbour conducted the Commission of Inquiry into Certain Events at the Prison for Women in Kingston (1996) and found that the CSC had a profound lack of respect for the underlying principles of justice and fairness in dealing with prisoners. She provided a damning indictment of the events:

> A guilty verdict followed by a custodial sentence is not a grant of authority for the State to disregard the very values that the law, particularly the criminal law, seeks to uphold and vindicate, such as honesty, respect for the physical safety of others, respect for privacy and for human dignity. Corrections officers are held to the same standards of integrity and decency as their partners in the administration of justice. (1996, XI)

Arbour was particularly dismayed to find that while the actions of officers in this case often violated both prison regulations and Canadian law, the CSC did nothing to address the officers' actions and instead blamed the prisoners for the events. It is worth noting that immediately following the release of the report, the then commission of the CSC resigned. On April 27, 2006, the CSC released its 10-year review of the issues raised by Arbour. While some progress has been made, particularly through the development of new regional centres for women, disturbing practices, including over-classification and inappropriate housing of women, still are issues of concern. This is particularly the case for Aboriginal women, according to the CI's report where addressing issues of human rights and equity have not met a standard acceptable to an external evaluator.

Since 1994, the federal and provincial governments have opened small, "women-centred" regional institutions for women prisoners. On July 6, 2000, P4W was officially closed and women prisoners were transferred to the smaller regional institutions. The majority of these women prisoners are non-violent offenders, many serving time for drug offences or, as Walford argues, for the crime of being a party to an offence. This latter crime is often referred to as "being in the wrong place at the wrong time." More common for women incarcerated at P4W was a history of being victims of sexual, psychological, emotional, and physical abuse. The new regional centres replacing P4W allow for visits by friends and family, more specialized treatment, and work and educational programs. They also provide better living conditions. Considering that P4W had been condemned in 1977 by a parliamentary committee as "unfit for bears, much less women" (Marron, 1996), the building of better facilities was long, long overdue.

Women in Prison Today

As we have already seen, there are far more men imprisoned in Canada than women. The number of women in federal prison has increased from 305 in 1999 to 379 in 2005. This represents an increase of approximately 25 percent in six years. Does this mean that women are becoming more criminal in their activities? Some criminologists believe that women will make up increasingly more of the prison population as their roles in society change to include many formerly open only to men. Aboriginal women make up a disproportionate number of incarcerated females at over 30 percent of all women inmates (108 persons). This is a serious concern in terms of the need to provide support services in institutions specific to Aboriginal women. Further, it highlights the clash of two cultures and a failure of our society to provide the kinds of educational opportunities and economic support that will permit Aboriginal women to live fulfilling lives free of crime.

The crimes of violence that bring women into prison have recently begun to mirror those of their male counterparts. Overall, women have traditionally been sentenced for economic crimes, for crimes of necessity and survival, and for acting as a party or an accomplice to more serious felonies.

Women have been entering the criminal justice system in increasing numbers in the past two decades. Explanations of this increase are often linked to a couple of intriguing theories. First, the disappearance of the justice system's chivalry toward females has had a decided impact. In the past, justice officials tended to view women as helpless and childlike, and so as less culpable for their actions. Second, as noted above, the increasing movement of women into full labour force participation and demands for equality have translated into the justice system's changed approach to female criminality.

In Canada, two-thirds of women who are sentenced federally are mothers. It is eye-opening to consider that single mothers make up 70 percent of that number. These female inmates report suffering physical abuse in 68 percent of cases, and more than half have reported sexual abuse. More striking, perhaps, is their lack of educational achievement. Over two-thirds of women in prison have

primary school education or less and have never held any form of steady employment. It is obvious that attempts must be made to address these core issues in terms of reducing the number of women incarcerated in Canada.

In penitentiaries throughout Canada, women prisoners are required to work or to take various educational or training programs. From Monday to Friday, prisoners work in the kitchen, school, or beauty parlour, and some toil in cleaning or office jobs in the prison. Women may also take university and secretarial courses, woodworking, ceramics, and word processing workshops. Provincial centres for women offer a variety of programs, including core courses in substance abuse, parenting skills, and life skills. Personal development and culturally specific programs focus on Aboriginal lifestyle and religion, and some institutions have programs in music therapy, chaplaincy, and health services. Educational, occupational, and vocational (e.g., canine) programs; and building maintenance, may be offered. There are also specific employment programs that train inmates to be kitchen workers, janitors, maintenance workers, library staff, and child care assistants. Several other programs focus on spirituality, health/well-being, and creativity. After an appropriate period of imprisonment, women prisoners may be chosen for work outside the institution, where they are paid a small wage for their efforts.

Prisons and the Future

In the twenty-first century, prisons are facing a growing number of challenges that will affect the kinds of services they provide and the ability of these institutions to carry out their punitive functions. These changes reflect, to a large extent, the changing nature of our society, and there is little doubt that prisons in the future will continue to be forced to adapt to rapidly changing conditions.

The Spread of HIV and AIDS

HIV and AIDS in prison combine to be one of the greatest challenges confronting Canadian prison administrations. This problem introduces many complexities into the prison environment. First, the number of prisoners who are testing positive for HIV and/or AIDS has continued to grow significantly in recent years. Jurgens (1996), writing on behalf of the Canadian HIV/AIDS Legal Network, reported on research conducted both nationally and internationally on this serious problem. He reported a 40 percent increase in the number of known HIV and/or AIDS cases discovered in Canadian federal correctional institutions in the period from April 1994 to August 1995. As Jurgens reports, one of the major difficulties that this increase presents for prisons is strictly economic. HIV/AIDS prisoners who require expensive medications and intensive care are becoming a substantial financial burden to prisons. More disturbingly, Jurgens found evidence of an increase in high-risk behaviours in prison. HIV and AIDS are spread not only through sexual contact among prisoners but also through shared needles. Jurgens found evidence to support the conclusion that as a result of these behaviours, HIV was being transmitted in prison.

The dilemmas facing prison officials as a result of this modern plague are many. Until recently, the attitude of prison officials was that supplying condoms was inappropriate in a same-sex environment. While sexual liaisons are specifically forbidden by prison regulation, there is little doubt that individuals will find ways to engage in sexual encounters in the closed society of the prison. Approaching the problem by denying condoms and making rules against consensual sex can be argued to promote the spread of HIV and AIDS and other sexually transmitted diseases. Prison officials have difficulty supplying fresh disposable needles to individuals for a similar reason—that is, drug use is strictly prohibited in prison. Yet, prison authorities understand that this behaviour does occur. To deny the inmates needles will lead to needles being shared and to a much greater risk of various diseases spreading. However, to supply needles might be seen as condoning illegal drug use. Needles also can be used as effective weapons in prison. Therefore, the dilemmas that authorities face are not simple, nor are solutions as easy as we might assume (see Box 8.4 on the next page).

A positive effort by correctional officials to address one cause of the transmission of disease has been the introduction of tattoo parlours into some institutions. Given the popularity of tattooing, both inside and outside the prison, the establishment of safe facilities will offer a positive alternative to "joint" tattoos done with sharpened pens and other unsterilized implements.

Parallel to problems with HIV and AIDS in prison are extremely high rates of hepatitis C. Three Canadian studies, reported in Jurgens (1996), discovered that from 28 to 40 percent of all prisoners have been infected. Given that a recent CSC survey of 4285 inmates revealed that a "high proportion" of prisoners engage in high-risk behaviours, there is considerable cause for concern. Jurgens rightly points to the Commission of Inquiry into Certain Events at the Prison for Women in Kingston (the Arbour Commission) as a ringing condemnation of the CSC's hypocrisy in comparing its statements regarding respect for rights of the individual versus their actions. The Arbour Commission found a system fraught with shortcomings and characterized by a culture of disrespect for individual rights. Furthermore, the Arbour Commission found clear evidence of insularity—that is, an unwillingness to consider external criticisms, whether emanating from the correctional investigator or from another source. This inability or unwillingness to respond severely hampered efforts to deal effectively with HIV, AIDS, and other diseases in the prison environment.

BOX 8.4

HIV AND AIDS: THE PRISON SYSTEM'S LEGAL RESPONSIBILITIES

What are the moral and legal responsibilities of the prison system in dealing with inmates who are suffering with HIV/AIDS? The Canadian courts have ruled that a Toronto detention centre had failed in its duty by not providing appropriate and adequate treatment for prisoners with HIV/AIDS. The administration had also failed in its legal duties by not educating staff. Under the law, employers have a duty to educate staff and to make reasonable accommodations for persons who are disabled. They also have a duty to educate employees about sexual harassment so that in legal cases they cannot claim that their employees were acting in ignorance of the law and of the rights of individuals. Do the prisons have a moral duty, if not a legal one, to protect inmates from unreasonable risks? Failure to do so could lead to a lawsuit being filed by an individual who became infected with HIV because he or she was not provided with condoms or sterile needles. An Australian prisoner has already brought such a case before the courts.

Source: Jurgens, 1996, p. v.

Kevin Marron's interview with prison AIDS activist Gerald Benoit, who was identified as suffering from the disease in 1987, revealed that prisoners with AIDS are now accepted in the general population of the prison. In fact, according to Benoit, "now the people ostracized are the ones who harass people with AIDS" (1996). According to Marron's investigation, prison medical facilities are hard pressed to provide the kinds of treatment that AIDS patients require. When prisoners develop full-blown AIDS, they are transferred to hospitals or hospices. Unfortunately, although prison authorities try to transfer inmates who are suffering from a terminal disease into the community to friends or family, it is not always possible to do so. Marron relates the story of a man who at age 35 was dying of AIDS and who could not find any agency, family, or friends to accept him in the community. Poignantly, the outsider status of prisoners may mean that there is no community outside of prison ready to accept them and meet their needs.

The Aging of the Prison Population

A further challenge for prisons is the growing number of geriatric prisoners, who, as our general population ages, will begin to overwhelm the capacity of the system to respond. This aging population is one of the reasons that community alternatives to prison will become necessary in future sentencing options. The functions of prisons are not aimed at treating people who are seriously ill. With adult-onset diabetes becoming epidemic and scores of other conditions increasing, including heart problems, stroke, and Alzheimer's disease, society must consider creative alternatives to prison that can meet the goals of criminal justice while balancing the needs of the aging prisoner.

Inmate Suicide

Suicide is another issue that has received insufficient response within the prison system. Research by Burtch and Ericson (1977), as well as others, has demonstrated a high rate of suicide among prisoners. Suicide is the most frequent cause of death within the Canadian custodial system. During 1997/98, there were 92 inmate deaths recorded in Canadian institutions. Suicide accounts for 35 percent of all deaths in institutions at the provincial and federal levels (Canadian Centre for Justice Statistics, 1999). The suicide rate in prison is twice that in the general population.

The reasons for suicide vary among prisoners, but it is apparent that two points in the prison career seem to be more problematic than others: the period immediately following incarceration and the time just prior to release. These periods of danger result from stresses associated with entrance into prison and fear concerning re-entry into the community. Marron reports that in 1993/94,

20 suicides occurred in federal institutions (this would exclude jails, detention centres, and provincial prisons). P4W was also plagued by suicides but at a lower rate than that in men's prisons. The methods of committing suicide are predominantly hanging and drug overdose. CSC research, according to Marron (1996), has revealed that higher suicide rates are associated with overcrowded prisons. Suicides are also associated typically with longer sentences.

Privatization of Prisons

Much consideration has recently been given to developing private prisons in Canada. Indeed, several private prisons are already up and running. Ontario opened a boot camp–style facility for juvenile offenders outside Barrie in 1998 as part of a "get tough" policy with young offenders. The much shorter period of incarceration required with a boot camp sentence is also in keeping with conservative fiscal policies, which predominate in government. A private owner/operator in these institutions may offer a daily rate per prisoner that is seemingly more cost efficient than that available under government schemes. However, studies of private prisons in the United States have failed to find evidence of the rosy predictions of cost savings that governments may have anticipated. While the initial offer to provide prison services may be lower, it is recognized that prisons, unlike other private businesses associated with human service providers, cannot simply close their doors in the face of financial difficulties. Governments must be prepared to provide economic bailouts to private prisons that cannot operate on budget.

Further scrutiny of private prisons also indicates that they are typically staffed by non-unionized employees, whose training may fall short of the level of expertise and experience required to ensure proper management of the institution and to deal with adult inmate populations. A further criticism is that as dealers in human misery, private prison operators have a vested interest in the expansion of the prison industry to provide more "raw product" for their institutions. New and alternative approaches to dealing with crime, including the possible abolition of prisons, run contrary to the private prison operators' interests.

Governments that have been faced with mounting costs for running prisons have chosen to move in two directions to effect cost savings. The first approach is a movement toward privatization, as discussed above. The second approach is the amalgamation of prisons into what are known as "superprisons." Under this latter approach, some institutions are closed and some are expanded and architecturally altered to allow a greatly reduced staff to supervise the inmate population. Maplehurst Correctional Centre in Ontario is "the flagship of the new system and the largest jail in Canada" (*Toronto Star*, 2000). Based on the marketing success of one-stop shopping outlets, the idea is to reduce costs from $126 a day per prisoner to roughly $76 per day. While the design has been called "radical," blueprints released by the Ministry of Correctional Services show clearly that the prison is based on Jeremy Bentham's panopticon. The prison is a series of self-contained units, or pods, each with its own exercise yard, dining room, and visiting area, constructed in a circular configuration. As reported, all of these areas are "visible from a central control point" (Fleming, 1995). The new "jumbo jails," which would house provincial prisoners, would take in approximately 87 000 inmates each year. The annual cost of running them is $500 million dollars (*Toronto Star*, 2000). Since there will be little movement within the institutions, the need for correctional officers will have more than halved, from 4000 to 1700 employees. The new Penetanguishene superprison will be privately run (after it has been built) as an experiment to see if costs savings will be realized. The private contractor would be penalized if recidivism rates among released prisoners exceeded a standard set by the ministry. However, given the current recidivism rate of roughly 66 percent, it is also likely that the standard will be very low.

This new approach to jailing inmates focuses more on economical management and easy control of prisoners than on the human aspects of control. Correctional officers' unions have expressed concern about the loss of the human dimension of service provision—that is, the services that are provided in human interaction. The new institutions provide a sterile, overcontrolled environment, where visiting will be by appointment and conducted by telephone through Plexiglas barriers. Each visit will be subject to a buzzer-controlled, strict 20-minute limit. While the ministry has claimed that the superprisons will allow people from small communities better access to services, in reality, they will remove the prisoner not only from contact with relatives and friends, but also from physical human contact while held within the system. How many inmates would prefer living in a clean, electronically gated fishbowl under intense supervision at all times to a drafty, but more human, county jail? However, inmates' experiences and desires have never been a priority with institutional planners, many of whom have never spent a day imprisoned in their own facilities.

Alternatives to Prison

The rising costs of imprisonment have caused governments to consider alternatives to simply putting criminals in the holding pens we call prisons. We have provided discussion throughout this chapter of the costs associated with running our national and provincial prison systems. Both Nils Christie (1994), a European criminologist and anti-prison activist, and Ruth Morris (1997), a Canadian prison abolitionist, have written impassioned books calling for the dismantling of the prison system. Penal abolition is a relatively new concept in Canada. The argument proposed is that prisons are not only ineffective at rehabilitating criminals but also a costly luxury that society can no longer afford.

Given the massive expenditures directed to prisons, there is little doubt that even a small portion of the corrections budget would support extensive community alternatives to imprisonment. Community corrections have recently gained in popularity, as the limitations of prisons from a rehabilitative perspective have been recognized. If community alternatives are more cost-effective and at least as successful, they may be worth considering. In Chapter 9, we consider some of the forms of community alternatives that are being developed in Canada.

Conclusion

Originally introduced as a method of containing and punishing individuals, the prison has evolved to serve a variety of functions, including rehabilitation. These new functions reflect changes in societal attitudes toward the confinement and treatment of prisoners. Canada's high rate of imprisonment ensures that prisons occupy an important place in discussions of societal values and expenditures in our society. Despite the efforts of prison abolitionists, the prison is unlikely to disappear as a means of dealing with crime. Therefore, dialogues on the structuring of the prison system and its functions are likely to continue to occupy academics, policy-makers, politicians, and the public during the twenty-first century.

Summary

In this chapter, we have provided an overview of the historical development of the prison system and have analyzed the evolution of various forms of prison systems. We have also focused on the nature of the inmate subculture and on prison violence. Additionally, we have examined prison conditions for both male and female inmates, along with new developments in the justice system's approach to imprisonment. Emerging problems in the prison system have been found to include the aging of the prison population, the increasing incidence of HIV and AIDS, and the growing costs associated with imprisonment.

Key Terms

Auburn system (p. 182)

correctional investigator (CI) (p. 197)

incarceration rate (p. 183)

inmate subculture (p. 193)

panopticon (p. 182)

Pennsylvania system (p. 182)

prison argot (p. 193)

prison industry (p. 185)

protective custody (p. 189)

security classifications (p. 186)

solitary confinement (p. 190)

Discussion Questions

1. Why did Canada adopt prisons as the main response to dealing with criminals?

2. What are the differences between the Pennsylvania and Auburn approaches to imprisonment?

3. Why does Canada have a higher rate of imprisonment than many other countries?

4. What are some causes of prison riots?

5. What problems will present the greatest challenges to prisons in the future?

Weblinks

www.csc-scc.gc.ca This Correctional Service Canada website is loaded with information on corrections and prison studies.

www.jpp.org The *Journal of Prisoners on Prisons* is the only journal written by prisoners themselves, with articles, poems, and other writings on prison issues.

www.fcnetwork.org The US-based Family & Corrections Network offers information on children of prisoners, parenting programs for prisoners, prison visiting, incarcerated fathers and mothers, hospitality programs, keeping in touch, returning to the community, the impact of the justice system on families, and prison marriage. The website is an excellent resource for policy and research on families of offenders.

CHAPTER 9

Alternatives to the Prison System

Objectives

- To explain the meaning of the term *probation* and its conditions.
- To outline the parole process, including hearings and the different forms of prerelease programs.
- To discuss the suspension and revocation processes and problems associated with parole.
- To discuss the concept of the life sentence.
- To describe various community-based alternatives.

Community Alternatives

Imprisonment has become the dominant method of punishment in the Canadian criminal justice system. The prison offers an established method of dealing with criminals that requires little in the way of community input. However, in both financial and human terms the prison is an extremely costly method of dealing with crime in Canadian society. Alternatives to prison have been slow to develop within our society, reflecting not only the complex issues that surround the punishment of crime in Canada but also the entrenched nature of the existing carceral network. The **carceral network**, a term coined by French writer Michel Foucault, is the extensive grouping of institutions, agencies, and staff who are part of the process of law enforcement, the judicial process, the prison system, and the ancillary programs and agencies that deal with offenders. While there is no means to accurately assess the entire cost of operating this vast network, it can be estimated to exceed several billion dollars. It employs hundreds of thousands of Canadians in direct and related services. Therefore, to say that crime does not pay is actually incorrect—it provides employment and revenues that exceed almost any business enterprise in Canada. It should not be surprising that there is a great deal of reluctance to find meaningful alternatives to prison in Canada, since so many individuals and communities depend on these institutions for their livelihood. Although our society is currently undergoing a technological revolution fuelled by computer technology and the global economy, the prison system remains largely unaffected by these shifts. However, in May 2006, the newly elected federal government of Stephen Harper introduced a bill that would provide mandatory prison sentences for repeat and violent offences, and offences involving handguns. If passed, this bill will create the need for building more prisons. The most significant threats to the current system of imprisonment are privatization and the further development and widespread use of alternative methods of punishment.

This chapter discusses alternatives to the prison system. Increasingly, the costs associated with prison and the debilitating effects of incarceration on prisoners have lead to the consideration of alternative methods of sentencing in an approach called **community corrections**. This term derives from the nature of these sentencing options, which place offenders in the community rather than in secure institutions. While the economic savings in the variety of community corrections programs will become apparent in the discussion that follows, there are also important philosophical underpinnings to this approach that support its use.

Advocates of community corrections view it as a more effective method of punishment, as it allows offenders to maintain or re-establish links with the wider community in which they live. Communities are seen as having the power to assist offenders in reorienting their lives to establish themselves as law-abiding members of society. Offenders benefit not only from being spared the pains of imprisonment but also from being able to maintain a stable life. Families and employment relationships, for example, are not fractured, as they would be in the case of an offender's entering detention. These sentences are court ordered and do require that the offender remain under supervision and abide by certain rules of behaviour that are expected by the supervising officer. There are a number of programs that can be included under the category of community corrections, including probation, parole, electronic tethering, and various new forms of confinement. Additionally, there are a variety of other community-based options, including restitution, community service, mediation, and conditional sentences, which will be considered in this chapter.

Probation

Probation is a widely used sentencing option that is most often associated with young offenders. This form of sentencing has a long history. Canada did not institute a system of probation until the early 1950s when the government responded to the Royal Commission to Investigate the Penal System of Canada, which had pointed out the need for a national body of social workers to assist the prison system by providing a parole and probation service.

Probation is a sentence imposed when an offender has either been found guilty or plead guilty in a criminal court. Probationers are provided with supervision and a variety of services in an effort to ensure their successful completion of the probation order. By leaving them in the community it is hoped that there will be less severe disruption of their ties to the community, and also less cost to the criminal justice system. Probation is a post-trial diversion involving a program that acts as an alternative to secure forms of custody such as jail or prison.

Canadian courts have made widespread use of probation. Currently, it is the most frequently awarded community sentence. While many community members view probation as a non-sentence, the reality is that probationers must adhere to a strict regimen of rules and supervision. Violation of the terms of probation can and do result in the offender's serving the remainder of the sentence in a correctional facility. Probation orders may range from several months to a maximum of three years; over the past decade, the average period of probation has been one year. In 2000, 100 000 people served terms of probation in Canada.

While criminologists have been concerned with the growth of the prison system and increasing rates of incarceration, rates of probation increased more rapidly than sentences of imprisonment during the 1990s. The median age of probationers is 29, the same median age as the homeless population in Canada, demonstrating that at this age people are most at risk for "falling through the cracks" (Fleming, 1993).

There are a variety of conditions that may be imposed upon the individual as part of an order of probation. Three of the conditions are mandatory and commonsensical: (1) the probationer may not change residence without informing the probation officer, (2) the probationer may not accept an offer of employment without permission, and (3) the probationer must report to a probation officer as required. Additionally, probationers are to refrain from associating with criminals in the community. Under section 737(2) of the Criminal Code of Canada, probationers are required to keep the peace, maintain good behaviour, and appear before the court when required, in addition to reporting to a probation officer. Further, conditions commonly reflect the nature of the offence committed and the need for personal change by the offender. Conditions could include participation in a substance abuse program, anger management classes, educational courses, community volunteering, or a course in money management.

Judges must consider a wide variety of factors when assessing an individual's suitability for probation. Some of these factors may include laws regarding eligibility for probation, input from the defence lawyer on the accused's character and criminal record (or lack thereof), the view of the prosecutor, presentence reports by social workers, and the circumstances of the offence. More serious offences or long records of criminality will usually disqualify an offender from consideration for probation.

Probation officers (POs) provide personal support to probationers, who must visit them regularly. POs can provide a helping hand to probationers by dispensing advise on problematic areas of social behaviour and guidance to prevent reoffending. However, POs also have a duty to enforce the orders of the court. This second role may serve as a barrier to effective rehabilitation of the offender. Since POs have wide discretionary powers to revoke probation if the probationer violates the conditions, it is difficult for probationers who are experiencing personal trouble to be forthright with their POs. Some offenders may view probation as a game of impression management and manipulation of the PO. They offer their POs an image of themselves that will not provoke incarceration or suspicion of wrongdoing but that also does not expose problem behaviours. Thus, criminal lifestyles are left relatively unhindered particularly for those who are not genuinely committed to the process.

Revocation will be recommended by the PO for two types of general violations. First, the commission of any new offence will initiate a recommendation for revocation. Offenders may also commit what are referred to as **technical violations** of the rules of the order. An individual might fail to report a change of address. We will assume that there is no intention to hide information from the PO, but rather he or she has been evicted from a residence, has stayed with relatives while finding a new place, and intended to report the change of address upon finding a new permanent accommodation. However, a one-week search for new accommodation turns into several weeks. The PO discovers the probationer has left the accommodation listed on his or her probation file. This forms of violation does not automatically result in revocation. POs have considerable latitude to use their professional discretion in assessing the seriousness of the violation. Officers may simply warn the probationer, or take the route of assigning further conditions to the order. In some cases, offenders may be required to spend a few days in jail in order to remind them that they are not fully free and to reinforce the seriousness of the order.

Probation is typically imposed following sentencing by a judge. At this point, the sentence is suspended, and a probation order is substituted. Probation may also be imposed as part of a conditional discharge, intermittent sentence, or split sentence, where the sentence combines another penalty, such as a fine or a period of incarceration. By the mid-1990s, approximately 66 percent of offenders in Canada were serving probation orders, representing an increase of almost 50 percent over the number at the beginning of the 1990s.

The courts have enthusiastically embraced probation as an alternative to imprisonment for several reasons. Probation is cost effective when compared with incarceration. As well, rehabilitation is more probable if the offender remains in the community. However, it is worth noting that little research has been conducted in Canada to examine the process of probation, its effects, and its ability to serve offenders' needs. Research conducted in the United States has shown that recidivism rates for probation have not varied significantly for those associated with imprisonment.

Parole

Parole is a reduction in the sentence of an offender as a reward for good conduct while incarcerated. As a form of conditional release, it has a long history in Canada's prisons, beginning in 1868 (one year after Confederation). In the latter half of the nineteenth century, the size of the prison population soared in Canada, resulting in the need for an innovative program to reduce the number of captive inmates. The "ticket-of-leave" program permitted prisoners to get out of prison early— given the harsh conditions at Kingston, this was no minor incentive for good behaviour. While inmates remained unsupervised until the beginning of the twentieth century, by 1910 the government had solicited the assistance of charitable and religious organizations as part of a remission service to manage the parole system. Parole is not a sentence that is imposed in a court hearing but is an early-release program for persons leaving prison who have shown good behaviour while incarcerated.

Parole has been a controversial measure in the last century and a half; some have criticized it as providing prematurely short sentences for dangerous offenders. It is often cited by conservative politicians and commentators as a "softening" of sentences. In a purely punishment-oriented model, incentives for good behaviour in prisons in order to gain early release are not supported. It should be noted that proponents of this approach invariably fail to discuss the astronomical economic costs associated with imprisonment or the importance of rehabilitation to maintaining a civil society. Prisoners have also criticized the parole process, arguing that subjective rather than objective criteria govern parole decisions. Inmates refer to parole hearings as "kangaroo courts," where rules and due process are distinctly absent. Inmates provide the responses that are expected in order to gain release, rather than honest answers.

Is parole a carrot dangled in front of the inmate to produce compliant, manageable behaviour in prison? Is it perhaps a stick used to psychologically beat the prisoners into submission? Or is it possible that it is nothing more than an illusion? In the sections that follow, we explore the reality of parole in Canada in an attempt to answer these questions.

The Parole Process

The process of parole begins at the time of sentencing. While judges should not consider the possibility of early release through parole when assessing sentences, there is obviously a tendency to do so. Judges are not elected in Canada, unlike in the United States, but rather are political appointees. As lawyers for the status quo and as community members, they cannot reasonably be expected to ignore public concerns regarding sentencing leniency (despite their purported neutrality). For some serious offences, judges may order offenders to serve half of their sentences before parole will be considered.

Since the chance of being granted parole is strongly influenced by an inmate's behaviour while in prison and by correctional authorities' assessment of the behaviour, prisoners must develop a realistic release plan to be considered seriously for parole. Case management officers aid them in creating this plan. The plan will address issues of possible employment, treatment plans, and residence. Inmates' chances of obtaining parole may be increased by their participation in appropriate programs—for example, substance abuse, anger management, or sexual offender therapy. However, two substantial criticisms of these programs should be noted. First, many programs are not readily available to inmates without a considerable wait of several months to several years. If successful completion of a treatment program is necessary for mounting a parole application, an inmate's release may be unreasonably delayed. Delays can result in other significant problems for inmates, including depression, heightened stress, and mental illness, which further delay their release. Second, inmates "playing" the parole system may enrol themselves in alcohol and substance abuse programs in order to demonstrate "change" to parole officials when they do not actually need these programs. As one former inmate related, "You just sit there and talk seriously and they give you certificates to wave at the parole boys. They're proof you've really changed."

The parole file contains information from the presentence report, institutional records, and various forms of criminal, medical, and psychiatric records. These documents are meant to assist the parole board members come to an informed decision.

Parole boards have been consistently criticized by legal authorities, criminologists, and former inmates. Some have viewed parole board decisions as arbitrary, with no objective criteria being employed to render decisions. Parole boards have consistently been unable to develop prediction instruments that can assess the suitability of particular inmates for parole; thus, decisions are often highly subjective. The Canadian Sentencing Commission (1987) commented that parole boards have more power than judges in determining the length of sentences. One of the more disturbing trends that researchers have observed is the decision to grant parole more readily to inmates serving long sentences of imprisonment. Therefore, although one individual may receive a much shorter sentence than another at court, both offenders serve roughly the equivalent amount of jail time. This means that more serious crimes are punished as though they are less serious crimes.

Another criticism is that inmates remain disadvantaged in parole hearings, since there are few guidelines to inform them of the criteria they must meet to gain their freedom. Another factor, rarely noted by researchers, is the limited ability of many prisoners to prepare a parole application, given their lack of academic achievement. Prisoners who depend on institutional assistance are often unable to make a convincing case before parole authorities.

The Parole Hearing

Parole board hearings are conducted on a rotating basis at all penal institutions. Members are essentially political appointees, called *order-in-council appointees*. They serve a term fixed by various levels of provincial and federal government. Parole officials often have no experience of corrections, but instead mirror the current thinking of the government in power concerning approaches to crime. Appointments in Ontario, during periods of conservative governments or in the wake of public concern about unacceptable or unusual levels of perceived higher crime have stressed a law and order approach to crime, thus limiting the granting of parole. Even during periods of more liberal governments, public demands to "get tough on crime" may exert considerable pressure on parole board members to deny parole to all but the most deserving. Members of parole boards serve on a part-time basis.

Inmates are required to apply for a parole hearing. However, as correctional investigator Ron Stewart found, many who are eligible do not bother to enter an application (Fleming, 1995). Most readers could not imagine forgoing any opportunity to gain release; however, this is a view from the outside. If the inside is "turned out" (Ericson, 1973), failure to apply is more readily understandable. Reasons given include lack of access to a necessary program or treatment, difficulty in finding employment outside the institution, lack of familial supports, and problems in locating a place of residence. Inmates who lack resources outside of prison walls (family, friends, assistance of religious groups, employer support) find themselves with little opportunity for parole success. Life skills acquisition is a major factor in the success of inmates seeking parole since it educates them in reinventing themselves for entry into civilian life.

Inmates are informed of their date for parole eligibility and can make an appointment to present their case to the parole board members. There are two types of parole that can be granted. *Day parole* is a more limited form of parole that provides some safeguards for the community through supervision of parolees. Parolees are required to live in a halfway house until ready for full parole. *Full parole* is granted to those who are ready for release to the community with their own living arrangements. Many parolees live with friends or relatives or on their own. However, since parolees are often short of funds and friends when released from prison, they frequently must live in homeless shelters. In Toronto, Seaton House, the largest men's shelter in North America, is home to many ex-inmates who need a place to live following incarceration.

The Parole Experience

Parole officers assist and monitor the parolee after he or she is released from the institution. The task of parole officers is to monitor the behaviour of inmates in the areas of employment, criminal activity, housing, and relationships to prevent a relapse into crime, which would lead to further incarceration. Parole officers, like probation officers, also serve an important function in providing counsel and a sounding board for parolees. Moving out of prison life proves to be a difficult transition for almost all individuals. The John Howard Society promoted a campaign in the 1990s that described the difficulties parolees experience reintegrating into the community: "Now the sentence is over, the hard part begins!"

Inmates on parole are required to live up to their parole conditions, including regularly visiting the parole officer and residing in a particular area. They may not leave the area they live in without the permission of the parole officer. Conditions that are regularly imposed include refraining from associating with known criminals, abstaining from alcohol consumption, and taking treatment for specific problems. These conditions act as controls on the types of behaviour and associations that have prompted criminality in the past.

Fleming's (1982) study on the reintegration of offenders demonstrated the difficulties that confront prisoners upon release. His study, conducted in England with long-term prisoners, showed the considerable difficulties that ex-prisoners must face. In some cases, the people had been institutionalized for so long that the monetary system of the country had changed. Many found it difficult to use a telephone or to cross a road—things that we take for granted in negotiating the everyday world. Returning to society is particularly difficult

for men and women who have no familial supports awaiting them, as noted in numerous studies conducted of prison life and release (Morris, 1965; Morris & Morris, 1963).

Parole board hearings predominate in the federal corrections system; however, almost 50 percent of parolees are released from provincial institutions. Some two-thirds of applicants for parole are successful in obtaining it.

Prerelease Programs

Prisoners are entitled to apply for a number of **prerelease programs**, including escorted and unescorted temporary absences, day parole, and work release. Escorted temporary passes are issued for a variety of reasons. The philosophy underlying them is that a way should be found to make it easier for the individual to re-enter society. By absorbing increasing, temporary freedom outside of prison walls, the individual can make a better adjustment to full freedom when it is eventually awarded. The inmate is assessed in terms of potential threat posed to the community if he or she were to escape on a temporary absence. Therefore, inmates must present a minimal risk to society before being awarded these forms of absence. Of over 40 000 passes granted each year (CSC, 1999), only a handful result in attempted or actual escape. Escorted passes generally apply for a day or two, with a maximum of five days if a person is seeking medical treatment. Most often, passes are granted to allow offenders to obtain further education or to visit relatives in the community.

Following a period of significant incarceration, inmates may apply for unescorted absences. Typically, these passes are for short periods of time, from several days to one week in duration (with some exceptional cases involving longer periods). In considering readiness for this form of freer release, authorities will examine various facets of the individual's life while in custody, such as the person's behaviour while incarcerated, as well as the planning that has gone into the proposed absence and the inmate's potential threat to the community.

Upon granting these absences, correctional authorities must notify the police. They also must give notice to victims who have made formal requests to be alerted when inmates will be released. Individuals who are serving time in a maximum-security institution and dangerous offenders are not permitted unescorted absences.

As inmates approach the end of their institutional sentence, they are permitted to apply for day parole. This program permits the inmate to spend the entire day in the community before returning to the prison at night. For some, day parole allows time for job searches or for seeking accommodation. Inmates at this stage in the carceral network will typically reside in a halfway house. These are facilities in the community that provide treatment for offenders to prepare them for bridging the gap between the institution and society.

Work release programs facilitate the transition back to society by permitting inmates to work in a full-time job, or in some instances in a voluntary position, while returning to the institution or halfway house at night. Alan Eagleson, the former NHL players' agent, inaugural union boss, and attorney, was permitted to work in a Toronto-area factory on such a program.

Full parole may be granted to persons who have served one-third of the sentence awarded by the court. Life prisoners are required to serve a sentence of 25 years. However, under section 745 of the Criminal Code (the so-called "faint hope" clause), offenders may seek an early eligibility date after serving 15 years. The most infamous inmate to seek early eligibility under this clause is serial murderer Clifford Olson. Time served before trial is not relevant in determining the time that must be served before an offender is eligible for parole.

Statutory release (formerly called *mandatory supervision*) begins after a prisoner has served two-thirds of a sentence. At this time, the offender may be eligible for release into the community. This is the most common form of release from federal facilities. Since those released must be supervised by a parole officer, some inmates prefer to wait until the end of their sentence before release. There is little debate that supervised release is preferable to an inmate's re-entering society completely on his or her own. Supervision forms part of the carceral network envisioned by Foucault (1977), who argued that the reinforcement of control messages throughout society was necessary to maintain adherence to societal norms. The question that arises for parole authorities is whether there is a danger that an inmate will hurt someone after release. In England until the mid-1970s, for example, supervision following release was not provided for criminally insane offenders. This lack of supervision led to several tragic murders by released individuals who, through regular contact and supervision, could possibly have been identified as being in danger of reoffending. This dilemma is discussed by Kevin Marron in his book *The Slammer*. An offender, Darren, was serving seven years for sexual and physical assault, and having served two-thirds of his sentence was applying for statutory release:

> The parole board would have no trouble deciding that Darren was dangerous. But would keeping him in jail for another two years lessen or increase the risk to the public? Would he benefit from more treatment in jail or would he become even more anti-social? Would it be safer to let him out now and insist that he attend treatment programs in the community? . . . Members of the parole board are frequently faced with impossible dilemmas, as they are asked to weigh imponderable risks. (A parole board member asked) "Do you think hitting her on the head was a failure to control violent impulses?" Darren responded, "The reason I did that was to stun her so she would stop screaming." The board members ordered that Darren be detained until the end of his sentence. (1996, p. 244)

Revocation of Parole

Inmates risk **suspension** of parole if they commit a technical violation of their parole. This violation involves breaching one of the conditions of their parole, most notably when it involves one or more of the behaviours involved in previous crimes. Committing another offence will automatically lead to suspension. Parole officers conduct unannounced visits to their parolees, including "curfew checks" (Marron, 1996). These checks are conducted by pairs of parole officers because many parolees are forced to accept accommodation in dangerous locales owing to their poor financial circumstances.

Most parole officers have a caseload of 25 to 35 offenders. Parolees are required to visit the parole officer approximately once a week to discuss their progress and problems. Marron's research reveals that the groups supervised by each officer are mixed: "About half of all offenders supervised by parole officers have been convicted of non-violent crimes, another quarter have been serving time for robbery, while the remaining quarter committed violent crimes or sex offences" (Marron, 1996).

When parole is suspended, the parolee is placed in custody. The parole board is then required to meet with the offender in the next 45 days to determine whether it will take the more serious step of revoking parole or whether it will release the person to continue parole. If the individual has committed a breach that is not of a serious nature and is not considered a serious risk to society, the parolee can be returned to the community. More conditions may be added at this time if it is felt they are necessary to ensure the success of the offender.

Revocation is initiated when the board considers the offender to present a significant chance of reoffending. The breaches that the parolee commits may signal a deterioration of his or her condition and so are taken seriously. For example, if an offender who has a long history of committing crimes while under the influence breaches parole in a tavern, considerable risk is demonstrated. Similarly, if an individual who has a history of committing sexual offences against children is found loitering near a school, the implications can be serious for the community. However, one of the difficulties in this approach is assessing which behaviours constitute merely a minor violation with no significant consequences, and which ones are serious and require intervention. According to Zamble, "We have no specificity of what is a serious violation and what is trivial lack of conformity" (2000, p. 3). For Zamble, parole officers are put in the position of acting like fortune tellers, since they have no specific tools for predicting an offender's behaviour. The research of Zamble and his colleagues points to the possibility of developing a model for predicting recidivism. Since he argues that offenders "appear to have had little or no perception of their movement toward recidivism" (p. 3), his model, which is based on the offender's choices of response to precipitating environmental situations, points to the individual's inadequate coping resources. The ineffective responding of the offender results in negative thoughts and emotions, which are "identifiable, distinctive and characteristic of offenders in similar circumstances" (Zamble, 2000, p. 5). Thus, officers could use this model to provide effective interventions when the behaviour is serious, rather than employing draconian measures when the behaviour is not serious. This model is not considered foolproof, however, since the complex nature of offending and the environment that either encourages or reinforces criminal behaviour must also be considered.

One of the questions most often addressed in complaints concerning the laxity of the parole system is whether it is an effective tool of rehabilitation. Three researchers (Nouwens, Motiuk, & Boe, 1993) studied a large sample of offenders released on parole over a 10-year period, from 1975 to 1985. In examining the cases of 42 000 parolees, they found that the majority were successful in completing parole. Roughly 20 percent had difficulties that involved committing a crime on parole, and 25 percent had their parole revoked either for a crime or for a technical violation, with the reasons being equally divided between each group.

PROBLEMATIC SITUATIONS FOR PAROLE SUPERVISION

A supervising officer must decide whether to suspend release when an offender commits each of the following breaches of parole:

1. is seen drinking in a local pub
2. is chronically late for appointments
3. leaves the district without permission to visit a girlfriend
4. appears somewhat depressed
5. breaks up with his wife
6. tests positive for cocaine through urinalysis
7. fails to appear for his monthly appointment and does not answer his phone

Which behaviours do you think constitute a serious breach of parole?

Source: Edward Zamble. 2000. "Community Supervision: Current Practice and Future Directions." CSC Canada website. Available: www.csc-scc.gc.ca.

Life Sentences in Canada

In 1976, bowing to world pressure and enlightened research, Canada revoked the death penalty for capital offences. No one had been executed in Canada since 1962, as during this period there had been a moratorium on the death penalty. In Canada, at least two cases played a significant part in ending the use of the death penalty. The execution of Wilfred Coffin was a clear case of the hanging of an innocent man (Belliveau, 1956). Coffin, a sometime trapper, guide, and woodsman in the Gaspé region of Quebec, was convicted of the murders of three US game hunters. The evidence against Coffin was circumstantial: he had been one of the last people to see the victims alive, he was in possession of a pocket knife owned by one of the victims (which he claimed was a gift), and he had US money in his pocket (in an era when Canadian and US money were at par and freely circulated as such). Coffin claimed to have seen a distinctive jeep bearing US plates and two men dressed in army fatigues in the area just before the murders occurred. During the trial Coffin's lawyer offered no defence, calling no witnesses on his behalf, and refused to let Coffin take the stand. After his conviction, several eyewitnesses came forward and confirmed his story regarding the jeep carrying the two Americans who had acted suspiciously; two of the eyewitnesses were doctors at a Toronto hospital, and another was the owner of a local gas station located just a few miles from the cut-off road for the woods where the victims were found. This evidence, though strong, was not heard by the court since the rules of evidence at the time did not permit an appeal on new evidence. Coffin went to his death an innocent man. One of the junior lawyers assisting on his case, Pierre Trudeau, later became the prime minister who repealed the death penalty.

The second case, that of Steven Truscott, has recently resurfaced as a matter of public debate, some 40 years after the original crime. In 1959, Truscott was convicted of the rape-strangulation murder of an 11-year-old girl, Lynn Harper. Both were residents of a military base in the small town of Clinton, Ontario. At the time, there was no other recorded case in common law involving a juvenile offender committing such a heinous crime. Truscott was convicted on circumstantial evidence. There were indications that the police and the military suppressed evidence in his favour, and that other suspects were not fully pursued (LeBourdais, 1966; Trent, 1971). Particularly suspicious was the military's transfer of Steven's family to Ottawa before the commencement of his trial for murder. As a young offender facing the death penalty, this separation from his family would have been particularly hard. Truscott was convicted and sentenced to death. His sentence was commuted by the cabinet of Prime Minister Lester B. Pearson to one of life imprisonment. Throughout his incarceration, and during his exemplary civilian life since release, Steven Truscott has told the same story of his actions and steadfastly maintained his innocence (Sher, 2001). Currently his case is under review.

Before the death sentence was repealed, murderers whose sentence was commuted served approximately 10 years before release. Following the repeal of the death penalty, the time served before release was increased to 25 years. Thus, an individual sentenced six months before the changes would serve less than half of the sentence of a person convicted six months later. The 25-year sentence was arbitrarily decided, rather than based on criminological studies and penological experience. It represented a concession to supporters of the death penalty. Little consideration was given to the costs involved in housing prisoners, the difficulties they would have adjusting to society upon release, and the effects of long-term imprisonment (Fleming, 1995).

The authors of the **Life-25** policy also instigated what is commonly known as the faint-hope clause. Under section 745 of the Criminal Code, inmates may apply for early parole after serving 15 years of their sentence. Those hearing the application can reduce the sentence remaining before parole eligibility or even order immediate release. A hearing is held before a judge and jury in the community where the original crime was committed. The original conviction is not revisited in court; instead, the behaviour and plans of the inmate while in prison are considered. Consideration is given to the nature of the original offence and the likely risk the inmate still poses to society. Over 2000 inmates will have been eligible for this review in the first few years of this new century. Research by criminologist Julian Roberts (2000) revealed, surprisingly perhaps, that "only a

LIFERS AND PAROLE ELIGIBILITY

Roberts (2000) demonstrated that few lifers apply for early parole eligibility despite the probability their applications would be successful in reducing their wait for parole. Which of the following reason(s) might explain this unexpected finding?

1. Lifers lack resources in their opinion to make a successful application so they do not proceed. These might include being illiterate, not understanding the process, or being unaware of how to apply. Given the average educational attainment of inmates it may be expecting too much to presume they will spontaneously exercise their rights in this matter.
2. Lifers just want to serve their full sentence and be free of parole restrictions upon leaving prison.
3. Lifers have misinformation about the relative success of applications.
4. Lifers think that section 745 hearings are not going to be fair and are a waste of time.

minority of eligible lifers, have, to date, applied for a reduction in their parole eligibility." While Roberts is unsure as to why this trend may be occurring, despite clear evidence that a positive response is more likely than a negative one, it might be interesting to try to explain this trend (see Box 9.2).

Early analysis of applications has shown a provincial difference in the granting of early eligibility. Quebec applicants have enjoyed a much higher success rate than their contemporaries in Ontario or Alberta. Some criminologists have questioned the criteria employed to assess eligibility, pointing out the apparent inequities in the present system. The case of Rene Vaillancourt, who as an 18-year-old killed a Toronto police constable during a bank hold-up, is interesting to compare with that of Larry Sheldon. Vaillancourt was denied early eligibility, despite an essentially model prison career. Sheldon, who was reported to be a model inmate, had been sentenced for abducting, raping, and dissecting a child near Gimli, Manitoba. Sheldon was successful in his section 745 application (Fleming, 1995).

Despite exceptions such as this, applicants who have committed horrendous crimes are unlikely to be successful in obtaining either early release or eventual release. Under legislation passed since the public outcry over Clifford Olson's application, multiple murderers have been excluded from applying for judicial review. Paul Bernardo, a multiple murderer and serial rapist, can legally be detained in prison for the remainder of his natural life. Since Bernardo poses such a continuing threat to the community, it is difficult to imagine releasing him into society for any reason.

Dangerous offenders are a special category under the Criminal Code. These individuals are declared a danger to society because of the violent, repetitive nature of their crimes. While there is some controversy surrounding the designation of persons as dangerous, particularly women, their long, repetitive and increasingly violent criminal careers and extremely violent nature of their offences make them poor candidates for parole.

Problems with Parole

It has already been argued that most inmates view parole board hearings as a form of kangaroo court. It is also interesting to note that many experts hold this same view. Their criticisms of the decision-making process in parole concern two areas: (1) the composition of parole boards and the relative competence of their members to render decisions and (2) a lack of clear criteria that can inform decisions. Regarding the first issue, the political nature of appointments to the parole board means that such positions are often given to individuals as a reward for party support, rather than as a reflection of their understanding of criminal behaviour. These positions command a pay scale approaching $100 000 per annum. Since few members of the board have any previous training in criminal justice or in human behaviour, it is difficult to establish working criteria that are understood by board members and that reflect objective assessment of issues. Often, the kinds of issues that have to be debated are complex and may be incomprehensible to members who lack the appropriate background.

Birnie (1990), a former member of the board who began her duties with minimal training, voices these criticisms. She critiques the arbitrary nature of decisions and argues that decisions reflect the inadequacy of training of members and board composition, rather than objective criteria. Therefore, the criteria by which individuals are judged suitable for parole in one jurisdiction may vary widely with those used in another location. Given that parole board members are informed of the success or failure of their decisions in terms of recidivism only in high-profile cases, they fail to receive the kinds of information that would allow them to reconsider or alter misguided decision-making processes. It should be acknowledged that the prediction of future behaviour poses difficult challenges even for trained professionals.

Parole board members are empowered to make decisions concerning the release or continuing incarceration of individuals even though they may be inadequately trained in human psychology and behaviour, fail to use objective criteria, and are unaware of the outcome of their decisions. Consequently, it is little wonder that parole board members may lean toward the conservative or seemingly safe decision of continuing incarceration. After all, a parole board that releases very few inmates has less chance of being blamed for the failure of its releasees. However, the safety of this approach can be questioned. If offenders are unjustly held in prison for no apparent reason after making serious efforts to reform their behaviour, they may re-enter society embittered by the justice system and with a grudge against society. Thus, holding a prisoner can result in more serious criminal exploits. Conversely, release at an earlier date may forge a stronger bond between a merciful society and the inmate.

The foregoing discussion of parole has considered both its benefits and drawbacks. For society and correctional officials, parole is both a carrot and a stick. It is a carrot to induce good behaviour and thus more efficient management of institutionalized persons, as well as a stick to punish those who do not conform. Outside the institution, parole can be used to continue the connection of the released prisoner with the institution, as disobeying a condition of parole may mean returning to finish out a sentence. Parole, under conservative governments, has become a way of further punishing criminals by denying it in all but the most "safe" cases, rather than using it as a tool for rehabilitation. If parole boards reject the dual role of balancing rehabilitation of the individual with the protection of society, and instead opt for concentrating on the latter consideration, then the intended purpose of parole is defeated. Some criminologists have called for determinate sentences of reasonable duration, followed by supervision in the community in the form of support rather than law enforcement. For inmates, parole is more of an illusion. Applying for parole is seen as a "crapshoot," reflecting the lack of due process safeguards in the parole procedure, the lack of training for board members, arbitrary standards, and the limited skills inmates possess in representing themselves at parole hearings.

Alan Manson, speaking on sentencing at a symposium held at the University of Windsor (1989), has addressed the importance of early release mechanisms. As one of the few attorneys who regularly represented inmates in various hearings, he has a unique perspective on the prison system. Given the high rate of imprisonment in Canada and the long sentences that are imposed, he argues that the possibility of early release is necessary to instill hope in inmates and to preserve and nurture the very skills necessary to constructive participation in a democratic society.

The increasing call for accountability in parole hearings, emanating on the one hand from governments that wish to impress society with their "hard line" regarding law and order and on the other hand from inmates who feel the process is questionable, seems to indicate the need for a more open process of parole. If society wishes to instill in inmates the recognition of the need for fair play and reasonableness in dealing with others, then it is incumbent upon society to construct a parole process that is marked by due process and by objective criteria, against which inmates can measure their progress toward release and make necessary adjustments to ensure success. It is only then that parole will be transformed into more than an illusion for Canadian prisoners.

DID YOU KNOW?

The yearly success rates in 2000/01 for day parole, full parole, and statutory releases are among the highest in recent years. From a public safety perspective, offenders granted a discretionary release (e.g., a day parole or full parole) and properly supervised in the community demonstrate very high levels of success.

Community-Based Alternatives

Increasingly, fiscal crises (O'Connor, 1973) have forced governments to consider less-costly alternatives to imprisonment. Researchers have identified other factors in the European context that could be transferable to Canada. Joutsen has identified trends in Canada that reflect the need for alternatives to incarceration:

1. Increasing fear of crime
2. Disillusionment with the effectiveness of treatment programs
3. Lack of confidence in the ability of the system to rehabilitate or produce law-abiding citizens
4. Increasing use of prisons as an administrative measure
5. Increasing attractiveness of a "just deserts" philosophy of punishment (CSC, 2000)

As Joutsen argues, it is difficult to muster the political will to move to alternative measures when public fear of crime is heightened. When a "politics of fear" prevails in society, fanned by media reports and self-serving politicians, few are strongly supportive of keeping convicted offenders in the community. Interestingly, fear of crime is typically unrelated to actual crimes committed in a community or to crime statistics. In an era of declining rates of serious crime, it is curious that fears of crime have escalated. A large measure of this fear seems to be intergenerational—that is, the aging population fears young offenders. Although we understand by reviewing statistics on young offenders that the overwhelming majority of their crimes are directed against other young people, fear of crime is fed not by hard facts, but by a media that seeks to exploit violent crime for readership. As well, governments have realized the value of fanning the flames of fear in the electorate. Put simply, if crime is "out of control," governments will argue, then people have reason to fear, and they can trust in government to crack down on criminals. The Ontario government, in the fall sitting of Parliament for 1999, identified the elimination of squeegee kids in Ontario as its number-one legislative priority. In passing the so-called Safe Streets Bill, it played to a the moral panic that it had created about the criminal intent of "aggressive panhandlers." This unrealistic fear of society's marginalized persons continues to be a view held by politicians and the public despite over 15 years of research on homelessness. Toronto city councillor Jane Pitfield, a co-chair of the city's committee on homeless and socially isolated persons, a position in which she is supposed to advocate on behalf of the marginalized, cited women's fear of persons begging as the reason she advocates passage of a bylaw prohibiting panhandling (CBC Radio, May 4, 2006). Extrapolating from the European experience, it can be argued that it is in the interests of politicians to "use harsher measures to draw attention away from the failures of society" (CSC, 2000).

For some observers, such as prison abolitionists Ruth Morris (1997) and Nils Christie (1994), prisons are an unacceptable form of punishment for the majority of offenders. In order to convince the public of the acceptability of alternative approaches, it is necessary to convince them both of the appropriateness of community sanctions and of their effectiveness when compared with institutional sentences. While rhetoric by law and order emphasizes the need to get tough with offenders, the grim reality of prison expenditure means that governments must consider alternatives. It is hypocritical for governments to suggest that health, education, welfare, and social services should be cut, whereas prison budgets should be permitted to expand exponentially. To that end, in April 1997 Parliament passed a series of sentencing and corrections reforms that allowed for the development or expansion of new community-based alternatives.

The movement of governments to cut costs is not new. During the 1970s and 1980s, governments deinstitutionalized mentally ill patients as a cost-saving measure. It was argued that living in the community was better for the mental health of individuals, who could benefit from outpatient clinic services and from social support and interaction with the community. However, some analysts, including Scull (1983) and Fleming (1982), have argued that such programs reflected the goal of saving costs, rather than a real transfer of resources to the community to assist the mentally ill. Unsupervised and living in substandard housing, the "walking wounded" posed a considerable problem for policing, hospitals, and the court systems in their community, which had few resources and little training to deal with mental health crises.

The philosophy underlying non-custodial sentences is that non-violent offenders who have committed crimes that are minor in nature are more effectively dealt with in the community (CSC, 2000). Public safety is not an issue with these offenders, so confinement serves no purpose other than retribution, which has been rejected as a valid goal by eminent legal scholars.

One alternative with significant potential to assist the justice system in its efforts to divert offenders from secure custody is **community service orders**. These orders, issued by a judge, compel a convicted offender to complete a requisite number of hours of work in the community. The centrality of the offender's bonds and attachments to the community in encouraging law-abiding behaviour has long been understood. The CSC believes that community service orders can be "far more meaningful, effective and less costly to taxpayers than a jail sentence. And better yet, it can help to instill good work habits, a sense of responsibility, and may even lead to stable employment" (CSC, 2000, p. 1). There is little doubt that individuals may benefit from remaining in their communities, as it may be unnecessary to remove the person from gainful employment, from familial relations and obligations, or from educational training. For those offenders who do not enjoy such bonds in their community, this experience teaches that the ends of justice can be met in the community, rather than in a prison cell. By leaving an offender in the community, we potentially extend to them the opportunity to atone for their crimes without suffering all of the pains associated with imprisonment.

A second developing area of community corrections is **mediation services**. This option is offered in co-operation with the office of the Crown attorney. The express aim of this option is to put the offender together with the victim(s) to provide victim–offender mediation. In this approach, victims are given the opportunity to confront the author of the crime committed against them. For offenders, it is a unique opportunity to gain insight into the consequences of their actions. Few criminals actually witness the impact the crimes they commit have on their victims. In a neutral mediated session, the victims are able to express pent-up feelings of anger about the criminal, the crime, and its negative effects on their life. For offenders, it represents a chance to learn and perhaps to apologize to the victim. Another component of mediation services is restitution. The offender, faced with the direct consequences of his or her actions, is asked to consider a means of making recompense to the victim. This restitution could take the form of financial compensation, work performed for the victim, community service in lieu of assistance to a victim who may feel uncomfortable with further contact, or another mutually agreeable option. The option must answer the needs not only of the victim but also of the offender, as well as the need for rehabilitation.

Sentencing circles and elder panels are further methods of dealing with the offender outside of prison walls. These options, which emerged in Canada from Aboriginal forms of justice, have recently received a great deal of public attention. In Aboriginal communities there has always been a greater emphasis on reclaiming the individual while maintaining the person in the community. In Aboriginal society, the community is seen as the centre of healing for offenders, and removal from society is rarely viewed as a positive option (unless it is a sentence that forces the individual to be isolated in a wilderness area to get back in touch with core spiritual values). The Aboriginal experience with the Canadian criminal justice system has never been positive. The location of prison facilities has typically meant that in Prairie provinces, Aboriginal offenders are removed from their reserve or home communities and are transported hundreds of kilometres away to serve their sentences. This process further disenfranchises offenders in terms of their own communities and unique sets of cultural values.

Elder panels are composed of respected members of the community who have knowledge of and respect for Aboriginal approaches to justice. This approach represents a meeting of the Canadian and Aboriginal justice systems, as elders sit with judges to assist them in constructing appropriate sentences for offenders. The advice, according to the CSC, can be offered either in open court or in chambers—that is, behind closed doors in the judge's chambers.

The **sentencing circle** reflects Aboriginal beliefs in the connectedness of all life. The offender is not cast out from the community but is kept part of it. Under this approach, the offender is involved with members of the community and elders in establishing how the case should be dealt with. The judge will make the final decision in the case but will take into account the recommendations of the sentencing circle or the elder panel. This approach allows the community that is most affected by the activities of the offender to have a direct input into sentencing options. The CSC has found that "the offender is more likely to heed the concerns and suggestions of the community rather than those of a judge acting alone" (2000).

Electronic monitoring, or tethering, is another form of alternative community punishment that has been in existence since 1987 (CSC, 1998) and is

administered by four provinces, including Ontario, British Columbia, Newfoundland and Labrador, and Saskatchewan. Recent improvements in technology have allowed the development of sophisticated electronic monitors, which permit offenders to serve sentences in their own homes. Offenders in this program do not simply remain in the household, since few would be able to sustain themselves throughout an extended sentence. Instead, most are employed, attend school, or are engaged in other programs that the judge approves as a condition of monitoring. The appeal of electronic monitoring is dual—it is an inexpensive alternative to custodial sentences, and it also permits offenders to benefit from remaining in the community with minimal disruption of their lives. However, certain conditions are attached to monitoring, including strict curfews and restrictions of movement. The tether, which is worn on the leg, is "read" by a telephone dial-in system to ensure that the offender is at the appropriate place at required times. A non-response at the home after curfew, for example, would send police to investigate the unauthorized absence.

Another program, **fine options**, is a response to previous inequities in the criminal justice system that disadvantaged poor offenders. Aboriginal Canadians have historically been overrepresented in the prison system, particularly in the Prairie provinces. They often have served prison sentences in provincial jails owing to an inability to pay fines ordered by the court. The CSC recently reported that over one-quarter of all people serving time in provincial jails were doing so because of their inability to pay fines. Enlightened reform indicates that alternatives, such as community service or probation, may be more equitable in serving both the offender and the community.

Another new development that has much promise is **restitution**. This is a new approach that permits judges to rule that the offender must compensate victims of property crime or for personal injuries sustained during the commission of a crime. While the pain the victim suffered may include emotional and psychological effects, there are personal costs as well, including loss of property, loss of employment income, and medical expenses, which can severely affect them. Crimes often have a complex impact on the victim that is difficult to measure. Understanding these costs requires the court to listen to victims and receive evidence regarding these costs. Restitution has recently experienced a renaissance, particularly in Ontario, where the provincial government introduced legislation to require the parents of young offenders to compensate the victims of crime. The restitution order is filed as a civil judgment. Enforcement of these orders, as might be expected, is often difficult, if not impossible, if the offender has few or no financial resources. If an individual is able to pay a fine but fails to do so, the province can refuse to renew licences until the fines are paid.

All of the above programs can be viewed as part of a movement toward what is called *restorative justice* (see Chapter 8). This approach focuses on a consultative process that brings together the offender, the victim, and the community in order to permit healing and repair (CSC, 2000). Derived from the writings of criminologist Richard Quinney, this form of "peacemaking criminology" focuses not on punishment but rather on "making things right" through a process of communication and problem solving between the parties. Two further programs that spring from this approach are family group conferencing and community sentencing panels. In the former, the victim, the offender, and family and supporters meet to resolve financial and emotional issues, as well as to examine means of providing restitution to the victim. The latter is a program that involves volunteers from the community. The panel can look at the issues that lie at the heart of offending through considering reparations, restitution, conciliation, and victim involvement. The panel is also empowered to make recommendations concerning the environmental factors in the community that may be conducive to crime or facilitate criminal activities.

Conclusion

Probation and parole have long been important components of Canada's criminal justice system. These approaches have been successful as alternatives to prison by providing both cost savings and opportunities for convicted criminals to benefit from serving their sentences in the community. A variety of community service options have become part of the correctional arsenal in the past two decades. These sentencing options allow the long-term reintegration of offenders into the community. Community alternatives, while relatively new in Canada, hold the promise of creating a more humane and effective criminal justice system.

Summary

This chapter has focused on alternatives to prison, specifically parole and probation, as well as community service models. We have explored both the strengths and weaknesses of probation as the most widely employed form of alternative sentencing in Canada. Parole, although effective as an early-release mechanism, has proved to present many problems, in terms of its administration and the ability of inmates to have fair and impartial hearings that ascribe to the dictates of due process and justice. We have explored a variety of prerelease programs, which allow inmates to re-enter civilian life more effectively. Finally, we have discussed the controversial "faint-hope clause," section 745 of the Criminal Code, in terms of its fairness and value as a rehabilitative tool.

Key Terms

carceral network (p. 210)

community corrections (p. 211)

community service orders (p. 228)

elder panels (p. 230)

electronic monitoring (p. 230)

fine options (p. 231)

Life-25 (p. 223)

mediation services (p. 229)

parole (p. 214)

prerelease programs (p. 218)

restitution (p. 231)

revocation (p. 221)

sentencing circles (p. 230)

statutory release (p. 219)

suspension (p. 220)

technical violations (p. 213)

Discussion Questions

1. Why have the courts made such wide-scale use of probation?

2. Do you think parole is a carrot, a stick, or an illusion? Explain why.

3. What are the prisoner's responsibilities to ensure a positive parole outcome?

4. Why do inmates refer to parole hearings as a kangaroo court?

5. How do the various prerelease programs differ in their purpose? Why do they enjoy a high success rate?

6. Is the process of parole supervision and revocation fair and effective, in your estimation?

7. Is Life-25 an effective sentence?

8. Why are community-based alternatives becoming increasingly popular with governments?

Weblinks

www.npb-cnlc.gc.ca The National Parole Board, as part of the criminal justice system, makes independent, quality conditional-release and pardon decisions and clemency recommendations. Their website provides information on the NPB and its role, as well as offering links to relevant legislation.

www.operb.gov.on.ca/english/intro.html The Ontario Parole Board site offers a wealth of information on parole statistics, fiscal reviews, parole criteria, the hearing process, review, and victim participation.

www.johnhoward.ca The John Howard Society of Canada works in an advocacy, research, community education, and crime prevention capacity with people who have come into conflict with the law.

www.lcc.gc.ca The Transformative Justice Project site is the work of the Law Commission of Canada and explores restorative justice issues in Canada and around the world. The site also provides an excellent resource for Canadian justice and law links.

ww2.psepc-sppcc.gc.ca/abor_corrections/publications_e.asp Published by the Solicitor General's Aboriginal Corrections Policy Unit, this study deals with community corrections and healing projects in Aboriginal communities.

CHAPTER 10

Victims of Crime

Objectives

- To define *victimization* and *victimology*.
- To describe the services and programs offered to victims.
- To note the patterns of victimization in Canada.
- To address some of the issues surrounding the emergence of victims' needs in justice administration.
- To describe the place of the victim in the criminal justice process.

The Place of Victims in the Crime Picture

Within the modern criminal justice system, victims often feel as if they have secondary status. They frequently feel neglected and abandoned by the very system in which they expect help. However, the role of the victim within the justice system was not always like this. Historically, written laws did not exist and there were no authorities to turn to for justice; thus the punishment of the offender fell to the victim or the victim's kin to carry out. The system was one of retribution, in which the offender would suffer for his or her transgressions. With the emergence of basic forms of law, the role of the victim shifted from a violation against the person to a violation against the state. The victim's status was diminished to that of a witness. Many critics of the modern criminal justice system argue that victims are forgotten and the rights of the accused outweigh the rights of victims. Obviously, we do not want to revert to the days when victims engaged in barbaric retribution, when the accused had few rights and laws were not applied. Yet we need to recognize that victims deserve basic rights and that they should be treated with respect and dignity and be duly informed of the sometimes complicated criminal justice process.

Currently, there are many advocates for victims, and the latter are recognized as an important part of the criminal justice process. Many victims have spoken out on their own behalf and urged lawmakers and officials of the criminal justice system to pay more attention to them. Much of the focus on the interests of victims in crime policy is a result of the efforts of reformers whose energies have been sparked by their own victimization in crimes. In this way, crime policy and, to a lesser extent, criminal procedure reflect times past, when victims used state resources to avenge or recoup their losses.

Until recently, it had been assumed that victims were being duly represented in the criminal justice system. After all, wasn't the state devoting considerable resources to prosecuting and punishing crime on the victim's behalf? In practice, however, victims were rarely consulted about their wishes, and pretrial and trial procedure gave them little or no opportunity to raise concerns about the plea or the sentence. Therefore, many observers and participants came to see the criminal procedure as officially furthering the victim's alienation and mistreatment through what is generally referred to as **secondary victimization**.

The recent surge of interest in victims—of placing them more centrally or at least less peripherally in the criminal justice process and policy development—is partly the result of politics. In this chapter, we will review some of the features of these political machinations. In addition, we will explore what is meant by **victimology**, a branch of criminology which studies the psychological, cultural, social, and political factors that contribute to victimization, and the societal processes that go into defining a victim. Finally, we will offer a statistical and normative portrait of victims and victimization by drawing on victimization surveys and self-report studies.

Victimology

Although the study of victimology is considered a relatively new and growing subcategory within criminology, the study of victims emerged in the 1940s and 1950s with the work of Hans von Hentig, Benjamin Mendelsohn, Stephen Schafer, and Marvin E. Wolfgang. However, in order to understand the criminal act, this early work was more concerned with the relationship between the victim and the offender as a possible factor in the victimization. In this sense, there was little in the way of compassion, sympathy, or understanding for victims of crime. Von Hentig described the *agent provocateur* or the crime provocative function of the victim, while Mendelsohn (the so-called "father of victimology") examined the interpersonal relationships between victims and offenders and developed a six-step legal classification of victim blame. Schafer furthered Mendelsohn's work by examining the responsibility of victims, which he described as *functional responsibility*. In a classic study of homicide, Wolfgang (1958) studied homicides in Philadelphia from 1948–1952. He found that 26 percent of all cases involved what he termed **victim precipitation**, in which the victim may in some way be responsible for his or her victimization. For Wolfgang, there were several factors, which included a prior interpersonal relationship, a small disagreement that escalated, and alcohol usage (after which the victim may lose inhibitions or lose the ability to defend him- or herself). Finally, in a very controversial, sexist, and methodologically flawed study, Menahem Amir (1971) reported that 19 percent of rapes were precipitated by the victim. Despite the inflammatory nature of Amir's work, the immense criticism did propel victimology in a new direction. Both victims' rights advocates and academics sought to redefine and reinvigorate the study of victims by moving away from the notion of victim precipitation (which had overrun the field of victimology). For example, victims' rights supporters advocated that victims should be deserving of assistance, not blame, and called for renewed interest in the victim. Academics and victim advocates gathered at Bellagio, Italy, in 1975 at the first ever International Conference of Victimology, which promoted a general approach to victimology, in an attempt to move away from traditional criminology and its inherent focus on the crime and criminal. More recently, critical victimology has emerged, with a focus on victims of the powerful, who often go without justice, such as those in developing nations, and the homeless and impoverished. Critical victimology focuses on such crimes as genocide, war crimes, state-sponsored torture, human slavery, and environmental crime. Today, there are several organizations that promote the study of victims and many criminal justice/criminology programs incorporate victimology into their curricula. But what is victimology? The definition varies. In his influential text, *Crime Victims: An Introduction to Victimology*, Andrew Karmen (2001) broadly defined victimology as

> the scientific study of victimization, including the relationships between victims and offenders, the interactions between victims and the criminal justice system— that is, the police and courts, and corrections officials—and the connections between victims and other societal groups and institutions, such as the media, businesses, and social movements.

The Emergence of Victims in Criminal Justice

As mentioned earlier, before the advent of our modern system of criminal prosecution, victims played a major role in the administration of justice. In sixteenth- and seventeenth-century England, prosecution relied on the complainant's initiative in bringing about an arrest, making a charge, and securing a penalty or compensation.

Gradually, with the arrival of the centralized state and the emergence of lawyers in the court (and later public police), criminal prosecutions came to be public and administered by professionals, with the state taking over the case of the victim in an adversarial contest with the accused. Both public police and public prosecutors came to represent the claims of the victim in the name of the state. With this representation, the victim's claims for compensation and reparation came to be secondary or even tertiary considerations, subordinate to the interests of the state in its own legitimacy and in maintaining the appearance of due process for the accused. The distinction between a civilian model and a state-based model of judicial administration is the relative weight given to the appearance of justice for the sake of society as a whole versus the special interest in the individual victim's experience of justice.

Throughout the nineteenth and most of the twentieth century, the administration of justice in nations based on the adversarial model developed into highly rationalized structures in which only well-educated specialists could find their way about. Because the interest of the victim was subsumed in the interest of the state in a just process, the victim of crime came to be excommunicated from justice delivery, and indeed was often treated as an afterthought or a nuisance.

There are differing accounts of the sequence of events that have led to the situation today, in which victim's rights have again come to influence judicial policy. In criminology in the late 1950s, several important papers and symposia on victimology appeared (Elias, 1986). A groundbreaking study by Wolfgang (1958) on victim precipitation in criminal homicide in Philadelphia also alerted scholarly attention to the dynamics of victim–offender interaction. In addition, attention to victims was supported by the first national survey on victimization in the United States in 1966. Victimology took off as a distinct field of inquiry, with several important papers published in the late 1960s and early 1970s.

In public policy, following the work of Sara Margary Fry in the 1950s, compensation schemes for victims of crime emerged first in New Zealand in 1963, and then in Great Britain and California in 1964 (Elias, 1986). Together with the proliferation of victimization surveys and a political and cultural backlash against the civil rights gains of the 1960s and 1970s, these schemes, known as Criminal Injuries Compensation Boards (CICBs), helped to focus attention on the rights of victims as a major political value (see Box 10.1).

BOX 10.1

COMPENSATION FOR CRIME VICTIMS IN CANADA

In Canada, most provinces have some type of criminal injuries compensation. In addition to recognizing the harm done to victims, these programs were started to help ease the financial burden that often follows criminal victimization. Although money cannot alone restore a victim's physical and/or emotional health, many provinces recognize that crime victims should not face additional hardships because of victimization.

Programs for criminal injuries are designed to compensate victims for expenses sustained as a direct consequence of a violent crime. This may include compensation for medical, dental, or counselling expenses; pain and suffering; and loss of wages. Legislation concerning criminal injuries does vary from province to province.

Who or What Is a Victim?

Under criminal law, a victim is person against whom a criminal act has been perpetrated. According to Quinney (1972) and others, under the law there is no crime without a victim (a person, a corporation, or some other entity) and a finding of guilt. Schneider (1982) defines a victim as a person, an organization, or a moral aspect of society that is harmed or jeopardized by a crime. Nagel (1974) argues that a victim is one who is acted against criminally.

However, when the legal system clears a defendant of responsibility for a criminal act—for example, when the defendant has committed only a technical violation of the law—it may clear the only person who has any factual causative responsibility for the act. This is also the case when the accused is found not criminally responsible owing to mental disorder. Unless a new suit is launched, this act of the court amounts to a technical declaration that there is, under law, no act that can definitively be said to have been criminal. And if there is no criminal act, then there is, under the strict legal definition, no victim. Therefore, strict legal definitions of *victim* and *victimization* are unsatisfactory, as they will negate instances of victimization and make validation of victimization dependent on legal authority alone.

A strict legal definition of either term is unlikely to validate the experience of many victims. Even victimization surveys may fail to reveal the full extent of criminal victimization because some respondents may be unwilling to acknowledge that an act committed against them was criminal. Many other acts that may engender loss or cause great harm, such as industrial polluting, may not be outlawed or considered criminal.

For these and other reasons, early victimologists went beyond the definition of *victimization* as loss from criminal wrongdoing to carve out the scope of victimology. One proponent of an inclusive view of the victim was Benjamin Mendelsohn (1976), who argued that people could even be victims of natural phenomena and of industrialization. Others, such as Marlene Young-Rifai (1982) and Robert Elias (1986), sought to use human rights violations as the template against which to define victims.

While we may not insist on illegality of acts as a condition of victimization, we also cannot rely entirely on subjective experience. Our definition of victimization should require recognition by a third party or external authority. Under this condition, only after a person is accorded the status of victim will a third party intervene on his or her behalf. There are limits on the capacities of social, political, and economic bodies to mobilize in the service of aggrieved parties, and thus there will be limits to who is accorded the victim status, or who is validated. There are even more limits on compensation. Here, it is important to recognize that there are a variety of contexts or stages in which a person may seek validation of victimization, and denial or invalidation in one context does not presume invalidation in another. For example, the mass media may define a person subjected to an illegitimate violation as a victim, even if the violation may not mobilize criminal or civil remedies.

What Is Victimization?

Victimization can be defined as "an illegitimate violation of a person by another, resulting in an experience of loss as recognized by a moral authority." Take, as an example, the execution of the individual by the state. In some societies, this practice is permitted both according to law and by popular consent. Stanley Tookie Williams, the 1960s founder of the infamous Los Angeles Crips gang and Nobel Prize nominee, was executed in California in December 2005. His person was violated when needles were inserted into his body and his heart was stopped. He was infringed, his life taken. But if we accept the legitimacy of the state in performing the execution—and some of us may not—the violation is neither unwarranted nor illegitimate, and therefore he was not a victim.

The phrase "experience of loss" in the definition above is important. The victim must experience a loss. When we say "experience," we refer to a *subjective* phenomenon. You *feel* the loss of your stolen bicycle. Why? Because it breached your personal circumference or your privacy wall. You expect to have a relationship with the social world in which your privacy, person, and property are protected. Because this expectation is part of the norms of society, you experience a general feeling of insecurity when your belongings are stolen. More specifically, you feel the loss because something you enjoyed is no longer there for you, leaving you with one less resource with which to take pleasure from your existence.

The clause "as recognized by a moral authority" is also significant in the definition above. This qualification is very important to the designation of victim status. Marlene Young-Rifai (1982) has argued that what is important in our definition of victimology is both whether there is an imbalance of power between the victim and the other and whether the action of victimization is seen as an injustice. When we think of events in terms of who has the power and what serves justice, we are not restricting ourselves necessarily to the acts forbidden under the law. Political scientists, psychologists, sociologists, and other expert authorities will differ in their perceptions of who rightfully belongs in the category of victims, but we depend on them, in addition to our legal authorities, to define this category. You may tell a police officer or a social scientist that you are a victim or have experienced a violation or loss, but until your definition of that experience matches legal, social scientific, and, to some extent, cultural designations, you will not be recognized as a victim.

The authority, once certifying that the loss is illegitimate according to its standard, takes some form of intervention. At a minimum, such intervention is merely the recognition that the violation suffered is illegitimate. Recognition is not to be underestimated, because it is prefatory to further intervention, such as compensation. The authority must then recognize the violation as being sufficient to meet some standard of third-party intervention. Violations that are seen as not requiring such intervention are eventually recast as normative actions.

The Context of Victimization

There are three considerations of context in assessing victimization: the balance of power, the rules of interaction, and the legitimacy of the authority granting the victim status. The balance of power is an essential consideration of any discussion of victims. Another way of conceptualizing victimization is as a person's exploitation of weakness in furthering an advantage. Victimization can be seen as the taking of power or autonomy from another; this, in many cases, is the essential loss that the victim experiences. The designation of victim status will in part be a consideration of the distribution of power between two or more parties. The question is, which of the parties to an interaction is in a position of advantage?

Take the idea of "playing the victim." What is meant by this accusation? Only when we consider the victim in the balance of power does it make sense. The person claiming the role of the victim does not deserve the status of the role because, it is implied, the aspirant has failed to present the case that she or he has been in a position of relative *disadvantage*. People may seek to gain the advantages of victim status by presenting the context or circumstances in which they have suffered a loss as overwhelmingly sided against them, in order to benefit from third-party recognition of their victimization. We would hardly see the United States as a victim in the context of international relations, unless we were given some very strong evidence of the country's powerlessness in a given arena. Similarly, we need to understand the victim within the context of relationships of power.

A second essential feature of context in assessing victimization is the *normal rules of interaction* governing conduct at the site at which the victimization is alleged to have taken place. Have both parties conducted themselves within the norms of communication and conduct that pertain to the site of their interaction? For example, in a queue at the cafeteria, a person who tackles the last in line violates the norms of interaction that apply to the situation. Even within the play of a CFL football game, such action is well circumscribed. But the ball carrier who is tackled during play has little claim to victim status, even if the play-by-play announcer claims that a "mugging" has occurred.

A third feature of context concerns the *legitimacy of the authority* who grants victim status. What is the degree of neutrality of the arbiter? What is used to measure violations? Are subjective or objective measures used? Does the interpretive framework itself adequately encompass the diversity of individual experience? Is the interpretive framework structurally biased in some way?

All of these questions go beyond the rules at the particular site and begin to apply to more universal evaluations, such as general principles of justice or human rights. For example, a totalitarian regime may imprison journalists who question the policy of the government. Such imprisonment may be sanctioned not only by the executive branch but also by the legislative branch and the judiciary. These parties will see the denial of rights and freedoms to the journalists not as an illegitimate violation but rather as an essential measure in promoting the internal security of the "just state." However, observers may argue that the legitimacy of the authority is questionable, and critical victimologists would likewise argue that a wider frame of reference than that offered by an individual nation's justice system is needed in determining injustice and illegitimate violations. Using a wider frame of reference, the attribution of victimization is made not by local or state authorities, but by the international community or by another moral authority, such as a religious or human rights group.

We may use human rights criteria or standards (although they are not free of cultural bias) to assign victimization within the prescriptions of cultural practices. Amnesty International and Human Rights Watch are organizations that "discover" victims who are not recognized by indigenous authorities. The practice of female circumcision in certain Muslim societies and

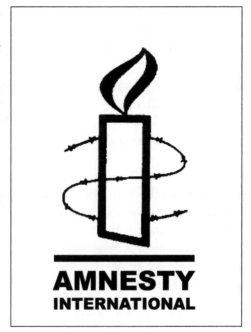

other communities, for example, may be a part of the normative rites of passage, falling within parameters of legitimate violation and loss. As well, certain states may sanction the incarceration of preadolescents or the execution of youths below the age of majority. Human rights agencies apply universal codes of conduct to review such practices. These acts may then be seen as crimes against humanity or as unjust and therefore falling within an expanded, international definition of crime. With the larger, international definition of illegitimate violation, there is also an expanded discovery of victims, as is the case in Amnesty International's "death watch" of executed inmates in the United States.

Recognition of victimization is often sought to achieve political empowerment, whether at the level of personal or state politics. Because victim status can be politically useful, parties or people often will seek recognition, even when the ultimate purpose is not to progress from the status of victim to the status of survivor. At bottom, this politicization of the victim draws on the fact that victim recognition is necessary before scarce resources will be allocated on the victim's behalf. Because victimization is dependent on recognition, it is not long before someone's real experience of loss becomes someone else's opportunity to advance a political agenda.

A Profile of Criminal Victimization in Canada

As noted in Chapter 2, in addition to the UCR, victimization surveys are used to reveal the extent of crime in society. These surveys are used with the idea that victims may be more willing to acknowledge their victimization anonymously and that many criminal incidents may go unreported to the police or unrecorded.

There have been a number of victimization surveys in Canada, beginning with the Canadian Urban Victimization Survey (CUVS), which surveyed 61 000 people by telephone in 1982. One of the most important findings was that, of the total offences unearthed, only 42 percent had been reported to the police.

In addition to the CUVS, Statistics Canada has carried out the General Social Survey (GSS) since the mid-1980s and included questions about risk of crime and victimization. The most recent survey, in 2004, asked approximately 24 000 respondents about their experiences with criminal victimization. Compared to 1999, there was no change in self-reported rates of violent victimization, such as sexual assault, robbery, or physical assault. However, rates increased 42 percent for theft of household property, 17 percent for vandalism, and 24 percent for theft of personal property. Rates of breaking and entering fell by almost one-fifth (CCJS, 2005). Table 10.1 provides an overview of the self-reported incidents communicated to police in 2004.

TABLE 10.1

SELF-REPORTED VICTIMIZATION REPORTED TO THE POLICE, 2004

CRIMES	INCIDENTS REPORTED TO POLICE		INCIDENTS NOT REPORTED TO POLICE		TOTAL # OF INCIDENTS
	000	%	000	%	000
Sexual assault	42	8	448	88	512
Robbery	127	46	144	53	274
Physical assault	519	39	789	60	1323
Total violent incidents	**688**	**33**	**1381**	**66**	**2109**
Break and enter	275	54	223	44	505
Motor vehicle/parts theft	281	49	285	50	571
Theft household property	330	29	786	69	1136
Vandalism	303	31	664	67	993
Total household property	**1189**	**37**	**1958**	**61**	**3206**
Total personal property	738	31	1623	67	2408

Source: Adapted from Statistics Canada's publication *The Daily*, Catalogue 11-001, Thursday, November 24, 2005. Available at www.statcan.ca/Daily/english/051124/d0511246.htm.

It appears that fewer victims are reporting incidents to police. In 1999, 37 percent of incidents were reported to the police, but by 2004, only 34 percent of incidents were reported to the police. However, there is no change in reporting violent victimizations, theft of property, and vandalism. Sexual assault remains the crime least likely to be reported at only 8 percent, compared to 54 percent of break-ins, 49 percent of motor vehicle/parts thefts, 46 percent of robberies, and 39 percent of physical assaults. However, compared to physical assault victims, sexual assault victims are twice as likely to seek help from support centres and social services, such as help lines, crisis centres, and counsellors. In general, the more serious the crime, the more likely it is to be reported. Victims who did not report an incident claim that it was not important enough, while the use of a weapon or the need to take off work (because of victimization) increases the likelihood that victimization would be reported. Probably because of insurance reasons, reporting household victimization and personal property theft is highest when there is significant financial loss.

Within Canada, violent victimization rates are generally higher in the Western provinces. However, Alberta and Nova Scotia experience the highest rates, while Quebec has lower rates (see Table 10.2 on the next page). Similarly, the Western provinces experience higher rates of household victimization, with Saskatchewan and Manitoba experiencing the highest, while Newfoundland and Labrador has the lowest, followed by Quebec (see Figure 10.1 on the next page).

FIGURE 10.1

RATE OF SELF-REPORTED VIOLENT VICTIMIZATION IN QUEBEC

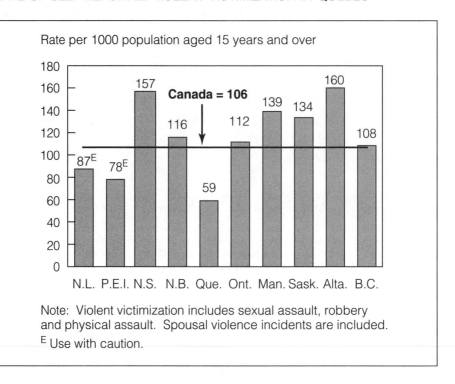

Rate per 1000 population aged 15 years and over

Note: Violent victimization includes sexual assault, robbery and physical assault. Spousal violence incidents are included.

E Use with caution.

Source: Adapted from Statistics Canada's publication *The Daily*, Catalogue 11-001, Thursday, November 24, 2005. Available at www.statcan.ca/Daily/english/051124/d051124b.htm.

KEY FACTS: GSS VICTIMIZATION SURVEY (2004)

- The violent victimization rate is 2.5 times higher for self-identified gays or lesbians.
- About 4 percent of self-reported victimization incidents are believed to be hate motivated (in two-thirds of incidents the motive is based in race/ethnicity).
- The risk of violent victimization is 1.5 times higher for those aged 15–24 compared to those aged 15–34 and 19 times higher compared to those over the age of 65.
- Single people (who tend to be younger) are four times more likely to be violently victimized compared to those who are married.

- Respondents who frequently participated in evening activities are four times more at risk for violent victimization.
- There are few differences between men and women; however, females are more at risk for sexual assault, while males are more at risk for physical assault.
- Aboriginals are three times as likely to report violent victimization.
- Short-term residents, renters, and high-income households are more at risk of household property offences. (Those who live in their residence for less than one year are most at risk of household victimization.)

Source: Adapted from Statistics Canada's publication *Juristat*, Catalogue 85-002, Criminal Victimization in Canada, 2004, Vol. 25, No. 7, November 2005. Available at www.statcan.ca/english/freepub/85-002-XIE/0070585-002-XIE.pdf.

FIGURE 10.2

HOUSEHOLD VICTIMIZATION BY PROVINCE

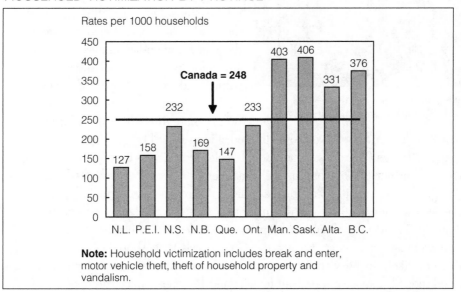

Rates per 1000 households

Canada = 248

N.L. 127 P.E.I. 158 N.S. 232 N.B. 169 Que. 147 Ont. 233 Man. 403 Sask. 406 Alta. 331 B.C. 376

Note: Household victimization includes break and enter, motor vehicle theft, theft of household property and vandalism.

Source: www.statcan.ca/Daily/English/051124/d051124b.htm.

The GSS Victimization Survey reveals that there are few differences in victimization between males and females. However, when seen over the course of a lifetime, rather than over the course of a year, violence against women is revealed to be a major social problem. In 1993, the Violence Against Women (VAW) survey of Statistics Canada inquired into various kinds of abuse experienced by Canadian women. It found that 29 percent of women experienced at least one sexual assault since turning 16, and that 29 percent of women who have lived with a spouse (married or common law) have experienced at least one episode of spousal violence (CCJS, 1995b).

The White Ribbon Campaign is a men's organization working to end violence against women.

Surveys like the VAW also reveal that while people most fear being victimized by strangers, victims are more likely to be assaulted by someone they know. Of the women in the VAW who reported being sexually assaulted, 79 percent said that they were assaulted by men known to them.

More current data reveals similar percentage of spousal violence for both males (6 percent) and females (7 percent). An estimated 546 000 men and 653 000 women experienced some form of violence by a current or former spouse. Those aged 15–24, those in relationships less than three years, those who had been separated, and those in common-law unions are most at risk for spousal abuse. However, the nature and consequences of spousal violence is more severe for women. Females are three times more likely to fear for their lives, twice as likely to be injured, and twice as likely to be targeted in more than 10 violent episodes. In addition, females are twice as likely to be stalked by a former partner. Stalking or criminal harassment is repeated or unwanted attention that causes a person to fear for their safety. Approximately 2.3 million people experienced stalking in 2004, with the majority of those people knowing their stalker. Roughly 11 percent of females and 7 percent of males report that they have experienced criminal harassment. Finally, the GSS reveals that Aboriginals are three times more likely to be victims of spousal violence, 21 percent of Aboriginals reported spousal violence (24 percent females and 18 percent males) as opposed to only 7 percent for non-Aboriginals. Aboriginals also experienced more extreme forms of spousal violence such as beating, sexual assault, choking, and weapon usage.

In addition to victimization experiences, the GSS also asks respondents about their fear of victimization and feelings of safety (see Box 10.3).

BOX 10.3

KEY FACTS: CANADIANS FEAR OF VICTIMIZATION AND FEELINGS OF SAFETY (2004)

- The vast majority of Canadians (94 percent) are satisfied that they are personally safe from crime, up from 86 percent in 1993 and 91 percent in 1999.

- There is increased fear of crime in three situations: 42 percent felt some fear when waiting for or using the transit system; 20 percent feared for their own safety when home alone; and 10 percent felt unsafe walking alone at night.
- Fear of victimization is higher for women—95 percent of males felt safe compared to 93 percent for females. However, the gap has narrowed since 1991.
- Gender differences are stronger when attributed to fear of transit use at night (males at 29 percent versus females at 58 percent); fear of being home alone (males at 12 percent versus females at 27 percent); and women are three times as likely to be afraid of walking alone at night compared to men.

Source: Adapted from Statistics Canada's publication *The Daily*, Catalogue 11-001, Thursday, July 7, 2005. Available at www.statcan.ca/Daily/english/050707/d050707b.htm.

Programs for Victims

In general, we can distinguish between two types of innovations when it comes to changing the relationship of the victim with the criminal justice system: victim-centred measures and restorative justice measures.

Initiatives such as victim–offender reconciliation programs, community justice forums, family group conferences, and justice circles are also part of the panoply of interventions that are aimed at giving the victim of crime a voice in the administration of justice. While some programs are intended exclusively to aid victims or to compensate them or offer retribution to others in their name, Cavadion and Dignan (1997) have pointed out that there is another group of strategies known as **restorative justice measures**. Restorative justice is an alternative approach in which the victim's voice is to be a major component of lasting redress and peacekeeping.

Victim-Centred Measures

Victim Impact Statement

A **victim impact statement (VIS)** is a testimony of loss suffered by the victim owing to the harm caused by the crime. It allows the victim or family of the victim to inform the court of the emotional and financial consequences of the act of victimization. In Canada, the Criminal Code requires the court to consider a VIS at the time of sentencing if the victim of the offence has prepared such a statement. The provinces or territories will stipulate the form of the statement. Under section 662 of the Criminal Code, a VIS takes the form of a written submission attached to the probation officers' pre-sentence report. A VIS may also be read aloud at the discretion of the judge. In general, the victim will get a VIS form from the police and may even get help in filling it out. The form will often have spaces for physical injury, financial and property loss, and so on, and can be withdrawn at any time at the victim's discretion.

The VIS is intended to help in victim rehabilitation by reducing the victim's feelings of helplessness and alienation from the community. VIS forms are believed to be of therapeutic value to victims. According to Wells (1991) the greatest benefit of the VIS is that it aids in the psychological recovery of victims (see Box 10.4).

BOX 10.4

THE BENEFITS OF VICTIM PARTICIPATION DURING CRIMINAL PROCEEDINGS

* Gives victims a voice for therapeutic purposes;
* Enables the interests and/or views of victims to be taken into account in decision-making;
* Ensures that victims are treated with respect by criminal justice agencies;
* Reduces the stress for victims in criminal proceedings;
* Increases victim satisfaction with the criminal justice system; and
* Increases victim co-operation, as a result of any of the above objectives.

Source: Sanders, Hoyle, Morgan & Cape, 2001.

In a study of six Canadian cities, Giliberti (1990) found that the majority of victims who completed statements deemed the experience to be positive and would participate again. However, Giliberti also points out that greater victim satisfaction is not just dependent on the VIS. Victims want information about the operation of the criminal justice system and their respective cases. Corns (1994) argues that victims who participate in VIS are less satisfied because they expect that their views will influence sentencing practices, which is not always the case. Other research has found that the use of the VIS has little impact on victim satisfaction or on the harshness of sentences (Davis & Smith, 1994, 1995). Furthermore, research has found that many victims fail to use the VIS to speak because they are unaware of it, have become disenchanted with the system, or fear some form of retaliation from the offender (Erez & Tontodonato, 1992).

Critics argue that VIS forms have no place in the courtroom, as the emotional quality of the documents may interfere with the neutrality and objectivity of the sentencing decision. Some also argue that they may create sentence disparity because statements are not always provided, and some statements are more rhetorically powerful than others. For example, Arrigo and Williams (2003) argue that VIS undermines prospects for fair and impartial trials by fuelling vengeance, danger, and hatred. While Myers, Godwin, Latter, and Winstanley (2004) suggest that VIS dehumanizes the offender, which may have an impact on the fairness of the trial.

Legal professionals have also argued that allowing time for these statements adds unnecessary length to the process. However, disparity is already built into the system in the discretionary purviews of officials, including police officers, defence attorneys, prosecutors, and judges. Furthermore, research has failed to find that the use of VIS forms contributes to making court proceedings any less speedy (Davis, Henley, & Smith, 1990).

Court-Ordered Restitution Orders

Restitution entails a court-ordered sanction involving the offender's payment to the victim for injuries suffered as a result of the criminal act. Federal law allows criminal courts to impose a sentence of restitution in addition to any other penalty for convicted offenders. Courts may impose a restitution order on their own motion or following an application by the prosecutor. Restitution may be ordered when the court is satisfied that the victim has suffered a property loss or has incurred medical expenses or other pecuniary costs owing to the offender's actions. The restitution order will specify a time period for payment, and if the order is not carried out, the victim may file the order in any civil court, where it will have the effect of a judgment of damages made in civil court. The sheriff can then seize bank accounts or place liens on property.

Compensation

Compensation comprises direct payment to the victim to cover financial losses resulting from injuries or death suffered as a result of a criminal act. During the fiscal year 2002/03, all jurisdictions except Newfoundland and Labrador and the three territories had compensation programs for victims of crime. These programs are intended to ease the financial burden victims and their families can sustain as a result of victimization. While the eligibility standards and the reasons for compensation payments differ from one province to another, compensation is provided for various reasons such as loss of wages, medical and counselling costs, and financial support for children whose parents have been killed.

The eight provincial compensation programs that responded to the first ever survey of victim services report a total of 10 874 applications adjudicated or concluded during 2002/03. Another 8927 carried forward to the following fiscal year.

Of the total concluded, 70 percent were allowed or granted and 14 percent were disallowed. The remainder had another status, such as decision pending, withdrawn, or abandoned by the applicant. Overall, $70.6 million in compensation was paid for the victims of crime in 2002/03 by the eight provincial compensation programs surveyed (*Juristat*, 2004).

In Ontario, the CICB will reward a financial compensation to victims of violent crimes, providing they make the application within a year of the event. Compensation is awarded for expenses, lost income, and pain and suffering as a result of injury or death. Compensation is also awarded for the maintenance of a child born as a result of sexual assault. The CICB also takes into consideration the extent of the injury and whether the victim has been awarded insurance or compensation at civil law. As well, the CICB will consider whether the victim's behaviour contributed to the injuries or death and whether the victim has received compensation from other sources, such as private insurance or worker's compensation schemes. It also weighs against the applicant any unco-operativeness he or she has shown with the police.

Victim Services

In 2002/03, there were 606 victim service agencies in Canada. The majority of the agencies are police-based (41 percent), followed by community-based (19 percent), then sexual assault centres (17 percent), court-based (10 percent), and system-based (8 percent). For this last type, system-based services are delivered by a provincial government program that supports the victim throughout his or her contact with the criminal justice system. Other types of services account for 3 percent of agencies and the criminal injuries compensation and financial benefit programs for victims of crime made up the remaining 1 percent (see Figure 10.3). Almost 75 percent of victims helped are female and almost 40 percent of females seeking help are victimized by a spouse, ex-spouse, or intimate partner. Children under the age of 18 account for 18 percent of those helped by victim services—in terms of violent victimization, 75 percent are boys and 90 percent are girls. Of the girls, 7 out of 10 are victims of sexual assault. However, of those who sought help at a sexual assault crisis centre, only 46 percent reported the incident to police, while 31 percent did not.

The Police

Many provincial police acts now mandate that the police provide victim services. Throughout Canada, assisting victims of crime is part of the core mission of police services. In Ontario, the Police Services Act, as amended in 1998, stipulates that police must offer services to victims. Following the passing of An Act Respecting Victims of Crime in 1996, police officers are specifically mandated to provide victims of crime with information on services and to treat them with courtesy and respect.

Consequently, Victim Services Units provide support initiatives for victims of crime and disaster. As well, awareness programs are required for police and correctional officers. These units offer counselling and referral services around the clock to victims. Through the Victim Crisis Assistance and Referral Service (VCARS), each community in Ontario is serviced by volunteers who are available 24 hours a day and who provide on-site assistance to victims.

The Courts

The courts serve the interests of victims in a number of ways, including, fundamentally, by providing the court of law itself. However, in the past and even now, victims

FIGURE 10.3

VICTIM SERVICES COMPRISE MOSTLY POLICE-BASED AGENCIES

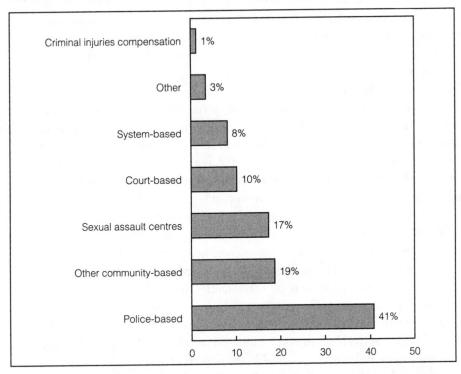

Source: Adapted from Statistics Canada's publication *The Daily*, Catalogue 11-001, Thursday, December 9, 2004. Available at www.statcan.ca/Daily/english/041209/d041209a.htm.

have often been an afterthought to procedure. Victims become witnesses who may be compelled to testify and who have often spent hours waiting outside the courtroom, only to be told that their case has been continued or to come face to face with the accused as he or she enters the courtroom. The courts have responded to criticisms that prosecutors are indifferent to the plight of victims by instituting court worker programs and Victim Witness Assistance Programs (VWAPs). The latter were created under the assumption that offering better services to victims would increase the likelihood of their being effective witnesses, as well as under the mandate of governments through legislation to recognize victims' concerns.

VWAPs offer a variety of services, including providing agency personnel to transport the victim/witness to and from court, crisis counselling, translators, and information pamphlets detailing what can be expected in the courtroom, which other witness-protection services are available, and how to apply for compensation. Some VWAPs also offer mediation services for victims who might want to reconcile differences with an offender.

Voluntary Organizations

The voluntary sector has been the main proponent of the need of the criminal justice system to incorporate victims' interests to a much greater degree. As previously noted, new initiatives often have their source in an individual instance of victimization, which has then been converted into a moral crusade. These crusades have brought victims and others together under a lobby banner alerting attention to some deficiency in our social policy.

For example, although now defunct, CAVEAT, which stands for Canadians Against Violence Everywhere Advocating for its Termination, was an organization that began when Nina de Villiers was abducted and murdered while jogging in Burlington, Ontario. The murderer was Jonathan Yeo, a man with a long history of violence who was out of prison on $3000 bail. A coroner's inquest was struck to examine Jonathan Yeo's 11-year history of attacks on women and the justice and mental health systems' apparent inability to prevent his continually slipping through the cracks. CAVEAT came into being as a vehicle to lobby the 137 recommendations of the inquest and to convert the outpouring of support for the de Villiers family into a reform agenda. A petition was signed by 2.5 million Canadians and delivered to Allan Rock, then federal minister of justice, in 1994. In general, CAVEAT seeks greater protection of communities from dangerous offenders through crime prevention, public education, changes to the justice system, and ensuring the rights of victims. Another important agency is Victims for Violence, which was founded in 1984 by parents of murdered and abducted children. Two key founders were Gary and Sharon Rosenfeldt, the parents of 16-year-old Daryn who was brutally murdered by the infamous Clifford Olson (the murderer of 11 children in BC in the early 1980s). The Rosenfeldts and other parents were frustrated and angry over the system's lack of empathy and inability to provide information. The parents were especially angry when, in a "cash for bodies" arrangement, $10 000 was paid to Olson's wife for information about the bodies that were missing. One of the most agonizing moments for the parents was when comments were made by prosecutor John Hall, who couldn't understand the frustration felt by the parents: "I don't know what you people are so upset about. Eleven children could just as easily have been killed in a school bus accident. I mean come on, if they're dead, they're dead." After moving back to Edmonton in 1984, the Rosenfeldts and other parents of murdered children formed Victims for Violence and helped propel the victim into being an important part of the fight for justice (for a more complete history of the organization and their services, please visit www.victimsofviolence.on.ca).

Current Legislation

Current legislation in aid of victims in Canada is found in the Criminal Code, the Corrections and Conditional Release Act, and the Youth Criminal Justice Act, as well as in provincial and territorial legislation. Federal, provincial, and territorial legislation is guided by the Canadian Statement of Basic Principles of Justice for Victims of Crime.

In July of 1988, Bill C-89 added amendments to the Criminal Code that established new legal rights for victims of crime, including a right to restitution and a right to make a victim impact statement.

Another provision of the Criminal Code is the victim fine surcharge (VFS). This is an additional payment that every offender convicted of a Criminal Code offence or of an offence under the Controlled Drugs and Substances Act is required to pay in addition to any other punishment, so that revenue can be collected to provide assistance to victims. Each province may then use this money to support the victim services programs as the lieutenant-governor in council directs, and the majority of provincial and territorial victim services are financed by this revenue. The maximum VFS is the lesser of 15 percent of any fine imposed, or $35.

The administration of justice is the jurisdiction of the province, and all provinces now have legislation aimed at helping victims of crime to recover losses. In Ontario, such legislation includes the Victim's Bill of Rights (S.O. 1995 c. 6), Compensation for Victims of Crime Act (S.O. 1990 c. 24), and Victims Rights to Proceeds of Crime Act (S.O. 1994 c. 39).

Ontario's Victim's Bill of Rights established a set of principles according to which judicial system officials are to treat victims of crime. These principles include the requirements that victims be treated with courtesy and compassion; that their privacy be respected; that timely access to information be afforded to them, including notification of the conditional release of offenders or their parole; and that their property be returned to them in a timely fashion.

The bill also states that a person convicted of a crime is liable for damages awarded in civil court. The offender's criminal sentence is not to be weighed against the victim's claim of civil damages; rather, a victim of domestic or sexual assault is presumed to have suffered emotional distress that may be cited as evidence at civil trial. Also under the bill, money collected under the VFS is expressly dedicated to a victim's justice fund.

The Ontario government also operates, funds, or otherwise assists several victims' initiatives. It provides funding for 34 community-based sexual assault crisis centres (SACS), which provide 24-hour crisis lines; counselling services; public education and referral; and court, police, and hospital accompaniment and support. Ontario also operates an automated victim support line (VSL) to keep victims informed of changes in the status of adult offenders who are provincially incarcerated and to provide information on victims' services and other general information on what to expect from the court process. Through the VSL, victims can register for automated updates on the status of an offender through a victim notification system, including information on escape from custody, parole hearing dates, changes in scheduled release dates, transfers or readmissions, and the name and phone number of the supervising probation officer.

In addition, the Ontario government helps to fund the Victim Crisis Assistance and Referral Services (VCARS), which is a community program providing round-the-clock help to victims of crime or disaster. VCARS volunteers are alerted by the police on the victim's request and provide short-term, on-site counselling services. As mentioned on the government's website, these local victim services programs allow police to meet their legislated mandate of responding to victims' needs.

Restorative Justice

Much of the emphasis on the traditional retributive model has focused on validating the victim's experience by punishing the offender. In general, studies have found that victims' satisfaction with the justice process, even when an offender has been sentenced to punishment, has been weak.

This finding has led to calls for alternative models of justice delivery that place the victim back in the centre of the judicial process. Christie (1977) was among the earliest proponents of a radical change in judicial administration, in which communities would have greater participation in conflict resolution. In New Zealand and Australia, experiments with family group conferences (Braithwaite & Mugford, 1994), and here in Canada with **victim–offender reconciliation programs (VORPs),** have reportedly been successful in bringing the wishes of the victim into the inner circle of justice delivery. In both such schemes, the interests of the community and of the state in certifying that justice is not totally civilianized have been secured with steps that also secure state and community representation.

The VORP allows an offender the opportunity to acknowledge his or her guilt and, under the authority of the judge, to make restitution according to an agreement hashed out in a meeting between victim and offender, which is mediated by a social worker, a probation officer, or some other official.

Conclusion

In the past 25 years, much activity has taken place to bring victims back into the circle of justice. Victims are now part of a powerful lobby for criminal justice reform and are now recognized as primary partners in justice delivery. What we need to watch for, as we continue to move away from retributive justice, is just how the public interest will be represented. A number of critics have argued that the wishes of the victim have no business informing criminal sentences because it is the public interest in condemning a criminal act that is of utmost importance. In this new millennium, we risk seeing a gradual erosion of the concern in justice policy for both the victim and the public interest. However, the failure of private forms of justice is precisely their inability to incorporate notions of fairness and equal treatment under the law.

It is important to recognize that during most of the past century, judicial administration was often hostile to victims' long-term interests. The adversarial process from the side of the prosecution, in the main, looks upon justice in terms of conviction. In their quest for convictions, prosecutors view victims as witnesses who are more or less likely to add to the chances of winning the case. When victims are perceived as instruments in this way, it is no wonder that their interests as suffering individuals tend to fall by the wayside. Today, this institutional indifference is being overturned, and it is now possible to ask whether a resolution serves the victim's interest. The pendulum has been swinging back.

Summary

In this chapter, we have explored the concept of victimization and the services to victims offered in Canada. It has also addressed some issues surrounding the emergence of the victim's needs in justice administration, and it has detailed some of the specific strategies and programs that are available. We have stressed that an understanding of victimization must include attention to the notion of the victim's loss. We also noted that there is a politicization of the victim's status and that the relationship between victim and offender can be a complicated one, in which the official designation of victim status may be preceded by victim precipitation.

Key Terms

restorative justice measures (p. 247)
secondary victimization (p. 235)
victim impact statement (VIS) (p. 247)
victimization (p. 239)

victim–offender reconciliation programs
(VORPs) (p. 254)
victimology (p. 235)
victim precipitation (p. 236)

Discussion Questions

1. Why is it important in conceptualizing victimization that we pay attention to the subjective experience of victimization?

2. Describe some of the factors that contribute to a person's likelihood of being victimized.

3. List the advantages and disadvantages of allowing victim impact statements to be read in court.

4. Describe the process involved in victim–offender reconciliation programs.

5. Describe some programs that are available for victims of crime.

Weblinks

www.caveat.org CAVEAT, an organization dedicated to the rights of victims, argues that the protection of the public must be the overriding goal of the justice system, and that the offender's rights should not be greater than those of the victim. Their website offers information, event listings, educational material, publications, and relevant links.

canada.justice.gc.ca/en/ps/voc The Department of Justice's Policy Centre for Victim Issues website has the text of the Canadian Statement of Basic Principles of Justice for Victims of Crime (2003), as well as information on legislation, funding, and news. The site also provides information on government programs and services, such as Aboriginal justice and child custody.

www.gov.ab.ca/justicesummit/process/dwb/delwork32.htm The report by the Alberta Summit on Justice entitled, "Victims—Their Rights and Their Involvement in the System," provides a detailed look at the treatment of crime victims in Alberta.

www.crcvc.ca The Canadian Resource Centre for Victims of Crime is sponsored by the Police Association of Canada and acts as a non-profit victim advocacy group in Ottawa. Their site offers information on their resources, publications, news releases, and links to provincial resources.

www.attorneygeneral.jus.gov.on.ca/english/about/vw This provides information about victim services for the province of Ontario.

www.state.gov/g/drl/hr The United States Reports on Human Rights Practices are submitted annually by the US Department of State to the US Congress. The reports cover internationally recognized individual, civil, political, and worker rights, as set forth in the Universal Declaration of Human Rights.

www.justice.gc.ca/en/ps/voc/rjpap.html The Law Commission of Canada endorsed restorative justice, this link provides an overview of restorative justice.

www.crimevictims.net This website provides numerous links to victims' rights and victims' issues.

www.victimsofviolence.on.ca/index2.html Victims of violence is a national, non-profit, non-government funded charitable organization founded in 1984, by founders of abducted in murdered children. Two leading founders were Gary and Sharon Rosenfeldt, the parents of Daryn Rosenfeldt who was murdered by Clifford Olson in BC in 1981.

CHAPTER 11

The Future of Crime Control

Objectives

- To discuss the concept of decriminalization.
- To describe community policing models and their limitations.
- To discuss international, computer, and high-technology crime in the twenty-first century.
- To discuss international terrorism.

Questions about Crime

In this final chapter, we consider the means of preventing, eliminating, and reducing the amount of crime that is committed in our communities each year. Having read the previous chapters on crime and punishment, readers are well equipped to understand both the nature and the extent of criminal activity in Canada. For most of us, the question of whether crime rates are rising or falling is a central issue. This question leads us to consider whether we are more or less likely to become the victim of particular crimes. But there are perhaps even more important questions concerning the nature of what we call crime and our attempts to police and punish these acts.

A Canadian criminologist, Peter McNaughtan Smith, posed an interesting question over a quarter of a century ago. He asked, "What is crime and why do we fight it?" This is a more significant question than it at first appears. The acts that society identifies as crimes have overwhelming significance for every member of that society, whether as victims, offenders, workers in the justice system or allied fields, or taxpayers who support the administration of justice. It is a simple fact that the more crimes we have "on the books," the more crimes we will record, and the more it will cost us as a society in both human and economic terms to uphold these laws. The current version of the Criminal Code of Canada contains over 1000 pages of prohibited acts and their prescribed penalties. The number of laws that circumscribe our lives is not diminishing, but rather has grown throughout the twentieth and twenty-first centuries. Spending on law enforcement and corrections is exponential in character. So, the question of what constitutes crime is worth considering in more detail, since its impact reverberates strongly in our society and shapes the lives of many members of our communities.

Decriminalization

Given the increasing number of laws governing our lives, we need to consider seriously the issue of **decriminalization**. This is a term used to describe behaviours that have been outlawed in our society but that have assumed the status of social norms. In other words, the behaviours or acts in question are now accepted as "normal" or perhaps "tolerable" by members of society (Stebbins, 1996). If this process has occurred, then criminologists and advocacy groups will raise the question of whether the penalties associated with these crimes should be reduced or whether the acts should be legalized. However, once an act has become defined as criminal through the legislative process (*mala prohibita* crimes), it is a long and difficult process to have it removed from the Criminal Code. Two forms of behaviour that are currently criminalized are worth considering in this context: marijuana use and acts associated with prostitution.

Marijuana Use

Vago and Nelson (2004) note that of the 92 000 people charged with offences under the Controlled Drugs and Substances Act in 2001 two-thirds of these offences involved marijuana use, and half of the charges were for possession. They recount that a survey of youth in 2000 reported that 50 percent of Canadian teens favour the legalization of marijuana use—up from 27 percent in 1992. In that year, 37 percent of Canada's teens indicated that they regularly smoked marijuana. Among certain specific groups such as street youth, the rate of illicit drug use—including marijuana—ranges from 70 to 85 percent. It would seem that such widespread use among youths and in the general population makes the present punitive approach a failure.

One alternative includes approaching drug use as a medical problem instead of a legal one. For example, in Great Britain, the Netherlands, and the Scandinavian countries, the official government approach is to treat the use of both soft drugs (e.g., marijuana) and hard drugs (e.g., cocaine, heroin) as a health issue instead of as a crime problem. In the Netherlands, marijuana is sold legally in "cannabis cafés" for personal use, and in Great Britain drug addicts can obtain prescribed opiates from doctors who believe that addicts cannot quit using the drugs on their own. The rationale is that if addicts are provided with drugs by the state, they will not resort to crime in order to support their drug addiction.

The second alternative is the legalization or decriminalization of marijuana. In April 1999, noting that roughly 2000 Canadians go to jail annually for cannabis possession at a cost of approximately $150 a day per offender, the board of directors of the Canadian Association of Chiefs of Police made a recommendation to the federal government that simple possession of marijuana and hashish be decriminalized. Decriminalization, they argued, would clear a backlog of drug cases in the courts and allow Canadian police services to focus their resources on more serious crimes like drug trafficking (Fife, 1999). Canada has already amended its law to allow those who require marijuana for medical purposes (e.g., to relieve symptoms associated with such conditions as HIV, cancer, and multiple sclerosis) to apply for an exemption under section 56 of the Controlled Drugs and Substances Act. In 2002, over 800 Canadians were permitted by Health Canada to possess marijuana for medical purposes. In addition, the Marijuana Medical Access Regulations permit people with authorizations to possess and cultivate marijuana for medical purposes (McLellan, 2002).

Prostitution and Associated Acts

A great number of Canadians think that prostitution is a crime. In reality, the act of prostitution is, in itself, not a crime in Canada. The federal government moved to liberalize its laws regarding prostitution following the report of several commissions that examined the state of prostitution in Canada. The Fraser Commission (1985) and the Badgely Report (1987) gathered information from prostitutes, their customers, politicians, interest groups, and academics in Canada. An earlier report in England, the Wolfenden Report, looked at the problems associated with prostitution and its control within an evolving capitalist society.

The Canadian government moved to liberalize its prostitution laws for several reasons. In the wake of the feminist revolution, it became increasingly apparent that female and male sex workers considered their services to be a job. The individual, rather than the state, had ownership of his or her body and the right to decide how it would be used (or abused). Yet government intervention had long been based on moral considerations of the undesirability of prostitution. Concerns about public health and the morality of communities also propelled a draconian approach to dealing with sex workers. However, most law enforcement authorities recognized long ago the futility of policing prostitution, and people arrested for prostitution were generally fined and released quickly. Attempting to police prostitution often placed officers in compromising situations that the courts considered entrapment; that is, the police induced people to commit a crime that they would not otherwise have committed (or brought the law into disrepute by acting as customers). Most community members viewed prostitution as a necessary evil that could be tolerated as long as it was not visible.

The form of prostitution that has caused the most concern for communities is referred to as *street walking*. Sex workers walk in areas, called *strolls* or *tracks*, that are well known to "johns" (customers). Most customers approach prostitutes in their automobiles. They "cruise" the hookers, find one who is appealing, and then stop to discuss a business transaction for sex. The hooker normally puts her head in through the window of the car and then discusses acts and prices. If a deal is struck, the prostitute and customer retreat to a dark parking lot or in some cases to a cheap motel room for sex. The greatest percentage of streetwalkers' sex exchanges involve oral sex or masturbation.

Streetwalkers have a number of negative effects on the locales they choose as a stroll. They can be loud and disturb the public peace, which is particularly annoying for residential neighbours. As well, since some sex acts take place in public places, they and their customers may leave behind used condoms and needles employed in drug use. Their garbage is both dangerous and disturbing for residents of the area. Cruising johns also cause traffic problems in the neighbourhood. Residents may feel that they are being prevented from quietly enjoying their homes, and they may be accosted while coming and going when sex workers are on the street. Prostitution also leaves other criminal, quasi-criminal, and illegal behaviours in its wake, including violence. All of these problems can have a serious, negative impact on a neighbourhood's quality of life and property values.

Consequently, Canadian laws were altered to reflect the overwhelming concern over streetwalkers and their customers. Currently, Canadian law targets several behaviours associated with prostitution. First, communication for the purposes of engaging in prostitution is illegal. Under this law, discussion of sex acts and their costs is reason for arrest. Second, solicitation is a crime. Solicitation involves a prostitute's asking the customer to engage in sex acts in exchange for money, or a customer's requesting sexual services in exchange for money. Since customers are often unable to distinguish prostitutes from other female pedestrians, these laws are intended to shunt prostitution off the streets. Police in Toronto, Vancouver, and other large urban areas regularly engage in operations to remove customers from the street. Female police officers pose as prostitutes in an undercover sting intended to catch johns. Once arrested, most customers are sentenced at court to a fine and mandatory attendance at "john school." This educational institution is run by the police in co-operation with former sex workers and is meant to educate johns about the substantial health risks associated with frequenting street prostitutes. Finally, living on the avails of prostitution, or pimping, is another crime associated with prostitution.

Current law additionally provides that those who profit from or participate in juvenile prostitution face more severe punishment than those who profit from or participate in adult prostitution. Since 1988, those who live on the avails of a prostitute under the age of 18 are liable for a maximum period of incarceration of 14 years. The offence of "aggravated procuring" imposes a five-year minimum sentence on individuals who live on and profit from the avails of child prostitution while using violence or intimidation to force a child or children to engage in such work. Amendments made to the Criminal Code have extended the jurisdiction of Canadian courts and allowed for proceedings to be instituted in this country against Canadian citizens who engage in child prostitution abroad (sex tourism) and permit police to charge tour operators or travel agents who arrange for such services.

Streetwalkers use, and are addicted to, a variety of drugs at significantly high rates—primarily crack cocaine. Prostitutes who are high on drugs or alcohol (or both) are far less likely to practise safe sex. Sex workers who are homeless and desperate for food, drugs, alcohol, or a place to sleep may not be in a position to insist on safe sex, particularly when customers offer substantial financial inducements to forgo the use of a condom. Therefore, street hookers are also more likely to contract and transmit venereal diseases and HIV than are prostitutes who work in more protected settings.

The difference in legal interest between streetwalkers and other kinds of prostitutes is evident in the different enforcement patterns that characterize relationships between the police and hookers. In all major Canadian cities, there are pages of listings in the business telephone directory for escort/massage services. Similarly, local entertainment newspapers such as *NOW* in Toronto and *The Georgia Straight* in Vancouver contain many pages of listings for escort/massage services and individual prostitutes' advertisements. Prostitutes working for escort/massage agencies provide sexual services in massage parlours, hotel rooms, or private homes. Individual prostitutes offer sex in their own homes (incalls) or in a client's hotel room or home (outcalls). Police rarely, if ever, arrest people who are engaged in these two forms of prostitution, except if there are public complaints.

What is the future of legal intervention in prostitution? John Lowman, a criminological researcher, has spent a great deal of time talking with and researching the lives and work of prostitutes. He and other researchers have recognized the need to focus on street prostitution as commerce and as part of the sex trade. Street prostitutes are perhaps unfairly targeted by the police, since their personal circumstances prevent them from having the capital to work out of their own apartments. In many cases, they are unsuitable candidates for working in massage parlours. Age, physical appearance, drug and/or alcohol problems, and day jobs that they would lose if their alternative source of income were discovered all prevent them from enjoying the relative safety of other forms of sex work. Should their acts be criminalized simply because they cannot afford to move off the streets?

It is apparent that current Canadian laws on prostitution seek to criminalize the acts of a specific form of prostitute and customer, while leaving others to engage in the same sexual acts without legal repercussions. Some criminologists have argued that prostitution is a victimless crime, as it involves two consenting adults engaging in conduct that some observers in the community consider immoral. Who is harmed by these forms of activities? The prosecution of street prostitutes through the criminal law is both costly and ineffective. Our concern over streetwalkers has more to do with our sensibilities regarding supposedly public spaces than with protection of the community.

Prostitution and acts associated with it will likely be removed from the public purview in the future. The costs associated with enforcement are high, and enforcement has little effect in reducing the amount of prostitution in any city. One alternative to criminalization is establishing a clearly demarcated red light district, where sex trade workers can offer their services. This approach has met with great success in Amsterdam, but it is less popular in some US jurisdictions. Prostitution's natural tendency of attracting other forms of criminal activity has meant that red light districts have the potential to deteriorate unless there is strict urban regulation through appropriate bylaws.

Another possible solution is retraining sex workers so that they will find alternative employment. For individuals who wish to move away from the sex trade, this may represent a positive investment in their lives. Street prostitutes are often caught in a cycle of extreme violence, as demonstrated by the murders of prostitutes in Vancouver, Toronto, and other major urban centres. The fact that prostitutes work in a profession that requires accompanying complete strangers to out-of-the-way locations for sex poses a serious threat to their physical well-being.

If street prostitution were decriminalized, would it follow that a free market in street sex should be permitted? Most observers who support the notion of the sex trade as commerce argue that, as with any legitimate business, prostitution must be regulated. This regulation would involve licensing, health and safety regulations (through testing for sexually transmitted diseases), the maintenance of business records, and the payment of taxes. Given the nomadic nature of street prostitutes, such regulation would likely be difficult if not impossible to achieve. Furthermore, even if prostitution were decriminalized, cities would undoubtedly pass bylaws restricting the activities of streetwalkers.

Crime Prevention

One of the most promising developments in Canadian criminal justice is crime prevention. On the surface, crime prevention seems to be a priority for most agencies that deal with crime control in Canada. However, crime prevention strategies have grown significantly in both depth and scope over the past decade as innovative approaches have been developed. Crime prevention techniques have focused on several key areas, which are worthy of brief discussion.

Crime Prevention Techniques

Many clinicians and criminological studies have pointed to the centrality of the family and parent–child relationships in controlling deviant and anti-social behaviour. Parental attitudes and skill levels can have a great impact in reducing delinquency and dealing with aggressive and inappropriate behaviour. Troubled youths often direct their inappropriate behaviour toward parents through lying and aggression. Studies of gang behaviours have found that minors are able to lie to their parents about school attendance and performance particularly when a language barrier exists between the school and the family.

Whatever the context and aggravating factors, it is certain that parents who improve their parenting skills are more able to control delinquent or unacceptable behaviour. As well, they can help their children to establish the kinds of inner and outer controls that will allow them to succeed in civil society. The focus on the importance of effective parenting is one of the most promising areas of crime prevention research and techniques.

Crime prevention also involves programs that protect neighbourhoods and their residents. One school of research has argued that crime prevention is best achieved through environmental design. Most of us are aware of some of the everyday methods for preventing victimization by criminals, such as stopping home newspaper delivery when on holiday, leaving lights on when out of the home during the evening, installing alarm systems, placing bars on basement windows (a common access point for break and entry), and allowing for a clear view of entrance points to the home. Environmental design goes one step further by actually engineering streets and homes that will make criminal activities difficult. Lighting, access points to housing, distance from the road, placement of windows and garages, and door and window types all can greatly affect the potential for victimization.

The Factors Behind Crime Prevention

Criminologists have identified certain key components for effective crime prevention models. Most important, there is a need for efforts to be proactive rather than reactive. It is important to take measures that will prevent individuals from having the opportunity to commit crimes. Gwynn Nettler (1984), a pioneering criminologist, argued that crimes are often the result of the intersection of opportunity with desire. If we remove opportunities, then desires can be thwarted. Thus, designing safe communities, streets, and houses is one approach to reducing crime.

Effective crime prevention is not a short-term process but rather involves planning; consultation among residents, police authorities, and planning experts; and investment in projects. While the desired effect may not be achieved immediately, there is some evidence that investment in crime prevention projects pays off in the long run. One example of an effective program is the **neighbourhood watch** system. This program is aimed at reducing residential theft, interpersonal crime, and property damage. Residents co-operate with the police by first marking all of their valuables for identification, which under an ancillary program—operation identification—assists police in identifying stolen goods. Community members post stickers at the entrances to their homes and on windows to indicate that they are part of neighbourhood watch. This process is called *target hardening*—it makes the home less desirable to the prospective thief since the items he or she steals will be less saleable and more identifiable. Under the neighbourhood watch program, community members are vigilant in noting people or automobiles in their area that do not belong to the neighbourhood, and report suspicious behaviour to the police. Through a telephone message

system, the police update watch captains in the neighbourhood on crimes committed locally so that neighbours can be informed and take precautions.

Crime prevention programs require active participation by the community and its members in attacking the opportunity for criminal activities. Therefore, citizens must be supportive of law enforcement efforts and be willing to assist rather than to think of the task of crime prevention as belonging solely to the police. The Regent Park neighbourhood of Toronto (which is now in the midst of an enormous renovation project aimed at gentrifying the area), for example, has had significant problems with drug dealing and drug use in housing projects. Consequently, residents engaged in a variety of activities that were intended to prevent the commission of crime and to reclaim their neighbourhood, rendering it safe for walking and family outings. The residents began to videotape drug deals, form groups to harass the dealers, install lighting in appropriate places, and hold family block parties in the middle of the dealers' territories. This proactive form of crime prevention proved successful in moving the drug dealers out of the neighbourhood. However, even though the dealers retreated from this area, there is a need for constant vigilance by residents—both in Regent Park and elsewhere—to ensure that criminals do not begin to infiltrate the streets again.

Crime prevention programs also require the infusion of government funds. Crime prevention is an interactive process that involves changing the nature of policing to be more effective and accountable to citizens, particularly in sharing information on local crime patterns. Many crime prevention programs reflect the basics of solid communities in which an investment is made in the lives of young people to provide alternatives to gang involvement, relieve the effects of poverty, and make available mentoring help and proactive role models. Gang recruitment, for example, targets youths who are alienated from society and disenchanted with their lives. These gang recruits are without the benefit of positive role models or mentors who can forge a link between the young person and society. Mentors can encourage youths to develop self-esteem, improve their school performance, and make career plans. When there are few opportunities for young people to interact in after-school programs, community-organized activities, or mentor–mentee programs, the chances of involvement in delinquent activities rise rapidly. They are youths with too much time on their hands.

Schools have an important role to play in crime prevention initiatives. Children and adolescents spend a large majority of their day in these institutions, and so the potential for positive intervention is enormous. School programs can focus on providing children with the skills to succeed in everyday life and on the career track by promoting high academic achievement in tandem with innovative skill training. Schools also need to establish and enforce daily clearly articulated norms of behaviour.

Community Policing

Community policing is not a new concept, and often involves collaboration between an accessible and accountable police force and community members. Many of the underlying precepts of community policing hark back to an earlier era of policing in Canada and as far back as Victorian England, when police "walked the beat" and were known and highly visible to community residents. Essentially, in community policing the police are involved in the neighbourhood as law officers who monitor the area through foot patrols (and bicycle patrols) and as participants in other activities to create a community presence. All of these factors require that police be removed from faceless, mobile response units and become recognizable people interacting within the community. The shift of a fraction of police resources from automobile-based policing to more accessible forms is ideal for urban communities with established neighbourhoods in which residents share elements of a common identity. Central to this approach is the notion that police officers may do more good by simply being visible in the communities they serve. This approach inspires confidence in policing measures and bolsters community co-operation. The focus on safe streets helps to preserve the community and its quality of life.

Foot patrols are essential to community policing in urban centres. They allow law enforcement officials to hear community issues and concerns that they would otherwise hear only in rare meetings between the police and residents. With this approach, the police officers are able to monitor directly and intervene in the types of activities associated with the decline of neighbourhoods. Street violence, graffiti spraying, vandalism, littering, property damage, and drug dealing are all much more controllable when officers are on the ground level in communities. Residents can assist officers in identifying culprits and pointing out areas where petty criminals congregate after dark. Under this co-operative model, citizens help to preserve their neighbourhoods while allowing police an opportunity to respond to community issues. Criminological research and police experience confirm that officers who are on foot are easily approachable and become privy to valuable information from an enforcement perspective when talking with community members. Rapid technological advances have meant that foot and bicycle patrols can be in constant communication with police command and often are able to respond to crime scenes more quickly when traffic jams are a problem.

However, critics of community-based policing have argued that this approach is ineffective. Police are viewed as having little impact on crime control and as functioning merely as peacekeepers in the community. Some also criticize the police for their view of what constitutes the "community." Rather than responding to communities' needs, police serve the community according to their traditional

administrative approach. Furthermore, instead of defining neighbourhoods in terms of the shared norms, values, or boundaries of the community, authorities tend to divide the community in terms of policing priorities and needs. Police have begun to develop a greater sensitivity to community issues, rather than administrative areas. Since neighbourhoods often have very different views of the police and their role in the community, it takes a great deal of effort and research on the part of police to sensitize themselves to community boundaries, views, and priorities.

Another problem is how to integrate a variety of police services, from foot patrols to bicycle patrols to mobile units. While communication is not a significant problem today, there is still substantial debate over how to use these services and whether they should act independently or in conjunction with one another. Most police forces combine the strengths of all the approaches, providing the most comprehensive response possible.

Community policing also makes certain assumptions about the desirability of a police presence in neighbourhoods. Some neighbourhoods both fear and loathe the police, owing to a number of important factors. Recent immigrants from countries in which the authorities are viewed as violent interveners with the potential to torture, jail, or even kill people have little reason to want more police on their streets. Given reported racism within police forces in Canada, there are neighbourhoods in which the police are not welcome. The presence of more officers in a neighbourhood, some analysts suggest, is a signal of neighbourhood decline and thus could have a negative impact on both quality of life and real estate values. Given the subculture of policing, with its emphasis on secrecy, isolation, and suspicion of the public, it is difficult to argue that police can adequately perform these new co-operative roles without training to prepare them for their new duties. It is obvious that concerns about racism and sensitivity to diversity warrant a directional change in policing that may appear quite radical to policing organizations. Police, in future, will likely be called upon to perform multiple roles that have not traditionally been part of the police mandate. To prepare the fully functioning police officer of tomorrow, police forces must take new directions in training, including the implementation post-secondary education and training in dealing with diversity and sensitivity to community members.

Computer and Internet Crime

Computer and high technology crime is a phenomenon of the twenty-first century, and until the last decade, laws relating to **computer crime** were unheard of. As Schmalleger et al. (2004) note, often the state had to use property offence laws to prosecute illegal entry into computer systems or anti-theft laws to prosecute stealing of digitized information. Today, the Criminal Code of Canada includes laws relating to the altering of data, unauthorized use of data, data manipulation, and the wilful destruction of data. Computer hacking, for example, can wreak havoc on the computer world by introducing hidden instructions called viruses on software that can spread from computer to computer. The challenge of software manufacturers is to install antivirus mechanisms that would prevent these problems. Computer criminals are highly educated and skilled, and often the crimes they commit are difficult to detect. Many large companies, because of the sensitivity of data stored in their data processing computers, have had to develop special departments staffed by experts in computer security to combat this new criminal activity. In fact, a new growing specialty of computer security consultants has developed in the business sector. Both police departments and government organizations have had great difficulty in keeping abreast of the sophisticated methods of computer criminals. In Canada, both the RCMP and provincial police departments complain of their limited resources in terms of trained and skilled officers to investigate this type of crime, and as well the many loopholes in laws relating to computer crime. The RCMP, in fact, have stated that they are ill-equipped to combat not only computer crime, but also white collar crime in general. Government policy needs to call for enlisting investigators and experts from the private sector who can aid in the apprehension and prosecution of this new wave of criminals. Unless a comprehensive enforcement policy is developed, these skilled and astute technical thieves will remain ahead of law enforcement and successful prosecution, to the detriment of Canadians in general and business organizations specifically. Cybercrime in terms of business losses amounts to hundreds of million of dollars in Canada, and the illegal copying of software programs, for example, costs over $15 000 000 000 worldwide. The challenge to combat this growing scourge and succeed in reducing its impact is imperative in this decade.

The internet, while the fastest growing source of information in the world, has also spawned many forms of criminal behaviour, including identity theft and online pornography. Marron (2002) terms identity theft the fastest-growing financial crime in Canada. Clark (2002) notes that the internet allows criminals to steal information offline, and then use stolen credit cards online while under the protection of anonymity. It is estimated that identity theft victims in Canada number in the thousands and growing each year. A lot of time and money are spent to clear the victims' names and restore good credit ratings—there is also the obvious personal anguish of being victimized in such a way. Law enforcement agencies are demanding new laws to protect individuals from **internet crime**, as well as tighter security in the dispensing by governments of official documents such as birth certificates, social insurance numbers, and driver's licences. Given the success of this type of theft, it is necessary that all the agencies involved in protecting the identity of Canadians review the documentation process, increase penalties under the Criminal Code, and improve the security of the banking system and other electronic databases where personal information on clients is stored.

There is a very disturbing and dangerous fallout to the ever-growing popularity of the internet: because of the ease of transmitting information on the web, it has become a purveyor of illegal material and an aid to cybercriminals. Research suggests that online pornography is a billion-dollar industry in the United States, with the porn business in Canada roughly one-tenth that size. The internet has facilitated both the illegal exposure of sexual images of minors to viewers, and the trafficking of pornographic pictures and videos. What the internet offers to its viewers are anonymity, security, and speed. Visual materials can be sent across the globe speedily, and through the use of passwords, security is improved and discovery minimized. Graham (2000) notes that the most beneficial factor of the internet to pornographers is its anonymity and privacy. The online pornography industry has preyed on children, with one in five surveyed children reporting being the object of sexual advances over the internet. Foss (2002) notes that girls were targeted twice as often as boys, and—most alarmingly—less than 10 percent of those targeted reported the advances to police, parents, or teachers. The Canadian government, in an attempt to protect children from internet pornography, amended the Criminal Code in 2002, addressing three areas: sexual exploitation, internet luring, and child pornography. It is a criminal act for an individual to communicate with a child over the internet for sexual purposes, as well as to transmit or export child pornography. Canadians who sexually exploit children in other countries can now be prosecuted in Canada under the Child Sex Tourism Law. Judicial powers have been strengthened so that judges can close down child pornography websites in Canada and prohibit those convicted of child pornography offences on the internet from associating with children. Because many sites and chat rooms originate outside Canada, effective law enforcement in this arena makes international cooperation and Interpol involvement imperative.

International Terrorism

That Canada is not immune from **international terrorism** has been shown on numerous occasions over the past two decades. The bombing of Air India flight 182 in June 1985 brought home the reality of terrorism to Canadians. Sikh fundamentalist extremists, fighting for an independent homeland, planted bombs on this plane, resulting in the deaths of 329 people. Canadians were eventually arrested and acquitted of the air-bomb crime plus absolved of any involvement in an international terrorist group. The al Qaeda attacks on the World Trade Center and Pentagon on September 11, 2001, affected all of North America, not only because Canadians died in the attacks, but also because suspected terrorists were arrested in Canada and abroad and some resided in Canada or were Canadian citizens. Most alarming of all is the recent news story about 17 alleged terrorists—all Canadian citizens—being arrested and charged in Toronto with plotting terrorist acts in various parts of southern Ontario. The prosecution alleges that all of these defendants had an al Qaeda connection. Sadly, seven of the accused were young offenders. It is clear, therefore, that Canada will have to take vigorous steps to improve its security and protect its sovereignty. The Anti-Terrorism Act of 2001 established procedures to follow for identifying, prosecuting, convicting, and punishing terrorists and their organizations. Also, the Act provided new powers to police as well as investigative and security agencies to apprehend terrorists. A further piece of legislation empowered the federal government and cabinet ministers to issue executive orders to deal with security threats. We should note that not all Canadians support stronger anti-terrorist laws. Civil libertarians point out that rights guaranteed by the Charter of Rights and Freedoms are being infringed by this legislation and other similar anti-terrorism steps being taken by the government and various agencies. At the time of writing, the Supreme Court of Canada is holding hearings on the legitimacy of the Canadian government in detaining, without charges or trial, foreign residents on suspicion of terrorist activities. The legitimate concerns raised that this legislation could likely lead to widespread racial profiling, undermine civil liberties and minority rights, and provide police agencies with too much power need addressing. The challenge for the state is to walk the middle road and find the balance between individual rights and freedoms and national/community security. Western democracies like Canada, with its curtailing of police surveillance and search-and-seizure restrictions, make it more difficult for the apprehension of terrorists. It is a sad state of affairs that law and human rights legislation, designed to protect the citizenry from tyranny (governmental or otherwise), plays into the hands of groups bent on destabilizing our government and its institutions. The al Qaeda terrorist network, operating in 50 countries, is well financed, deadly, and has a fanatical following, including many acolytes in Canada. Al Qaeda is a classic example of the threat we face. It is clear that only a coordinated, international approach to achieving world safety can have any hope of countering faceless terrorism. The role of the United Nations in instituting and coordinating strong anti-terrorism measures is crucial.

Conclusion

That the debate about crimes associated with morality continues in Canada is not surprising. Many argue that the criminal justice system has no place in policing prostitution or marijuana use. While community concern about street prostitution is ongoing, other forms of the sex trade are allowed to carry on without police involvement. Escort services, massage parlours, and call girls practise their profession openly in many of our cities. Similarly, the issue of decriminalization of marijuana use has been debated and discussed for decades. Sufficient public attitude change has occurred for the Liberal government in 2005 to introduce legislation decriminalizing simple possession of small quantities of the drug. While the government was defeated before the bill could be debated, it is likely that eventually Canada will cease prosecuting marijuana use. Widespread popularity of the drug, the difficulties and costs associated with enforcement, and the minor status of this criminal offence all point to a shift in attitudes toward the use of marijuana.

Although community policing is in its infancy in Canada, pilot programs across the country have shown its popularity and success. It is a tool that allows for greater co-operation and accommodation between the public and police. Most importantly, it allows for proactive policing, rather than maintaining the traditional reactive policing methods and procedures. As well, greater accountability by the police to the public will improve trust, confidence, and efficiency of operations.

Computer and internet crime, two newer forms of deviant behaviour in the last two decades, have challenged the criminal justice system to develop new crime-fighting approaches. Amendments to the Criminal Code have been necessary to meet the sophistication of technically astute criminals. Both national and provincial police agencies, for example, lament the fact that they are under-resourced and under-trained in competing with cybercriminals. Although the laws have been strengthened, it remains a difficult task to detect, apprehend, and prosecute offenders. More law enforcement officers trained in computer-related crime-detection techniques are desperately needed.

The internet, the fastest growing source for the dissemination of information in the world, is also the source for the growth of identity theft, which is a burgeoning financial crime in Canada and elsewhere. Victims of identity theft number in the thousands, and increased security measures are integral to reducing this criminal activity. As well, the internet has become a major source for the transmission of child pornography, estimated to be a $100 million industry in Canada. The government has tightened the laws covering all aspects of child pornography on the internet. The courts have prosecuted many transgressors for possessing images or videos of children performing sexual acts or soliciting children for sexual acts. However, because of its worldwide utility, only through international co-operation of police agencies can the prevalence of child porn activity be reduced.

That international terrorism has found its way to Canada is not surprising. The September 2001 bombings in the United States were a wake-up call, but not this country's first involvement with acts of terror. Terrorists have operated from Canada, planning illegal activities in other parts of the world. While we have an anti-terrorist act with teeth, many human rights activists complain that individual civil liberties and freedoms have been curtailed. However, the recent arrests of Canadian citizens planning attacks on some of our cities have alarmed many citizens. The challenge is to establish a middle ground, where the government can successfully intercept and monitor terrorism, while at the same time maintaining our democratic traditions and values.

Summary

In this chapter, we have explored the issue of crime control in Canada. We have discussed decriminalization, focusing on both prostitution and marijuana use as controversial offences that may be candidates for decriminalization. We have also examined the rise of community policing in Canada and described some of the innovative programs that move police officers from the patrol car to the street, allowing greater involvement in the communities they monitor.

Computer and internet crime has become a challenge to law enforcement agencies because of its complexity, sophistication, and worldwide nature. We have discussed the criminal justice system's response to these newest forms of deviant behaviour, and the system's successes and failures. Finally, this chapter discusses the scourge of international terrorism, its impact on Canada, and the government's response through its anti-terrorist act. It seems inevitable that changes to individual and societal freedoms and rights will be altered as the state responds to the terrorist threat at home.

Key Terms

decriminalization (p. 258)

foot patrols (p. 266)

neighbourhood watch (p. 264)

internet crime (p. 269)

international terrorism (p. 270)

computer crime (p. 268)

Discussion Questions

1. Discuss arguments both in favour and against the idea of legalizing prostitution.

2. Should marijuana use be legalized? Why or why not?

3. Why do advocates of community policing consider foot patrols important?

4. Discuss the strengths and weaknesses of community policing.

5. Discuss the changes in Canadian society resulting from the impact of international terrorism.

6. How have Canadian law enforcement agencies adapted to computer crime?

Weblinks

www.crime-prevention.org/english/main.html The National Crime Prevention Centre website offers information about crime prevention projects in Canada, the National Strategy on Community Safety and Crime Prevention, the National Crime Prevention Centre, and its programs and services.

www.blockparent.ca The website of the Block Parent Program of Canada— the neighbourhood program which emphasizes children's safety issues.

www.lcc.gc.ca The Law Commission of Canada is an independent law-reform agency, responsible to the Parliament of Canada. Its website includes information on its current and past projects.

www.crime-prevention-intl.org The International Centre for the Prevention of Crime is a Canadian initiative, with the purpose of assisting cities and countries to reduce delinquency, violence, and insecurity. Their website is a great resource for information on crime prevention programs around the world.

Glossary

Actus Reus The criminal act (literally, "the guilty act"), which leads to criminal liability when *mens rea* is also present.

Arrest The detaining of a suspect in legal custody. Involves suspension of the individual's rights and freedoms.

Auburn System An approach to imprisonment in the 19th century based on the idea that hard labour was the path to reform of the convict. It has also been referred to as the *silent system*, since prisoners were forbidden to speak to one another.

Canadian Charter of Rights and Freedoms (the Charter) A document, established in the Constitution Act of 1982, that formally states the rights and freedoms of all Canadians.

Carceral Network The institutions, agencies, and staff that are part of law enforcement, the judicial process, the prison system, and the ancillary programs and agencies that deal with offenders.

Case Law Laws based on precedence in both criminal and civil cases.

Choice-Structuring Properties The situational elements that lead individuals to choose to commit particular crimes.

Circumstantial Evidence Evidence that is ambiguous and that will have to be evaluated by the judge and jury to determine its veracity (e.g., testimony given by a witness who saw the accused running from the crime scene or who previously heard the accused threatening the victim).

Civil Law Laws dealing with noncriminal relationships involving persons, businesses and other organizations, or government agencies. Civil lawsuits seek compensation, rather than punishment, for alleged wrongs.

Classical Criminology A school of criminology based on the Enlightenment thinking that morality was influenced by social institutions, rather than God, and thus these institutions needed to be reformed. Classical criminologists asserted that criminal law should operate primarily to deter crime and that this function could best be achieved through principles of rationality, transparency, proportionality, and humaneness.

Community Corrections Methods of sentencing as alternatives to prison that involve placing offenders within the community.

Community Policing Policing by officers who are knowledgeable about or part of the communities they patrol.

Community Service Orders Orders, issued by a judge, that compel a convicted offender to complete a requisite number of hours of unpaid work in the community.

Comparative Criminal Justice a new field of criminology where experts compare institutions of justice, procedures, and problems in different countries and re-evaluate aspects of criminal justice from a world perspective.

Computer Crime Crimes such as illegal entry into computer systems or the online stealing of digitized information.

Concurrent Sentence A form of sentencing that requires a person sentenced on several charges to serve only the longest term imposed (e.g., an offender sentenced to three years for one charge and ten years for another would serve a total of ten years).

Conflict Criminology A perspective in criminology that aims to explain not what causes criminal behaviour but rather the process by which certain behaviours and individuals are designated as criminal. The conflict perspective holds that there is an ongoing contest for power in society, and that the criminal law and agencies of law enforcement act, both directly and indirectly, in the interests of the powerful.

Conflict Perspective A criminological viewpoint that emerged during the 1960s as some observers began to question if there was an overall consensus in society regarding important matters pertaining to the law.

Consecutive Sentence A form of sentencing that requires a person convicted on several charges to serve the sentence imposed for each charge in sequence (e.g., an offender sentenced to three years for one charge and ten years for another would serve a total of thirteen years).

Consensus Perspective Asserts that society's ability to maintain law and order is the result of a social contract that all of our citizens are a party to.

Containment Theory Walter Reckless's 1967 theory which claimed that each person has inner and outer controls that pull or push potential offenders toward delinquency.

Corporate Crime Crime committed by businesses (e.g., polluting the environment, forming illegal monopolies, fixing prices of goods and services, or manipulating the stock market).

Corporate Interest Group As defined by Larsen and Burtch (1999), in alliance with others, these groups have the ability to exploit human and natural resources, pollute the environment, form illegal monopolies, fix the prices of goods and services, and manipulate the stock market, and yet can have all of these activities classified as legal behaviour.

Corpus Delicti The essential facts and features that are evidence of a crime (literally, "the body of the crime").

Correctional Investigator (CI) A position that is mandated by law. This person acts as an ombud on behalf of federal offenders.

Corrections The system of treatment of criminal offenders through incarceration, parole, community sentencing, etc.

Court System In Canada, the area of the justice system that hears and submits rulings on cases at law and comprises the provincial courts, the superior courts, and the appeal courts.

Courts of Appeal Superior courts that hear cases that have been decided in a lower court but sent for appeal against the court's judgment. The court of appeal usually consists of a panel of judges who examine the evidence and the findings of the original judge and extensively question the defence and prosecution lawyers. The judges review the transcript of the lower court to ensure that the hearing was fair and in accordance with statutory and case law.

Crime Control Model A system, typical in many US jurisdictions, that puts the emphasis on the arrest and conviction of offenders, the enforcement of law, and the maintenance of order.

Crime Map A graphical presentation of the official crime statistics published by Statistics Canada.

Crime Rate The number of offences that occur per population, calculated by totalling all the offences occurring in a given population and dividing that number by the population.

Crime Acts that violate the law and that are punishable upon conviction.

Criminal Code of Canada The federal statute comprising the criminal laws of Canada and requirements for criminal procedures and sentencing.

Criminal Insanity Defence A defence based on the premise that a person cannot be held legally accountable for crimes committed at a time when he or she could not comprehend the illegality or moral reprehensibility of the act.

Criminal Justice System The police, the courts, and corrections.

Criminal Law A body of rules for prosecuting crime set out by political authority and applying uniformly to all members of society.

Criminal Offence The official name for a charge against an accused for committing a crime against the state.

Criminal Sanctions Penalties intended to enforce obedience to the law.

Criminology The study of criminal justice and criminal behaviour.

Crown Attorney The prosecutor who acts on behalf of the government in prosecuting indictable charges.

Cultural Deviance Theories Offer the premise that we live in a complex society in which there is disagreement about conduct norms, particularly among different levels of the class structure and across ethnic groups.

Dark Figure of Crime The amount of actual crime in society, a figure that is unknown because not all crimes are reported.

Decriminalization A term used to describe behaviours that had been outlawed in our society but have assumed the status of social norms and thus have been legalized.

Defence Counsel The legal counsel for the accused.

Delinquent Boys Refers to Albert Cohen's 1955 argument that at least some of the crime attributed to people from lower-class backgrounds is committed by delinquent boys who act to show their rejection of middle-class values, which they cannot hope to measure up to.

Demographics Statistics that reveal patterns or distributions in a population.

Deterrence The attempt to prevent crime by imposing penalties that are constructed to convince potential offenders that they will lose, rather than benefit, from committing criminal acts.

Deterrence Theory The theory that people can be discouraged from committing crime through punishment and prevention. **General deterrence** refers to the use of punishment to inhibit crime rates or the behaviour of specific populations, rather than individuals. **Specific deterrence** refers to discouraging the activity of a particular individual through such steps as incarceration, electronic monitoring, or shaming.

Deviance Behaviour that does not conform with societal standards.

Differential Association States that criminal behaviour is learned within intimate personal groups, and the learning includes techniques for committing crimes and the motives, attitudes, and rationalizations that the groups use to favourably define the behaviour, even though it may violate the law.

Differential Opportunity States that while people may be strained in their ability to meet set goals with the means at their disposal, people do not necessarily have access to the means of crime—thus the name of this term.

Differential Reinforcement Purports that criminal behaviour is learned within close, intimate personal groups; however, experts further argue that the mass media can also influence the learning of behaviour.

Direct Evidence Factual evidence, such as wiretaps, videos, photographs, or eyewitness testimony.

Diversion Programs Programs for young offenders that intend to reconcile the offender and victim, to compensate the victim, and to divert young offenders from the youth court system.

Due Process In law, the system of following established rules in order to obtain fair justice for all accused and to protect the legal and human rights of those charged with criminal offences.

Duress A legal defence claiming that a defendant should be excused from criminal liability because he or she was forced to commit the criminal act under threat of death or bodily harm for failing to do so.

Elder Panels A community sentencing option in which elders in Aboriginal communities assist judges in constructing appropriate sentences for offenders. Elder panels may offer their advice either in open court or behind closed doors in the judge's chambers.

Electronic Monitoring The use of electronic devices, such as wristbands, to supervise sentenced offenders, who are allowed to remain in the community provided they adhere to certain conditions, including curfews and restrictions to their movements.

Espionage The gathering of secret information related to national defence by spying.

Federal Court of Canada A court that is not involved in criminal cases, but instead deals exclusively with legal actions brought against the federal government and federal agencies. The court is divided into a trial and an appellate division.

Felony The most serious crime carrying the most severe punishment, usually imprisonment for more than one year. Examples include first or second degree murder, manslaughter, armed robbery, drug possession, aggravated assault, sexual assault, burglary, and arson.

Fine Options Alternatives to fines, such as community service or probation, especially for poor offenders who might be imprisoned if unable to pay fines ordered by the court.

Foot Patrols The patrol of neighbourhoods by police officers on foot. Foot patrols are essential to community policing, as they allow officers to hear community issues and concerns and to monitor and intervene in the types of activities associated with the decline of neighbourhoods.

Formal Social Controls Controls that are legislated and form the written body of our civil and criminal legal codes.

General Deterrent refers to the use of punishment to inhibit crime rates or the behaviour of specific populations, rather than individuals.

Hedonistic Calculus Jeremy Bentham's theory of the weighing of pleasure and pain: the individual seeks to maximize his or her own happiness and to minimize pain, and thus the pain from crime must be greater than the pleasure derived from it.

Incapacitation A sentencing approach that, in Canada, involves imprisonment of offenders.

Incarceration Rate The number of people jailed per 100 000 population.

Incidence of Crime The average number of offences per offender, measured by dividing the number of offences by the number of offenders.

Indictable Offences More serious crimes prosecutable under the Criminal Code, such as murder, robbery, sexual assault, kidnapping, or fraud. People charged with these offences are tried before a judge and jury, and if convicted can be sentenced to prison terms or placed on probation.

Informal Social Controls The unwritten codes of behaviour that the majority of small groups follow in everyday social interaction.

Inmate Subculture The norms and rules within prisons. New inmates learn codes of conduct by talking to other inmates and by observing interactions among prisoners and between correctional officers and prisoners.

Interest Group A group of people with a common interest or goal.

International Terrorism Perhaps the most contentious issue of the 21st century, it usually involves horrifically violent crimes committed in one country by an aggrieved faction from another place (e.g., the hijacked-plane bombings of the World Trade Center and the Pentagon on September 11, 2001).

Internet Crime Crimes, such as fraud and harassment, perpetrated on the internet.

Intoxication A legal defence stating that a defendant is not responsible for a crime because at the time of the act the person was intoxicated and could not comprehend his or her actions as criminal.

Just Desserts A sentencing approach that focuses on the act or events that led the individual to be convicted; the underlying philosophy is that the criminal has benefited from the crime and now must pay society back for his or her misdeeds.

Labelling Theories The theory that societal reactions help to shape the individual's identity. For example, when a judge tells a youth that he is a thief, the youth is more likely to act according to this label.

Law Enforcement A duty of the police to both reactively and proactively enforce the law by preventing crime from occurring and by apprehending violators of the law.

Life–25 A sentence of 25 years, which murderers must serve in full.

Macro Theories Theories developed by criminologists to explain the operation of society and the beliefs that produce a consensual social order.

McNaughtan Rules The standard by which mental disorder is judged in our laws. The rules state that in order for an accused to be found not guilty by reason of mental disorder, the person must not "know the nature and quality of the act they have committed."

Mediation Services A community sentencing option that involves bringing the offender and victim together to encourage victim–offender mediation and to allow the offender to make restitution to the victim.

Mens Rea The intent to commit a criminal act (literally, "the guilty mind").

Mental Disorder A defence plea for an accused (i.e., not guilty by reason of a mental disorder).

Misdemeanour Minor crimes, such as petty theft, disorderly conduct, or possession of marijuana. Punishment is usually a fine for first-time offenders and probation or a short prison sentence for repeat offenders.

Mistake of Fact A legal defence stating that the defendant committed the ***actus reus*** of the offence but had no reason to believe that he or she was committing a crime.

Mistake of Law A legal defence stating that the defendant committed an act in the belief that it was not criminal because he or she misinterpreted the law.

Moral Behaviour Behaviour reflecting societal standards of right and wrong.

Necessity A legal defence based on the contention that although the defendant committed a crime, he or she should not be convicted because breaking the law was the only option and thus was necessary.

Neutralization or **Drift Theory** According to the theory, in order to commit delinquent acts, youth learn ways to neutralize conventional values or attitudes. A youth will drift back and forth from conventional and criminal behaviour and learn how to rationalize his or her actions before the behaviour.

Neighbourhood Watch A crime prevention program that involves residents of a community marking their valuables for identification by police and noting suspicious activity in their neighbourhood.

North West Mounted Police (NWMP) A precursor to the **Royal Canadian Mounted Police (RCMP)** and established in 1873 by an act of Parliament, this force was modelled after the Royal Irish Constabulary and was mobilized with the tacit responsibility of easing adversities of settlers in the West, appeasing Aboriginal resistance, and deterring US colonization of British land. For its last fifteen years of existence (1905–1920), it was known as the Royal North West Mounted Police (RNWMP).

Official Statistics Crime statistics recorded by the police, the courts, and corrections agencies.

Ontario Civilian Commission on Police Services (OCCPS) In Ontario, the provincial body that oversees the police forces.

Ontario Provincial Police (OPP) Ontario's provincial police force. It was established in 1909.

Order Maintenance A more passive role of the police in deterring crime, such as ensuring that public demonstrations are peaceful. The presence of police acts as a sufficient general deterrent.

Panopticon A circular, multi-tiered institution designed by Jeremy Bentham in the 17th century. Few guards were required to maintain control because tiers permitted them to "lock down" segments of the prison, whole tiers, or individual cells.

Parole Release of a prisoner before serving the entire the sentence as a reward for good behaviour while incarcerated. Parolees granted day parole are required to live in a halfway house. Full parole is granted to those who are ready for release into the community and to their own living arrangements.

Peacekeeping A role of police that involves taking an active role in settling disputes and preventing them from escalating.

Pennsylvania System An approach to incarceration in the 19th century that was strongly connected to religious and moral ideals. Prisoners were confined to small cells, where they were to read the Bible, contemplate their acts, and repent, and were allowed less than one hour of exercise in a small yard per day.

Plea Bargaining An arrangement whereby the Crown and the defence together decide on a common plea and sentence that they present to the judge. The defendant pleads guilty to a lesser charge in order to obtain a more lenient sentence.

Police Accountability The requirement that police account for actions taken or not taken through various mechanisms, such as internal investigations, external review by monitoring agencies, and civil lawsuits.

Police Discretion The freedom of police officers to choose between two available courses of action.

Police Powers The authority of the police to enforce warrants of the court, pursue arrests, preserve the peace, search premises with a search warrant, and use force when justified.

Positivist Criminology An approach that focuses on the idea that the human condition is determined but changeable, and therefore crime can be prevented or remedied through social engineering.

Preliminary Inquiry A stage of the criminal court process where a provincial court judge determines whether the Crown has sufficient admissible evidence in a case to send it to a superior court for trial.

Prerelease Programs Programs that allow temporary release from prison, including escorted and unescorted temporary absences, day parole, and work release, to allow the offender to reintegrate in the community.

Presumption of Innocence Law stating that everyone in Canada is presumed innocent of crimes that they are charged with until proven guilty.

Prevalence of Crime The number of people participating in crime at a given time, measured by dividing the number of offenders by the size of the population.

Prison Argot The jargon developed by prisoners.

Prison Industry Some criminologists argue that the ever-expanding number of prisons has produced what some might call a prison industry. This industry is a huge employer of thousands of prison employees and tens of thousands employed in support industries.

Probation A community sentence, ranging from several months to a maximum of three years, whereby an offender's sentence of incarceration is suspended providing that the offender adheres to strict rules under supervision.

Protective Custody The separating of prisoners, often rapists, pedophiles, and informers, from the general inmate population for their own protection.

Provincial Courts Courts that hear less serious civil and criminal cases. The provincial court system has separate divisions, including small claims, family, youth, traffic, and criminal courts. The provincial governments appoint provincial court judges and pay their salaries.

Rational Choice Theory The belief that some offenders are rational decision makers who seek to benefit themselves through their criminal behaviour. According to this theory, potential offenders can be deterred when the choice-structuring properties of an offence are altered.

Reasonable Person In a criminal trial, it is incumbent on the defence lawyer to prove that the mistake is an honest one, and that the mistake would have been made by a reasonable person.

Rehabilitation A sentencing option that provides training, education, and treatment programs in order to allow offenders to change themselves and thus avoid future involvement in crime.

Restitution A sentencing approach that involves the offender's compensating victims for loss of property owing to the crime or for personal injuries sustained during the commission of a crime.

Restorative Justice Measures A sentencing approach that brings together the offender, the victim, and the community to deal with the harm caused to the victim. The focus is not on punishing the offender, but rather on restoring peace and permitting healing through communication and problem solving.

Revocation The ending of parole and reincarceration of the offender for breaching conditions of parole.

Right to Remain Silent An accused's right not to speak when apprehended by the police.

Routine Activities Theory A theory that attempts to explain changes in crime rates over time by considering social and economic conditions that determine the chances of a crime being committed. According to this theory, people will, in the absence of deterrence, exploit illegal chances that come their way. Routine activities theory argues that we can understand changes in crime rates if we look at changes in three variables: suitable targets, capable guardians, and motivated offenders.

Royal Canadian Mounted Police (RCMP) Established in 1920 by the merger of the Dominion Police and the Royal North West Mounted Police (RNWMP), the RCMP became Canada's first and only federal police force. It still operates today.

Secondary Victimization Many observers and participants have come to see the criminal procedure as officially furthering the victim's alienation and mistreatment through what is generally referred to as secondary victimization.

Security Classifications The classifications given to inmates based on the risks they present. Incoming prisoners are assessed for classification according to the risk they pose for escaping, for being a danger to other inmates or correctional officers, and for breaking the rules of the prison. In Canada, prisoners are classified as minimum security, medium security, maximum security, and multilevel.

Self-Defence A criminal defence arguing that a criminal act was justified because it was necessary to avoid personal harm.

Self-Report Survey A survey that asks people to report on their own delinquency or criminal past.

Sentencing Circles An approach to corrections in Aboriginal communities in which members of the community and elders meet with the offender to establish how the case should be dealt with. The judge will make the final decision in the case but will take into account the sentencing circle's recommendations.

Situated Transaction Edwin Luckenbill's term for the emphasis on the dynamics between the participants in a criminal event, rather than on what one person does to another.

Social Bond Theory Travis Hirschi's 1969 theory, which claimed that a person's bond to society prevents him or her from engaging in criminal behaviour.

Social Contract Allows that criminal law may be viewed as an instrument to redress damage to the state as well as individuals.

Social Control The way in which societies encourage conformity.

Social Control Theories Assume that humans are born bad but learn to be good.

Social Disorganization Clifford Shaw and Henry McKay's belief that highly transient communities are more crime prone because they are socially disorganized.

Social Learning Theories Maintain that socialization plays an important role in the development of criminal behaviour. Proponents of social learning theory suggest that youthful offenders are taught to believe that criminal or deviant behaviour is acceptable and possibly legitimate behaviour.

Social Process Theories Criminological theories that are based on the idea that criminal behaviour is normal, learned behaviour and that examine how people come to have beliefs and knowledge that predispose them to criminality.

Social Reaction Theories Criminological theories that purport that criminal behaviour is learned, but the interaction between social control agents, such as the courts, the police, and schools, also contributes to criminality. Situations that are favourable to the commission of crime are followed by societal reaction to the criminal act.

Solitary Confinement The isolation of incarcerated offenders in order to punish them for failing to obey institutional rules or for committing violence against others.

Specific Deterrent refers to discouraging the activity of a particular individual through such steps as incarceration, electronic monitoring, or shaming.

Statutory Law Laws passed by legislation and known as the Criminal Code.

Statutory Release Release of an offender into the community after he or she has served two-thirds of a sentence of incarceration.

Strain Theory Robert K. Merton's theory that societies promote certain goals but that the legitimate means to achieve these goals are unequally distributed.

Summary Conviction Offences Less serious types of crimes under the Criminal Code, such as trespassing, vagrancy, and petty theft. People charged with these offences are usually tried in provincial courts without a jury and punished by a fine, or for repeat offenders, by not more than six months in prison.

Superior Courts The highest provincial courts, with federally appointed judges. Superior courts hear serious cases, such as first-degree murder cases.

Supreme Court of Canada The highest court of appeal in Canada. The Supreme Court hears cases from the Federal Court of Canada and provincial courts of appeal involving some aspect of case or statute law or an issue of national importance.

Sûreté du Québec (SQ) Quebec's provincial police force. It was the first provincial force established in Canada, in 1870.

Suspended Sentence A sentence that is handed down but is unenforced provided the offender commits no further crimes.

Suspension The cessation of parole by the parole officer because the parolee has breached the conditions of parole or committed a new crime. At this point, the parole board holds a hearing to determine whether the parole should be continued or revoked.

Technical Violation A way that an offender on parole might violate that parole (e.g., not reporting a change of address).

Tipping Level The point at which the probability of being arrested is high enough to act as a deterrent.

Treason The crime of helping a foreign government to overthrow or make war against one's own government.

Unfit to Stand Trial An individual who is deemed so mentally ill that he or she is unable to instruct counsel on how to conduct his or her defence.

Unofficial Statistics Crime statistics that are estimated based on self-report and victimization surveys.

Victim Impact Statement (VIS) A testimony of loss suffered by the victim owing to the harm caused by the crime. It allows the victim or the family of the victim to inform the court of the emotional and financial consequences of the criminal act.

Victimization An illegitimate violation of a person by another, resulting in an experience of loss as recognized by a moral authority.

Victimization Surveys Questionnaires that ask people to provide information about their experience as victims of crimes.

Victimless Crimes Crimes, such as drug use and prostitution, that are considered to have no victims because the participants are willing.

Victim–Offender Reconciliation Programs (VORPs) Program that allow an offender the opportunity to acknowledge his or her guilt and, under the authority of the judge, to make restitution according to an agreement reached in a meeting between victim and offender, mediated by a social worker, a probation officer, or another official.

Victimology A branch of criminology that deals with the psychological, cultural, social, and political processes that contribute to victimization and the societal processes that contribute to the conferral of the victim status.

Victim Precipitation Crimes brought about by some action of the victim, such as brandishing a weapon.

Youth Court The courts that deal specifically with cases involving young offenders—those from 12 to 17 years of age.

Youth Criminal Justice Act (YCJA) An Act passed by Canada's federal Parliament in February 2002. The YCJA replaced the Young Offenders Act (YOA, which had been enacted in 1984). The YCJA builds on the strengths of the YOA and introduces major reforms that were highlighted by critics of the YOA.

References

Abbot, J. 1981. *In the Belly of the Beast*. New York: Random House.

Adler, F. 1975. *Sisters in Crime: The Rise of the New Female Criminal*. New York: Basic Books.

Akers, R. 1985. *Deviant Behaviour: A Social Learning Approach* (3rd Ed.). Belmont, CA: Wadsworth.

Amir, M. 1971. *Patterns of Forcible Rape*. Chicago: University of Chicago Press.

Arbour, the Honourable Louise, Commissioner. 1996. *Commission of Inquiry into Certain Events at the Prison for Women in Kingston*. Ottawa: Public Works and Government Services Canada.

Arrigo, B. A., & Williams, C. R. 2003. "Victim Voices, Victim Vices and Restorative Justice: Rethinking the Use of Impact Evidence in Capital Sentences, *Crime and Delinquency*, 49, 603–626.

Badgely, R. 1987. *The Badgely Report on Prostitution*. Ottawa: Government Printing Office.

Barsh, R. L. & Marlor, C. 1999. "Alternative Paradigms: Law as Power, Law as Process" in N. Larsen & B. Burtch (eds.), *Law in Society: Canadian Readings*. Toronto: Harcourt Brace, pp. 132–151.

Beccaria, C. 1963. *On Crimes and Punishment*. Trans. Henry Paolucci. Indianapolis: Bobbs-Merrill. (Original work published 1764.)

Becker, H. S. 1963. *Outsiders: Studies in the Sociology of Deviance*. Glencoe, IL: Free Press.

Beddoes, D. 1989. *Pal Hal*. Toronto: Macmillan.

Belliveau, J. E. 1956. *The Coffin Murder Case*. Toronto: Kingswood House.

Bentham, J. 1988. *An Introduction to the Principles of Morals and Legislation*. Buffalo, NY: Prometheus Press. (Original work published 1789.)

Bernard, T. 1987. "Testing Structural Strain Theories." *Journal of Research in Crime and Delinquency*, 24: 262–280.

Birnie, L. H. 1990. *A Rock and a Hard Place: Inside Canada's Parole Board*. Toronto: Macmillan.

Black, D. 1983. "Crime as Social Control." *American Sociological Review*, 48: 34–45.

Blau, J., & Blau, P. M. 1982. "The Cost of Inequality: Metropolitan Structure and Violent Crime." *American Sociological Review*, 47: 114–129.

Bonger, W. 1916. *Criminality and Economic Conditions*. Boston: Little, Brown.

Bonta, J., & Cormier, R. B. 1999. "Corrections Research in Canada." *The Canadian Journal of Criminology*, 41: 235–247.

Booth, A., & Osgood, D. W. 1993. "The Influence of Testosterone on Deviance in Adulthood: Assessing and Explaining the Relationship." *Criminology*, 31: 93–117.

Boyd, N. 1989. *The Last Dance: Murder in Canada*. Scarborough, ON: Prentice Hall.

——. 1991. *High Society*. Toronto: Key Porter.

——. 1998. *Canadian Law. An Introduction* (2nd Ed.). Toronto: Harcourt Brace.

Brady, P. 1990. *Sentencing Environmental Offenders: Individuals versus Corporations*. Master's thesis, University of Windsor, Ontario.

Braithwaite, J. 1997. "John Braithwaite's 'Control Balance' and 'Criminological Theory.'" *Theoretical Criminology*, 1(1): 77–98.

Braithwaite, J., & Mugford, S. 1994. "Conditions of Successful Reintegration Ceremonies." *British Journal of Criminology*, 34(2): 139–170.

Brantingham, P. J., Mu, S., & Verma, A. 1995. "Patterns in Crime" in M. A. Jackson & C. T. Griffiths (eds.), *Canadian Criminology: Perspectives in Crime and Criminality* (2nd Ed.). Toronto: Harcourt Brace, Chapter 6.

Brockman, J., & Rose, V. G. 1996. *An Introduction to Canadian Criminal Procedure and Evidence*. Scarborough, ON: Nelson Canada.

Brown, S. E., Esbensen, F. A., & Geis, G. 1998. *Criminology: Explaining Crime and Its Context* (3rd Ed.). Cincinnati, OH: Anderson.

Bugliosi, V. 1996. *Outrage: The Five Reasons Why O. J. Simpson Got Away with Murder*. New York: Island Books.

Bureau of Justice Statistics Data Report. 1989. Online. Available: www.vix.com/pub/men/abuse/studies/murder.rate.html

Burnside, S., & Cairns, A. 1995. *Deadly Innocence*. New York: Time Warner.

Burtch, B. 1992. *Sociology of Law*. Toronto: Harcourt Brace.

Burtch, B., & Ericson, R. V. 1977. *The Silent System*. Toronto: Centre of Criminology.

Callwood, J. 1990. *The Sleepwalker: The Trial That Made Canadian Legal History*. Toronto: Lester & Orpen Dennys.

Campbell, K. (ed.). 2005. *Understanding Youth Justice in Canada*. Don Mills, ON: Pearson Canada.

Canadian Centre for Justice Statistics (CCJS). 1994. "Trends in Criminal Victimization: 1988–1993." *Juristat*, 13(3).

_____. 1995a. "Factfinder on Crime and the Administration of Justice in Canada." *Juristat*, 15(10).

_____. 1995b. "Victims' Use of Police and Social Services." *Juristat*, 15(6).

_____. 1997. "Canadian Crime Statistics, 1996." *Juristat*, 17(8).

_____. 1999a. "Justice Spending in Canada." *Juristat*, 19(4): 4.

_____. 1999b. *Police Resources in Canada* (Cat. no. 85-225-XIE). Statistics Canada: Minister of Supply and Services Canada.

Canadian Sentencing Commission. 1987. *Report of the Canadian Sentencing Commission*. Ottawa: Supply and Services Canada.

Canadian Urban Victimization Survey. 1982. Ottawa: Solicitor General of Canada, Program Branch, Research and Statistic Group.

Caputo, T., Kennedy, M., Reasons, C., & Brannigan, A. 1989. *Law and Society: A Critical Perspective*. Toronto: Harcourt Brace.

Carlen, P., Christina, D., Hicks, J., O'Dwyer, J., & Tchaikowsky, C. 1985. *Criminal Women*. Oxford: Polity Press.

Caron, R. 1978. *Go-Boy!* Toronto: McGraw-Hill.

_____. 1985. *Bingo!* Toronto: Methuen.

Carrington, P. & Schulenberg, J. 2003. *Police Discretion with Young Offenders*. Ottawa, Department of Justice Canada.

Cavadion, M., & Dignan, J. 1997. *The Penal System: An Introduction* (2nd Ed.). London: Sage.

Cayley, D. 1998. *The Expanding Prison*. Toronto: House of Anansi.

CBC Radio. 2006, May 4. News report interview with Jane Pitfield on Radio One.

Chambliss, W. (ed.). 1975. *Crime and the Legal Process*. New York: McGraw-Hill.

_____. 1967. "Types of Deviance and the Effectiveness of Legal Sanctions." *Wisconsin Law Review*, 3: 703–719.

Chamelin, M. 1991. "A Longitudinal Analysis of Arrest–Crime Relationship: A Further Explanation of the Tipping Effect." *Justice Quarterly*, 8: 187–199.

Chesney-Lind, M. 1977. "Judicial Paternalism and the Female Status Offender: Training Women to Know Their Place." *Crime and Delinquency*, 23: 121–130.

Chessman, C. 1954. *Cell 2455 Death Row*. Englewood Cliffs, NJ: Prentice Hall.

Christie, N. 1977. "Conflicts as Property." *British Journal of Criminology*, 17(1): 1–15.

_____. 1994. *Crime Control at Industry: Towards Gulags Western Style* (2nd Ed.). New York: Routledge.

Clairmont, D. H., & Magill, D. W. 1987. *Africville: The Life and Death of a Canadian Black Community*. Toronto: Canadian Scholars' Press.

Clark, T. 2002, February 9. "Ontario Laws Toughened to Combat Identity Theft." *The Globe and Mail*.

Clarke, R. 1995. "Situational Crime Prevention" in M. Tonry & D. Farrington (eds.), *Crime and Justice: A Review of the Research* (vol. 19). Chicago: University of Chicago Press, pp. 91–150.

Clarke, R. V., & Homel, R. 1997. "A Revised Classification of Situational Crime Prevention Techniques" in S. P. Lab (ed.), *Crime Prevention at a Crossroads*. Cincinnati, OH: Anderson.

Cleaver, E. 1967. *Soul on Ice*. New York: McGraw-Hill.

Cloward, R., & Ohlin, L. 1960. *Delinquency and Opportunity*. Glencoe, IL: Free Press.

Cohen, A. K. 1955. *Delinquent Boys*. Glencoe, IL: Free Press.

Cohen, S., & Taylor, L. 1976. *Prison Secrets*. London: Radical Alternatives to Prison.

Constitution Act, 1982. Canadian Charter of Rights and Freedoms, Ottawa, Queen's Printer.

Cornish, D. B., & Clarke, R. V. G. 1987. "Understanding Criminal Displacement: An Application of Rational Choice Theory." *Criminology*, 25(4): 933–947.

Correctional Officers of Canada. 2004."We Are Also Doing Hard Time." CD-video. UCCO/SACC.

Correctional Service of Canada (CSC). 1998, 2000. Website. Available: www.csc-scc.gc.ca.

Culhane, C. 1985. *Barred from Prison*. Montreal: Black Rose.

_____. 1987. *No Longer Barred from Prison*. Montreal: Black Rose.

Currie, E. 1998. "Market, Crime and Community: Toward a Midrange Theory of Post-Industrial Violence." *Theoretical Criminology*, 1(2): 247–272.

Curtis, D., & Blanchfield, C. 1985. *Kingston Penitentiary: The First One Hundred and Fifty Years, 1835–1985*. Ottawa: CSC.

Davis, R. C., & Smith, B. 1994. "Victim Impact Statements and Victim Satisfaction: An Unfulfilled Promise?" *Journal of Criminal Justice*, 22: 1–12.

_____. 1995. "Domestic Violence Reforms: Empty Promises or Fulfilled Expectations." *Crime and Delinquency*, 41: 541–552.

Davis, R. C., Henley, M., & Smith, B. 1990. *Victim Impact Statements: Their Effects on Court Outcomes and Victim Satisfaction*. Washington, DC: National Institute of Justice.

Delisle, R. J. 2002. *Canadian Evidence Law in a Nutshell* (2nd Ed.). Scarborough, ON: Thomson Carswell.

Denno, D. 1988. "Human Biology and Criminal Responsibility: Free Will or Free Ride?" *University of Pennsylvania Law Review*, 137(2): 217–671.

Desroches, F. J. 1995. *Force and Fear: Robbery in Canada*. Scarborough, ON: Nelson Canada.

Doob, A., & Marionos, V. 1995. *Youth Crime and the Youth Justice System in Canada: A Research Perspective*. Ottawa: Department of Justice Canada, Research, Statistics and Evaluation.

Dowler, K. 2004. "Comparing American and Canadian Local Television Crime Stories: A Content Analysis." *Canadian Journal of Criminology and Criminal Justice*, 46(5): 573–596.

Durkheim, E. 1951. *Suicide: A Study of Sociology*. New York: Free Press. (Original work published 1897.)

Ekstedt, J., & Griffiths, C. T. 1988. *Corrections in Canada: Policy and Practice*. Toronto: Butterworths.

Elias, R. 1986. *The Politics of Victimization: Victims, Victimology and Human Rights*. New York: Oxford University Press.

Erez, E., & Tontodonato, P. 1992. "The Effect of Victim Participation in Sentencing on Sentence Outcome." *Criminology*, 28: 451–474.

Erickson, P. 1980. *Cannabis Criminals*. Toronto: Addiction Research Foundation.

Ericson, R. V. 1974. "Turning the Inside Out: On Limiting the Use of Imprisonment." *Community Education Series*, 1(3), John Howard Society of Ontario.

Ericson, R., Baranek, P., & Chan, J. 1987. *Visualizing Deviance*. Toronto: University of Toronto Press.

_____. 1989. *Negotiating Control*. Toronto: University of Toronto Press.

Felson, M., & Cohen, L. E. 1979. "Social Change and Crime Rate Trends: A Routine Activities Approach." *American Sociological Review*, 44: 588–609.

Fife, R. 1999, April 22. "Police Chiefs get Through to the Top." *National Post*.

Fishbein, D. 1996. "Selected Studies on the Biology of Antisocial Behaviour" in J. Conklin (ed.), *New Perspectives in Criminology*. Needham Heights, MA: Allyn and Bacon.

Fitzgerald, M. 1986. *Prisons in Revolt*. London: RAP.

Fleming, T. 1974. *The Chronic Drunkenness Offender and the Courts*. Unpublished honours B.A. thesis, University of Toronto, Ontario.

_____. 1982. *The Release of Mentally Disordered, Dangerous and Psychopathic Offender-Patients from a Special Hospital*. London: Unpublished Ph.D. thesis.

_____. 1993. *Down and Out in Canada: Homeless Canadians*. Toronto: Canadian Scholars' Press.

_____. 1995. "The Dark Factory" in L. Visano & K. McCormick (eds.), *Canadian Penology: Advanced Perspectives*. Toronto: Canadian Scholars' Press, pp. 291–317.

_____. 1998. "Serial Murder Investigation: Prospects for Police Networking" in R. Holmes & S. Holmes (eds.), *Contemporary Perspectives in Serial Murder*. London: Sage, pp. 218–226.

_____. 2000. *The Science of Criminology*. Toronto: Academic Press.

Fleming, T., & Jorgenson, B. 1982. *Stolen Property*. Toronto: Solicitor General.

Foot, D., with Stoffman, D. 1996. *Boom, Bust, and Echo*. Toronto: Macfarlane Walter and Ross.

Forcese, D. 1999. *Policing Canadian Society* (2nd Ed.). Scarborough, ON: Prentice Hall.

Foss, K. 2002, September 14. "Winnipeg Man Among First Charged with Internet Luring." *The Globe and Mail*.

Foucault, M. 1977. *Discipline and Punish: The Birth of the Prison*. London: Vintage.

The Fraser Commission on Pornography and Prostitution. 1985. Ottawa: Government Printing Office.

Friedenberg, E. J. 1985. "Law in a Cynical Society" in D. Gibson & J. Baldwin (eds.), *Law in a Cynical Society: Opinion and Law in the 1980s*. Vancouver: Carswell.

Gall, G. 1995. *The Canadian Legal System* (4th Ed.). Toronto: Carswell.

Giliberti, C. 1990 (November). *Study probes effectiveness of victim impact statements*. Justice Research Notes No. 1.

Gittens, M., Cole, D., Williams, T., Skanda-Rajah, S., Tam, M. & Ratushny, E. 1995 (December). *Final Report of the Commission on Systemic Racism in the Ontario Criminal Justice System*. Toronto: Queen's Printer.

Goff, C. 2004. *Criminal Justice in Canada: An Introduction* (3rd Ed.). Scarborough, ON: Thomson Nelson Learning.

Goffman, E. 1961. *Asylums*. Garden City, NY: Anchor Books.

Gomme, I. 1998. *The Shadow Line*. Toronto: Harcourt Brace.

Gosselin, L. 1977. *Prisons in Canada*. Montreal: Black Rose.

Graham, W. R. 2000. "Uncovering and Eliminating Child Pornography on the Internet." *Law Review*. Michigan State University. Summer.

Grana, S., & Ollenburger, J. 1999. *The Social Context of Law*. Upper Saddle River, NJ: Prentice Hall.

Greenspan, E., & Jonas, G. 1987. *Greenspan: The Case for the Defence*. Toronto: Macmillan.

Hagan, J. (ed.). 1989. *Structural Criminology*. New Brunswick, NJ: Rutgers University Press.

_____. 1974. "Extra-legal Attributes and Criminal Sentencing: An Assessment of a Sociological Viewpoint." *Law and Society Review*, 8(3): 357–383.

_____. 1985. "The Class Structure of Gender and Delinquency." *American Journal of Sociology*, 90: 1151–1178.

Hagan, J., Gillis, R., & Simpson, R. 1985. "The Class Structure of Gender and Delinquency: Toward a Power-Control Theory of Common Delinquent Behavior." *American Journal of Sociology*, 90(6): 1151–1178.

Hann, R. G. 1973. *Decision Making in the Criminal Court System: A System Analysis*. Toronto: Centre of Criminology.

Hartnagel, T. 1978. "The Effect of Age and Sex Compositions of Provincial Populations on Provincial Crime Rates." *Canadian Journal of Criminology*, 20(1): 28–33.

Hartnagel, T., & Lee, J. 1990. "Urban Crime in Canada." *Canadian Journal of Criminology*, 32(4): 591–606.

Hastings, R. 1997. "Crime Prevention and Criminal Justice" in T. Fleming (ed.), *Post-Critical Criminology*. Scarborough, ON: Prentice Hall, pp. 315–329.

Hills, S. 1971. *Crime, Power and Morality*. Scranton, PA: Chandler Publishing.

Hindelang, M., Hirschi, R., & Weis, J. 1981. *Measuring Delinquency*. Beverly Hills, CA: Sage.

Hirschi, T. 1969. *Causes of Delinquency*. Berkeley: University of California Press.

Hogg, P. 1992. *Constitutional Law of Canada* (3rd Ed.). Scarborough, ON: Carswell.

Huizinga, D., & Elliott, D. S. 1986. "Reassessing the Reliability and Validity of Self-Report Delinquency Measures." *Journal of Quantitative Criminology*, 2(4): 293–327.

Hylton, J. 1983. "The Growth of Punishment: Imprisonment and Community Correction in Canada" in T. Fleming & L. Visano (eds.), *Deviant Designations: Crime, Law and Deviance in Canada*. Toronto: Butterworths, pp. 411–430.

Irwin, J. 1970. *The Felon*. Englewood Cliffs, NJ: Prentice Hall.

Jackson, M. 1983. *Prisoners of Isolation*. Toronto: University of Toronto Press.

James, C. E. 1989. *Seeing Ourselves: Exploring Race, Ethnicity and Culture*. Oakville, ON: Instructional and Human Resource Development, Sheridan College.

Johnson, H. 1986. *Women and Crime in Canada*. Ottawa: Solicitor General of Canada.

Jonas, G. & Amiel, B. 1978. *By Persons Unknown: The Strange Death of Christine Demeter*. Toronto: Signet.

Jones, M. A., & Krisberg, B. 1994. *Images and Reality: Juvenile Crime, Youth Violence and Public Policy*. Washington, DC: Office of Juvenile Justice and Delinquency Prevention.

Jurgens, R. 1996. *HIV/AIDS in Prison: Final Report*. Ottawa: Canadian HIV/AIDS Legal Network.

Karmen, A. 2001. *Crime Victims: An Introduction to Victimology*. Belmont, CA: Thomson Wadsworth.

Katz, J. 1988. *The Seductions of Crime: Moral and Sensual Attractions in Doing Evil*. New York: Basic Books.

Kelling, G., Pate, T., Dieckman, D., & Brown, C. 1974. *The Kansas City Prevention Patrol Experiment: Final Report*. Washington: Police Foundation.

Kennedy, L., Silverman, R., & Forde, D. 1991. "Homicide in Urban Canada: Testing the Impact of Economic Inequality and Social Disorganization." *Canadian Journal of Criminology*, 16(4): 397–410.

Klein, J. F. 1976. *Let's Make a Deal: Negotiating Justice*. Lexington, MA: Lexington Books.

Krisberg G., & Austin, J. 1993. *Reinventing Juvenile Justice*. Newburg Park, CA: Sage.

Kymlicka, W. 1989. *Liberation, Community and Culture*. Oxford: Clarendon Press.

LaPrairie, C. 1983. "Native Juveniles in Court: Some Preliminary Observations" in T. Fleming & L. A. Visano (eds.), *Deviant Designations: Crime, Law and Deviance in Canada*. Toronto: Butterworths, pp. 337–350.

Larsen, N., & Burtch, B. (eds.). 1999. *Law in Society*. Toronto: Harcourt Brace.

LeBourdais, I. 1966. *The Trial of Steven Truscott*. Toronto: McClelland & Stewart.

Lemert, E. 1967. *Human Deviance, Social Problems and Social Control*. Englewood Cliffs, NJ: Prentice Hall.

Lemieux, F. 2003. "Evaluation of the Impacts of Crisis Management: A Case Study." *Criminologie*, 36(1): 57–88.

Lewis, D. O., Pincus, J. H., Feldman, M., Jackson, L., & Bard, B. 1986. "Psychiatric, Neurological, and Psychoeducational Characteristics of 15 Death Row Inmates in the United States." *American Journal of Psychiatry*, 14: 838–845.

Linden, R. 1996. *Criminology: A Canadian Perspective* (3rd Ed.). Toronto: Harcourt Brace.

Lipton, D., Martinson, R., & Wilks, J. 1975. *The Effectiveness of Correctional Treatment*. New York: Praeger.

Luckenbill, D. F. 1977. "Criminal Homicide as a Situated Transaction." *Social Problems*, 25(2): 176–186.

Manson. A. 1989 (April). Lecture presented at "The Fifteen-Year Review of Life Sentences Symposium" conducted at the University of Windsor, Ontario.

Marron, K. 1996. *The Slammer: The Crisis in Canada's Prison System*. Toronto: Doubleday.

_____. 2002, June 28. "Identity Thieves Plunder the Net." *The Globe and Mail*.

Martinson, R. 1974. "What Works? Questions and Answers about Prison Reform." *The Public Interest*, 35: 22–54.

Marvell, T. B., & Moody, C. E. 1996. "Specification Problems, Police Levels and Crime Rates." *Criminology*, 34(4): 609–645.

Matthews, R., & Young, J. 1992. "Reflections on Realism" in J. Young & R. Matthews (eds.). *Rethinking Criminology: The Realist Debate*. London: Sage Publications, pp. 1–24.

McDonald, L. 1969. "Crime and Punishment in Canada: A Statistical Test of the 'Conventional Wisdom.'" *Canadian Review of Sociology and Anthropology*, 6: 212–236.

McLellan, Anne. 2002, August 29. "Medical Marijuana." *National Post*.

McNaughtan Smith, P. 1974. *What Is Crime and Why Do We Fight It?* Toronto: Centre of Criminology.

Meithe, T. D., & Meier, R. F. 1990. "Opportunity, Choice, and Criminal Victimization: A Test of a Theoretical Model." *Journal of Research in Crime and Delinquency*, 27(3): 243–266.

Melnitzer, J. 1995. *Maximum, Minimum, Medium: A Journey Through Canadian Prisons*. Toronto: Key Porter.

Mendelsohn, B. 1976. "Victimology and Contemporary Society's Trends" in E. Viano (ed.), *Victims and Society*. Washington, DC: Visage.

Merton, R. K. 1938. "Social Structure and Anomie." *American Sociological Review*, 3: 672–682.

Messner, S., & Rosenfeld, R. 1994. *Crime and the American Dream*. Belmont, CA: Wadsworth.

Miller, W. B. 1958. "Lower Class Culture as a Generating Milieu of Gang Delinquency." *Journal of Social Issues*, 14: 5–19.

Morris, N. 1982. *Madness and the Criminal Law*. Chicago: University of Chicago Press.

Morris, N., & Rothman, D. (eds.). 1995. *The Oxford History of the Prison*. New York: Oxford University Press.

Morris, P. 1965. *Prisoners and Their Families*. London: Allen and Unwin.

Morris, R. 1997. *Prison Abolition*. Toronto: Canadian Scholars' Press.

Morris, T., & Blom-Cooper, L. 1963. *A Calendar of Murder: Criminal Homicide in England since 1957*. London: M. Joseph.

Morris, T., & Morris, P. 1963. *Pentonville*. London: Routledge and Kegan Paul.

Morton, J., Addison, H., Addison, R., Hunt, L., & Sullivan, J. 1953. "A Clinical Study of Premenstrual Tension." *American Journal of Obstetrics and Gynecology*, 65: 1182–1191.

Muncie, J., McLaughin, E., & Langen, M. (eds.). 1997. *Criminological Perspectives: A Reader*. London: Sage.

Murphy, P. J., & Johnson, L. 1997. *Life-25: Interviews with Prisoners Serving Life Sentences*. Vancouver: New Star Books.

Myers, B., Godwin, D., Latter, R. & Winstanley, S. 2004. "Victim Impact Statements and Mock Juror Sentencing: The Impact of Dehumanizing Language on a Death. Qualified Sample." *American Journal of Forensic Psychology*, 22, 39–56.

Nagel, W. H. 1974. "The Notion of Victimology in Criminology," in I. Drapkin & E. Viano (eds.), *Victimology*. Lexington, MA.: Lexington Books.

Nergard, T. B. 1993. "Solving Conflicts Outside the Court System: Experiences with the Conflict Resolution Boards in Norway." *British Journal of Criminology*, 33(1): 81–94.

Nettler, G. 1984. *Explaining Crime*. Cincinnati: Anderson.

Nouwens, T., Motiuk, L., & Boe, R. 1993. "So You Want to Know the Recidivism Rate." *Forum on Corrections Research*, 5(3), 22–26.

Nye, F. I., & Short, J. 1957. "Scaling Delinquent Behaviour." *American Sociological Review*, 22: 326–331.

O'Connor, J. 1973. *The Fiscal Crisis of the State*. New York: St. Martin's Press.

Olweus, E. 1987. "Testosterone and Adrenaline: Aggressive Antisocial Behaviour in Normal Adolescent Males" in S. A. Mednick, T. E. Moffitt, & S. A. Stack (eds.), *The Causes of Crime: New Biological Approaches*. Cambridge, UK: Cambridge University Press, pp. 263–282.

Osgood, W., Wilson, J., O'Malley, P., Bachman, J., & Johnsston, L. 1996. "Routine Activities and Individual Deviant Behaviour." *American Sociological Review*, 61: 635–655.

Packer, H. 1964. "Two Models of Criminal Process." *University of Pennsylvania Law Review*, 113: 1–68.

Peak, K. 1997. *Policing America: Methods, Issues, Challenges*. Englewood Cliffs, NJ: Prentice Hall.

Perkins, C. A. 1997. *Age Patterns of Victims of Serious Crimes* (NCJ 162031). Washington, DC: Bureau of Justice Studies.

Quinney, R. 1972. "Who Is the Victim?" *Criminology*, 10: 314–322.

Ramcharan, S., de Lint, W., & Fleming, T. 2001. *The Canadian Criminal Justice System*. Don Mills, ON: Pearson Canada.

Ramcharan S., & Ramcharan, C. 2005. *Law Order and the Canadian Criminal Justice System*. Toronto: Canadian Educators Press.

Regoli, R., & Hewitt, J. 1996. *Criminal Justice*. Englewood Cliffs, NJ: Prentice Hall.

Reiman, J. 1990, 2004. *The Rich get Richer and the Poor Get Prison* (3rd and 7th Eds.). Upper Saddle River, NJ: Prentice Hall.

Riedel, R. 1989. *The Victim's Guide to the Canadian Criminal Justice System*. Scarborough, ON: Centennial College Press.

Roberts, J. V. 2000. *Criminal Justice in Canada: A Reader*. Totonto: Harcourt Brace.

Rosenbaum, A., Hoge, S. K., Adelman, S. A., Warnken, W. J., Fletcher, K. E., & Kane, R. L. 1994. "Head Injury in Partner-Abusive Men." *Journal of Consulting and Clinical Psychology*, 62(6): 1187–1193.

Ross, J. I. (ed.). 1995. *Violence in Canada: Sociopolitical Perspectives*. Don Mills, ON: Oxford.

Ruby, C. 1996. *Sentencing* (3rd Ed.). Toronto: Butterworths.

Rush, G. 1994. *The Dictionary of Criminal Justice* (4th Ed.). Guildford, UK: Dushkin Publishing.

Sacco, V., & Kennedy, L. 1998. *Crime Victims in Context*. Los Angeles: Roxbury.

Sanders, A., Hoyle, C., Morgan, R., & Cape, E. 2001. "Victim Impact Statements Can't Work, Won't Work." *Criminal Law Review*, 447–458.

Schmalleger, F. 1997. *Criminal Justice Today: An Introductory Text for the Twenty-First Century* (4th Ed.). Upper Saddle River, NJ: Prentice Hall.

Schmalleger, F., MacAlister, D., & McKenna, P. F. 2004. *Canadian Criminal Justice Today* (2nd Ed.). Don Mills, ON: Pearson Canada.

Schneider, H. J. 1982. "The Present Situation in Victimology in the World" in H. J. Schneider (ed.), *The Victim in International Perspective*. Berlin: Walter de Gruyter.

Scott, G. (with B. Trent). 1982. *Inmate*. Toronto: Optimum.

Scull, A. 1983. *Decarceration*. Englewood Cliffs, NJ: Prentice Hall.

Sellin, T. 1958. *Culture, Conflict and Crime*. New York: Social Science Research Council.

Senna. J. J., & Siegel, L. J. 1995. *Essentials of Criminal Justice*. Minneapolis/St. Paul: West Publishing.

Shaw, C. R., & McKay, H. D. 1969. *Juvenile Delinquency and Urban Areas* (rev. ed.). Chicago: University of Chicago Press. (Original work published 1942.)

Sheldon, W. H. 1949. *Varieties of Delinquent Youth: An Introduction to Constitutional Psychiatry*. New York: Harper.

Sher, J. 2001. *"Until You Are Dead": Steven Truscott's Long Ride into History*. Toronto: Knopf Canada.

Sherman, L., & Weisburd, D. 1995. "General Deterrent Effects of Police Patrol in Crime 'Hot Spots': A Randomized, Controlled Trial." *Justice Quarterly*, 12: 625–648.

Siegel, L. J., & McCormick, C. 1999. *Criminology in Canada: Theories, Patterns, and Typologies*. Scarborough, ON: Thomson Nelson Learning.

Silverman, R. A. 1980. "Measuring Crime: A Tale of Two Cities" in R. A. Silverman & J. J. Teevan (eds.), *Crime in Canadian Society* (2nd Ed.). Toronto: Butterworths.

Smith, J. C., & Hogan, B. 1992. *Criminal Law* (7th Ed.). London: Butterworths.

Spierenburg, P. C. 1984. *The Spectacle of Suffering: Executions and the Evolution of Repression*. Cambridge, NY: Cambridge University Press.

Sprott, J. B., & Doob, A. 1998. "Understanding Provincial Variations in Incarceration Rates." *Canadian Journal of Criminology*, 40(3): 305–322.

Stansfield, R. 1996. *Issues in Policing: A Canadian Perspective*. Toronto: Thompson Educational Publishing.

Stebbins, R. 1996. *Deviance: Tolerable Differences*. Toronto: McGraw-Hill.

Stenning, P. C. 1983. *The Legal Status of the Police*. Ottawa: Land Reform Commission of Canada.

_____. 2003. "Policing the Cultural Kaleidoscope: Recent Canadian Experience." *Police & Society*, 7, 13–47.

Strategic Planning Committee on Police Training and Education: A Police Learning System for Ontario: Final Report and Recommendations (D. Scott Campbell, chair). 1992. Toronto: The Committee.

Sutherland, E. 1966. *Principles of Criminology* (7th Ed.). Philadelphia: J. B. Lippincott.

Sutherland, E., & Cressey, D. 1970. *Principles of Criminology* (8th Ed.). Philadelphia: J. B. Lippincott.

Sykes, C. 1992. *A Nation of Victims: The Decay of the American Character*. New York: St. Martin's Press.

Tappan, P. 1960. *Crime, Justice and Corrections*. New York: McGraw-Hill.

Tittle, C. 1995. *Control Balance: A General Theory of Deviance*. Boulder, CO: Westview.

Tittle, C., & Rowe, A. 1973. "Moral Appeal, Sanction Threat, and Deviance: An Experimental Test." *Social Problems*, 20: 488–498.

Toby, J. 1957. "Social Disorganization and Stake in Conformity: Complementary Factors in the Predatory Behaviour of Hoodlums." *Journal of Criminal Law and Police Science*, 48: 12–17.

Trent, B. 1971. *The Steven Truscott Story*. Toronto: Pocket Books.

Turk, A. 1969, 1976. *Criminality and Legal Order*. Chicago: Rand McNally.

Udry, J. R. 1988. "Biological Predisposition and Social Control in Adolescent Sexual Behaviour." *American Sociological Review*, 53: 709–722.

Vago, S. 2000. *Law and Society* (6th Ed.). Upper Saddle River, NJ: Prentice Hall.

Vago, S., & Nelson, A. 2004. *Law and Society* (Canadian Ed.). Don Mills, ON: Pearson Canada.

van den Bergie, P. 1974. *Race and Ethnicity* (2nd Ed.). New York: Basic Books.

van Dijk, J., & Mayhew, P. 1997. *Criminal Victimisation in Eleven Industrialised Countries: Key Findings from the 1996 International Crime Victims Survey*. Amsterdam: Netherlands Ministry of Justice.

van Dijk, J., Mayhew, P., & Kilias, M. 1991. *Experiences of Crime Across the World: Key Findings of the 1989 International Crime Survey*. Boston: Kluwer Law and Taxation Publishers.

van Rijn, N. 1999, July 24. "Police Caseload Doubles in 36 Years." *Toronto Star*, p. A1.

Verdun-Jones, S. 1997. *Criminal Law in Canada: Cases, Questions and the Code* (2nd Ed.). Toronto: Harcourt Brace.

Vincent, C. 1990. *Police Officer*. Ottawa: Carleton University Press.

Visano, L., & McCormick, K. 1992a. *Canadian Penology: Advanced Perspectives*. Toronto: Canadian Scholars' Press.

_____. 1992b. *Understanding Policing*. Toronto: Canadian Scholars' Press.

Volovka, J. 1987. "Electroencephalogram among Criminals" in S. Mednick, T. Moffit, & S. Stack (eds.), *The Causes of Crime*. Cambridge, NY: Cambridge University Press.

Von Hentig, H. 1948. *The Criminal and His Victim*. New Haven, CT: Yale University Press.

Walford, B. 1987. *Lifers: The Stories of Eleven Women Serving Life Sentences for Murder*. Montreal: Eden Press.

Wallerstien, J. S., & Wyle, C. 1947. "Our Law-Abiding Lawbreakers." *Probation*, XXV(April): 107–112.

Weinberg, L. S., & Weinberg, J. W. 1980. *Law and Society: An Interdisciplinary Introduction*. Washington, DC: University Press of America.

Weisburd, D. 2005. Hot spots policing experiments and criminal justice research: Lessons from the field, *The Annals of the American Academy of Political and Social Science*, 599 (1): 220–245.

Wilson, E. O. 1975. *Sociobiology: The New Synthesis*. Cambridge, MA: Belknap-Harvard University Press.

Wilson, J. Q. 1975. *Thinking about Crime*. New York: Basic Books.

Wilson, J. Q., & Kelling, G. 1982, March. "Broken Windows: The Police and Neighbourhood Safety." *Atlantic Monthly*, 127: 29–38.

Winterdyk, J. (ed.). 2000. *Issues and Perspectives on Young Offenders in Canada* (2nd Ed.). Toronto: Harcourt Brace.

Witkin, H. A. 1977. "XYY and XXY Men: Criminality and Aggression" in S. A. Mednick & K. O. Christensen (eds.), *Biosocial Bases of Criminal Behaviour*. New York: Gardner, pp. 165–197.

Wolfenden Committee on Prostitution, Pornography and Homosexuality. 1966. London: Home Office.

Wolfgang, M. 1958. *Patterns in Criminal Homicide*. Philadelphia: University of Pennsylvania Press.

Wolfgang, M., & Ferracuti, F. 1967. *The Subculture of Violence*. Beverly Hills, CA: Sage.

Wolfgang, M., Figlio R. M., & Sellin, T. 1972. *Delinquency in a Birth Cohort*. Chicago: University of Chicago Press.

Young-Rifai, M. 1982. "Victimology: A Theoretical Framework" in H. J. Schneider (ed.), *The Victim in International Perspective*. Berlin: Walter de Gruyter.

Zamble, E. 2000. "Community Supervision : Current Practice and Future Directions." CSC website. Available: www.csc-scc.gc.ca.

Index

Photo and Illustration Credits